Characters in Literary Fictions

MEDIATED FICTIONS

STUDIES IN VERBAL AND VISUAL NARRATIVES

Series Editors: Artur Blaim and Ludmiła Gruszewska-Blaim

Editorial Board
Antonis Balasopoulos
Joanna Durczak
David Malcolm
Fátima Vieira

VOLUME 9

Jadwiga Węgrodzka (ed.)

Characters in Literary Fictions

PETER LANG
EDITION

Bibliographic Information published by the Deutsche Nationalbibliothek
The Deutsche Nationalbibliothek lists this publication in the Deutsche Nationalbibliografie; detailed bibliographic data is available in the internet at http://dnb.d-nb.de.

Library of Congress Cataloging-in-Publication Data
Characters in literary fictions / Jadwiga Wegrodzka (ed.).
   pages cm. — (Mediated fictions ; 9)
Includes index.
ISBN 978-3-631-64056-2
1. Fiction—History and criticism. 2. Characters and characteristics in literature. 3. Character in literature. 4. Fiction—Technique. 5. Narration (Rhetoric) I. Wegrodzka, Jadwiga, 1956- editor.
PN3411.C47 2015
809.3'927--dc23

2015014334

This publication was financially supported
by the University of Gdańsk.

Cover illustration printed with kind permission of Jerzy Durczak.

Reviewed by Wojciech Nowicki.

Typesetting: Mateusz Liwiński.

ISSN 2194-5918
ISBN978-3-631-64056-2 (Print)
E-ISBN 978-3-653-02466-1 (E-Book)
DOI 10.3726/978-3-653-02466-1

© Peter Lang GmbH
Internationaler Verlag der Wissenschaften
Frankfurt am Main 2015
All rights reserved.

Peter Lang Edition is an Imprint of Peter Lang GmbH.

Peter Lang – Frankfurt am Main · Bern · Bruxelles · New York · Oxford · Warszawa · Wien

This publication has been peer reviewed.

www.peterlang.com

Contents

From Character to Identity … and back?

URSZULA TERENTOWICZ-FOTYGA
JADWIGA WĘGRODZKA

> It is the privilege of novelists to create characters
> who kill those of the historians. The reason is
> that historians only evoke mere ghosts, while
> novelists create persons in flesh and bones.
>
> Alexandre Dumas, *Memoirs*

Most readers would agree that literature is written for and about people. A great majority of non-professional readers, "gentle skimmers" as Beckett called them, read books to find out about other people, their worlds, thoughts, emotions, fortunes and adventures. It is the characters that focus the readers' attention and are usually most vividly remembered long after the reading of a fictional text. Some characters are so fascinating and memorable, that they may acquire some mode of existence apparently independent of their original text (like Hamlet or Don Quixote, for example). They may even pass the threshold of the fictional narrative and – in the belief of many readers – live or have lived their lives in the actual geographical locations in the readers' reality associated with the characters in their original texts. Umberto Eco mentions an amusing incident of Alexandre Dumas who, on visiting the Chateau d'If, "discovered that the visitors were shown the 'real' cell of Montecristo, and the guides were speaking of him, Faria and other characters of the novel as if they had really existed" (Eco 2009: 82). Similarly, many readers believe that Sherlock Holmes was a real detective lodging at 221B Baker Street (Eco 2009: 87).

The appraisal of characters from moral, psychological and sociological perspectives in various critical analyses seems to suggest that critics may sometimes partly share the (ordinary) readers' tendency to treat characters as people. The person-like aspect of fictional figures becomes particularly prominent in the consideration of fiction belonging to the realist tradition; for instance, Bernard J. Paris claims that it becomes possible to "appreciate the distinctive achievement of the genre" only by treating characters as real people (1974: 4). Virginia Woolf, writing from the other end of the literary communication process, argues that any creative work grows out of an interest in a human being and his or her experience of reality. In her essay "Mr Bennet and Mrs Brown", in a characteristically playful tone, Woolf argues that writing fiction starts with a human figure taking shape in the writer's mind and demanding attention:

> Most novelists have the same experience. Some Brown, Smith, or Jones comes before them and says in the most seductive and charming way in the world, "Come and catch me if you can." And so, led on by this will-o'-the-wisp, they flounder through volume after volume, spending the best years of their lives in the pursuit, and receiving for the most part very little cash in exchange. Few catch the phantom; most have to be content with a scrap of her dress or a wisp of her hair.
>
> My belief that men and women write novels because they are lured on to create some character which has thus imposed itself upon them has the sanction of Mr Arnold Bennett. In an article from which I will quote he says: "The foundation of good fiction is character-creating and nothing else … Style counts; plot counts; originality of outlook counts. But none of these counts anything like so much as the convincingness of the characters. If the characters are real the novel will have a chance; if they are not, oblivion will be its portion…" (1996: 23)

Literary interest in a human being has an important cognitive function. As David Lodge argues, among the different forms of communication, both artistic and non-artistic, literature allows one to experience what it means to be someone else most fully; it enables one to look at reality from a different point of view, to know and experience the world as someone else does: "Literature is a record of human consciousness, the richest and most comprehensive we have. Lyric poetry is arguably man's most successful effort to describe qualia. The novel is arguably man's most successful effort to describe the experience of individual human beings moving through space and time" (2002: 10).

Although the experience of an individual human being is central to literature and to literary appreciation, the study of the character has long remained on the periphery of contemporary literary studies. Theories that dominated the study of literature in the twentieth century, not only those of structuralist tradition programmatically disapproving of "personalistic studies" (Zgorzelski 1999: 164), focused much of their energies on questioning the conventional reading of the literary character as a person, a socio-psychological figure representative of its time and place. Such an approach, however, did not really resonate with the readers. In fact, the importance and function of the literary character is the area in which professional and non-professional interpretations of the text – the approaches of literary scholars and ordinary readers – probably differ the most. For non-professional readers the concepts and models constructed within literary studies tend to be either too theoretical or too complex to evoke much interest. And while scholars might be tempted to blame the readers for not absorbing the intricacies of contemporary theory and clinging onto naïve beliefs in characters as real people, it would be justified to argue that in the anti-anthropomorphic climate of the twentieth-century, theory did not provide a satisfactory account of the literary character.

The following consideration of the critical approaches to character will focus on the three traditions that dominated the post-war landscape in the humanities – structuralism, poststructuralism and cultural studies – tracing their struggle to absorb the character into their vision of textual reality and to account for the "human context" (Harvey 19667: 231) of the literary text. As we shall demonstrate, structuralism and poststructuralism effectively marginalised the study of the character while cultural studies, though returning to socio-psychological considerations, ended up locking the actual and the textual people in the paradigm of race-class-gender.

One of the key premises of structuralist poetics which aimed to establish literary studies as a systemic and objective discipline, was turning away from the focus on the personal – from the biographic interest in a literary text as a personal statement of an individual author and from the literary character as a speaker for a particular vision of reality. Inclined towards abstraction and generalisation, structuralism was not interested in the character as an expression of individual experience, and it effectively distanced itself from psychological focus on the mind and from the consideration of character types or personalities. As Jonathan Culler writes:

> Character is the major aspect of the novel to which structuralism has paid least attention and has been least successful in treating. Although for many readers character serves as the major totalising force in fiction – everything in the novel exists in order to illustrate character and its development – a structuralist approach has tended to explain this as an ideological prejudice rather than to study it as a fact of reading. (1975: 230)

Structuralism in its Western variant searched for the underlying general rules, the "grammar" of a literary text, and thus, if interested in fictional characters at all, it analysed them as parts of the more systemic aspects of the text, such as plot or setting. Characters were defined as functions of the text, participants rather than beings (Barthes 1975: 257). Yet the "grammar of characters" proved a blind alley, well-illustrated by the conclusions that Tzvetan Todorov draws when analysing the characters in *Les Liaisons dangereuses*: "if A loves B he attempts to make B love him; if A discovers that he loves B then he will endeavour to deny or conceal that love" (quoted in Culler 1975: 235). One can hardly imagine offering Todorov's conclusions as inspiring theoretical material capturing the complexity of Pierre Choderlos de Laclos's characterisation. Structuralism in its Eastern European variant defined the very term structure differently and did not aim to define the underlying "grammar" of literature but explored various textual, generic and cultural levels of literary structures. In spite of differences between Eastern and Western variants of structuralism, neither treated fictional characters as particularly worthy of attention except as a part of the whole network of structural relations under scrutiny.

Although structuralist interest in character analysis was limited, its impact remains significant, mainly due to a broad redefinition of the theoretical framework of the whole discipline. In the area of character studies structuralist poetics separated the literary character from the author; it drew attention to the paradoxes resulting from treating literary characters as real people and interpreting their experiences as a factual record of human life. More importantly, it worked out the tools that allowed for the analysis of different aspects of character construction and their relations with other elements of the text. At the same time, however, as it moved away from personal and psychological considerations, it separated fictional characters from human beings and from the discussion of philosophical and cultural models of subjectivity. Speaking metaphorically, it locked characters within the text and failed to provide a framework allowing for the analysis of their individuality, psychology or relationships with extra-textual reality, the aspects that many readers see as most vital in their appreciation of literature.

Poststructuralism shared structuralist suspicion of personalistic and psychological approaches, and its conviction that "the psychological person (belonging to the referential order) has nothing to do with the linguistic person, which is never defined by natural dispositions, intentions or personality traits, but only by its (coded) point of insertion in the discourse" (Barthes 1975: 263). The "death of the literary character" became both the symptom and the reflection of the "death of the subject", and critical thinking on the literary character became part of a broader reflection on the crisis of subjectivity.

At the same time poststructuralism shifted attention from grammar to rhetoric. Critical analysis took the form of a complex process of multiplication of language tropes, an infinite deferral of meaning. In the poststructuralist multiplication of meanings the literary character came to embody the plural arbitrary sign. Writing, argues Barthes in "The Death of the Author", becomes the "neutral, composite, oblique space where our subject slips away, the negative where all identity is lost, starting with the very identity of the body writing" (1977: 142). If, alongside the death of the author, poststructuralism brought the death of the literary character, it consisted in de-anthropomorphised exegesis that did not aim at synthesis. The character, like other aspects of the text, was not seen as a coherent construct but as "a triumphant plural, unimpoverished by any constraint of representation" (Barthes 1974: 5).

A good illustration of an early poststructuralist analysis of the literary character can be found in *S/Z*, in which the protagonist Sarrasine is construed as a transitory site producing an "uninterrupted exchange of the codes" (1974: 179). Sarrasine, argues Barthes, should not be seen as a person but as "an impersonal network of symbols combined under the proper name" (1974: 94). It is only by scraping the anthropomorphic readings that the critics can capture the full complexity of the literary work – as the death of the literary character is the true marker of modernity and a pre-requisite of experimental art:

> We occasionally speak of Sarrasine as though he existed, as though he had a future, an unconscious, a soul; however, what we are talking about is his *figure* (an impersonal network of symbols combined under the proper name "Sarrasine"), not his *person* (a moral freedom endowed with motives and an overdetermination of meanings): we are developing connotations, not pursuing investigations; we are not searching for the truth of Sarrasine, but for the systematics of a (transitory) site of the text: we mark this site (under the name Sarrasine) so it will take its place among the alibis of the narrative operation, in the indeterminable network of meanings, in the plurality of the codes. [...] All subversion, or all novelistic submission, thus begins with the Proper Name. [...] What is obsolescent in today's novel is not the novelistic, it is the character; what can no longer be written is the Proper Name. (Barthes 1974: 94-5)

Poststructuralist "rhetoric" of the literary character ultimately proved as restricting and unproductive as structuralist "grammar". Perhaps its most important contribution to the study of the character consisted in providing the tools for the analysis of experimental fiction, for example, the French *nouveau roman*. As Henryk Markiewicz argues, before the poststructuralist probing into the field of shifting meanings, the texts that deliberately reduced, eliminated and deconstructed the subject, in critics' and readers' reception often appeared more stable and coherent than their authors intended (1984: 149). Poststructuralist thinking sensitised readers to the subversion of codes in character construction and put greater emphasis on its narrative and intertextual aspects. These questions and perspectives clearly had an important function in the reinterpretation of the role and function of the literary character that came with the "cultural turn".

Cultural studies brought an important redefinition of the disciplinary boundaries of the humanities. Rooted in Marxist ideology of the Frankfurt School, it defined culture as the lived dominance of particular classes and offered a new conceptualisation of where social and political struggle was taking place. It was an intellectual and a political project which strongly politicised the terms of the debate. Critical attention focused on the interplay of representations and ideologies, and underlined the questions of power and agency.

A growing interest in the *politics of signification* led to a greater concern with *politics of identity*. Cultural studies held onto the poststructuralist belief in the crisis of the subject and shared its conviction that literary characters should be seen as symptoms of this broader crisis. An important theoretical inspiration was provided by the Foucauldian idea of the discursive production of the subjects, which argued that the self is constructed in the process of internalisation of discourses of power. The individual and textual self was conceptualised as an "effect" or "personalisation" of various disciplinary structures, analyzed in terms of the dominance of hegemonic ideologies. Social identities were defined as "complex fields of multiple and even contradictory struggles; [...] the product of the articulations of particular social positions into chains of equivalences, between experiences, interests, political struggles, and cultural forms, and between different social positions" (Grossberg 1997: 180). With the focus on the interplay of representations and ideologies, critical attention shifted onto the periphery, to the margins of class, gender, race and nationality. It centred on the subjects previously marginalised, women within feminist studies, sexual minorities in queer studies and "other" races in postcolonial studies.

An important aspect of the "cultural turn" was the shift of focus from character to identity. The character came to be viewed as a representative of the culturally and ideologically embedded self, a product of a given set of discourses. As textual analysis came to focus on the underlying narratives that construct the individual sites within the networks of determinations, literary characters, like other forms of self representation, came to be seen as a battleground upon which dominant views contest and try to secure their hegemony. No longer a stable self but a narrative "spoken" by different discourses, the character was construed as a complex field of multiple ideological struggles. The understanding of the fictional character as a bundle of discourses no longer centred on the intertextual dialogue but on the hegemonic narratives that determine different subject positions.

On the one hand, the "cultural turn" clearly broadened the scope of the debate. Texts and practices, representations and languages came to be seen as part of a broader cultural field and social experience, while the study of the literary character was inscribed in more general considerations of the philosophical and cultural models of subjectivity. Critical

analysis put emphasis on the relation between the character and its social, cultural, historical and political contexts and by doing so it re-
embraced the link between the fictional and the extra-textual. Politicis-
ing the debate, cultural studies offered the grounds and the conceptual
framework for the consideration of the literary character as an expression of a certain vision of reality or ideology, "multiplicitly constructed
across different, often intersecting and antagonistic, discourses, practices
and positions" (Hall 1996: 4).

On the other hand, however, the perspectives that dominated the in-
terpretational frameworks of the "cultural turn" proved seriously reductive. While broadening the terms of the debate by re-embracing the political and cultural context, they rooted literary analysis in very clearly
demarcated ideological discourses. The analytical perspectives in the
study of subjectivity were defined by the growing importance of feminist, postcolonial and queer studies, and the self came to be defined in
terms of excluded histories and displaced narratives. The study of the
literary character, though conducted within a potentially broader framework of identity, was largely limited to the mantra of race, class, and
gender.

Inscribing the study of the literary character in a broader study of
identity is one of the most valuable legacies of the "cultural turn". Identity became a buzz word in the humanities and social sciences: it "infus-
es a wide variety of new social knowledges, from psychoanalysis to
feminism to postmodernism" (Elliott 2007: 23). At the same time, the
crisis of cultural studies as a discipline exposed some of the limitations
of the project as well as major problems resulting from too close a marriage of literature and ideology. The discipline that started from a critique of the exclusionary logic of literary studies and claimed to offer a
new paradigm by taking seriously the cultures of those it taught (Hartley
2003: 3), ended up treating literary texts as mere "pegs on which to hang
some clanking theoretical argument" (Norris 2003: 97).

*

Contemporary landscape in the humanities does not offer universal theories and methodologies. Postmodernity brought an end to old securities
and certainties but at the same time it made room for new explorations
and alliances: "after the period of apocalyptic doom and gloom, of
brooding over the death of the humanities, a more hopeful vision is be-

ginning to prevail. There is a growing sense that in the crisis lie opportunities as well as difficulties and that what is really at stake is the new
face of the humanities" (Terentowicz-Fotyga 2013: 520). The profusion
of research perspectives means that new approaches to the study of literary and cultural texts have to do without a pre-defined, systematic theory. A pragmatic and functional approach to analytical tools is often more
justified than the search for an all-embracing methodology. Yet, as the
brief sketch of structuralist, poststructuralist and culturalist approaches
to the literary character has aimed to demonstrate, the grand theoretical
and methodological "narratives" that dominated the humanities in the
twentieth century did not fulfil their promises of capturing the totality of
the literary universe either. New trends and approaches often have local,
grass-root character; they grow out of and build on individual problems,
hypotheses and perspectives. The fact that they evolve through critical
praxis rather than out of a coherent theoretical or methodological position need not be a disadvantage as grass-root initiatives may prove most
useful in providing answers to individual problems and the crisis of the
discipline as such (Terentowicz-Fotyga 2013: 528-9).

In the context of the literary character study, two trends can be traced
in the recent decades. One of them builds on the shift from character to
identity proposed by the "cultural turn" in an attempt to forge new interdisciplinary alliances and perspectives; the other returns to the notion of
the literary character with the aim of constructing more satisfactory theoretical models and methodological tools. Although seemingly contrasted, they can be seen as largely complementary, especially when we take
into account that in both the most interesting voices are formulated on
the ground of narratology.

In a recent book entitled *Travelling Concepts in the Humanities*
Mieke Bal calls for a shift in methodology within the interdisciplinary
projects of the humanities from method-based to concept-based. Interdisciplinarity, she argues, "necessary, exciting, serious, must seek its
heuristic and methodological basis in *concepts* rather than *methods*"
(2002: 5). Concepts are the backbone of interdisciplinarity as they are
the principal tools of intersubjectivity. They are valuable "[n]ot because
they mean the same thing for everyone, but because they don't" (Bal
2002: 11). It is through the process of negotiating different meanings of

the seemingly shared ideas that the different disciplines, research perspectives, hypotheses and methodologies can come together.

> If well thought through, they offer miniature theories, and in that guise,
> help in the analysis of objects, situations, states, and other theories. [...]
> But concepts can only do this work, the methodological work that discipli-
> nary traditions used to do, on one condition: that they are kept under scru-
> tiny through a confrontation with, not application to, the cultural objects
> being examined. For these objects themselves are amenable to change and
> apt to illuminate historical and cultural differences. The shift in methodol-
> ogy I am arguing for here is founded on a particular relationship between
> subject and object, one that is not predicated on a vertical and binary oppo-
> sition between the two. Instead, the model for this relationship is interac-
> tion, as in 'interactivity'. (Bal 2002: 22-24)

Identity is one of the key concepts capable of focalising intersubjective
and interdisciplinary dialogue both within the humanities and between
the humanities and social sciences[1]. Putting identity in the centre of attention brought together different approaches to the study of the human
aspect of cultural texts and practices, and was an important step in the
construction of interdisciplinary dialogue. In this dialogue, literature and
literary studies can fulfil an important role. Literature because of its potential for expressing the complexity of human experience. Literary
studies because, regardless of the limitations of individual theories and
methodologies, the discipline has constructed a wide range of tools and
methods capable of exploring the human aspect of cultural texts and representations.

Recent developments within narrative theory – in both cognitive and
rhetorical narratology – suggest a growing interest in the literary character (Margolin, Schneider, Phelan). Relying on some aspects of structuralism and semiotics, reception theory and the theory of fictional worlds,
Uri Margolin, for example, insisted on seeing characters as semiotic elements of the narrative worlds, ontologically independent from any verbal expression (1983: 7)[2]. He also emphasised the variety of the characters' ways of existence – from factual and counterfactual, through hypothetical and conditional, to subjective (1995: 375). Though Margolin can

---

1   Although Bal mentions identity, subjectivity and agency among the key terms in the
     humanities, they are not analysed as part of the book.
2   The claim is also formulated, for instance, by Seymour Chatman in his *Story and Dis-
     course* (1987: 117-118).

be perceived as "one of the first to argue for considering characters' different aspects as non-actual individuals in fictional worlds, as thematic elements, as topical entities of discourse, and as artificial constructs" (Eder, Jannidis, Schneider 2010: 16), it was James Phelan who formulated a consistent, comprehensive and flexible approach to the character analysis in his 1989 book *Reading People, Reading Plots. Character, Progression, and the Interpretation of Narrative*. Because Phelan's analytical terms are extensively applied in the present volume, his proposal requires a more detailed presentation.

Phelan's model of character analysis may be perceived as an attempt to harmonise the approaches that in the literary studies tended to be treated as separate or even exclusive. In contrast to scholars who refuse to grant characters any similarity to real persons, Phelan attempts to accommodate the well known tendency of the readers to treat characters as such. In Phelan's model, character construction involves three components: mimetic, thematic and synthetic. It is the *mimetic* aspect that embraces elements responsible for construing a character as a person, a plausible human being. Best exemplified by realist fiction, the character perceived from the perspective of the mimetic aspect answers to the expectations of readers who are inclined to treat characters as actual people and to focus on their psychology, personality or appearance. The mimetic component is supplemented by the *thematic* one, which refers to the literary character as a representation of an idea, group or class larger than the individual character (1989: 12). In terms of literary approaches the mimetic aspect is dominant in psychological studies of character, which are definitely not prevalent in the current reflection though they are by no means absent[3]. The thematic focus on the other hand may be said to dominate in the political and ideological approaches that define cultural studies. The *synthetic* component in Phelan's triad refers to the level of discourse and concerns the character's artificiality as a "literary construct" (1989: 3). This is the aspect that might be said to dominate in the structuralist and poststructuralist approaches in literary studies. It is significant in Phelan's model that a comprehensive analysis has to take

---

3   Compare, for instance, Bernard J. Paris's *Imagined Human Beings. A Psychological Approach to Character and Conflict in Literature* (New York: London, 1997) or Margaret Rustin and Michael Rustin's *Narratives of Love and Loss. Studies in modern children's fiction* (London and New York: Karnac, 2001) both employing broadly defined psychoanalytical perspectives.

into account all three components of character construction and their mutual interrelations. As Phelan claims, "the mimetic and thematic components may be more or less developed, whereas the synthetic component, though always present, may be more or less foregrounded" (1989: 3).

It is also important for Phelan's proposal that he places the character within what he calls *progression* which refers to the narrative "as a dynamic event, one that must move, in both its telling and its reception, through time" (1989: 15). Progression is always dynamic by virtue of various instabilities and tensions inscribed into the narrative. *Instabilities* refer to the story level and occur "between the characters, created by situations and complicated and resolved by actions" (1989: 15). *Tensions* belong to the level of discourse and describe conflicts "of value, belief, opinion, knowledge, expectation – between authors and/or narrators, on the one hand, and the authorial audience on the other" (1989:15). The notion of progression is also essential in Phelan's model for the consideration of the characters' *dimensions and functions* within each of the three components. "A dimension is any attribute a character may be said to possess when that character is considered in isolation from the work in which he or she appears. A function is a particular application of that attribute made by the text through its developing structure. In other words, dimensions are converted into functions by the *progression* of the work" (1989: 9; emphasis original).

The notion of authorial audience, mentioned above in connection with tensions in the progression, is juxtaposed with that of the narrative audience: "the *authorial audience* is the ideal audience that an author implicitly posits in constructing her text, the one which will pick up on all the signals in the appropriate way. [...] The *narrative audience* is that group of readers for whom the lyric, dramatic, or narrative situation is not synthetic but real. For the mimetic illusion to work, we must enter the narrative audience" (1989: 5). The two terms, taken over by Phelan from Peter Rabinowitz, seem close to the notions of the implied reader and the addressee of the narration. In the present volume the term "reader", unless used with some modifiers, always refers to the authorial audience or the implied reader in the sense of the ideal recipient.

Phelan's model, valuable in accounting for the experiences and attitudes of ordinary readers as well as scholars, and combining various critical perspectives, is by no means the only comprehensive and multiaspectual approach to the character. A similar division was designed in 2008 by Jens Eder who proposed to view characters as fictional beings (considering their features in the fictional world), as symbols (analysing the meanings communicated through them), as symptoms (studying the reasons for their makeup and their effects), and as artifacts (observing their textual structures) (Eder, Jannidis, and Schneider 2010: 16). Though Eder primarily dealt with characters in film, his model is generally applicable to characters in fictional worlds, and does not exclude other media.

The theoretical advances in the study of the literary character, while explaining and clarifying numerous issues, still leave many questions and problems unresolved, especially within the area of the recipient/audience/reader's engagement with the characters. Notions such as identification or involvement are notoriously difficult to define. So are other aspects of character processing by the reader, especially since

> contemporary narrative theory has amply demonstrated, by exploring aspects such as the unreliable narrator, changes of focalization and free indirect style, how extremely complex literary discourse can be. A satisfactory theory of character cannot ignore discourse but, on the contrary, will have to concentrate explicitly on textual patterns and determine accurately what information is given about a character, who gives this information and how this information relates to other, possibly incompatible and conflicting data. Such a theory, which combines discourse analysis and reader's response (generating images on the basis of words and imaginative involvement) might be developed by using insights and concepts of cognitive science, the relevance of which in literary theory seems to be rapidly increasing. (Weststeijn 2007)

The contributions of the cognitive approach, such as top-down and bottom-up processing or frame theory, seem interesting and promising, though the need to account for multiple reception levels painstakingly distinguished by narratology still seems to constitute an important challenge.

Interesting issues also seem to arise in connection with character typologies – which are numerous, but frequently overlapping or contradictory, and often based on not entirely consistent criteria. Are general typologies of character possible? Or can they only be genre (or media) specific? Character typologies may be closely linked with social and cultural contexts (involving stereotypes, clichés, and evaluations) and with their variations across time. A comprehensive historical view of changes connected with the understanding, techniques of creation, and possible functions of characters, as well as audiences' engagements with fictional figures might offer valuable theoretical insights and prevent critics from universalising theories which may be in fact relative to a given cultural period. As has been already noted here it is obvious that theoretical approaches to character respond to the type of fiction focusing the attention of readers, critics, and theoreticians – which is noticeable in the correspondences between the literary production and theoretical proposals within the last hundred years.

However, despite evident need for further research and reflection, it is manifest that theoretical reflection enriches the understanding of literary characters and supplies tools that reveal new complexities not only within this notion itself but also in the numerous and various contexts which the readers and/or scholars employ in their engagement with fictional figures. Some more recent proposals, such as Phelan's, appear particularly valuable in attempting to account for the experiences and expectations of both professional and non-professional readers, and to combine structuralist, post-structuralist and culturalist perspectives. The extension and development of such proposals seems to open a way for defining various aspects of identity formation and representation within different projects of the interdisciplinary humanities.

*

The present monographic volume is an attempt to make use of various aspects of literary character theories and analytical models by putting them to practical test in detailed examinations of characters in selected literary texts. Following the plurality of possible approaches within the current paradigm in the humanities, no single theoretical stance has been adopted for the whole book – each study focuses on a different fictional text and applies theoretical and analytical tools in accordance with interpretative challenges posed to the reader/scholar. *Characters in literary fictions* is divided into three parts, each of them gathering studies which explore three different analytical contexts: textual in Part I, generic in Part II, and extra-textual in Part III.

Part I, "Characters in textual contexts", focuses on examining characters in particular texts. The part opens with an analysis of the ballad

"Sister Helen" (1881) by Dante Gabriel Rossetti and ends with a discussion of Charles Williams's novel *Shadows of Ecstasy* (1933). Both articles – opening and closing Part I – combine analytical considerations with defining distinct paradigms for the understanding of the character. In his study of Rossetti's ballad Professor Andrzej Zgorzelski outlines what he calls "a functional approach to the literary characters" carefully tracing its roots in Russian Formalism, the Prague school structuralism, and the Tartu school of semiotics. Zgorzelski opts for treating the character as a strictly textual phenomenon existing as "an intricate network of sign relations". The analysis emphasizes the necessity of a careful examination of "every trait of a literary character" in order to determine "its function within the larger structure of the whole text". It is the stress on functions of different textual elements in relation to various structural levels of the text – from phonological to generic – that explains the name of the approach. Zgorzelski's sensitivity to language patterns is echoed in the next article which analyses characters in Joseph Conrad's story "The Partner" (1912). Karolina Trapp studies Conrad's intricate hierarchy of narrators with their "rich diversity of languages" responsible for "the delineation of particular characters", and emphasises "that character is structured by the literary language". The character's involvement with the fictional space in Peter Straub's *Shadowland* (1980) is the focus of Sławomir Studniarz's examination of the novel's central figure in what he calls liminal space of the initiation experience understood in the anthropological sense. The following study also employs a culturally based perspective by analysing characters marginalised due to their "age, gender, or ethnicity" in Anita Desai's two novels and a short story. Joanna Pasternak links the cultural marginalisation with the textual technique of apparently removing a central character from the reader's metaphorical field of vision. While the first four articles in Part I focus on the main characters in the considered literary texts, the final two shift attention to minor figures. Magdalena Kuźniar scrutinises secondary characters in A. S. Byatt's *The Children's Book* (2009) carefully distinguishing between "flanks" defined as sharing the same diegetic level with the main figures, and hypodiegetic characters called "ficelles". With the help of the analytical model proposed by James Phelan, the study traces the functions of minor figures in contributing to the main character's mimetic, thematic and synthetic components. The final contribution in Part I focuses on a secondary character from Charles Williams's *Shadows of Ecstasy* (1933). Andrzej Sławomir Kowalczyk attempts to explain numerous conflicting interpretations of Williams's character advanced in criticism, by adopting the cognitivist approach to literary character and to literature in general. The examination of both the character and its various critical interpretations leads the scholar to question objectivist approaches to literature and to postulate drawing "a clear borderline between text-bound character analysis and reader-bound interpretation".

Part II, devoted to "Characters in generic contexts", opens with the study of early modern utopia by Professor Artur Blaim who examines a wide variety of texts analysing modes of construction as well as functions of the figure of 'utopian Jew' as both an individual character and a collective. Claiming that "Jewish characters offer an interesting insight into the dialectic of centre and periphery in utopian fiction", Blaim scrutinises techniques of peripheralisation of the figure of Jew or Jewishness. The following article also examines a wide range of texts within one genre and attempts to capture the changes within the generic convention of Secondary World Fantasy. Grzegorz Trębicki observes altered qualities and functions of SWF protagonists who, nevertheless, preserve their heroic features. The four subsequent articles in this part of the monograph are narrower in the analytic scope since each of them focuses on one text in its particular generic context(s). Thus Żaneta Nalewajk analyses William Faulkner's *The Sound and the Fury* (1929) as an illustration of the modernist rejection of "the conventions of objective, realistic presentation of literary characters – typical of the nineteenth century realistic novel" – for the sake of "a more personal type of narration" with its multiple points of view and stream-of-consciousness technique. The next study also involves the realist and modernist contexts but focuses on the fantastic transformations of the character sketch on the basis of H. G. Wells's short story "The Crystal Egg" (1897) which is used to illustrate the writer's artistic techniques of character creation. Starting from the story's primary generic convention of the character sketch, Halszka Leleń relates Wells's modifications of this genre to the contexts of nineteenth century realist tradition, modernist re-evaluation of the character's role, as well as to the cultural ambience of the turn of the century. The exploration of nonmimetic fiction is continued by Marta Komsta who analyses Shirley Jackson's *The Haunting of Hill House* (1959) in the context of the Gothic tradition. James Phelan's division into mimetic, thematic and synthetic components of the character, is employed to trace the gradual merging of the protagonist and the villain defined as the central element of the Gothic setting. Elżbieta Perkowska-Gawlik's study returns to the mimetic genre conventions. The author scrutinizes characters in Joanne Dobson's campus mystery *The Raven and the Nightingale* (1999) and shows how the novel's constitutive genre conventions of academic fiction and detective story shape the characters' mimetic, thematic, and synthetic components. The closing article by Ludmiła Gruszewska-Blaim, wider in scope, continues the subject of academic characters by focusing on techniques of constructing and construing "possible people" – men and women of science – in the mainstream college fiction. Examining numerous American college novels, Gruszewska-Blaim discusses various techniques of familiarisation or estrangement of the professor figure. She argues that mimetisation, rethematisation and gothicisation may also be observed in filmic representations of scientists and academics.

The third and final part of the monograph, "Characters in extratextual contexts", considers aspects of intertextuality, transtextuality, and the reader's cultural knowledge necessary for the interpretation of characters. It begins with exploring the category of the transtextual character – a term proposed by Brian Richardson to refer to characters appearing in more than one text[4]. The opening article employs what is probably the most primary sense of this term, examining a character featured in several different texts by the same author. Kamil Karaś suggests important semantic functions played by a secondary character in Terry Pratchett's Discworld fantasy series, resorting, among others, to the character types (or roles) in the plot as described by Vladimir Propp in relation to the magic folktale. The next study deals with a more complex case of a character's transtextuality on the example of Ursula Le Guin's novel *Lavinia* (2008) whose main figure is taken from Vergil's *Eneid*. Katarzyna Pisarska traces intricate relationships of the two texts describing multiple facets of Le Guin's protagonist predominantly within James Phelan's framework. The problem of transtextual characters is continued in the context of Phelan's model linked with certain cognitive concepts by Patrycja Podgajna, who compares parallel characters in E. M. Fos-

---

4   Umberto Eco applies the term "fluctuating characters" to such a situation (2009: 87-89).

ter's *Howard's End* (1910) and its adaptation by Zadie Smith in *On Beauty* (2005). Podgajna focuses on intertextual (or hypertextual) relationships and on examining the degree of their recognisability for the readers. The following two studies take up the problem of fictional characters' connections with historical figures. In the first one Barbara Klonowska analyses Beryl Bainbridge's novel *Young Adolf* (1978) which employs the strategy of deflating and ridiculing the historical character through irony and humour, simultaneously inviting reflection on the "constructedness" of historical characters both in fiction and in the cultural images within the readers' knowledge. While the potential for historical referentiality is clearly marked (though questioned) in Bainbridge's novel, William Golding's "The Scorpion God" (1971), examined by Jadwiga Węgrodzka, seems to obscure its connection with history. The article shows how the activation of the reader's historical and/or cultural knowledge changes the understanding of the main character as well as the generic status of Golding's novella. In the final study Dominika Szwajewska raises the problem of the relation between the character and the author by examining the complex case of the central character in J. M. Coetzee' semi-(auto?)biographical novel *Summertime* (2009), who appears as a counterfactual persona of the author in a complex postmodern narrative of multiple perspectives constantly oscillating between the referential and the fictional.

Part I

Characters in Textual Contexts

Dante Gabriel Rossetti's "Sister Helen": A functional approach to the literary character

ANDRZEJ ZGORZELSKI

Literary character appears to be one of the most complex and difficult textual relationships to analyse. Moreover, although numerous studies on the topic have been presented, it seems that their interpretative results have not yet been most illustrative or outstanding. If I were asked to undertake the challenge of such a demanding analysis, I would be bound – as in the case of all other aspects of the literary text – by some elementary methodological precepts that I have been taught by Russian Formalists, by the Prague School structuralists (not to be mistaken with French structuralism represented by Tzvetan Todorov, Claude Lévi-Strauss and others), and finally by semioticians from the Tartu school of semiotics. In my opinion these assumptions ensure the only consistent and logical paradigm of literary study in general and are also applicable to the particular aspect of the literary text that we recognise and refer to as a literary character.

To begin with: I have been taught to view a literary character as a *textual phenomenon* woven from an intricate network of sign relations, which exists only within a given utterance, within the text subjected to observation and interpretation. Such a perspective defines the basic directive of my scrutiny: to discover how this phenomenon reveals itself, how a given literary character "is made". In the broader context of humanist endeavour my aim is to understand how "beauty" comes into being – the aesthetic value being the paramount feature of literary art. It is the "beauty" that draws us and enchants but the question still remains: how? How does a literary work of art draw us and enchant? It was the Formalist school that first introduced such an angle of interest into literary studies and asked the question about a literary text: "how is it made[1]?"

When I learned that a literary character is concealed within an intricate network of sign relations, that it is a phenomenon of a *structural nature* (where structure is defined as a functional whole of relationships, which cannot be reduced to a simple sum of its components), I understood that a literary character is not a human being who can meet you or can consult a psychologist. I also realised that every trait of a literary character has its function within the larger structure of the whole text. In my view it is precisely this *function* which should be the object of literary investigation, while psychological analysis, which treats the character as if it were a real living person, does not really belong to the area of literary studies.

In practice, however, it is easy to blunder for the simple reason that we all tend to read within a cultural framework of reference, and not a literary one: we treat a literary text as if it referred to the real world we live in. Even literary scholars may find it hard to shed the impression – shared by all readers – that characters encountered in the text are persons like living people. If this happens, then scholars often become interested in the characters' inner-life and their interpersonal relationships. Then they are inclined to judge characters' attitudes, ideologies or deeds, to reconstruct characters' life stories ("how many children had Lady Macbeth?"), and on this basis to discuss historical or else contemporary reality. In fact, however, a literary character is simply a part of a certain model, to be more precise – a model of a different reality, not the world we live in.

Semiotics prompts here another sharply defined directive by declaring that the *textual* is recognised *in opposition* to the *extra-textual*. These are two different realities that are governed by different sets of rules. My own studies on fantastic literature made me realise that any attempts to compare those two (or even more numerous) realities in terms of their similarities or differences, possibility or probability of their existence, are ill-founded and fail to render any valuable interpretative conclusions. As it is, in contradistinction to our phenomenal reality, the literary model of the world is not random or chaotic but is a highly organised structure with a communicative purpose, the structure in which the function of

---

1 See B.M.Eichenbaum's "Jak jest zrobiony 'Płaszcz' Gogola" (1970: 491-513) .

each and every element is carried out only in relation to the whole structure and not to any external factors.

Moreover, semiotics – both in the variant developed by the Tartu School and by Umberto Eco – emphasises that a literary utterance is subjected not only to linguistic rules but is additionally complicated by its subordination to the rules of a *supercode*[2], called by Umberto Eco the "textual idiolect" and by Yuri Lotman the "secondary modelling system"[3]. Thus, a literary text – whether considered as discourse (narration) or as a world model – turns out to be entirely different from our reality not only by virtue of the semiotic nature of language itself, but also because of the semiotic nature of the supercode, which seems to raise this difference to the second power. For my scholarly purposes such recognition of the "ontology" of a literary text (and all its elements) becomes entirely satisfactory, so that Ockham's razor effectively cuts all other (philosophical?) speculations about the status of literary characters or other textual phenomena.

The recognition of the different nature of the two realities, the textual and the phenomenal, allows me to distinguish the textual world model as the object of my observation and – on the other hand – to define the use which can be made of my knowledge and understanding gained from the textual observations. The recognition of the difference helps to draw a line between what exists actually in the text and what is evoked in my mind by reading and analysing the text. The experience of encountering many literary world models leads – I trust – to a better understanding of our own reality as well, though this aspect does not properly belong to the literary studies even if it defines their sense and purpose in most general terms.

If I were to analyse a literary character, I probably would also suspect – besides observing the above strict methodological directives – that the substructure we call a character reveals its secrets through *the language* of the literary text: both through the language that describes the characters and their actions as well as through the language in which the characters speak. It is probably the first textual level on which the

---

2   See A. Zgorzelski's "Against methodological compromise in literary studies" (1996: 231-242).

3   See U.Eco's *Pejzaż semiotyczny* (1972:101-108) or his *Nieobecna struktura* (1996: 85-89) and J. Lotman's *Struktura tekstu artystycznego* (1984: 18).

structuring of a character takes place and where we can recognise primary signals of how a character is made. Practically everything is structured in language: motivations of actions, relationships between the character and various types of tellers, including the narrator (especially the first-person narrator-character or "focaliser" whose perspective determines the narration), interactions between characters and also relations with events and spatiotemporal settings. Polish readers may remember that the expression "a pine torn apart" is not just a part of the space setting, but brings important information about one of the characters in the novel *Ludzie bezdomni* by Stefan Żeromski. Obviously, analysing the language of a literary text I would also remember that we deal not only with linguistic rules but always with additional supercode rules, too.

In order to apprehend the role of the character in the *context of compositional patterns* or in the course of narration it would be necessary to go beyond simple observation of language and to delve deeper into the complex structures of the supercode: the interplay of various points of view, the patterning of lyrical, dramatic and narrative situations, or even into the intricate plot development, narrative structures, and the range of thematic topoi. The analysis of the supercode would probably reveal the relationship of the character with the textual organizing principles, with the text's construction, with its *dominant*.

It has to be emphasised that a specific element of a literary work (such as a character) never exists in isolation from other elements, from relations with other aspects of the text and with the text as a whole (it is always good to remember that the textual structure is a functional whole made of relationships within *the hierarchy* of various structural levels: phonological/phonetic, morphological, lexical, syntactical and compositional). Any textual interpretation scrutinizing this variety of structures-within-a-structure of an individual work is a *functional* one.

At some point of the analysis it would be necessary to examine literary conventions used in the text, beginning with genre conventions and finishing with the axiological systems evoked in the text. This may open a broad literary-historical perspective allowing to place a given literary text among other works that precede or follow it. But such an analysis may not always bring verifiable results; the further we depart from the

observation of concrete textual phenomena or the higher levels of abstraction we reach, the more dubious our conclusions may turn to be.
Let us return for a while to the beginning, to our most general methodological directives: what makes me adhere to them so stubbornly? What makes me limit myself to just one scholarly paradigm? In not so distant past the label of a formalist (applied to my own Father, Professor Czesław Zgorzelski) was not only offensive but also dangerous as a political denunciation. Today structuralism has a bad name: it is dishonoured and compromised. So what is the point of obeying principles which appear outmoded, rejected, forgotten and often evidently misunderstood?

As it is, I am really afraid of the uncritical acceptance of new theories and paradigms which, for instance, often seem to bring back the danger (among others) of returning to the crude division of the text into form and content. The division, to all appearances, has been successfully eliminated from literary studies but currently returns dressed up in various terminologies. I am also afraid of the new approaches to literature which frequently offer unverifiable and subjective critical statements and, what is more, again shift the scholar's attention from the text (which I take to be the proper object of literary studies) to, for example, the characters' psychology, the author's ideological convictions or the mental processes involved in reading. I am anxious for the distinctness, discreetness and "clarity" of literary studies, and I am particularly wary of the so-called interdisciplinary approaches which muster isolated examples culled from literary material to support newly coined theories. And I believe that, as a complex and challenging phenomenon, the literary character certainly deserves examination in the context of a long-established and well-tested, more traditional paradigm of literary studies.

*

Perhaps the general directives suggested above ought to be illustrated by more or less exemplary observations of characters in a particular text. But, instead of a monograph study, I can offer here only some sketchy remarks on Dante Gabriel Rossetti's ballad "Sister Helen" and the characters there[4]. At the outset let us see what characters we are to deal with

---

4   The original version of what follows was published in Polish in a handbook for students entitled *O analizie tekstu literackiego* (Lublin 1974) compiled in cooperation with

in this text. They are revealed to us neither in description or narrative nor fully and instantly – at first, we can only hear their voices engaged in a dialogue. The order of responses remains the same throughout the whole text: the first three lines are uttered by Little Brother, with the iterative second line, the following two lines belong to his sister Helen, each stanza repeating her second line, while the next two lines – closing the stanza – contain a prayer-like apostrophe to Mary Mother, which constitutes a kind of commentary put in parenthesis and printed in italics[5]. The first stanza, with its introductory dialogic exchange, provides basic information about the situational context of the dialogue:

> 'Why did you melt your waxen man,
> Sister Helen?
> To-day is the third since you began'.
> 'The time is long, yet the time ran,
> Little brother'.
> (*O Mother, Mary Mother,*
> *Three days to-day, between Hell and Heaven!*)

Thus the opening informs of Sister Helen's actions: for three days she has been melting a wax figure of a man. Cultural competence allows us to recognise this activity as a magic ritual designed to bring about someone's death. This suggestion is indirectly confirmed by the parenthetical part of the stanza: three days have elapsed in suspension between damnation and salvation, "between Hell and Heaven". In contrast to the reader, however, Little Brother is unaware of his sister's intent. He asks about the purpose of her time-consuming work because, as the second stanza reveals, he is waiting for the playtime she promised to him: "You'll let me play, for you said I might". What is more, Sister Helen's subjective perception of the fast flow of time is suggested by the words: "Yet the time ran!". Let us notice a crucial juxtaposition between the dialogic nature of the text, determining its dramatic[6] character, and the lyr-

---

Wiesław Krajka. Ten years later Artur Blaim undertook the challenge of translating the text which subsequently was published by Państwowe Wydawnictwo Naukowe as *On the Analysis of the Literary Text*. The study of "Sister Helen" contained in these two editions will serve as a springboard for my argument here.

5   I refer to the text from the D.S.R. Welland's edition of *The Pre-Raphaelites in Literature and Art*, London 1953.

6   The word "dramatic" is popularly used to refer to the rising tension of a dangerous situation, but here, as a theoretical term, it designates "presenting" as opposed to "narrat-

ical strategy of implication (as opposed to straightforward statement) which suggests both the innocence of Little Brother and Sister Helen's subjective perception of the world. Evidently, the text communicates much information by implying rather than by stating explicitly.

Our understanding of the situation in which the characters find themselves at the beginning of the ballad, as well as of their characteristics, becomes often enhanced by a number of reticent passages in the dialogue. This strategy of hinting, implying and suggesting is based mainly on the device of equivalence, owing to which some words acquire multiple meanings, and refer not only to their immediate context but also to the past and future situations. This is what happens, for instance, in the fifth stanza of the ballad:

> 'See, see, the sunken pile of wood,
> Sister Helen,
> Shines through the thinned wax red as blood!'
> 'Nay now, when looked you yet on blood
> Little brother?'
> (*O Mother, Mary Mother,*
> *How pale she is, between Hell and Heaven!*)

The information contained in the parenthetical part of the stanza indicating Sister Helen's paleness suggests that she is worn out by the three days of work and, perhaps, by the morbid character of the effort. Additionally, her uncertainty and anxiety about the efficacy of her magic was also emphasised in the initial stanzas where to her brother's words "all is well", the sister replied "even so – nay, peace! you cannot tell" (III). Helen's exhaustion is confirmed by her reaction to the words of Little Brother: when he says "Now close your eyes, for they are sick and sore", the girl answers: "Aye, let me rest - I'll lie on the floor" (VI).

Moreover, the word "pale" is linked by phonological correspondence with the word "pile" in the phrases "pile of wood" and "how pale she is". That correspondence establishes an equivocal cause-and-effect relationship between the words, which may be interpreted in numerous ways (this is how the supercode is built!). Perhaps it is the sight of the pile of

---

ing" (connected with the epical) and "expressing" (characteristic of the lyrical). The dramatic, the epical and the lyrical constitute three ways (modes, kinds) of transferring information both in literary and non-literary texts. Compare the understanding of kinds in E.Steiger, *Grundbegriffe der Poetik*, Zurich 1956.

burning wood, blood-red when seen through the wax, that reminds the girl about the usual punishment for witches: burning at a stake. Maybe that is why she turns white? It has to be stressed that the reticence of the descriptive elements is not incidental here – the alliterated words are placed in such strategic positions of the stanza, in the first and last line, that they have to be semantically functional: "pile"-"pale" correspondence indicates what may happen in the future and thus suggests the possible *Nachgeschichte* of the situation presented in the dialogue. At the same time, however, it implies what may be happening in the main heroine's psyche here and now.

Rossetti's text often juxtaposes repetitions of words and motifs in the span of its forty-two stanzas. The motif of Sister Helen's pale face recurs in the heavily alliterated description of the former fiancé's wife ("Pale, pale her cheeks, that in pride did glow"; XXXII) and makes us compare the appearance and the situations of both women, establishing yet another equivalence, this time between the characters. And again it seems important that the text only suggests such a comparison, never developing it fully.

The shadow of the stake will also lurk in the alliterations of "fire" and "forgive" in the twenty seventh stanza, in the middle of the ballad:

'Oh his son still cries, if you forgive
Sister Helen,
The body dies but the soul shall live'.
'Fire shall forgive me as I forgive,
Little brother!'
(*O Mother, Mary Mother,*
As she forgives, between Hell and Heaven!)

The stanza allows to observe the ways of suggesting multi-layered meanings – as well as to illustrate the creation of the textual supercode. The word "forgive" in the first line carries its ordinary dictionary sense and means "to absolve, excuse and let something go", while in subsequent lines it is used ironically and acquires a completely opposite meaning: the fire of the stake will not forgive the witch just as she will not forgive her victim. What is more, the ambiguity extends to the word "as": not only may it suggest a comparison ("as I forgive" = in the way I forgive) but also brings temporal connotations ("as I forgive" = when I forgive) foreshadowing the main character's future.

Since we are dealing with poetry, juxtapositions of words challenge dictionary meanings and establish semantic values not only in the horizontal syntactic patterns of English grammar, but also in the vertical arrangements of rhymes. When Little Brother reports the "cry" of the messenger informing about the lover's agony (XIII), the rhyme signals the main theme of the message by the juxtaposition of rhyming words: "cry", "die", "I". What is also highlighted is the ambiguity of the word "cry" which can suggest shouting or lamenting. Stanza XXI exhibits a similar pattern of rhymes while the rhyming phrases from stanza XVI constitute almost sentence-like structures: "cry to-day", "curse away", "but pray". Likewise the previously quoted stanza suggests a strong imperative expressed in the rhyming sequences "forgive", "live", "forgive". Rhymes contribute also to the description of Lady of Ewern: "fair", "hair", "despair". Moreover, anaphoric patterns in the neighbouring stanzas emphasise the emotional value of the text.

The ballad unfolds unhurriedly; initially, up to stanzas VI-VII, the central motif of magic ritual develops in the carefully sustained atmosphere of peril which is conveyed through a selection of appropriate linguistic elements: triple repetition of the word "dead", double occurrence of the word "blood", alliteration of "sick and sore", accumulation of exclamations (5), and questions (6) which are often rhetorical: "what is this...?" (IV); "now, of the dead what can you say...?" (IV); "now when looked you yet on blood...?" (V). There arises a clear tension between the gloomy character of the stormy night as a spatiotemporal location of the opening scene, entirely congruous with the dreary intent of Sister Helen's actions ("to-night" II, VI, VII; "the moon flies" VII; "wind's wake", "shaken trees", "the chill stars shake" VIII) and Little Brother's behaviour suggesting his pristine perception of the spatial setting ("let me play..." II, "outside it's merry" VIII, "I'll play without the gallery door" VI).

We learn about the further course of events from Little Brother responding to successive requests and questions from Sister Helen: "Aye, look and say whatever you see..." (VII), "Whence come the three...?" (IX), "do you know them who they are ...?" (X). Then Little Brother reports on what he can see or hear "without the gallery door" as the ex-fiancé of his sister keeps sending messengers (his two brothers, father and his newly wedded wife) begging Sister Helen to lift the curse she has cast. In this way, through Little Brother's words, the ballad reveals the third – epical – mode evident in the descriptive fragments evoking landscape characteristics: "the hill-verge from Bygone Bar" (X); "the wind is sad in the iron chill" (XL); "in the frost" (XLII) or depicting the messengers' appearance – "the white mane on the blast" (XL); "A lady [...] by a dark steed brought" (XXX); "Pale, pale her cheeks, that in pride did glow" (XXXII). The epical mode appears also in short narrative passages: "it's Keith of Eastholm rides so fast" (XI); "He stops to speak, and he stills his horse" (XX); "He looks at me and tries to speak" (XXVI). So the character of Little Brother turns into a narrator who also reports in the indirect speech the messengers' words: "he says that Keith of Ewern's cry [...] is ever to see you ere he die" (XXI), "he prays you [...] to save his dear son's soul alive" (XXVIII).

The ballad, however, does not reveal whether Sister Helen's reaction is made known to the messengers, and whether it is thus forwarded to her former lover. The heroine directs the answers solely to her brother, and there are no indications that they are passed on. This remarkable economy of the dialogic structure – a special case of a "minus device" – seems to diminish the importance of a rather stereotypical and pretextual action. The character of the brother becomes the sole witness of his sister's cruelty and derision (though, of course, the reader is a witness too!), and thus attention is directed not so much to the events taking place outside, "without", but to what is "within", to the characters' psyche, thoughts and feelings.

An important analogy should be noticed at this point: divided into three parts and based on dialogue, the construction of each stanza reflects three mutually intertwined modal aspects: firstly, the dialogue represents the dramatic mode; secondly, Little Brother's utterances function within the epical mode broadening the information about the *Vorgeschichte* of the presented situation and determining the events of action by informing of new messengers who bring Keith of Ewern's requests; and thirdly, Sister Helen's replies have a lyrical function and complement the heroine's characterisation. Not only do these replies reveal her emotional state, but also testify to her verbal skill at coining mocking answers. Her anaphoric and repetitive "What else he broke will he ever join? (XXII), "What else he took will he give again" (XXVIII) work as an ironic commentary on Keith's sending back the ring and the broken coin. Let us observe that there is no direct information about the broken promise and lost virginity – these are only suggested by the protagonist's implications as well as by the partly explained *Vorgeschichte*. It has to be noted, however, that our reconstruction of modal dominants is definitely simplified. We have not considered, for instance, the constructional expression (connected with the lyrical and not the epical mode) of the evolution of the young narrator's awareness: at the beginning he just wants to play and perceives the cold landscape of wind-shaken trees as "merry", but at the end of his experience he views the world differently: "Oh, the wind is sad in the iron chill [...] And weary sad they look by the hill" (IL).

How does the third part of each stanza contribute to the structuring of the characters? This part is the most repetitive and refrain-like (though the second and fifth lines also have a similar, burden-like nature). The third voice revealed there (Oh, how those ballads love triple patterns!) is not directed to any of the parties involved in the dialogue. Shaping its utterance as a repetitive invocation to the Mother of God, the voice reiterates one of the phrases taken from the dialogue and then combines it with the second part of the refrain, "between Hell and Heaven". First, the stanza acquires a distinctive frame since the name of the sister from the title, repeated in the second line of each stanza, constitutes a combination of morphemes from the final words of each stanza: "Hel-l" and "Heav-en". This reiterative echoing evokes the heroine's inner conflict and her ethical situation ("between Hell and Heaven" - between the evil of hatred and the virtue of love), endowing it also with a more universal dimension. Second, the phrases lifted from the dialogue and inserted into a different syntactical context in the third part of each stanza, gain additional meanings. They echo the character's words (repeating their original sense) and simultaneously place them in a new perspective of another point of view, signalling extra its importance by a highly emotional exclamation or a question mark. Thus, the third part of each stanza, introducing a voice external to the characters' situation and dialogic exchanges, appears to establish the most dynamic tensions between the personal frames of reference in the ballad.

Let us look at some examples. Incorporating a phrase from Sister Helen's reply in stanza VI ("...of the dead what can you say...?") into the refrain part: "what of the dead, between Hell and Heaven?", changes the girl's rhetorical question signalling her doubt in Little Brother's knowledge and experience into a generalizing reflection on the situation of the dead suspended "between" (oh, this "between"!) damnation and salvation, between despair and joy, between punishment and reward. The personal and individual sense becomes shifted into a universal and more abstract perspective.

On a different occasion, the refrain part adds valuable "stage directions" to the on-going dialogue, as it happens in stanza XII:

'Oh tell him I fear the frozen dew,
Little brother'.
(O Mother, Mary Mother,
Why laughs she thus, between Hell and Heaven?)

Actually, the quoted refrain not only introduces additional information about the situation, but also emphasises the girl's derisive mockery in her refusal to converse with the messenger. Sometimes, the third voice's comments play an important part in constituting the supercode equivalences, as, for instance, in stanza XVIII:

'But he calls for ever on your name,
Sister Helen,
And says that he melts before a flame'.
'My heart for his pleasure fared the same,
Little brother'.
(*O Mother, Mary Mother,*
Fire at the Heart, between Hell and Heaven!)

The equivalence of the alliterated words: "flame"-"fared"-"fire" suggests a whole range of new semantic intimations. First, the words placed in the relation of equivalence refer to the performance of the magic ritual, however, it is not a wax figure here that melts in the flame but the man. Significantly, the word "flame" will reappear in the final description of the fire consuming the melted wax, signalling the quick progress of the agony: "the flames are winning up apace!"(XLI). Second, the alliterated words juxtapose the torture of the dying lover with the girl's suffering (through the rhyme "flame"-"the same" and a wide ironically indistinct semantic range of "fared"). Moreover, the metaphorical "heart" appears twice: in "my heart for his pleasure..." and "fire at the Heart". An explicit semantic extension of the word "heart" is signalled by means of the capital letter, which is rather difficult to justify here.

The potential range of the metaphor may possibly extend to the conventional iconographic representation of Christ's heart in the flames of love. Read in this context, the whole apostrophic refrain (though only within this particular stanza) may among other things express the admiration for this Love, or else it may simply juxtapose two contrasting kinds of love (only erotic "for his pleasure" and a true love "at the heart") or even signal the opposition between love and hate, enhancing the sense of "Hell and Heaven".

Another example of semantically important equivalences appears in stanza XXI with its intertwined situational and metaphoric associations, evoked by the linking of the words "see" and "soul":

'Oh he says that Keith of Ewern's cry,
Sister Helen,
Is ever to see you ere he die'.
'In all that his soul sees, there am I,
Little brother!'
(*Oh Mother, Mary Mother,*
The soul's one sight, between Hell and Heaven!)

While the former lover wants to see (meet) her, Sister Helen refuses to see (meet) even his messenger. Her lover's pleas reach her only through the double mediation of, firstly, the messenger and, secondly, Little Brother (so that she *does not see* but only hears). The girl, however, actually maintains the contact with the lover, albeit on a mental level, in his thoughts that are totally focused on her: "In all that his soul sees, there am I...". This "seeing", as the last line suggests, applies to both the lover and the girl ("seeing"-"meeting") since each is the focus of the other's thoughts: "The soul's one sight". Yet the latter phrase may also carry such suggestions as the exclusiveness of infatuation which sees only the object of love or – for that matter – a look of hate fastened on its object, or even the concentration of beseeching. Definitely the characters' psyche is not created here to give the impression of univocality!

The complexity of semantic relations established between the dialogue and the refrain-like commentary in each stanza should not be reduced only to the generalisation owing to which a particular situation of a girl, her brother and her ex-fiancé is transformed into a deliberation on the universal human condition. Such a function, though, can certainly be traced, for instance, in the semantic wealth of the phrase "for a space" in stanza XVI. Temporal and particularised sense of "burn for a space" meaning "burn for a while" is followed there by a clear spatial generalisation: "here for a space" in the sense "in earthly life", "between Hell and Heaven".

Greater semantic complexity is inherent in the very nature of the repetitive, litany-like invocations to Mary Mother. Perceived in terms of the litany, the "unfinished" syntactic format of the third part of each stanza lacks the verb in the imperative form to voice the appeal to the addressee of the supplication. After a series of forty such cases of reticence ending each stanza, the reader might be effectively tempted to provide the missing verb at least in the last line of the text: "O Mother, Mary Mother, lost, lost, all lost, between Hell and Heaven!"

Confronting the third part of each stanza with literary tradition will immediately suggest an association of the final refrain and its commenting function with the chorus in the ancient Greek tragedy. The third voice concluding each stanza in "Sister Helen" is subject to special unique rules: the voice is separated from the dialogic part by the graphical layout and by the parenthesis and as such, it is not heard by the characters participating in the dialogue. The parenthetical part of the stanza is an apostrophe addressed to the supernatural power but it is obviously directed also to the addressee of the whole text. This chorus-like refrain not only introduces additional semantic fields into the meanings of a given stanza, but also functions in relation to the whole poem by foregrounding the role of the addressee in structuring the final shape and sense of the implied litany. This in turn proves somehow contradictory to the previously observed predilection towards the interest in the characters' psyche and leads to yet another tension determining the inner dynamics of the text.

Needless to say, the dynamic tensions are also manifest in the three traditional but diverse genre conventions in "Sister Helen". The persistent use of the commenting chorus of the ancient tragedy does not agree too well with the dialogic construction characteristic of the ballad, though both genres serve the dramatic mode and can successfully present the characters' fates and are even able to analyse their internal conflicts. On the other hand the convention of the refrain with litany-like structure seems rather distant from taking on such themes. Moreover, though the litany shares the compositional repetitiveness with the ballad genre, yet the former seems to diminish the dramatic with its strong monologic tendency. The successive interweaving of dialogue and monologue, together with the constant exchange of the speaking voices – so characteristic of the analysed text – eventually serve not only to highlight each individual speaker, but also to build the complex semantic network of the textual supercode.

Finally I would like to return to the introductory methodological remarks. Numerous pitfalls await the literary scholar who becomes seduced by the technique of selective observation, exclusively concentrating on summarizing themes, attempting to unravel the intricacies of the relations between action and narration, focusing on the spatial and temporal relations within a text, or analysing characters. In all such endeavours one is in danger of being beguiled by a single aspect of the intricate network of structural relations whereas no scholarly task can be satisfactorily fulfilled if one ever loses sight of the supercode as a whole. But the most dangerous trap opens when we become infatuated with theoretical terminology accepted before starting the interpretation, which may lead us to observe only what the theory presupposes and to prove only what we assumed at the start. Accordingly, if we really want to see how a literary character "is made", then we have to examine the text in its totality, using solely these theoretical tools which the text really demands.

Translated by Joanna Pasternak and Jadwiga Węgrodzka

Joseph Conrad's "The Partner": Character and language

KAROLINA TRAPP

"And that tongue of his"

Critical discussions of literary characters in Conrad's prose provide for a popular trend running in the scholarly reflection on this writer. Much of that commentary approaches literary character as a psychological construct (sometimes in relation to the author's personality and life). One might mention for example works such as Albert Guerard's *Conrad the Novelist*, Robert Hampson's *Joseph Conrad: Betrayal and Identity*, or Joseph Dobrinsky's *The Artist in Conrad's Fiction: A Psychocritical Study*; among the more recent publications, *Hearts of Darkness: Melville, Conrad and Narratives of Oppression* (2010) combines postcolonial and psychoanalytical interpretations of Conrad's texts[1]. The present paper offers observations from a different angle. Here, the figures populating the fictional world of "The Partner" – one of the less frequently studied short stories from Conrad's *Within the Tides*[2] – are discussed strictly as literary phenomena. This seems to me an approach perhaps more faithful to the general notion of Conrad as a consciously artistic

---

1   Among its chapter-papers, a psychoanalytical perspective typifies for instance "The Ironic Rescuer in *Pierre* and *Victory*" by John T. Matteson, the examination of women's suffering in "The Stories of Agatha, Hunilla, Amy Foster and Winnie Verloc" by Sanford E. Marovitz, or "The Tragedy of Trauma" by Anna Marta Szczepan-Wojnarska – who proposes a reading of Ahab and Kurtz as shaped by traumatic experience in three works by Melville and Conrad.

2   This paper is based on an electronic copy of the 1915 J. M. Dent edition of Joseph Conrad's collection *Within the Tides* (which includes "The Partner"), available online as The Project Gutenberg eBook (#1053). The online version does not provide pagination. For the sake of clarity, all quotation marks used in this paper indicate original citations from Conrad.

writer who repeatedly directs the reader's attention to the process of literary creation and craftsmanship (compare Zgorzelski 1984a: 7).

A recognised strategy Conrad uses to this end is often that of multiple narrations[3]. This is also the case with "The Partner". In this text, the main narrator learns about the unfortunate partnership of two businessmen from a company stevedore in the smoking-room of a coastal hotel; the introduction of more than one narrating voice is accompanied by other elements and motifs betraying an underlying thematic focus on the art of storytelling (compare Greaney 2002: 16-17). Not only does the second narrator engage in relating the tale to contest its previous version (critiqued right from the outset as "a silly yarn"), but he also decides upon presenting his account to the frame narrator because he learns that the latter is a "writer of stories"[4]. The "old fellow" starts the conversation owing to his interest in "the process by which stories – stories for periodicals – were produced". Consequently, the chat overflows with direct observations on the literary process and technique: he asks his interlocutor about "how do [tales] ever come to your head?", for instance, or receives feedback such as suggestions of possible phrasings ("we usually say: some years passed").

At the first glance, the tale's impact seems to be attributed to the "striking effect of the [secondary] narrator", who is described as "impressive", "powerful", and "extraordinary". These are, however, rather vague traits (of personality? – as suggested by the remark "of individuality he had plenty"). A closer look reveals that it is his manner of speaking which becomes a primary point of interest. The text's second paragraph does provide some descriptive detail; nevertheless, such detail seems prevailingly to serve as evidence supportive, complementary, or subservient to the main narrator's observations concerning the raconteur's verbal expression:

---

3   See e.g. Modrzewski (1992: 89-95, and passim), or Zgorzelski's discussion of Conrad's "The Inn of the Two Witches" (1984a: 50-67).

4   One could note here that the very existence (in the fictional world) of two versions of the story that is the subject of Conrad's text – the one told by the "old ruffian" of a stevedore and the one told by boatmen to the summer visitors, the latter spoken of as a potential alternative literary material and even endowed with the tentative title "In The Channel" – seems to underline the issue of narrative choices and thereby indirectly orientate the reader to the autothematic drift of the text.

His great, flat, furrowed cheeks were shaven; a thick, square wisp of white hairs hung from his chin; its waggling *gave additional point to his deep utterance*; and his general *contempt* for mankind with its activities and moralities was expressed in the rakish set of his big soft hat of black felt with a large rim, which he kept always on his head. [emphasis mine]

Although the epithet "deep" can simply refer to the grave manner or the pitch of the speaking voice, it also carries associations with such qualities as profundity or the ability to affect powerfully, and "deep utterance" might be interpreted as attributing the power of impressing to the articulation itself. Moreover, the little chin puff is mentioned only in relation to the "utterance" (as an enhancer of its effect), while the disregard for social conventions perceivable in the ruffian's style of wearing the hat remains in strict cooperation with the derision tainting his enunciation: his "scornful tone", whenever he "growled out contempt". Otherwise, the occasional short bits of description focus mostly on the speaker's "immobility" (other examples might, for instance, be "without moving a muscle of his face", or "without moving he seemed to lend an attentive ear"). The function of such delineation seems to be to emphasise – by contrast – the rare moments of movement, which usually are also moments particularly strongly filled with emotion (e.g. "The turning of his head slightly toward me at this point was like a sign of strong feeling in any other man") and/or significant in terms of plot development and creation of tension (e.g. "He drew a breath, and I noticed his hand, lying loosely on the table, close slowly into a fist. In that immovable man it was startling, ominous, like the famed nod of the Commander").

Apparently, the "imposing old ruffian" does not perform particularly greatly as a storyteller: it is through descriptors such as "vague growls", "as an old dog growls", or "hoarse, fragmentary mumble" that his narrating style is presented to the reader. He is essentially, a "taciturn man" and when we first eye his utterances, they consist of short, incoherent, abruptly suspended clauses (rather than smoothly-flowing, fully-fledged sentences):

'I – no such foolishness – looking at the rocks out there – more likely call to mind an office – I used to look in sometimes at one time – office in London – one of them small streets behind Cannon Street Station'.
'Stare at the silly rocks – nod their silly heads [the visitors, I presume]'.
[comment as in the original]

His seems to be a simple, colloquial language, marked by swearwords and exclamations, unsophisticated sentence structure, often resorting to repetition (his range of adjectives fails to extend far beyond "silly") – as in his "Damn silly yarn!", "Devil knows", "I don't know why they do it!", or "What do they think a man is – blown out paper-bag or what? – go off pop like that when he's hit". His comparisons grow out of common every-day experience – blowing out paper bags, "drinking weak lemonade" or "plums in a slice of cold pudding" (of "silly lot of rocks"). This lack of refinement is brought to the reader's attention through contrast with the rivalling description of the rocks by the main narrator, focusing on subtleties of shape, hue, and atmosphere[5]. Hence perhaps the closing claim of the tale's inconsequential value – it is "not worth many thanks", nor does it deserve the effort of "cook[ing] it for the consumption of magazine readers".

One might observe at this point, however, that the presented story must have been not entirely without merit since the listening "writer" ultimately commits himself to retelling it. Given that he serves it "raw", apparently not paraphrased but faithful to the original utterances of "this statuesque ruffian", there must be something of interest not only in the individuality of the raconteur – which attracted the frame narrator's attention "at first" – but also in the vein in which he was delivering his tale. After all, it is through verbal means that narration (itself an utterance) forms and fleshes out the fictional world and its protagonists, as Conrad's text reminds us by persistently returning to the theme of linguistic artistry.

Importantly, it is not only the secondary narrator who is characterised by his manner of delivering words. He himself also displays interest in language matters, and repeatedly directs the main narrator's (and thereby also the reader's) attention to his characters' turns of expression. "Any squirming skunk can talk like that", "you know the way these chaps put it", "that sort of talk" (appearing three times in the text), "And that tongue of his [...]. Don't forget that tongue" and similar remarks flag this concern. Such preoccupation with language is particularly manifest in the depiction of Cloete – the fraudulent "partner" – who emerges in the text as a master of words and wields the power of convincing, af-

---

5   For more on this contrast, see Jóźwiak 2005: 27.

fecting and influencing people[6]. From the very moment when he enters the scene, his skills in this respect are highlighted, and to a substantial degree he is discussed in relation to the activities of speaking and/or writing:

> 'Cloete would come in to have his chop and make the girl laugh. No need to talk much, either, for that. Nothing but the way he would twinkle his spectacles on you and give a twitch of his thick mouth was enough to start you off before he began one of his little tales. [...] Talks plenty about himself. [...] Writes advertisements and all that. Tells me funny stories. [...] jocular way of speaking – in a low voice... [...] Never laughed so much in my life. The beggar – would make you laugh telling you how he skinned his own father'.
> 'Think they can carry off anything and talk themselves out of anything'.

As the story unfolds and Cloete unleashes his verbal (and plotting) talents onto the unsuspecting George Dunbar, not only his utterances but also the narratorial observations concerning him are conveyed in smoother and more fluent utterances, richer and more sophisticated in terms of vocabulary and sentence structure. Admittedly, the narrator's rough and abrupt clauses are still conspicuous in introducing the protagonist for the first time; yet, the fragmentariness here no longer functions just as a characterisation tool for the speaking voice. This style makes it possible to summarise the history of Cloete's *Vorgeschichte* life in a curriculum-vitae manner:

> 'First I *saw* him – *comes* off a ship in dock from the States – passenger. *Asks* me for a small hotel near by. *Wanted* to be quiet and have a look round for a few days. I took him to a place – friend of mine... Next time – in the City – Hallo! You're very obliging – have a drink. *Talks* plenty about himself. *Been* years in the States. All sorts of business all over the place. With some patent medicine people, too. *Travels. Writes* advertisements and all that. *Tells* me funny stories'. [emphases mine]

Repeatedly beginning with, or even just limited to a verb, fragmentary clauses indicate here the character's active personality, hinting at his role as the *spiritus movens* for the events to come, as well as suggesting that Cloete (in contrast to George and Harry Dunbar) can boast considerable

---

6 Phrases like "let me tell you" or "I tell you" – in Cloete's utterances – stress this protagonist's authority. In turn, the depiction of Cloete as deprived of his verbal potency during the climax – he turns "numb", he "forces himself to answer", or remains "without a word" – serves to emphasize his qualities through contrast.

experience. Thus, the fragmentary and peculiar syntax contributes to the presentation of Cloete as a character with power, even though gradually the narrator's sentences referring to Cloete become relatively long and complete.

Moreover, while the narrators employ a diversity of literary devices throughout the whole story, the articulation of Cloete attracts attention owing to the intensity and frequency with which figurative applications of language feature there (especially in comparison to other protagonists). Thus, utterances on or by Cloete are permeated with ambivalence and metaphor. This includes, for instance, the motif of "fire" when Cloete argues his case to George Dunbar and "warming his back at the fire, goes on" – seemingly a literal description of Cloete standing with his back to the fireplace but for the fact he "was [already] all *on fire* from the contact with this unique opportunity" [emphasis mine], later even reaching the state of "boiling". A case in point, however, is Cloete's proposing to wreck the ship through the metaphor of "tomahawking" (underlined by the narrator's remark and repetition – both immediate and throughout the text):

> 'Tisn't selling your old Sagamore wants. The blamed thing wants *toma-hawking* (seems the name Sagamore means an Indian chief or something. The figure-head was a half-naked savage with a feather over one ear and a hatchet in his belt). *Tomahawking*, says he'. [emphasis mine]
> 'The Sagamore must be tomahawked – *as he would call it*; to spare George's feelings, maybe'. [emphasis mine]

As can be seen in this case, metaphor in Cloete's mouth is often enlisted in the service of his general strategy to avoid naming things as they are and to speak indirectly.

This leads us to another type of ambivalence permeating Cloete's language, namely irony – which assumes a spectrum of shapes and shades here. Sometimes such irony consists in Cloete's tendency to use wordings which – in the reader's eyes – seem inadequate to a given situation: "Go in and win", he says to Stafford, as if he was cheering a player in a sports game (whereas the reader is aware of the rather sinister scheme being brewed up). A striking example can be found in Cloete's saying "by chance" (in "should she by chance part from her anchors in a north-east gale and get lost on the beach, as many of them do…") while weaving the web of intrigue to sink the ship *on purpose*, or in his naming Mr Stafford as a "noble sailor" despite the awareness of Stafford's corruption and despicability. Such exaltation of the evil is completed with Cloete's frequent debasement of things otherwise considered good, such as Sagamore. In contrast to the general high opinion of the ship (as revealed for instance in the newspaper article informing about its wreck), Cloete persistently calls it "that silly ship of yours" or "the blamed thing", and complains that "the blamed old thing wouldn't fetch half her insured value". In many instances, irony results from purposeful yet unnecessary emphasis and exaggeration – a technique most often applied by Cloete to the brothers Dunbar or the relationship between them. This happens for instance in the comment: "Model brothers, says Cloete – two love-birds – I am looking after the tinned-fruit side of this cozy little show... Gives me that sort of talk". The epithet "tinned-fruit" would with all probability refer here to one of the types of business George's company ran. However, we learn only later of the firm's involvement in such trade, while the word's embedment in a sentence describing the relationship between the two brothers – in terms such as "two love-birds" and "this cosy little show" – seems to suggest that its metaphorical, emphatic use hinges on its connotations of sweetness. Thereby, a critique of such a too-sugary bond is implied under the pretence of appreciation. In cases such as this, irony becomes Cloete's weapon serving to ridicule affection.

The roots of irony are always in discrepancy (between what is stated *expressis verbis* and the underlying meaning which the reader is able to decipher from the shape of the utterance, or else between what is being said and what the speaker and the reader know – but not necessarily what the addressee of Cloete's words knows). Ironic tension marking Cloete's ingenious verbalisation often grows out of an opposition defined in ethical terms: the good (degraded into a negative phenomenon) and the bad (toned down not to appear evil anymore). Consequently, irony constitutes an essential instrument in portraying the protagonist as reversing the traditional hierarchy of values, and thus, to use Conrad's words, as a "man of easy moral standards". By the same token, Cloete's evaluations of the surrounding world tamper with social prescriptions for the sake of satisfying his needs at a given moment. The swindler harnesses words to support his argument by downplaying the negative aspect of his proposition, by exaggerating its positive side, and by ridiculing the dominant standards of good – in a bid to thereby justify his plan to enrich himself illicitly. This is to say, the style used by Cloete is an example of a persuasive, manipulative language. The verbal ordering of Cloete's depiction in "The Partner" presents him as a deceptive and dangerous – but also pragmatic – character, a master of seductive language (also because of its literariness)[7] who puts his skills to questionable uses.

Cloete's highly individual interpretation of good and bad defines him also by setting him apart from and even against the other characters – the discrepancy between the underlying *common* moral hierarchy and the *reversal* of it in his words is illustrative of a difference in perception between Cloete and others.[8] Thus, the encounter between the two company partners, which determines the development of the action and constitutes the thematic dominant of the text's surface structure, reveals its nature on a deeper level as a clash of values and personalities, a collision of points of view – as well as a conflict of languages, so to say.

Accordingly, George Dunbar's depiction (and even more so the one of his brother Captain Harry) is governed by contraposition to Cloete's. The discord between the idealistic George and his financially-oriented associate is forcefully brought to the fore in the juxtaposition of their respective "an honest man for father" and "a rich man for father". Motifs disclosing the rationality and pragmatism of one character are complemented with those expressing emotional nature of the other (e.g. "He almost loses his head, while Cloete keeps cool"). When Cloete speaks of George as a coward, he uses the term "funky". The word, however, possesses also the sense – applied usually to jazz or similar music – of "uncomplicated and emotional"; and, it may well be used in this particular sense to characterise George's artless and straightforward language. Thus, for instance, on learning about Cloete's proposition, "George gnashes his teeth with rage". As his unprincipled partner spells out the details of the fraud scheme, he becomes "too upset to speak – only gurgles and waves his arms", "feels more upset than ever", "shudders", and

---

7   Greaney draws a parallel between the false in Cloete's language and the literary fiction (2002: 16-17).

8   The discord between the common and Cloete's interpretations of the world occasionally reaches even the degree of a quasi-paradox, as in the following examples: "Whenever Cloete looks at the sky he feels comforted; it looks so threatening", "it's the devil, says Cloete, cheerfully", or "It's a bad business, Mr Cloete, he says. And Cloete rejoices to hear that".

"shuts his eyes tight at that sort of talk". As can be seen in the above examples, the depiction of George focuses on feelings. His utterances are often accompanied with a gesture, which emphasises his emotionality and translates the underlying sentiment into visual form, as well as manifesting thereby his openness and honesty. When George speaks, short sentences, emphatic phrasings and exclamations help to convey emotion:

> 'George nearly chokes... So you think I am of that sort – you think me capable – What do you take me for?... He almost loses his head'.
> 'Do shut up. What's the good? No money. Hardly any to go on with, let alone pouring thousands into advertising. Never dare propose to his brother Harry to sell the ship. Couldn't think of it. Worry him to death. It would be like the end of the world coming. And certainly not for a business of that kind!'
> 'I wouldn't even dare think of such a thing...'

Indeed, instead of just speaking, he "cries" and "gasps". Moreover, he is presented like, and compared to, a child:

> George "bursts out weeping with a great bellow. He throws himself on the couch, buries his face in a cushion, and howls like a kid".
> 'You had nothing to do with it any more than a baby unborn'.

The above strategy contributes to the depiction of George as emotional, as well as suggesting his innocence and naïveté. By the same token, it also underlines his weakness: he is, after all, a "weak fellow" that "weakens" even more as Cloete's corrupting power gains momentum.

The delineation of George through gestures also helps to illustrate this process of weakening, the gradual loss of happiness, life energy and power: from violent bursts and gnashing teeth, waving arms and banging on the desk, George's portrayal veers into a picture of fear and fright: he "crumples all up inside", is "scared at his own shadow", "sits up in a sudden panic", or "lays his arms and his head on his desk, so that Cloete feels sorry for him". Gradually, vocabulary associated with fear begins to dominate. George's utterances also evolve from exclamatory to tentative, brimming with questions, and even assuming the shape of abrupt fragmentary grunts expressive of lack of self-confidence (compare "trembling voice"):

> 'Perhaps it would be best to sell. Couldn't you talk to my brother?'
> 'Humbug! There can be no such man. And yet if there was such a man it would be safe enough – perhaps'.

'H'm! H'm! Oh yes – unfortunately – sorry to disappoint – my brother – made other arrangements – going himself'.

Gradually, the process goes as far as even to prohibit any possibility of vocalisation: "George too upset to speak – only gurgles and waves his arms", "[a]nd George can't speak, throat too dry". Thus, in opposition to his "partner", George appears in the text as lacking in verbal power.

Harry Dunbar's language resembles the one of George in many respects. His lack of experience, vulnerability and innocence are expressed through the narratorial critique of sea life as offering "no opportunities, no experience, no variety, nothing", through comparison to a helpless and insignificant fly ("no more chance in the world if put to it than fly"), and through numerous equivalences with a child (e.g. "no more up to people's tricks than a baby", "sat in a corner like a good boy"). The key word in the delineation of Harry is "heart" and its relatives repeatedly used in reference to him. Thus, for instance, "in his hearty way" portrays him not just as energetic but also as a magnanimous person exhibiting general goodwill and warmth of affection. Love determines his relationships – with his wife, his brother, and his ship. Hence, George's argument against destroying Sagamore is that Harry "would break his heart". Indeed, following the ship's destruction, the Captain dies "[s]hot through the heart".

After discussing the main protagonists, a brief commentary may be advanced on the portrayals of the remaining characters. The languages embodying Mr Stafford, Mrs Dunbar, or Mrs Harry Dunbar also assume their own individual qualities. The delineation of Mrs Dunbar, for instance, focuses on clothing of "that piece of goods". That of Stafford, in turn, abounds in negatives, with the view partly to stressing his nature of a thug, and partly to conveying the rogue's mysteriousness (as a person careful not to reveal too much about himself). Thus, he is "a slinking chap", always "quiet" and "hanging about the dark", with his eyes repeatedly "half-shut" or "downcast". One might also point out here the accumulation of the [l] sound in the description of Stafford ("lazy", "loaf", "languid", "listless", "asleep", "small cheating at cards, wheedling and bullying his living out of some woman"), due to which the crook's remissness and his nature of a petty criminal gains accentuation.

Thus, while the individuality of character is more conspicuous in the verbal shaping of the main protagonists, it is nonetheless perceivable with regards to all characters: each is ascribed a certain language – which, importantly, concerns both their own utterances and the narratorial descriptions[9]. The narrator's rough and flawed enunciation dissolves as the story develops – to resurface only occasionally for brief spells – bringing particular figures into the spotlight: one might say his style's dominant feature is no longer fragmentariness as much as flexibility, or diversification. To an important degree this is of course connected to the narrator's reliance on seemingly indirect speech, which brings about the lack of proper differentiation between the description of a given character and the quotation of his/her words. We need to remember here that the stevedore's relation is a mixture of the third-person and first-person narrating voices, and that he was a witness to only some of the related situations:

'I run up against him again in Mr. George Dunbar's office. Yes, THAT office. It wasn't often that I... However, there was a bit of his cargo in a ship in dock that I wanted to ask Mr. George about'.
'How he gets on board I don't know'.
'It was then that Cloete, unembittered but weary, told him this story...'

Thus, the introduced narrator learned about the majority of events and circumstances from other characters, such as Cloete or a parson to whom Stafford made his final confession. By the same token, protagonists in possession of a fuller knowledge of the affairs do not figure as narrators in the text, and do not tell of events directly but through the filtering personality and mind of the narrator. In this light, the narrator's degree of faithfulness to the original utterances remains uncertain, and the language the characters use does not really appear to be their own. In other words, the device of modelling the language according to which protagonist is being spoken of reveals itself as narratorial strategy, and the shape of the characters' thoughts or utterances also manifests itself as an invention of the narrator – or narrators. In spite of the frame narrator's assertion that he conveys the story "raw, so to speak – just as it was told to me", he could not have escaped putting his own stamp on the relation, and what we read is *his* version of it. Expressions such as "you know the way these chaps put it", "that sort of talk", or "You must make her up

---

9   This is perhaps what Dalgarno has in mind when she mentions the "union between teller and tale, the creation of which was one of Conrad's chief distinctions as a writer" (1975: 43).

out of your head. You will know the sort" show that the ruffian leaves much room for the main narrator's activity.

With such a multi-levelled narration hierarchy, it remains not entirely clear which narrator provides the deciding voice in the creation of characters. What is clear, though, is that it is the figure of the narrator, or combination of narrators, though which the implied author formulates all the elements of the text (see Lothe 1996: 161), including the fictional world with its characters. They are shaped by a rich diversity of languages with which the text operates – each language being useful for the delineation of a particular character. In other words, Conrad's story reminds us of the fact that character is structured by the literary language.

Peter Straub's *Shadowland*:
Character in the liminal space

SŁAWOMIR STUDNIARZ

The present study focuses on the development of the protagonist in relation to the spatial setting of events which are crucial for the process of
his becoming[1]. First, however, to provide the ensuing discussion with
theoretical grounding, it seems reasonable to address briefly the issue of
characterisation and its place in contemporary narrative theory. What is
striking is the relative neglect of fictional characters in twentieth-century
literary studies, so acutely perceived by many scholars. Alex Woloch's
monograph *The One vs. the Many. Minor Characters and the Space of
the Protagonist in the Novel*, published in 2004 by Princeton University
Press, one of very few studies dealing with characters in fiction, opens
with a survey of the complaints voiced by various prominent literary
theorists. The catalogue of the shortcomings presented by Woloch includes relevant statements by Jonathan Culler, Seymour Chatman,
Shlomith Rimmon-Kenan and Mieke Bal. It is Culler who sets the tone
by stating that "character is the major aspect of the novel to which structuralism has paid least attention and has been least successful in treating"; he is echoed by Chatman who observes that "it is remarkable how
little has been said about the theory of character in literary history and
criticism" (both scholars quoted in Woloch 2004: 14). In the same vein,
Rimmon-Kenan points out that "the elaboration of a systematic, non-
reductive but also non-impressionistic theory of character remains one of
the challenges poetics has not yet met" (quoted in Woloch 2004: 14).

Mieke Bal attributes this perceived failure of literary studies to construct "a complete and coherent theory of character" to its "human as-

---

1   The notion, related to the process of initiation, will be explained later.

pect"; as she explains, "the character is not a human being, but it resembles one" (quoted in Woloch 2004: 15). Following Bal, Woloch poses the crucial question: "How does an interpretive practice that focuses on the syntax of narrative *as* a system conceptualise the implied resemblance between 'the character' and 'the human being'" (2004: 15)? Bal's stress on the problematic "human aspect" of characterisation comes out of the tension within twentieth-century literary theory, the opposition between the recognition of the protagonist as an anthropomorphic construct, that is as an imaginary individual, and the fitting of the character into the narrative pattern, the emphasis on the protagonist chiefly as the function of the plot. Woloch sees the origins of this theoretical clash in the new insights offered by the Russian Formalists and New Critics, who attacked the psychological and moralistic basis of traditional character-criticism and spoke against the anthropomorphic aspect of characterisation, which defines fictional figures by their referential or mimetic component (2004: 16). According to Woloch the groundbreaking approach of the Russian Formalists was best formulated by Boris Tomashevsky, who analysed the protagonist not as the central person whose story the literary text elaborates, but rather as a central device that acts as glue for the text itself, "a sort of living support for the text's different motifs" (2004: 15). But, as Woloch emphasises, "some recent studies have been increasingly troubled by the elimination of the human element from narratology" (2004: 16). As a countermeasure, Woloch in his work puts forward a conceptual system that incorporates the tension between the authenticity of a character in-and-of-himself and the supposed reduction of the character into the thematic field resulting from the structuralist approach. His methodological proposal offers the way in which the "human aspect" of a character is dynamically integrated into the narrative structure as a whole.

Fictional characters are indeed verbal anthropomorphic constructs, but they are created to fulfil certain functions within the context of a larger narrative pattern. Uri Margolin states that characters can be approached from different theoretical perspectives, each yielding a different conception and theory of character: character as a fictional figure, that is, an artistic product constructed for some purpose; character as a non-actual but well-specified individual presumed to exist in some hypothetical, fictional domain; and character as a text-based construct or mental image in the reader's mind (2007: 66). Characters in fiction are abstract constructs; they are not open to direct perception, since they are mediated verbally. They can be known only through textual descriptions and inferences drawn from those descriptions; in fact, as Margolin rightly observes, they are these complexes of descriptions and inferences, deprived of any independent existence (2007: 68).

Closely related to this conception of a fictional character is the term *great semantic figure* introduced by Janusz Sławiński in his essay "Semantyka wypowiedzi narracyjnej" (1979). The Polish scholar explains that his term applies not only to characters but to the narrator and the plot as well. A semantic figure is composed of small particles of information which accumulate and interact with each other, undergoing modification. The process of forming a great semantic figure proceeds in two dimensions. First, meanings of relevant sentences are simply combined with the previous ones, which means that they are accumulated in a linear way. But these newly added elements as new semantic particles interact with the meanings of the previous sentences and modify them. These added semantic particles bring new information and they are capable of reinterpreting the already created senses. Hence the construction of a character in a narrative work is a dynamic process. A fictional character as a semantic figure emerges as the sum total of the meanings of all sentences spoken by and about the character, but those meanings are configured by the specific rules of the literary work, by its supercode[2].

Tracing the development of the central fictional figure in a narrative text one must inevitably focus on its anthropomorphic component, and treat it as an imaginary individual, endowed with salient characterizing features. These features, however, fall into two distinct sets: the array of properties that determine its essential humanity, common to all people, and the cluster of qualities that are unique, peculiar to this imaginary individual only, and that shape his/her identity as a person. But these defining features are not ascribed to this fictional figure permanently, once and for all. For a character to be dynamic, to change in the course of the action, new properties must be added, while some of the previously assigned qualities must be lost. Finally, the process of the character's development should not be examined in isolation from the remaining components of the literary work; it cannot be abstracted from the narrative

---

2   Compare the use of the term by Andrzej Zgorzelski in Part 1.

pattern. The protagonist's internal growth comes about as the result of the complex interplay of many factors, one crucial determinant being the fictional space.

*

Peter Straub's *Shadowland*, whose protagonist will serve as the focus of the present analysis, begins with the character-narrator meeting after many years Tom Flanagan, his schoolmate and the protagonist of his story. In this way, a wide time distance is opened between the events and their narratorial reconstruction. The narrator, however, immediately draws attention to another distance, more relevant to the present discussion: "I measured another distance: that between the present man and the boy he had been" (Straub 1981: 5). He emphasises the difference between Tom's adult self and his former, adolescent personality. In this way from the outset the theme of personal transformation is introduced into the narrative. The idea of progress toward maturity is reflected also in the significant choice of the literary works alluded to in the novel. The Grimms' fairy tales feature the relevant motif of magical transformation[3], the *Odyssey* highlights the motif of the quest, while *Great Expectations* and *Huckleberry Finn*, as novels unambiguously focusing on the psychological and moral growth of their young protagonists, resonate deeply with the plot of *Shadowland*.

The titles of the first two parts of the novel, "The School" and "Shadowland", highlight the specific localities in which the process of the protagonist's becoming is enacted, Carson School in Arizona, and Shadowland, an estate located deep in the Vermont woods that belongs to a powerful and unpredictable magician. Entering Carson School is clearly associated with taking first steps toward adulthood, which is thematised in the narrative report fraught with such lexical items as "change", "process", and "growing up". Mr. Thorpe, the teacher of Latin, in his introductory speech makes Tom and the other pupils distinctly aware of the professed aim of the school: "We have to reshape you boys, mold you. Turn you into our kind of boy. Or you will be *doomed*, boys, doomed, an adjective meaning consigned to misfortune or destruction"

---

3   Bill Sheehan in his inquiry into the fiction of Peter Straub in *At the foot of the Story Tree* (Subterranean Press 2000), extensively discusses the thematic importance of several fairy tales for *Shadowland*.

(Straub 1981: 52). The prep school appears as a threatening, vaguely to-
talitarian institution, having no regard for individuality, and demanding
from the pupils discipline and obedience.

Carson School is no ordinary educational institution in yet another,
even more sinister sense. The description of the school building foreshadows the nature of events that are to take place there. The heart of the school
is an old Gothic mansion that "somehow shrank the modern addition, sub-
sumed it into itself" (Straub 1981: 17). The ominous atmosphere of fore-
boding pervades Registration Day, the first day the boys spend at school.
Failure of electricity creates gloom and pupils are led through the dark corridors by teachers with candles or flashlights. It is no accident that the
menacing headmaster, introduced by the narrator as "a minor devil", has
his office situated at the heart of the old Gothic mansion.

The macabre underside of the school life comes into focus in the figure of Steve Ridpath, fittingly nicknamed "Skeleton", a pupil obsessed
with violence. The narrative role of Skeleton Ridpath is that of Tom's
double, his negative counterpart. Both are abandoned by their fathers,
Skeleton virtually and Tom literally, and both despise the Carson way of
life and the suburbia, but Skeleton openly hates it and dreams of destroying it. His room, the collage displayed on its walls, the montage of images taken from the magazines, becomes equivalent of his mind, of his
inner self:

> He had begun by selecting pictures of the objects he hated, things that rep-
> resented the Cason way of life: new cars and grotesquely large refrigera-
> tors piled with food; manor houses, well-dressed suburban women, football
> players. Because he hated these things, because his father and his father's
> colleagues accepted them as values because they were elements of a world
> he wished would blow to pieces, they gave him a perverse thrill: hating
> them, he liked looking at them. Now he cut out every grotesque picture he
> saw, and welded horrors onto the representations of the suburban life he
> detested. (Straub 1981: 64)

In Carson School Tom meets Del Nightingale, a pupil whose parents
were killed in a plane crash, a strange, lonely boy, an aspiring magician.
It is Carson School that brings them together but it is their interest in
sleight-of-hand tricks and the passion for magic that cement their friendship. The two teenagers have much in common, since Tom, too, loses
his father. Bereft, Tom Flanagan feels acutely the pain of growing up
and for the first time in his life faces the fear of death and loss: "Death

has never been so real to him as it is now, and when he thinks of a future without his father, without a father, he sees a black valley bristling with threats" (Straub 1981: 94).

His father's death leaves him vulnerable, without protection, and propels him into maturity. Tom finds himself at a crossroads, he is forced to think about his future. The training or rather the shaping the boys are undergoing at Carson School is meant to prepare them for the conventional, bland, comfortable middle-class life in the suburbia, incarnated in the novel in the district called Quantum Hills, "the city's most artificial and dream-struck setting, this place of pools and tennis dresses" (Straub 1981: 119). And it is his father's death and friendship with Del that make him rethink his options and, above all, steer clear of Quantum Hills and everything it stands for:

> If he had not met Del, if his father had not died, he would never have seen its absolute remoteness from him. He would have (he imagined) slid toward Quantum Hills as if on greased rails. He could not, now. He could only invent his future as Del was doing; he had been shaken from his frame. (Straub 1981: 119)

Thanks to the dream in which he encounters the figure of the benign wizard, he realises that the final and decisive stage of his becoming will take place not in Carson School, but in another realm altogether, as he is forewarned by the magician about what is to befall him:

> 'Oh, yes. You'll find what you have to find. It'll be all right. You'll have to fight for your life, of course, you'll have tests to pass – tests you can't study for, hee hee – and there'll be a girl and a wolf, and all that, but you're no idiot'. (Straub 1981: 16)

The end of the first stage of Tom's becoming is marked by the fire that destroys the school auditorium and nearly kills the pupils gathered there to watch his and Del's illusionist show. The key to the mystery that culminates in the wreckage and the death of one of the pupils lies in Shadowland, the mysterious realm presided over by Del's uncle. Tom Flanagan shares this observation with the narrator "in the present", looking at the events from the perspective of many years, now clearly realizing the truth:

> *Tom said: 'You see, there was a mystery in our school, and the end of the mystery was the awful thing that happened when Del and I were doing our magic show. But that wasn't the answer to the mystery, just its conclusion.*

The answer was at Shadowland; or the answer was Shadowland.' (Straub
   1981: 65)

The initially suggested opposition between Carson School and Shadowland, as two distinct places of Tom's education and passage to adulthood, thus becomes dissolved: to the adult Tom the school reveals itself
now as an extension of Shadowland. Del's uncle is the force influencing
the public happenings and Tom's private "daymares" and "nightmares",
too. His powerful presence is hidden for most of the time, but he manifests himself as a dark figure manipulating the characters. Through the
magician's visitations, Shadowland invades the space of Carson School
and the difference between the two domains becomes purely nominal.
He appears to be the cause of Tom's "daymares", terrifying visions experienced by the boy during his waking hours, in which the fabric of reality becomes momentarily ripped. The threatening dark figure as the
representation of the magician Coleman Collins enters Tom's dreams,
his "nightmares", premonitions of things to come, which are full of hints
about his experiences in the magician's realm, in Shadowland. In one of
his visions, inside the fairy-tale house formerly occupied by a benign old
wizard, Tom glimpses the true face of Shadowland, "the magic world
warped into evil". The spectacle of shadows arranged for his benefit, the
"shadow play", shows a boy's violent death, and Tom realises that he
has to accompany Del on his visit to Shadowland, because he feels responsible for his friend's life:

> The men kicked the boy's body aside, fluttered apart just as if they were
> hands after all, and reformed as a word: SHADOW. Then another series of
> letters flew together. LAND. Shadowland. The laughter built up around
> me, nasty and knowing, and I didn't know if all those twisted faces watch-
> ing me were laughing because they were warning me away from Shadow-
> land, or because they knew I would identify the dead boy with Del and
> would know I had to go there. (Straub 1981: 125)

The extension of Shadowland beyond its physical boundaries, evidenced
by the intrusions of Del's uncle into the school life and his manipulation
of Del (and also of Skeleton), seems permanent rather than sporadic, a
rule rather than an exception. Borders in the fictional reality become
permeable and flexible, as Shadowland incorporates other areas and domains of the mimetic space, investing them with supernatural properties,
in fact transforming them into the fantastic space. Traveling to Shadow-

land, the boys go by train to Hilly Vale where they are to meet Del's uncle, the magician. Actually, the boys' journey to Shadowland is already a part of the experience of Shadowland. Even the name of the station where they get off, Hilly Vale, contains a contradiction in terms, by itself signaling the disruption of the order of things.

As Tom and Del are on their way to Hilly Vale train station, Tom notices an extra car, inexplicably attached to their train, that "had somehow been magicked onto the end of the train" (Straub 1981: 156). The presence of the strange car turns out to be the first performance arranged by Del's uncle for the visiting boys, but the trick involves even more than may initially appear. Both the interior and the occupants of the extra car seem to come from another era, adding to the bafflement and disorientation of Tom, who feels that he has gone fifty years back in time.

Also the railway disaster that kills dozens of people and causes the boys' delayed arrival at their destination is later revealed as the magician's doing. Collins makes Tom experience the train crash and he virtually puts Tom inside one of the compartments moments before the disaster:

> [Tom] realised that the magician had known at the Hilly Vale station that he was going to put him on the wrecked train (*Not just a little spilled coffee, a little bump on the tracks, a little messy commotion?*), and in the second before the forest disappeared as finally as Coleman Collins, Tom had time to think that Collins had somehow caused that wreck in order to put him inside it six hours later. (Straub 1981: 202)

The wreckage of the train and the "incidental" death of dozens of innocent passengers had been brought about by the magician in order to enlighten Tom about the nature of reality, as part of his education in the new realm. The continuity of the boy's learning process is underscored by the perceived resemblance between Carson School and Shadowland, which is to be the stage of Tom's initiation into the mysteries of reality: "It looked faintly like a compound – faintly like something else. 'The school,' Tom said. 'I mean . . . it sort of reminds me of our school'" (Straub 1981: 168). Shadowland, because of the candles that "give a welcoming glow", echoes the candle-lit gloom of Registration Day, their first day at Carson School. But as Collins brings home forcefully, there is a difference: "'This is far more important to you than your schooling, boy. This is your real schooling'" (Straub 1981: 327).

The location of the estate in "deep wood" corresponds to the un-known reality, which the two characters, like their predecessors in so many traditional fairy tales, are about to penetrate. From the very begin-ning Collins assumes the role of a powerful and knowledgeable master, treating Tom and Del as his disciples, promising them knowledge and experience: "'Oh, yes, the knowledge. You'll see. You'll *experience*. And that is all I will say at present'" (Straub 1981: 167). Collins intro-duces the adepts to the mysteries of Shadowland and the realm of magic. Of the two boys, Tom, possessing unique qualities and aptitude, from the start wins the favour of Del's uncle, who predicts his becoming a true magician: "'So this is the summer of Tom Flanagan's growth as well as the summer of my unburdening. You are a very special boy, Tom'" (Straub 1981: 209).

He alerts Tom to the danger inherent in the practice of magic: "The smile was taut now, and directed straight at Tom. 'I am saying that the practice of magic is the courting of self-destruction – that is one of its great secrets'" (Straub 1981: 174). As befits the master, he explains to him the nature of things that he is about to experience in Shadowland, as caused by the interaction of their uniquely gifted, creative minds:

> 'Everything you will see here, and you will see many odd things, comes from your own mind – from within you. From the reaction of your mind with mine. None of it exists elsewhere'. (Straub 1981: 209)

Collins hints here at semi-theatrical, semi-magical shows, visions sent and performances staged for the benefit of Tom, in which the fabric of reality becomes dissolved and the line separating truth and illusion is all but erased. The first in a long series of displays in store for Tom, the ex-perience of being inside the crashing train, seems so real to the boy as to prompt him to doubt its illusory character. Collins clearly grooms Tom for his successor: "You are mine. Nothing that is in magic will be un-known to you, boy. For you are no one else's but mine" (Straub 1981: 216). He promises him not only secret knowledge and magical power, but also his dominion:

> Above it, on the far end, Shadowland sat on its cliff like a jeweled doll-house. Its windows gleamed.
> 'Pretend that is the world. It is the world. It can be yours. Everything in the world, every treasure, every satisfaction, is there'. (Straub 1981: 217)

The temptation is great but it carries a high price – Tom must embrace a completely amoral life: he is expected to go "beyond good and evil". Magic, as it is understood by Tom, means an extension of human abilities, mastery over time and space, but this transcendence of the human condition requires moral responsibility. Magic must not be used for selfish purposes, for satisfying one's thirst of power. Resisting Collins's temptation, Tom struggles to become free from the corrupting influence of the magician, which contributes to his moral and psychological growth.

The protagonist's struggle is also intertwined with his experience of the fictional space of Shadowland. First of all, Tom realises that Shadowland is a trap. It is not only cut off from the external world by the natural boundaries of the lake and surrounding woods, but it is fortified and guarded like a prison:

> He went up to the gates. The spikes on top of each bar looked more than ornamental. And the brick wall, he could now see, was topped with thick jagged pieces of glass embedded in concrete. Barbed wire snaked over the glass. (Straub 1981: 321)

But the space functions here not only as a trap in the literal sense; much more important is its mirage-like, deceptive quality. The seemingly solid physical space frequently dissolves, revealing its make-believe character:

> White fluted pillars took shape as suddenly as if blown into being. The ground shifted, became harder, less resilient. With his next step forward, he whanged his leg against the metal back of a padded chair.
> 'Oh, my God,' he whispered. He was standing in a large vaultlike room with a curtained stage at one end. [...] He was in the big theater where Collins was going to teach them to fly.
> 'Oh, God,' he said. 'I wasn't even outside'. (Straub 1981: 202-203)

The quoted example demonstrates that the fictional reality seems to be composed of layers upon layers of illusions, deprived of any tangible, solid core. On one hand Shadowland reveals itself as a fairy-tale like realm of enchantment:

> 'You may be within a wood ... within a storied wood...'
> 'Or fur-wrapped in a sleigh in deep snow . . .'
> 'Or dying for love of a sleeping princess . . .'
> 'Or before a dwindling fire with your head full of pictures . . .'

'Or even asleep with a head full of cobwebs and dreams . . .'
'And still you will be in Shadowland'. (Straub 1981: 225)

As one of its inhabitants puts it: "Everything here is a lie. [...] Just because you saw it doesn't mean it really happened" (Straub 1981: 374).

Not only space is subject to the magician's power. Part of Shadowland's deception is its distortion of time, too. In Shadowland time flows according to its ruler's will, as seen in the following exchange: "'It's July? We've been here a month?' [...]'How can he do that?' 'He just can. One summer he made Del think that six or seven weeks went by in a day'" (Straub 1981: 302). Temporal progression may be simply an illusion. Time is collapsible, the present merges into the past, which can be freely revisited, as demonstrated by Tom re-experiencing the fire at Carson School or other important events.

The way time flows in Shadowland without any distinct markers, brings to mind Bakhtin's chronotope of the *threshold*, in which "time is essentially instantaneous; it is as if it has no duration and falls out of the course of biographical time" (2006: 248). As the Russian scholar explains, "highly charged with emotion and value", the chronotope of the threshold "can be combined with the motif of encounter, but its most fundamental instance is as the chronotope of *crisis* and *break* in a life" (2006: 248). It is, Bakhtin goes on, "connected with the breaking point of a life, the moment of crisis, the decision that changes a life (or the indecisiveness that fails to change a life, the fear to step over the threshold)" (2006: 248).

For the young protagonist of Straub's novel, thresholds are not only the particular "crises", the endless enigmatic situations that he faces. In fact the whole space of Shadowland reveals itself to be a transitional zone, one huge trial that he must go through:

> Shadowland, as much as he knew of it, was a test harder and more important than any he had ever taken at Carson; and he could not let Shadowland defeat him. (Straub 1981: 229-230)

It is precisely the constant metamorphosis of space in Shadowland that challenges the young protagonist and plays a significant role in his development. The protean, shifting space becomes invested with hidden meanings that are to be decoded by Tom as part of his initiation; he has to learn to see through the illusion, "to distinguish reality from its shadow".

Despite his ambivalent attitude toward the whole undertaking – "part of him was fascinated by Shadowland, and intrigued by the powers Coleman Collins might be able to find in him" (Straub 1981: 273) – Tom in a moment of insight makes a conscious decision to oppose the magician. In this way he proves his moral maturity. He rejects Shadowland and its legacy; he realises its evil nature and Collins's perversion of the true spirit of magic: "And he thought that Shadowland, an ugly name for a house, was anywhere secretive and mean, anywhere that deserved shadows because the people there hated light" (Straub 1981: 320). Tom is also deeply concerned about Del and wants to protect him from his uncle, who as Tom clearly sees now, is a dangerous person. But he has to overcome Del's hostility and jealousy because in Del's eyes he is a traitor and a usurper. The two friends have drifted apart and Tom tries desperately to regain Del's trust and get him out of Shadowland safely.

Another important factor in Tom's development is his sexual awakening owing to his attraction to the mysterious inhabitant of Shadowland, Rose Armstrong. The girl's ontological status is ambiguous, though: "The girl seemed as perfect as a statue. *Living Statue*. 'He made me,' Rose said with an air of bravery'" (Straub 1981: 242). Rose polarises the tension inherent in the magical domain, her "yearning brooding uncertain beautiful face" is perceived by Tom as the essence of Shadowland. Though she tantalizingly admits that she is the magician's creation, for Tom she is the most desirable girl on the earth.

Tom's moral and sexual maturity is complemented by his development as a magician, evidenced first of all by intensity of perception: his senses seem "tuned and burnished", he sees and hears with "great clarity". More importantly, however, he acquires the ability to project himself into other people's minds, which he first tests by entering the minds of Skeleton and Del. This magical skill proves decisive during his ultimate confrontation with the magician, after Tom's attempt to escape with Del from Shadowland has failed. He resists the final temptation when Collins promises him that he can still walk away and save his life, if he betrays Del and Rose, and gives up his skills as a magician:

> 'I will give you yet another choice. The choice of giving up your song. Leave Del. Leave Rose – you will have to do that anyhow. And leave magic. Let me have your gifts. You could just walk out of Shadowland, and be precisely the boy you thought you were when you came here'. (Straub 1981: 428)

Tom defeats Collins proving both his own superiority as a magician and his ineradicable humanness. Yet, despite his personal triumph, he fails to save Del: "the wise magician who enters at the end to set everything right was only a fifteen-year-old boy kneeling on bloodied floorboards and reaching for the transformed body of his closest friend" (Straub 1981: 429). The loss of the friend leaves an indelible mark on Tom, and the pierced palms through which he has been nailed to the wall become a permanent and visible counterpart of his scarred psyche.

Tom's confrontation with the dark aspects of human nature, with its yearnings for the ultimate power and freedom personified in the *Übermensch*-like figure of the amoral magician, and his psychological transformation belong the type of a formative experience that is richly portrayed in American literature. The passage of a young, inexperienced protagonist to adulthood triggered by the loss of innocence usually results from his exposure to hidden or hitherto unknown aspects of reality. In the American canon, Nathaniel Hawthorne's "Young Goodman Brown" stands out as the prototypical story that shows a young member of the Puritan community losing the naïve and childish view of the world and of humanity. But fictional works dealing with the theme of initiation range from Herman Melville's *Billy Budd*, Mark Twain's *Huckleberry Finn*, Stephen Crane's *The Red Badge of Courage*, through Henry James's *Daisy Miller* to such twentieth-century works as *The Catcher in the Rye* by J. D. Salinger, *Birdy* by William Wharton, or *Shadowland*, a Gothic *Bildungsroman*, the focus of the present study.

The process of initiation is almost obligatorily enacted in the unknown and threatening space, which can be called *liminal*. The term *liminal* and the corresponding noun *liminality* derive from the Scottish anthropologist Victor Turner, himself influenced by the ethnographical writings on preindustrial societies by Arnold Van Gennep. In Turner's framework the term *liminality* serves to designate the middle, transitional stage of a three-stage paradigmatic rite of passage (Turner 1991: 94). The adjective *liminal,* from the Latin *limen*, "threshold", as Roisin O'Gorman points out, in anthropology denotes a peculiar condition of the initiate, which "can be broadly defined as a transitional place of becoming, a state of flux between two different states of being" (2009:7).

The stage of the character's becoming could be the dark forest in the American wilderness visited by Goodman Brown, the man-of-war *Bel-*

lipotent into which Billy is "impressed", an unnamed battlefield in *The Red Badge of Courage*, the Mississippi shores in *Huckleberry Finn* or even the deceptive social environment of Rome in *Daisy Miller*. In *Shadowland*, Tom is first confronted with the strict, hierarchical and essentially hostile microcosm of Carson School into which he is admitted as a freshman. But the painful process of his growing up and education is completed during his stay in Shadowland. There he is exposed to a series of elaborate theatrical performances and magical displays that put him at a loss, lead him to question the very basis of reality and ultimately, to expand his knowledge.

Tom's immersion in this dangerous, strange, seemingly hallucinatory realm corresponds to what in anthropology is meant by entering a site of transition, the threshold, a zone "betwixt-and-between". It signals "the quality of being socially segregated, set apart and divested of status, and relates to associated characteristics and qualities: indeterminacy, ambiguity, selflessness, and becomingness" (Joseph 2011: 138). The initiate's condition in this *liminal space* is explained as "a borderland state of ambiguity and indeterminacy, a transformational state characterised by a certain openness and relaxation of rules, leading those who participate in the process to new perspectives and possibilities" (O'Gorman 2009:7). Joseph points out that liminal spaces are projected outside of society and symbolise a borderland through which the protagonist passes in order to re-enter a social structure (2011: 139). In other words, the borderland or the threshold zone "holds a promise of growth, change and possibilities that can come into actuality through the ritual processes of transformation" (O'Gorman 2009: 11). From this liminal condition the protagonist in Straub's Gothic *Bildungsroman* may emerge as a transformed, adult human being. Alternatively, he may be stuck in it and, consequently, perish. The process of his becoming crucially depends on his negotiating and mastering the pitfalls and threats of Shadowland, the perilous and protean reality in which he is trapped. Tom Flanagan, however, manages to resolve all the epistemological conundrums posited by Shadowland, passes through its ontological ordeals and proves his maturity and integrity.

The focus of the present study was on the development of the protagonist; hence he was treated as an anthropomorphic entity, an imaginary person equipped with the features that define him both as a typical adolescent and as a unique individual. As the presented analysis has demonstrated, the creation of a character in fiction is a dynamic process that is not completed until the narrative reaches its end. It is the final actions and their outcome that ultimately determine a fictional character.

Moreover, the process of the protagonist's becoming was traced in relation to the larger framework of the spatial organisation of the fictional reality. The particular spatial domains and the challenges they presented to the protagonist were examined as crucial determining factors in Tom's development, unfolding simultaneously on three levels, as the crystallisation of his moral sense, his sexual awakening, and his growth as a magician. It should emphasised that while studying characters in fiction, it is hard to avoid the excessive focus on the anthropomorphic aspect, i.e. their resemblance to real-life people. On the other hand, treating fictional figures as abstract components of the pattern of relations projected by the literary text may appear dismissive. A reasonable solution, then, would be to steer clear of the two extremes, thus avoiding the pitfalls of the exclusively mimetic approach, and the possibly detrimental reduction of a character to merely one of the narrative's constituent elements.

Anita Desai's fiction: Marginalisation as a technique of character creation

JOANNA PASTERNAK

One of the characteristic features of Anita Desai's writings is almost a complete absence of political or social ideology in her novels, which is explained by the novelist herself who firmly declares in interviews that "[her] writing is a process of discovering the truth – the ninety percent of the iceberg that lies submerged beneath the one tenth visible portion [...] called Reality. Writing is the way of plunging to the depths and exploring this underlying truth [...] to discover and convey the true significance of things [...]" (Amanuddin 1898: 154-156). She takes her readers on an inward journey into the realm of the minds of the characters she creates. Having said that, a working assumption can be made that Desai uses a literary character as an essential material to weave the story line in the fictional world of her novels. The novelist focuses on exploring the depths of consciousness and reveals major problems of the novels through the inner life of her characters. Human nature is analysed by Anita Desai not through heroic deeds of the characters but through their psyche. It is not an exaggeration, therefore, to say that the world of Anita Desai's novels is the inner world of her characters, who represent individual human beings with their uniqueness, complexity and also moral flaws (Nityanandam 2000: 18-40).

The chief goal of the present article is to explore the techniques Anita Desai uses to structure her characters and shape some aspects of the fictional world. The task will be carried out with the attention to the following aspects: alienation of characters, their mutual complementation, and the impenetrability of the inner worlds they represent.

A close reading of Desai's novels gives rise to a hypothesis that there is a distinct regularity that governs the way in which the writer structures her characters and organises the fictional world. Firstly, her characters are described as alienated for they often possess certain deformities or inferiorities which place them on the margins of the fictional society to the point of being rejected. Secondly, the rejection that the characters experience evokes tension between two or more protagonists, which in turn binds them as complementary and inseparable pairs of protagonists. Thirdly, it can also be noticed that one of the consequences of the fact that the protagonists are given contrastive and complementary characteristics is that they live in worlds impenetrable to one another; so the narrator, and thus the reader, have access to the separate worlds of only one character at a time. This is turn gives rise to a phenomenon which may be metaphorically referred to as the 'dead centre of the reader's field of vision', which means that the main characters remain undescribed because they are placed too close to the central point of the narration and thus, in a sense, they remain invisible. It may be seen as an important feature of Desai's technique that the portraits of the main characters are in fact incomplete. Information gaps in the depiction of character are recognised as an obvious feature of literary communication (e.g. Eder, Jannidis, Schneider 2010: 11-13). What I intend to describe on the example of Anita Desai's fiction is the use of such gaps as an important part of the literary technique purposefully employed in the creation of characters.

The analysis will focus on one short story and two novels by Desai, which depict characters deemed inferior either because of their age, gender, or ethnicity. Victor, a child protagonist in the short story entitled "Pineapple Cake" from the collection *Games at Twilight* is an example of a character who is patronised and stripped of dignity by his overbearing mother. A character whose otherness and rejection are rooted in her gender is Uma from the novel *Fasting, Feasting*, a mentally retarded woman who becomes her family's servant and slave carrying out the most menial chores. Finally, a protagonist whose difference is perceived as the most unsettling, is a German Jew from the novel *Baumgartner's Bombay*.

In one of the interviews on the art of her fiction, Desai admits that she "is interested in characters who are not average but have retreated, have been driven into some extremity of despair and turn against or make a stand against the general current [...]" (Pandit 1995: 156-157). That is why Desai resorts to portraying her characters as abnormal or inferior and opposed to others, which brings at least three consequences noticeable from the reader's perspective. The first consequence is that the characters are perceived in terms of contrasts which stem from age, gender or ethnicity, and bind characters into inseparable oppositions. Secondly, the difference between the characters turns them into a self-regulating system which is never in a state of equilibrium and thus fuels the development of the plot. Thirdly, not only are the characters inseparable, but their inner worlds are defined by their points of view and thus their worlds remain impenetrable to each other. The initial division of characters into three groups depending on the reasons of their suffering and rejection, should be treated as introductory orientation, since the problems considered in Desai's novels reach far beyond the issues of age, gender and ethnicity, as will be discussed below.

In "Pineapple Cake" Victor's rejection stems from brusque and abrasive attitude of his mother, Mrs Fernandez, towards him and manifests itself on the physical level. The boy is pushed away, shoved and squeezed into the corners of the taxi or the church, which can be interpreted as an attempt to eliminate him on the physical level. The boy is dominated by his mother to the point where there is almost no place for him. Victor is also oppressed by Mrs Fernandez on the mental level when he is subjected to her psychological manipulations and humiliations best reflected in the way the pineapple cake is used as a bait for Victor whenever he might feel reluctant to comply with his mother's wishes. Victor's individuality is not respected and, treated as a mere object, he suffers psychological rejection as a human being.

Uma, the protagonist in *Fasting, Feasting*, is also exposed to rejection which originates from the fact that she is female, which in Indian patriarchal society means being a second rate citizen. Her position becomes even more inferior when it transpires in the course of the story that she suffers from mild epilepsy. Three aspects – age, gender and mental handicap – make Uma's future in the society unpromising. And indeed, she continues to live with her parents until she becomes their rather old servant, doing menial jobs in their house. Desai depicts Uma as a person deprived not only of her family's love which she deserves, but also of personal space or even belongings. Uma's rejection is manifested through the fact that she is treaded by her family like an object, which is the result of the strange mixture of her being a female and mentally handicapped.

Rejection that verges on ostracism is presented in the strongest terms in *Baumgartner's Bombay*. In this novel the characters' otherness and thus lack of acceptance has ethnic rather than psychological background. Hugo Baumgartner is a German Jew born in Berlin in the 1930s, where his family experiences Nazi persecution. The atrocities of the Second World War are depicted in an extremely subtle manner here: Hugo Baumgartner's father, having been arrested and imprisoned in one of the early concentration camps in Germany, returns but is unable to talk about the camp experience. It is his silence, however, that speaks loudest, and implicitly points to the danger that threatens their lives, which lurks outside their home. In this novel, rejection and social ostracism are connected with persecution and expulsion.

Desai is very reserved in depicting this aspect of rejection which to European minds speaks in a transparent manner. On the narration level, this social ostracism is revealed through the Baumgartners' living space that is continuously shrinking. Firstly, they lose their family business, then their house is acquired by their German business partner so that Hugo with his mother are forced to live in just two rooms in what was formerly their own big house. The lethal loop of persecution is becoming ever tighter and Hugo is sent to India as a timber merchant. In Venice while waiting for his vessel, Hugo experiences yet another rejection, brilliantly depicted though subtle use of detail. In the scene where Hugo eats breakfast in the kitchen of the house where he stays, the landlady is busy sweeping and cleaning the floor, she pretends not to notice him and sweeps the floor exactly around Baumgartner's feet so that he stands in the middle of a dry and dusty circle (Desai 1988: 56).

In India, Baumgartner's prevailing sense of social incompatibility and thus rejection do not ease. As a European, he stands in sharp contrast to the indigenous local community, while his Jewish origins are instantly recognised by the German-speaking community and thus he is not fully accepted there. Ironically, when the war breaks out, he is detained in an internment camp along with other Germans for the simple reason that his mother tongue is German. Baumgartner's character seems to be defined by the fact that he has no homeland and that no social ties anchor him in the fictional world.

However, Anita Desai uses the principles of inferiority, otherness, and rejection not only to define her characters, but also to set them against the backdrop of the character system of the fictional world. Thus the characters are often set into pairs governed by the principle of contrast, understood here not as sheer opposition but rather as a complementary relation of contrasting figures who are mutually dependent and thus create the basic unit of characters. This mutual dependence and complementation create a powerful tension between opposed characters and thus fuels the plot development in the fictional world.

In "Pineapple Cake", a transparent juxtaposition can be observed between two characters: Victor and his mother. Mrs Fernandez is depicted as a domineering person who derives a sense of power from the fact that her small son is physically dependent on her. Taken to a wedding by his mother, he is too small to be able to see anything and has to rely on the senses of hearing and smelling in his perception of the adult world. The limitation of perception, suggesting an image of a blind mole, makes him dependent on his mother and extremely vulnerable. The more vulnerable Victor gets, the more powerful Mrs Fernandez grows so that she can use him as an excuse for activities which are only her whims. The eponymous pineapple cake is an effective bait as well as a long-awaited reward for Victor's good behaviour during a wedding reception on a blistering hot day. However, in the last scene of the story it is Mrs Fernandez who cannot contain her greed and eats the cake, paying no attention to her son who is unable to recover from the shock evoked by the death of one of the wedding guests. One has to bear in mind that this dependence is mutual and has fundamental importance for the structure of the story. Mrs Fernandez would not seem so powerful if she could not dominate her small and fragile son. It is the game of power which generates tension between the characters and seems to underlie the plot development.

A similar power game between the strong and the weak recurs in Desai's novel *Fasting, Feasting* in which the submissive role is played by Uma with her family placed in the position of power. She has neither the mental capacity to excel in learning nor is she capable of making her two marriages work, arranged and executed as it later turns out for purely financial reasons by the family. As the narrator explains: she "cost her family two dowries and brought no family in return" (Desai 1999: 94-95). Yet, as in the case of Victor and his domineering mother, there is an unexpected twist to the plot which reveals that this power game serves a well-defined purpose, namely the stronger feeds on the weaker. It is reflected in the intricately hierarchical structure of the family which is ready to bear the highest sacrifice in order to provide for their eldest son Arun and his education in America. In this intricate system one character lives at the expense of the other: Uma suffers from physical and emotional malnutrition whereas her younger brother Arun is virtually overfed and as a consequence unable to devour what is showered on him. Paradoxically, he also suffers from emotional starvation though in a different way than his sister does.

It would be misleading to label *Fasting, Feasting* as a novel about the equality of rights and opportunities for men and women in still patriarchal India although there is a significant number of scholars who would support such an interpretation[1]. However, the author structures a symmetrical world of mutually complementary oppositions – as also the title *Fasting, Feasting* suggests – with the view to presenting the novel's main problems: the arbitrary inequality of giving and taking as well as malnutrition which may stem from both abundance and shortage. These problems are reflected in the opposition of the two main characters, which is consistent with the structure of the presented world (India vs. America) and makes the plot divide into two separate story lines. The opposition is present, firstly, in the relationship between Uma and her abusive family where she is not given the attention and emotional support she needs. Secondly, it recurs in the unbalanced relationship between the siblings, Uma and Arun, where the former suffers from emotional deprivation whereas the latter, though not hungry, is only apparently surfeited. It soon transpires that the problem is not confined to only the Indian family as Arun encounters a similar inability to cater for both

---

1   At the initial stage of her career as a writer, Anita Desai developed mainly female characters and thus the plots pertained to the domestic environment. For that reason Desai was regarded a feminist writer, which is clearly reflected by the criticism in the 1980s and 1990s; compare: Sharma, S.P. (1984) "A Vindication of the Feminine" in *Perspectives on Anita Desai*; Gopal, N.R. (1995) "Feminine Psyche" in *A Critical Study of the Novels of Anita Desai*; the trend still prevails: Dengel-Janic, E. (2011)."Home Fiction. Narrating Gendered space in Anita Desai's and Sashi Despande's Novels".

emotional and physical needs in an American family. The notion of "fasting" (starvation) and "feasting" (excess) is recognised globally and sets the East (represented by Arun's family), and the West (the American family), in contrasting opposition. What has been presented as an individual problem between two siblings in an Indian family, turns out to be a problem of universal significance.

The characters in *Baumgartner's Bombay* are set also against one another in order to highlight the multi-faceted relationships between them and also to fuel the development of the plot in the novel. The characters are organised so as to fulfil the principle of complementary opposition between: the strong and the weak (the Baumgartners vs. Herr Pfuehl, the German merchant who takes over their timber trade business); the pursuer and the pursued (Hugo Baumgartner vs. a German backpacker); those who are present and those who are absent (Hugo and his mother who is present only through letters sent from Germany, whose flow ends abruptly indicating her death). However, what becomes apparent is that the complementary opposition on which the character system is based does not have a static but a dynamic nature. Characters are paired up and the oppositions change depending on which feature is highlighted in a given moment of the novel's progression.

The characters in Desai's novels are placed in contrastive pairs in order to enable the reader to perceive these characters as in fact complementary because the contrasts highlight their relations. Thus Hugo Baumgartner's ethnic 'otherness' can only be appreciated against the German or Indian backdrop; Victor's frailty becomes obvious when juxtaposed with his mother's ruthlessness; and Uma's deprivation is set against the favours bestowed on her brother.

Moreover, contrastive and complementary pairs of characters are presented with the help of an interesting narrative technique. The narrator tends to carry out the narration from the point of view of only one protagonist, so that only one character is actually described while the other remains undescribed or his/her description is significantly incomplete. Consequently, the reader's field of vision appears to have a dead centre, or a blind spot. This in turn creates a sense of understatement or mystery in relation to those protagonists that receive scant description.

In "Pineapple Cake", the narrator tells the story mainly from the perspective of Mrs Fernandez who thus seems to occupy a much larger space than her son. This seems particularly emphasised when the narrator momentarily switches to Victor's point of view and describes the world underscoring the boy's perception as limited to smell and hearing, while he is not able to use his sight (Desai 1978: 52). As a consequence, the reader's knowledge of the world presented form Victor's point of view is limited to such an extent that Mrs Fernandez' exact description remains unknown. In this way, Victor's mother stays in what has been referred to in this paper as the dead centre. The reader does not know what Mrs Fernandez looks like, which in turn evokes several questions.

Similarly, in *Fasting, Feasting*, there is a significant imbalance between the world presented from the perspectives of the two characters, Uma and Arun. The lack of balance lies not in the disproportion between the worlds presented from the points of view of both protagonists, but in the phenomenon named in this paper a dead centre which manifests itself as a temporary though complete absence of one of the characters at a given moment of narration. That is why the reader is not made aware of the other character until the second part of the novel. In the first part, which focuses on Uma's grotesquely miserable existence, Arun is scarcely mentioned and is treated as a background character; whereas in the second part set in America, it is Uma who turns into a secondary character. The reader observes the world only from either Uma's or Arun's perspective which reinforces the impression that the worlds presented are mutually impenetrable for the characters who are then doomed to a solitary existence, unable to share their burden of being emotionally starved or overfed.

This phenomenon becomes visible in the scenes depicting the moment of Arun's preparation and departure to America. This is the moment their eyes meet for the first time in the entire novel. The characters see each other almost at the same time. The realisation that ensues from this moment is that the siblings may be set at the opposing poles of their family system but they both constitute an inseparable unity:

> Uma watched Arun too, when he read a fateful letter [which informs Arun of his acceptance at university]. She watched and searched for an expression, of relief, of joy, doubt, fear, anything at all. But there was none. All the years of scholarly toil had worn down any distinguishing features Arun's face might once have had. They had left the essential: a nose, eyes, mouth and ears. But he held his lips tightly together, his nose was flattened, [...] and his eyes were shielded by the thick glasses his relentless

studies had necessitated. [...] Uma gave a sigh of disappointment and turned away, ungratified. [...] Then the day of departure arrived, and he was getting into the train to Bombay from where he would leave for the States. Looking back, he saw Uma on the platform beside her parents and suddenly he noticed how old she looked: his sister Uma, already beginning to stoop and shrink. He threw her a stricken look. (Desai 1999: 122)

The exclusion of one character from the other's mental world and field of vision suggests that the subjective worlds of the protagonists remain impenetrable to one another.

A similar phenomenon can be observed in the case of the title protagonist in *Baumgartner's Bombay*. The narrator in this novel, although consistently presented as maintaining an objective view of the world presented, predominantly stands close to the main character and thus his world and his point of view which entails one of the most striking consequences. Namely, the fact that Hugo Baumgartner's appearance remains practically undisclosed but for scant details such as: "[...] purplish warts on his nose, shortsighted eyes disappearing in the nest of wrinkles [...]", which is virtually all information the reader is given. More details concerning Hugo are given indirectly, through the reference to his clothes, e.g.: "[...] Baumgartner rarely washed his clothes, they emanated a thick, cloudy odour that he found comforting but others offensive [...] (Desai 1888: 9).

It would be inaccurate to state that Desai's narrators refrains from providing descriptions of the characters in her novels because other figures in *Baumgartner's Bombay* are portrayed more than vividly; for instance, the murderer of Hugo Baumgartner is depicted with an abundance of detail and colour:

[his arms were] two solid baked brick-red arms of human flesh [...], his head was covered with such a mass of blond curls [...], he was Nordic possibly, it was so pale - if not Teutonic. His arms that sprawled about sunburnt to a raw, meaty red on which the bracelets he wore seemed incongruous in their delicacy, their femininity. Angel-child, raw meaty man, helpless lad – he was all three [...]. (Desai 1988: 12)

The discrepancy in the narrator's attention devoted to the two characters suggests that Hugo Baumgartner, the main character in the novel remains as if unknown. Baumgartner's character is placed in the centre of the novel and simultaneously in what we have designated as the dead centre of the reader's field of vision, compelling the receiver to focus on the protagonist's mystery.

The three texts by Anita Desai have been selected to demonstrate three principles that govern the world of literary characters created by the novelist. Desai creates characters that feature almost grotesque abnormality or inferiority. The characters are paired up so as to emphasise their features and thus the protagonists are perceived not only as contrastive but complementary as well. It has a phenomenal importance to the characteristics of the fictional world, as it creates the tension between the protagonists, fuels the plot development by making it viable in psychological terms, and divides the presented world usually into two impenetrable parts. The latter division contributes to the phenomenon called here the dead centre of vision, which manifests itself in one of the characters always remaining undescribed, though not totally unknown because the undescribed character – as the focaliser – makes the fictional world accessible to the reader. The fact that the presented world in Desai's novels can be observed from the point of view of only one of the protagonists at a time, evokes the impression of understatement and makes one of the characters apparently blank or invisible. This marginalisation through lack of description, creating the information gap in the presentation of character, seems to constitute an important technique in the structuring of characters in Anita Desai's novels. The technique emphasises the mystery of the character, and focuses the reader's attention on what is not accessible, especially that the inner worlds of the alienated characters are impenetrable to other figures in the fictional world.

A.S. Byatt's *The Children's Book*: The functions of flanks and ficelles

MAGDALENA KUŹNIAR

The present study will focus on the role of secondary characters in rela-tion to their prominent figural counterparts from the foreground. It can be argued that the figures who are present in the projected world of a novel as 'objects' filling the background and, therefore, appear – at least at first sight – to be less significant or even completely unimportant for the progression of the plot, may in fact considerably influence the read-er's perception of the protagonists. In point of fact, it is the attributes of minor *dramatis personae* that frequently shed light on the main charac-ters, either by analogy, highlighting some of the protagonists' traits, or by contrast, hyperbolising some of their not unequivocally presented at-tributes.

The figures under analysis here are of twofold type – those that are defined by secondary characters present at the diegetic level of the nov-el, inhabiting the same projected world, and the ones whose essence is brought to the forefront of our perception when juxtaposed with some hypodiegetic or intertextual characters mentioned at some point in the text. Baruch Hochman applies the term flanking characters to the literary extras in the novel who are expected to flank the protagonists so that they are "experienced in all [their] vividness, complexity and coherence" (1985: 68). They support the central characters, providing a background for them and making the presentation of the protagonists more lifelike, shown rather than told of. Henry James, in turn, applies the term *ficelle* to characters whose main function is to support the protagonists "like a *ficelle* (a piece of string to hold a bundle together)". A *ficelle* in a novel does not necessarily act as an original, clearly defined model of a person but rather is present in the text "to express as vividly as possible certain

things quite other than itself" (quoted in Fokkema 1991: 22-23). Because
the term "flank" may bring to mind certain spatial associations, let us
reserve the name for those characters that in fact appear side by side
with the main protagonists at the same diegetic level, whereas hypodiegetic or minor intertextual characters that help characterise the protagonists will be here called "ficelles".

In A. S. Byatt's *The Children's Book* (2009) the characters that are
presented with the use of flanking characters are Olive Wellwood and
Benedict Flood, who are defined by members of their families. Hedda
Wellwood's characterisation is deepened intertextually by Hedda Gabler
from Henrik Ibsen's drama, whereas Julian Cane is defined hypodiegeti-
cally by Alice from poems of his authorship.

The main objective of Byatt's *The Children's Book* seems to be the
presentation of the Victorian epoch and therefore the cast of characters is
immense, without a single protagonist that would come across as the
most important of all the foregrounded dramatis personae. However, if
we were to choose the character whose story seems to weave through
most of the text, encompassing a large number of motifs, it would definitely be Olive Wellwood, a writer of children's stories and mother of a
considerable group of children. Judging by what is said in the novel
about Olive *per se*, we may come to the conclusion that she is a happy,
independent, and artistically talented woman as well as a good wife and
caring mother, who writes a separate story for each of her children and
gives them much freedom to spend their time as they wish. Her caring
posture seems even more evident as the reader learns that she invites a
foundling boy to stay in her house.

It is Olive's children and their wellbeing that most accurately point
to Olive's attributes and in so doing considerably modify our first impression of the character. Byatt's novel is divided into four parts that
correspond to the stages of development of the young characters as well
as human life in general and even civilisations – the Beginnings, the
Golden Age, the Silver Age and the Age of Lead. The names of subsequent periods that mark the regression towards an increasingly bleak
state of subsistence, also refer to the nature of Olive that is delineated
along the stages of her children's lives as more and more negative. The
dark side of her mind is gradually revealed to us thanks to the secondary
characters.

Thus, at first, the carefree existence of her children, "who were not hidden away in nurseries, but present at family meals, where their developing characters were taken seriously and rationally discussed, over supper or during long country walks" (29), reflects quite well upon her. We are informed that she was hyped by the press as a perfect mother, when the fact that she wrote several stories customised to the emotional and intellectual needs of each of her children was made public. However, we gradually begin to suspect that there is something wrong with the stories, since the children stop reaching for them. The signal implies some rift between the children and the parent – we are no longer convinced of her being endowed with an attribute of an empathetic mother artist. The characters that make us suspect that the reason for such behaviour is less innocent than, for instance, poor quality of the texts in question are the young Warrens, homeless siblings taken care of by Olive's family. We are surprised that the way she talks about them, when introducing them to her friends, instils them with an impression of her being "witchy", in spite of the pleasant appearance that she is said to have (114). The Warrens turn out to function as indicators that Olive has an attribute of destructive creativity that makes imagination influence real life. As the critic June Sturrock observes, Olive creates a story around any newly met person (2010/2011: 118). For instance, she outlines complete scenarios of the young Warrens' biographies after she learns that they have been neglected and homeless. She turns their harsh lives into gripping stories, their real life into fiction. The Warrens notice it and, acting as focalisers, they filter to the audience their own conviction that she is rather a wicked person who makes use of her special gift to steal and manipulate the material that does not come exclusively from her imagination but belongs to other people. All these attributes of Olive are joined together in the novel, suggesting the thematic function[1] of the character concerning the distinction between life and art, and the consequences of failing to keep them apart. An individual at the mimetic level, when analysed from the thematic perspective, Olive turns into a representative of all artists, with their inherent propensity to prioritise the imaginative at the cost of the real.

---

[1] The terms introduced by James Phelan in his *Reading People, Reading Plots* are explained in the Introduction.

In fact, Byatt, when asked about the motives for writing *The Children's Book,* explains that she was always curious about the lives of children whose parents actually wrote children's books. Although it could be assumed that the children's lives were made fabulous by the parents who managed to fascinate thousands of young readers with the worlds of their making, Byatt mentions several tragic events that affected the families of children's books' writers:

> I started with the idea that writing children's books isn't good for the writers' own children. There are some dreadful stories. Christopher Robin at least lived. Kenneth Grahame's son put himself across a railway line and waited for the train. Then there's J. M. Barrie. One of the boys that Barrie adopted almost certainly drowned himself. This struck me as something that needed investigating. (quoted in Leith 2009)

It is, among others, with Olive that Byatt tries to probe into this question and provides her own view of what it is like to be an artist and what it is like to have an artist as a parent.

Another flanking character that sheds some more light on Olive is her daughter Hedda, whose mimetic attributes of incurable curiosity and rebelliousness make her eavesdrop on conversations between adults and consequently reveal another attribute of Olive, that is her infidelity. The little girl learns that some of the siblings were born out of wedlock. However, because her detective skills are not sufficient to answer the question: who, in fact, is and who is not Olive and her husband Humphry's child, all of them start to suspect themselves of being changelings, cuckoos' children, out of place in their house. As a result, the worldview that has hitherto been obvious for their innocent minds is suddenly shaken and they must "rearrange the family patterns in their heads, like chessboards which suddenly lacked a bishop and had too many knights, or where the queen ran amok in zigzags" (Byatt 2009: 315). This obviously causes in them an identity crisis and a sense of being betrayed. The adults are seen as treacherous and unworthy of their trust. The effect for the audience is, first of all, a cognitive tension – the omniscient, third person narrator does not reveal to us the whole truth at once but directs our thinking with the use of the characters' statements, and makes us formulate divergent hypotheses and answers to the questions voiced by the characters. However, the most important mimetic function of the children's feelings of uncertainty and insecurity is to act as a stimulus to the authorial audience for judging Olive and her notorious and incurable propensity to engage in love affairs, to look for new experiences and to disregard the gravity of potential consequences. The audience empathises with the confused children and adopts their negative attitude towards Olive, modifying the initial good opinion about her.

The flanking character that acts as the most emphatic expression of the view of Olive as a destructive mother and artist is her favourite son, Tom. He seems to be Byatt's *puer aeternus*, modelled on Peter Pan who refused to ever grow up. Tom, like Barrie's character, has his Neverland in the woods in a tree-house that functions as a secret base, at first for all the children when they need to discuss something that should not reach the ears of the adults. He is, however, the only child that never grows out of the need to run away from time to time to the tree-house and his own imaginary world. He makes it into his green utopia, where he can hide away from the world and read escapist books whose subject matter does not touch upon issues that both bore and frighten him, such as "sexual intrigues" or "the angry descriptions of the condition of the working class, in Manchester, London, Liverpool and Birmingham" – the subjects very popular among his peers. He chooses books on natural science or utopias, such as William Morris's *News from Nowhere*, reading only to kill time, not with any prospects for a future career. It is him that Byatt uses as the main object of the analysis of the destructive influence of the parent artist. The boy's inability to grow up may be blamed partly on Olive – it symbolises her distorted perception of her beloved son, who has always appeared to her as a fabulous creature, a perfect child that will stay forever by her side. The boy seems to Olive always so young, beautiful and dependent on her, as in one of the scenes, in which she perceives him in an unrealistic light:

> He was the most graceful creature she had ever seen. It was noon. The sun was high and shone directly down on her golden boy, who was not reflected in the moving surface of the sea, which he had broken into shining particles, myriads of slanting glassy fragments, a mosaic of surfaces, as there were myriads of glittering water-drops catching the light and making rainbows along his shoulders and in his long hair. [...] She loved Tom. She could not keep him. Tom loved her – this was still her time, with him too – but he would go away and be changed. (Byatt 2009: 187)

With the use of her overactive imagination she recreates the world and the people around her, imposing identities of her own making onto them, and because most of her tales are based on her family life, the children become her toys that she plays with rather than brings up. This danger-ous propensity to take advantage of real people and make stories based on their lives is dramatised in the most extreme form on the example of her last tale. It is a story which projects a boy, modelled on Tom, who, as an infant, had his shadow bitten off by a big rat. This lack of a physi-cal element that all other earthly beings have, instils the child with a feeling that he is different, incomplete in a sense, and as a result not ful-ly normal. Unable to accept his peculiar nature, he sets off on a long journey to regain his shadow and become a standard human being, like all other people. The story-boy's attributes seem to metaphorically rep-resent the attributes of Tom, who also seems to lack something – he is immature, excessively sensitive and afraid of contact with the things that his peers are attracted to, like sex or social and political problems, as if he was not fully male. Like the hypodiegetic character of Barrie's mak-ing, Byatt's Tom feels different than typical teenage boys.

Thus, in her tale, Olive makes public her own, probably quite accu-rate, vision of her son. This is also a vision that Tom himself recognises while watching the play based on the story, but that he is unable to ac-cept. This view of his personality has been so far safely kept hidden, un-til the moment when it is very skilfully dramatized and made public, leaving him stripped of privacy and painfully humiliated. It is with the act of writing the story that Olive deals a lethal blow to her beloved son, brought up in a clime of fairy stories and unequipped with means of de-fence that would enable him to cope with harsh reality. Tom's act of committing suicide after the staging of the play is probably the final and most extreme act of critique against Olive, carried out in the novel with the use of the flanking character.

Thus, starting with an impression of Olive as a liberal, empathetic and caring mother, going through the stage of perceiving her as an artist who takes advantage of her family by stealing some facts from their lives and turning them into stories as well as a woman who cannot help cheating on her husband to the detriment of her children, the reader fi-nally sees a murderess in her. Fotis Jannidis refers to this kind of pro-gress of the reader's understanding of a character as a "deferred identifi-cation", i.e., the final establishment of the identity of a character that is initially presented equivocally and inspires divergent assumptions as to his or her real identity. This progress in shaping the reader's attitude towards Olive depends in Byatt's novel on the presentation of the children's perspectives. Without the scars Olive has left on their perception of the world, she would be for us just another pleasant fictional figure of a children's stories writer, an acknowledged authoress of a bestselling tale modelled on Peter Pan's story, but never a dangerous type of artist making immoral use of her intrapersonal skills to penetrate other people's psyches and rob them of privacy by making their personal dramas public.

The last function for Tom to play in the novel is the one that he performs actually after his suicide, when Byatt uses his multiplied figure to present Olive's despair after his death. The distressed mother sees a "forest of coeval boys, all eternally present, crowding her room". Her mind is bombarded with images of her son at various stages of development:

> ...every Tom that had ever been, the blond baby, the infant taking his first, hesitant steps, the little boy clutching her skirt, the besotted reader in too low a light, his brows pulled into a frown, the adolescent with his skin broken out, the young man walking, always walking or about to walk. They were all equally present because they were all gone. (Byatt 2009: 536)

The vision of a multiplied boy is an effective way of reflecting the thinking processes of Olive. She rapidly scans her memory in search of all the moments when Tom was still alive.

Some minor characters, that themselves are not particularly significant for the progression in the novel, yet who add to the general presentation, or, to use Genette's term, revelation of Olive, are her sons Robin and Harry, whose attributes are as if purposefully neglected by Byatt, even though their presence in the novel is not meaningless. Olive's youngest sons as characters are made barely noticeable, almost unknown to us, however, they swell the progress of the figure of Olive as a mother – for they are also hardly visible to her, until they unexpectedly die in the war. Only then does she realise her parental mistake of privileging one child at the cost of so many others, which leaves her with "the useless thought that she should have protected them, that she had thought of Tom, and taken her attention from these boys, and lost them" (2009: 588).

The scene in which Olive reads the letter informing her that her youngest son got killed is one of very few moments in the novel when the relationship between her and the boys is presented as that of the parent and her children. In most episodes the children seem to surround her as completely independent figures, housemates rather than her own offspring. Thus it can be argued that like other secondary characters in the novel, the two youngest boys are there to perform the function of revealing their mother's character. Their premature deaths make Olive's realisation of her own mistakes more dramatic and poignant.

There is also Florian, the boy that was born by Olive's sister Violet, whom Olive accepted to bring up as her own child. His function in the novel is also subordinated to the presentation of Olive. In her distress after the loss of her biological sons, she starts to hate him and would gladly sacrifice him for the lives of her own dead boys. Byatt presents the young survivor as somebody

> ...gaunt, [who] limped heavily, and his skin was puckered and stained and scarred all over. All of his eyelids drooped. His golden curls which had been shaved off for the draft, were growing back only sparsely and in tufts [...]. Worst of all, he emitted a heavy, painful, wheezing sound, having briefly breathed in blown-back English gas. (2009: 592)

His, almost scary, appearance helps the audience understand Olive's dread at his sight and her persistent impression that she "liv[es] with a monster, a changeling, a demon" (593), apparently her son, yet born by another woman and changed physically by the war to the point that he is hardly recognisable. Florian, therefore, helps to delineate the workings of her desperate mind in a vivid way. Similarly, when Olive tries to avoid contact with him by listening to the sound of his limping steps, only to realise that it is she that should be hated instead of the young man, his battered image once again helps us empathise with the woman torn between contradictory emotions – disgust at the dreadful sight of the invalid and self-hatred, when she realises that he is actually a victim rather than a monster.

Thus, at the end of the story Olive seems to be flanked by all of her sons and mimetically defined by them. They bring out the complex workings of her mind and make them perceptible to us, the readers of the story. This is the final stage of the authorial audience's formation of judgments about Olive. Her distress at the loss of so many sons mitigates slightly our negative attitude towards her formed so far along the progression of the story in our minds.

Another artist whose house is presented in Byatt's novel is Benedict Fludd – a genius potter in the perception of his neighbours, yet a monster for his family. In one of the first scenes where he appears, his characterisation is drastically delineated by a comparison to tyrannical Bluebeard. The analogy made by his young apprentice, Philip Warren, is, in fact, very apt not only with regard to Fludd's fiery temper but also because of the secret room that is always kept locked, where he stores pornographic sculptures of, among others, his underage daughters. This synthetic attribute, stylised on Bluebeard's habit of keeping the evidence of his degeneration in a locked room, is one of many effects of Byatt's use of metatextual techniques. By means of what Ralf Schneider refers to as the literary categorisation,[2] we create a mental image of Fludd as a stereotypical literary villain and formulate a set of expectations regarding his personality and his potential future actions. He seems much less convincing than other characters from Byatt's novel, as if taken out of some fairy tale – a monster that, on the one hand, is supposed to scare us, yet on the other, prevents us from excessive immersion in the story. Phillip Warren is therefore the first focaliser that helps the authorial audience formulate our initial impression about Benedict Fludd as a tyrant.

However, the most shocking attributes are actually conveyed to us implicitly thanks to Fludd's family members that flank him and act as foils against which we formulate our distaste at him. In a sense, the whole Fludd family is synthetic[3] as all of its members are modified copies of well-known characters from fairy tales. In spite of being very vividly described and endowed with clearly defined attributes, they do not primarily function as plausible persons. Benedict is a Bluebeard-like tyrant and the rest of the family, with their victim-like attributes, hyperbolise his monstrosity even more convincingly than he does himself when he bursts out with uncontrolled fury or retreats into madness.

The three Fludd women, Benedict's wife and his two daughters, are presented as unnaturally listless, quiet and inactive, they move about the house dreamlike, rarely talking to each other or engaging in any housework. They often walk in the countryside, but always separately – word-

---

2   A mental process of recognizing in a character the features of a literary stock character, that is a stereotypical type of person, with overall characteristics that recur in numerous works of literature, such as *femme fatale* or rich miser (Schneider 2001).

3   In Phelan's sense; see Introduction.

less and almost ghostlike. Fludd refers to them as "pallid silk moths" (211). Pomona, one of the daughters, in one of very few scenes where she seems to be logical and perceptive, paradoxically admits that she feels the family is

> under a spell [...], behind one of those thickets in stories. [They] trail out to the orchard and back to the kitchen. And up to bed, and out to the orchard, and back to the kitchen. [They] sew. That's part of the spell. [They] have to sew things or something dreadful will happen. (Byatt 2009: 338)

Her figurative comparison is later supported by Philip, the apprentice potter. When the illiterate boy practises reading on fairy tales, he instinctively makes associations between the fictitious characters and the people that he presently lives with. He compares Seraphita, Benedict's wife, to the automaton Olimpia from Hoffmann's *Sandman*, when he sees her

> look[ing] straight ahead, dreamy and distracted, her mouth composed in a pretty, unchanging half-smile [...] as though she was skating on unseasonal ice – or rolling along on invisible balls or wheels. [...] She walked, sat in her chair and stared pleasantly forwards till lunch, stitched a little, operated a loom a little, waited a little more, and arrived at supper time. (Byatt 2009:134)

Her older daughter Imogen does not differ much from her – statuesque, scentless and unnaturally unemotional, resembling "ceramic madonnas in the Museum" or Sleeping Beauty, who "pricked her finger and [is] sleep-walking" (133). The youngest Pomona, in turn, is "all the Cinderella daughters in the hearths, woebegone and unregarded" (133). Whereas Imogen sleepwalks only figuratively, Pomona does it literally, mooning about the house at night and regularly slipping into the bed of confused Philip, who never finds out why she does it and whether she is really asleep or only acting.

The three women's attributes add much to our perception of Fludd who, with the family as the foil, gradually assumes the shape of a vampire figure, sucking out life from his slave wife and daughters, unable to bear the departure of any of his daughters when they want to start their own lives, as if he were drawing energy and inspiration from them. The flanking effect of the women is further reinforced by their meaningful names – Seraphita, alluding to the female angel from Balzac's story, similarly passive, spiritual and critical of men's possessive treatment of women; Imogen, probably an allusion to Shakespeare's good-natured heroine from *Cymbeline*, punished by her father for making a misalliance; and finally Pomona, pointing to the Roman goddess of orchards and gardens, a perfectly fitting model for Byatt's passionate adolescent character. Thus, the additional meanings hidden behind the names can be summed up in the following way: the three women – one angelic, another one an attractive and blameless heroine, adored by men, and a goddess, symbolizing blossoming fruit trees – stand for three types of female perfection that are contrasted here with the male degenerate nature.

It can be argued that if it was not for the attributes of the Fludd women, Fludd himself would probably come across as a less vicious and complex figure – an impulsive freak, yet not necessarily a serious victimiser whose unpredictable behaviour turns what should be a family hearth into a concentration camp where nobody feels secure. It is the women that give our "narrative intelligence"[4] food for thought so that we make an attempt at combining facts and forming hypotheses about potential acts of maltreatment of the women and about child abuse on the part of Fludd, although Byatt does not state anything clearly in the novel.

With the progress of the plot however, the bleak, monstrous image of Fludd's character is slightly minimised. Byatt uses a similar technique to the one she applies to Olive at the end of the story, namely she turns Fludd into a tragic figure. This is done by means of superimposing on him some borrowed attributes that make him miserable rather than monstrous. These are all the mimetic elements of his personality that suggest his inability to cope with the world around him and the strong emotions that are always ready to burst out of him. A very suggestive synthetic technique that Byatt uses to turn Fludd into a tragic character is to suggest his similarity to King Lear. The last moments of his life are stylised on the final moments of Shakespeare's tragic king. Having learnt that he lost his daughter after she decided to leave her father's house to get married, Fludd re-enacts Lear's behaviour – he first utters the famous words: "howl, howl, howl", copied from Shakespeare's hero mourning his daughter, and later walks away to the marshes like the mad king. Thus, Shakespeare's character acts as an intertextual flank here, an objective

---

4   The ability to organise experience into narrative form, to think in narrative and to understand narrative forms already created as a being continuums of causally linked sequences of events (Mateas and Sengers)

correlative that helps reflect Benedict's emotions very vividly and emphatically. The moments when the monster manifests some human weaknesses, which we are taught to recognise through Shakespeare, make us decategorise[5] Fludd to some extent and perceive him not as a flat fairy-tale character but, paradoxically, as a more mimetic figure with complex personality which makes us empathise with him, even in spite of his being endowed mainly with negative attributes. It is true that Byatt's characters, even if they happen to be degenerate freaks, are characterised in such a way that there always seems to exist some explanation for their asocial behaviour (Leith). Like Olive – an artistic vampire mother – Fludd also appears pitiable rather than only despicable.

A character constructed by Byatt, whose attributes or, more specifically, states of mind are conveyed to us not so much by pure description but rather with the use of a ficelle character, is Julian Cane. Julian is a young, sensitive student of fairy tales, who has to take part in the war, in spite of his characterological maladjustment to military action. Byatt applies a skilful technique of presenting his traumatic experiences and the confusion that he felt on the battlefield by means of overt allusions to Lewis Carroll and a superimposition of Alice's feelings of something inexplicable and illogical happening around her onto the young soldier. Julian's confusion during the war is so strong that he does not even recognise himself in a mirror: "He caught sight of someone else, standing quietly in a corner, a thin, grim-looking, middle-aged man with a scarred face and weary eyes. He raised his hand to greet him and saw, as the other raised his hand, also, that he had failed to recognise himself" (Byatt 2009: 591). A scene where he feels particularly overwhelmed is the one in which he gets wounded in an explosion, losing consciousness and, as it later turns out, also his episodic memory. What comes to his mind at this moment is the wood from *Through the Looking Glass*, where things have no names. This objective correlative successfully reflects the puzzlement that he feels after a shrapnel sticks in his head, causing a kind of dysphasia in him. He cannot remember the names of ordinary things, including his own name. The physical disorder is cured later on, yet the preoccupation with names does not leave him. He sud-

---

5   In Schneider's meaning of the term suggesting the reformulation of our former perception of a character after having acquired information that contradicts our previous image of him or her.

denly realises that such words as "honour, glory, heritage, joy" (590) can no longer be used after the war, the belief in the existence of any signifieds that these words would refer to having been verified with a negative answer. Even the names of the other soldiers who are killed lose their significance and become empty labels, torn off their carriers:

> the dead who were buried had their names on temporary grave-markers, which were often blown to bits in the endless gunfire. Their name liveth after them for evermore. He had a drugged vision of names, like scurrying rats searching the battlefield for the flesh they had been attached to. [...] Men and their names were provisional: he realised he learned their names with a kind of dull grief, because there were already so many he did not need any longer to recall, because they could not be recalled, they were spattered and scattered in the churned-up mire that had been green fields and woodland. (Byatt 2009: 589)

Overwhelmed with these experiences, Julian tries to commit his emotions to paper and starts writing poems, all alluding to the story of Alice to some extent. The soldiers from his poetry are no longer certain what their names are – "a worm, a maggot, [...] a smell, a scapegoat, a smashed snail, a toad, a broken teacup". They are told that even these statuses are too much for them to desire, because what they, in fact, are is "null [...] nothing [...] zilch, nichts" (596). The lyrical I of one of his poems suffers from overburdening of memory with names, which makes it impossible for him to remember any new names:

> My head is packed with names. Names of dead men. I cannot learn the live?
> Names that come late, boys to replace the boys
> Who marched away [...]
> Today they stand and smile
> Numbered and nameless. And they march away.
>
> (Byatt 2009: 597)

All their identities seem to be blurred and blended together with their names after they have been equalised by the same fate – they seem nondistinct to him.

In one of his poems he draws the figure of Alice herself wandering through the forest that is the site of a battle and examining remnants of this event, all of them strange to her, because of being incomplete, vestigial, "stumps of wood and stumps of flesh and metal" (596), useless and nonsensical. The landscape that surrounds her is impossible to de-

scribe in normal frames of cognition, the only forms of expression that
are suitable here are oxymorons, as

> no shapes hold. [She] watched a wood
> Mix four elements so air was flame
> And earth was liquid: nothing stood
> Trees were wild matchsticks [...]
> and men were mud. [...]
> There was no light, no skyline, up and down
> Were all the same. (Byatt 2009: 595)

This virtual, transtextual intrusion of the little girl into the frame[6] of the
battlefield may at first seem only a postmodernist misattribution[7], but in
fact not only has the synthetic function of highlighting the constructedness of Alice and as a result also of Julian, but also performs a significant mimetic function. The emotional state of the child character in the
poem, who gets lost in an ontologically and genologically alien world,
and who is terrified and overwhelmed with strong feelings caused by
cognitive dissonance, is superimposed on the adult man figure. This
quite successfully performs the mimetic function of conveying the state
of mind of the young soldier. The audience reads about the war and the
soldier who takes part in it, yet it is the intertextual Alice that speaks
louder about Julian's impressions and confusion than the passages describing the battles in which he takes part. The effect is the reader's
emotional engagement with the experiences of the character associated
with the little girl, who is familiar from childhood reading.

Byatt also created a character whose most vital attributes are to be
inferred by the reader from what is associated with the character's name.
The *dramatis persona* in question is Hedda, one of Olive's bevy of children. The girl is named after Ibsen's Hedda Gabler and, in spite of this
association being mentioned only once in *The Children's Book*, this intertextual character (transworld identity) seems to be always present in
the novel when Hedda Wellwood is mentioned. The name seems to have
a significant mimetic function in the presentation of Byatt's character.

---

6   Frames are one of the basic cognitive structures of story grammars, referring to our "ex-
      pectations about how domains of experience are likely to be structured", e.g. what ele-
      ments are congruent with a particular setting (Herman Cognitive Narratology) .
7   Placing an element from one sign system into a different, dissimilar sign system
      (McHale 1994: 47).

Although Olive's daughter is described as one that shares attributes with many literary celebrities,

> she was the traitor in all tales of chivalry and in myths. She was Vivien, she was Morgan le Fay, she was Loki. She despised the cow-eyed and the gentle, Elaine the lily maid, faithful Psyche, Baldur's weeping wife, Nanna. She was a detective, who saw through appearances. No one was as nice as they seemed, was her rule of judging characters. She was the darkest of the children, with long black hair and very solid black brows, drawn in a frown more often than not. (Byatt 2009: 216)

it is Ibsen's heroine that most of all models our perception of Byatt's character. Hedda's individualism, rebelliousness and disdainful attitude towards her siblings, with whom she cannot find common ground[8], are seen in a bleaker light when the story of Ibsen's heroine is superimposed on hers. For all of her childhood years Byatt's Hedda suffers from boredom and lack of purpose, which she tries to cope with by engaging her detective inclinations in spying on the mysterious adults. Because of associations with Hedda Gabler, our initial, quite positive, reaction to a clever, nonconformist child character, always suspicious and defiant, peeping through keyholes or hiding in tall grass to overhear the treacherous adults, gives way to suspicions of what could her need of excitement, combined with a feeling of superiority over others, lead to if she had not found her purpose in the suffrage movement. Her social activity, presented as dangerous in itself, makes "her sure she [is] alive, and that life ha[s] a meaning, which she [was] always uncertain about" (484). While reading about her determined fight for equality – public speeches given in chilly weather and returning home bruised and bleeding – the reader feels that her "capacity for indignation [and] rage" (482) must be given vent to, one way or another. The superimposition of Ibsen's heroine upon Byatt's Hedda only increases the impression of the strength of cumulated emotions.

In fact, if it was not for the ficelle character that is carried in her name, Hedda would probably be construed as an average naughty child figure at first and then a typical rebellious feminist. It is the ficelle Hedda,

---

8   "Phyllis was an idiot. Florian was a baby. [...] Pomona was an idiot, too, of the same kind as Phyllis. Dorothy was who she hated, because she was older, and in the way and got things Hedda didn't get. And because she had Griselda and they were together, and Hedda had no one" (Byatt 2009: 216).

Ibsen's heroine, that gives us a hint that the Wellwood girl may also be ascribed strong emotions that can eventually become destructive. Hedda Gabler, when superimposed onto Hedda Wellwood, makes the attributes of Byatt's character flicker in our eyes – we are especially prone to hyperbolising her negative attributes. Keeping Ibsen's character in mind we pose the following questions: is Byatt's Hedda simply bored or is she crazy with the lack of purpose in life; is the decision of joining the suffragists a conscious, well-considered step in her life or is it just a whim motivated by the desire to do anything rather than devoting her life to repetitive household chores; is her disrespect for the rules and ideas of others a manifestation of individualism or is it strong craving for freedom from limitations imposed by the society? These and many other questions may come to our minds when we juxtapose the two Heddas and their attributes, the final effect being obviously dependent on our interpretation of the intertext and the ficelle that is borrowed from it.

To sum up, the four abovementioned characters are perceived by the authorial audience as changing textual constructs throughout the whole progression of the text. We come across their attributes in descriptive passages of the novel as well as in the scenes where it is the flanks that provide various stimuli for the main characters to manifest their attributes. We add up the data and form opinions on the dramatis personae, yet because the sources of our information about the characters are multiple and at times provide inconsistent, if not conflicting, sets of attributes, what is constructed in our minds as a result are images of characters that have no static and clearly defined features but undergo a process of constant transfiguration, which depends, among others, on additional information a flanking or ficelle character brings to the text at a particular moment. And all these techniques obviously remind us of the fictiveness of Byatt's characters and of fiction in general, since with our realisation of the importance of all the syntagmatic relations between particular characters and their influence on our perception of them, we are brought round from the false impression that the protagonists are independent, unified, humanlike beings.

Charles Williams's *Shadows of Ecstasy*: Cognitive aspects of character interpretation

ANDRZEJ SŁAWOMIR KOWALCZYK

If, generally speaking, the novels of Charles Williams (1886-1945) have won little critical appreciation—to say the least[1], it is even more so with his first one. The book, written in 1925 and originally entitled *The Black Bastard*, was rejected, revised, and finally published in 1933 as *Shadows of Ecstasy* (Hadfield 1983: 81; 92-93). Many a scholar observes that the novel stands apart from Williams's other fictional works, characterisation being one of its principal shortcomings. Thus, for instance, Humphrey Carpenter notices the author's aversion to describing the characters (1999: 124), Don D. Elgin writes about Williams's "unclear attitude toward his characters" and their being "ultimately contradictory" (1985: 122), Thomas Howard suggests that "[if] you want the subtleties of a Henry James novel then you cannot have your characters lined up holding placards the way they do in *Shadows of Ecstasy*" (1983: 36), while Stephen M. Dunning associates "[t]he greatest difficulty in coming to grips with what goes on in the novel" precisely with the characters, "who appear and disappear without any apparent pattern" (2000: 19)[2].

Since it is impossible to fully investigate the problem of characterisation in a novel within the limitations of an article, my aim is humbler. I

---

1   Patricia Meyer Spacks, for instance, states that "Williams' work seems full of false notes, unable to justify its pretentions, lacking in imaginative energy" (1979: 150); Stephen Medcalf regards the books as "overall rather poor" (1995: 207); Don D. Elgin criticizes "the lack of consistent character development; the uneasy marriage of psychological, theological, and supernatural elements; the reliance on abstract rhetoric instead of concrete symbol and/or incident to develop plot, character, and theme" (1985: 97).

2   Significantly, in her biography of Williams, Alice Mary Hadfield observes that "Charles himself was not fascinated by personalities as such, in life or fiction" (1983: 95).

intend to address certain theoretical questions associated with character-building and character-interpretation with reference to Ian Caithness, whom critics regard as a "minor" or "secondary" figure in *Shadows of Ecstasy*. My chief concern will be the role of the reader/interpreter in creating this literary character as well as the possibilities offered by cognitive poetics within the discussed area of literary studies.

Apparently, both literary scholars and Williams's biographers have focused upon the novel's central (hero-)villain, Nigel Considine[3], usually paying less attention to subsidiary characters[4]. *Shadows of Ecstasy* is indeed constructed around the said Nigel Considine, a European who spent a number of years in Africa and managed to discover the esoteric secret of "transmutation of energy", which allowed him to prolong his life beyond known human limits. He believes he ultimately will be able to conquer death forever. Later on, we learn that Considine, as the mysterious "High Executive", is the leader of an African revolution aimed at liberating the continent from the white race. When European governments disregard the Proclamation he issues and send troops to pacify the rebellious colonies, the African forces are "compelled to open war upon Europe" (Williams 1933/2003: 58)[5]. In the end, even London is threatened by air raids and by the landing of African armies[6].

These political events, however far-fetched they may seem nowadays, form a background against which the conflict of ideas is portrayed – a theme Williams seems to be interested in the most. The eponymous "shadows", such as art/poetry, love/sex, religion, material goods, or kingship – each related to a given character in the novel – are, according to Considine's teaching, only deterrents to "the realm of pure and undying ecstasy of which all these shadows are merest hints" (Howard 1983: 24). Considine believes that if the energy mortals devote to the pursuit of the aforementioned "earthly" aims is absorbed into the powerful imagi-

---

3   Major commentaries upon the character of Considine are comprehensively summarized in Dunning 2000: 24-27.
4   One of the most radical statements positions Considine as "the *only* viable centre to the text [emphasis added]" (Dunning 2000: 19).
5   All references in the present study are to the Regent College Publishing edition of *Shadows of Ecstasy* (Williams 1933/2003), based upon the 1933 Gollancz version. The corresponding page numbers are given in parentheses.
6   Howard authoritatively claims that these events "never convince [...] us in the smallest degree" (1983: 48).

nation of people's being alive, death will be vanquished. So far, for ages the human species has been deluding itself:

> This was the beginning of sex when far away in the ages the world divided itself in its primal dark instinct to destroy death which seemed its doom. And when man came he desired immortality, and deceived himself with begetting children and with religion and with art. All these are not ecstasy but the shadow of ecstasy. Kingship and dynasties he created and cities and monuments and science, and nothing satisfied that hungry desire. (Williams 1933/2003: 177)

However, according to Considine, it will be possible to take "the ghost of man" out of the place s/he wanders at death, "stripped of all powers", by coming to this place "armed with passion and high delight" and finally to return from the other side (Williams 1933/2003: 178-179). Such is the aim of the experiments Considine has made, himself serving as a *sui generis* proof positive.

On the level of ideas, as Howard puts it, Considine's mistake "is to insist that this world here is an illusion and that it can be overcome by one's own [...] imagination" (1983: 24), which visibly clashes with the Christian perspective, both intra- and extra-textual[7]. To spread his gospel, the self-proclaimed messiah does not refrain from sacrificing people's lives, himself becoming a master of puppets:

> 'I have let the English feel panic, panic such as they have not felt since the Vikings raided their coasts and burned their towns a thousand years ago. [...] As for my Africans, they ask for death and they shall have death. Most of them will kill themselves or one another to-night; those who survive till to-morrow will die before your soldiers. I do not pity them; they are not the adepts; all that they are capable of I have given them. They die for the Undying. How many martyrs would the Churches offer me of such a strain?" (Williams 1933/2003: 176-177)

And yet, to a far greater degree the novel depicts Considine's influence upon the particular characters, Williams juxtaposing their personal "shadows" with the new tidings. Thus, there is Roger Ingram, a "Professor of Applied Literature" (Williams 1933/2003: 4) for whom poetry

---

7 For numerous scholars, Williams's status of a Christian "lay theologian" is indisputable. Importantly, though, Dunning observes that the "*a priori* conviction that Williams was simply an orthodox member of the Church of England and that all his writings comprise a unified testimony to that orthodoxy [...] is quite simply false" (2000: 25-26).

constitutes the core of life[8]. He becomes fascinated with Considine's teachings to the extent of being ready to leave his exemplary wife, Isabel, and join the guru in his trip back to Africa. There is Philip Travers, a son of a retired surgeon, Sir Bernard, who lives by his idealised love of Rosamund Murchison, Isabel's sister, characterised as "stuckup and not quite intelligent" (Williams 1933/2003: 13). Considine provides Philip with the vision of transmuting his sexual desire into immortality – a trail he once blazed himself[9]. Another character is Inkamasi, the hereditary Zulu king living in London, who worships the idea of genuine royalty and chooses an honourable suicide rather than mere existence "without his majesty" (Williams 1933/2003: 212). Considine's aide, Colonel Mottreux, should also be mentioned, since his "shadow", i.e. the desire for precious jewels, manifests itself towards the end of the book, pushing the story to its climax. Mottreux shoots his master teacher dead only to find death from the hand of another adept (Williams 1933/2003: 255).

Apart from the abovementioned characters, there is Rev. Ian Caithness. The manner in which he is introduced already reveals much about his status as a literary character. His entrance interrupts the conversation between Sir Bernard and his son, Philip. Welcomed with a simple "Hello, Ian", Caithness is immediately asked the question of "how's the Archbishop?" (Williams 1933/2003: 15), which creates the impression of his being a priest whose position in the ecclesiastical hierarchy is somehow significant. After that, the third person narrator takes over:

> Ian Caithness was the vicar of a Yorkshire parish and Philip's godfather. He was a tall man of about Sir Bernard's age and looked like an ascetic priest, which was more by good luck than by merit, for he practiced no extreme austerities. But he took life seriously, and (as often happens) attributed his temperament to his religion. He was therefore not entirely comfortable with other people of different temperaments who did the same thing, and a lifelong friendship with Sir Bernard had probably survived because the other remained delicately poised in a philosophy outside the Church. As a Christian, Sir Bernard would have probably irritated his

---

8   Ironically, the narrator draws attention to Roger's "definite and continuous despair that words which meant so much to him meant so little to others" (Williams 1933/2003: 11).

9   Much later, Considine himself admits: "I myself carried out the great experiment, and I laid my imagination upon all the powers and influences of sex and love and desire. In the adolescence of my life I did this, and I have thriven upon that strength ever since. [...] I have gathered from many women all that imagination desired, and I have changed it to strength and cunning and length of days" (Williams 1933/2003: 178-179).

friend intolerably; he soothed him as a – it was difficult to say what. (Williams 1933/2003: 15)

The passage provides us with information concerning several aspects of Caithness's fictional "existence;" significantly enough, it is the most detailed one in the entire book. First of all, a personal link between the priest and the other characters is established ("Philip's godfather", "a lifelong friendship with Sir Bernard"). The reader learns that the priest lives "in a Yorkshire parish", which, to a degree, dispels the former expectations of his belonging to the upper circles of clergy, as he is but a modest "vicar". There are also a few seemingly dispassionate facts about Caithness's appearance (height, age, general impression), but, in general, irony can be traced in the narrator's comments, which apparently reflects Sir Bernard's vantage point[10]. Thus, the priest's austere image is attributed to "good luck" rather than "merit", and his serious attitude to life is underscored, with the accompanying generalisation on the relationship between one's temperament and religion ("as often happens"). As the story develops, Caithness becomes characterised through utterances and actions rather than via direct definition (*sensu* Rimmon-Kenan 1983/1994: 59-60), but these key moments will be discussed in greater detail later.

Shadows of Ecstasy ends with the fundamental questions unanswered: *is* Considine permanently dead? *Will* he return? *Was* he a genuine messiah, "the Master of Love" and "the Deathless One" (Williams 1933/2003: 174)? Or rather, did he fall victim to the false, infectious vision he had shaped himself[11]? The final paragraph leaves both Considine's disenchanted neophyte, Roger Ingram, and the reader in limbo:

> If he returned. If he carried out the experiment of his vision, the purpose of his labours. If, first among his peers, when all believed him lost, he thrust himself from the place of shades back into immortal and transmuted life, if he held death at his disposal, if he knew how the vivid ecstasy of experience dominated all shapes and forms, all accidents of time and place. […] If now, while the world shouted over the defeat of his allies and subjects,

---

10   Sir Bernard's ironic disposition is mentioned twice in the passage where the narrator introduces him to the reader (Williams 1933/2003: 6-7).

11   Interestingly, John Heath-Stubbs finds a parallel between Nigel Considine and Adolf Hitler in that they both represent "the canalization of primitive, unconscious forces for evil ends" (1998: 156).

[...] if now he came once more to threaten and deliver it. If – ah beyond,
beyond belief! – but if he returned. (Williams 1933/2003: 260)

And although the book's inconclusiveness, compared by one critic to a
"foreplay leading only to an [...] act of coitus interruptus" (Dunning
2000: 23), is sometimes treated as another weakness of *Shadows of Ecstasy*, it is, arguably, one of the factors owing to which the novel remains within the domain of literature rather than applied theology.

Coming back to Ian Caithness, it is enlightening to look at a few representative points critics make with regard to this character. The least
"academic" commentary presents him in clear opposition to Considine.
We learn that "[i]n the chaos that ensues [from Considine's actions] two
people alone *stand firm*—Ian Caithness, *the quiet vicar who knows the
true meaning of death and resurrection*, and Isabelle [sic!] Ingram,
whose love and faith leave her nothing to fear [emphasis added]" (Williams 1933/2003: blurb). One critic also claims that "Isabel and Caithness [...] are *patently in the right* [emphasis added]", although the reader's feelings are not "quite squarely" on their side (Howard 1983: 36).
He explains this failure in terms of "the drama being too pageant-like for
any very complex subtleties" (1983: 36). Focusing upon Caithness,
Howard argues that he "is obvious enough" since – taking into account
the masque- or pageant-like nature of *Shadows of Ecstasy* – "[h]e is a
priest" (1983: 36). His role, therefore, amounts to reminding others of
the metaphysical dimension of this world (1983: 36) as well as "supply-
ing a certain plausibility to what might otherwise seem to be merely
primitive sorcery" (1983: 37). In addition, according to Howard, Caithness is a static character—one who "does not develop" except for becoming "a sadder and wiser man" at the end of the novel (1983: 37).

A similar note is present in the considerations of Patricia Meyer
Spacks. Though not concerned with *Shadows of Ecstasy* exclusively, she
nonetheless notices affinity between Williams's novels and science-
fiction in that both utilise the principle which Kingsley Amis names
"idea as hero" (Meyer Spacks 1979: 153). She further argues that it is
Williams's "apparent interest in psychology" that conceals his real theological involvement (1979: 154). By analogy, Caithness would be a representative of the Church of England, or, more accurately, its voice. According to Meyer Spacks, it goes without saying that Williams fails: although his novels are "*fundamentally allegorical*, [...] he cannot commit

himself to the limitations of allegory [emphasis added]" (1979: 158). One final example comes from a study by Gareth Knight; there, Caithness "*represents the attitude of the Church* to the powers promised and enacted by Considine [emphasis added]" (1990/2010: 183).

This allegorical/figural role of characterisation in *Shadows of Ecstasy* is called into question by Dunning, who plainly states that scholars are "wrong to conclude [...] that the characters correspond to the types found in traditional morality plays" (2000: 28). "Neither is Caithness 'simply Priest,'" he argues, "nor is Roger Ingram 'Poet'[...]" (2000: 28). More significantly, Dunning explicates Williams's approach to characterisation from an utterly different standpoint: "Williams's *evident psychological interest in his characters* [...] leads readers to expect a commitment to *realistic* and *methodological* documentation of character development, but Williams *frustrates* these expectations [emphasis added]" (2000: 28). Dunning disagrees with those who describe the characters in *Shadows of Ecstasy* as "static", but, contrary to numerous critics, he reasons in favour of the "fine psychological interest displayed in [Williams's] characterisation" (2000: 37). This interest is construed within the "Kierkegaardian" frame of existential stages (aesthetic vs. ethical), the characters being treated *collectively* (Dunning 2000: 29), which, in turn, engages the reader in the central conflict of the novel: one between Christianity and Hermeticism (2000: 38).

It is also worth considering a recent remark upon the novel in question, for it is strikingly dissimilar from everything that has been written so far. Namely, Scott McLaren argues that rather than being a Satan-like character, Nigel Considine "lives and functions as a Christian saint in everything but name" (2004: 110). McLaren further claims that Williams's new messiah is both a "catalyst for sacramental epiphanies in others" and "a sacramental [...] image in his own right" (2004: 117). Granted that, the novel's antagonist must be identified with an agent leading to the destruction of the sacramental image (2004: 118). Ian Caithness, therefore, though not the most fundamental opponent[12], would not only "resist Considine's agenda" but could also be read as "a functional atheist" (2004: 119).

---

12   According to McLaren, it is Rosamond, Philip's fiancée, who is the character "most visibly set against [Considine's] goals and person" (2004: 118).

In a nutshell, if one were to believe the critics, Caithness would be 1) an allegorical entity/figure *and* a psychologically involving character; 2) an individual *and* a part of a collective of characters; 3) a "patently right" representative of Christianity *and* an atheist; 4) a (generally) positive character *and* a "bad guy" (i.e. Considine's antagonist). The list provokes numerous questions of theoretical nature. How is it possible that the "flat", "static", and "secondary" – i.e. apparently uncomplicated – character is read in such diverse and even mutually exclusive manners? Does a non-subjective and at least roughly unequivocal method of character analysis exist? Is it achievable to draw a clear borderline between text-bound character analysis and reader-bound interpretation? And finally, to what extent is a particular reader, rather than the text-projected implied one, "responsible" for creating literary characters?

According to the traditional critical paradigm, meaning is a fixed, unchangeable – and thus objective – entity associated with the text (Zgorzelski 1999: 18-21). Interpretation could then be defined as an activity aimed at explaining the "text's nature" (Collini [2008] referring to Eco) or, as Andrzej Zgorzelski puts it, at elucidating the practices responsible for "the additional organisation of signal material" so as to discover and comprehend its "superimposed meaning(s)" (1999: 22). In such understanding, if there are mutually exclusive interpretations, at least one of them must be false, this interpretative fallacy being more often than not caused by a critic's "blindness to the text" (1999: 22-23).

Whereas in some cases the true-or-false principle allows us to reject certain interpretations as "text-blind" or text-contradictory, I will argue that with regard to the literary character the issue is more complex. For instance, McLaren's claim that Considine, Williams's (hero-)villain, "lives and functions as a Christian saint" (2004: 110) is nonsensical in the light of the character's statements concerning Christ and Christianity[13]. And yet, the remark of Caithness's being a "functional atheist" should not be dismissed without thorough examination (to be performed later).

---

13 Suffice it to say Considine refers to Christianity in terms of "an erring principle" (45), to Christian martyrs as "misguided instances of that imagination [...] the Christian religion dimly proclaims" (45), and to Christ as one being "ignorantly worshipp[ed]" (177). Opposing Christian teachers, Considine declares: "I tell [men] that they are themselves gods, if they will" (208). Does it all make him, as McLaren (2004) would like, "a Christian saint in all but a name"?

Let us begin with Caithness's allegorical vs. non-allegorical and "representative" vs. individual status. From the outset, it will be remembered, we learn about the priest's relatively lowly position in the ecclesiastical hierarchy (he lives "in a Yorkshire parish" [Williams 1933/2003: 15]). On the other hand, his close relation with the Archbishop of the Church of England is mentioned in a number of places in the novel (e.g. 15, 25, 109), creating the impression of a unison of views. There is not much information pertaining to the priest's appearance or idiosyncrasies, which implies his being a type rather than individual. It appears, therefore, that Caithness is to be read as a "thematic or ideational element" rather than "an image of a possible person" (Margolin 1990, web). Likewise, Caithness's pseudo-individual reactions are in fact identical with the voice of the Church he belongs to. When, for instance, asked about the reasons behind the Archbishop's averseness to the government's policy of taking military action to avenge the death of Christian missionaries in Africa, the priest explains:

> 'Because it is their [the missionaries'] duty, their honour, to die, if necessary, […] it is a condition of their calling. Because the martyrs of the Church must not be avenged by secular arms. […] We can't, of course, object to any steps the Government think it wise to take in their own interests, so long as they don't use the missions as a reason. The Archbishop has intimated to the Societies who sent them out that no material ought to be given to the papers – photographs or what not'. (Williams 1933/2003: 16)

Later on, during a conversation with Sir Bernard Travers, the priest learns that Inkamasi, the Zulu king, seems to have been spiritually entrapped by Considine. The vicar's reaction is unsurprising and somehow appropriate for a Christian minister:

> 'I don't like it,' he said. 'I don't like the sound of any of it. And especially I don't like a Christian to be under this man's [Considine's] influence or in his power. […]'
> 'He evidently thinks he's got hold of some infernal power,' Caithness went on, 'and if – if by the wildest possibility he were mixed up with this African delirium – are we to leave one of the Faith exposed to his control? He's done it harm enough already. God knows what he may be doing to him. […]'
> '[…] Are we to have a Christian spiritually martyred here among us?' (Williams 1933/2003: 102)

Caithness and Sir Bernard – the latter reluctant but obliged to follow his friend – sneak into Considine's house, where they find Inkamasi in a bizarre lethargy. There, the vicar attempts to cast Considine's demon out of the Zulu. The priest acts like a typical Christian exorcist, evoking the authority of "the Eternal and Everlasting" or "Immanuel" (Williams 1933/2003: 105). The sleeper, however, admits he "do[es] not know them", which is rather surprising in the context of what the *New Testament* reveals about the expelling of evil spirits[14]. The first rift in the so far monolithic figure can be noticed exactly here, as Caithness's evoking "the union of Man with God" and intercession of "the Mother of God" turns out to be ineffective (1933/2003: 106). Even the name of the holy Trinity and the sign of the cross fail to yield spiritual victory, the battle remaining unresolved (1933/2003: 106).

The question arises why this seemingly emblematic (or "allegorical") priest cannot set Inkamasi free? Does it mean that Christianity, whose voice Caithness is to be identified with, is not powerful enough against Considine's magic? Is Sir Bernard right in explaining the event in terms of "one magic against another" (Williams 1933/2003: 108)? Or, perhaps, is Caithness only *formally* a vicar but in fact one whose faith is intellectual rather than spiritual? Should the reader take for granted Sir Bernard's observation that "Caithness [...] had always been a little inclined to call up *his own* spiritual reserves under such a quite honest pretence of invoking direction, though he was always rather careful to keep the command in *his own hands* [emphasis added]" (1933/2003: 102)? Is the main narrator authoritative when he observes that the author of the claim, an ironist and sceptic, "couldn't remember that God had ever

---

14   "And when he [Jesus] had called unto him his twelve disciples, *he gave them power against unclean spirits, to cast them out*, and to heal all manner of sickness and all manner of disease [emphasis added]" (Matt 10: 1; KJV, web); "And he [Jesus] said unto them, "Go ye into all the world, and preach the gospel to every creature. He that believeth and is baptized shall be saved; but he that believeth not shall be damned. And these signs shall follow them that believe: *in my name shall they cast out devils*; they shall speak with new tongues; they shall take up serpents; and if they drink any deadly thing, it shall not hurt them; they shall lay hands on the sick, and they shall recover [emphasis added]" (Mark 16: 15-18; KJV, web); "Wherefore God also hath highly exalted him [Jesus], and given him a name which is above every name: that *at the name of Jesus every knee should bow*, of things in heaven, and things in earth, and things under the earth [emphasis added]" (Phil 2: 9; KJV, web).

been known to disagree with Ian, anyhow in ecclesiastical affairs" (1933/2003: 102)?

Elsewhere, Caithness acts in a manner which might be classified as anti-Semitic, expressing his scorn towards a Jewish millionaire who committed suicide after the death of his wife, for whom he used to collect "the most wonderful [...] jewels in the world" (Williams 1933/2003: 26). In an exchange of opinions between Sir Bernard and Caithness, it is actually the former who tends to be understanding and empathetic, the brunt of his irony being directed towards Caithness, whose attitude, reflected in his manner of speaking, is hardly Christian. The reader, then, is more likely to share Sir Bernard's perspective, classifying the priest as insensitive and prejudiced. It is not impossible, however, to think of a reader for whom such anti-Semitic sentiment would be justified, especially if we take into account the socio-political situation in Britain in the thirties[15]. Furthermore, Caithness turns out to be a kind of a racist, expecting nothing good "out of Africa", as Philip observes (1933/2003: 53). Does it mean, though, that the Church Caithness (apparently) embodies is not only helpless in confrontation with magic/the occult but also discriminatory and xenophobic? Taking into account what *Shadows of Ecstasy* reveals about the Archbishop's attitude towards the situation in Africa[16], as well as his spiritual ministry to Inkamasi (1933/2003: 116-119), the answer must be negative. If so, is Caithness a figure of an anti-priest? And can one go as far as calling him "a functional atheist" (McLaren 2004: 119)?

First of all, Caithness does pray and does take active part in Christian service (Williams 1933/2003: 102, 111, 116, 175), no matter how Sir Bernard interprets his intentions. It should also be reminded that the latter represents the most sceptical vantage point in *Shadows of Ecstasy*

---

15 In his study of anti-Semitism in pre-Holocaust Europe, William I. Brustein comments upon the religious, racial, economic and political roots of the sentiment in European countries, including Britain. He argues that "[u]ntil very recently, regular Christian events and practices [...] have kept alive Christian hostility toward Jews" (2003: 57). He attributes Christian anti-Semitism among other things to "the beliefs that Jews were collectively responsible for the death of Jesus and that Jews failed to accept Christ as the Messiah" (2003: 52).

16 Caithness himself declares that "[t]he Archbishop's very anxious that the [British] government shan't use [the massacre] as a reason for military operations" (Williams 1933/2003: 16).

(Carpenter 1999: 128; Howard 1983: 30; Dunning 2000: 30-31).[17] And it is Caithness himself who arranges and participates in a mass in the Archbishop's chapel during which Inkamasi is finally liberated (Williams 1933/2003: 109). Furthermore, in this scene we see the priest smiling, perhaps for the first time (1933/2003: 119). Earlier, in Considine's house, Caithness is described as a *zealous* spiritual warrior. The narrator mentions his "voice of energy" (1933/2003: 105), "superb and deep confidence" (1933/2003: 105), and the concentration of his "will and intention" (1933/2003: 106), whilst Sir Bernard himself talks about "Ian's passion" (1933/2003: 108). Also, when Roger, as Considine's neophyte, attacks Caithness for his lack of understanding of the new African faith, he refers to the priest's beliefs in pejorative terms ("your own damned dogmas" [1933/2003: 133]), which may suggest the latter's religious consistency. The same Roger latter alludes to what the narrator calls "Caithness' own integrity" (1933/2003: 220). Furthermore, the priest turns out to be a prophet, for he – not quite realizing it – foresees Considine's death: "Your friends may fire at you one day" (1933/2003: 180). Finally, the vicar spiritually accompanies Inkamasi at the end of the Zulu's earthly journey, kneeling next to his bed, a crucifix in his hand (1933/2003: 243-244).

The textual examples I have provided seem ample enough to justify the conviction that Caithness is not an allegory of the Church, nor is he a figure of an anti-priest in the sense of embodying a corrupted representative of institutional Christianity. His middle-of-the-road position arouses even more confusion when the scenes of the direct clash between him and Considine are taken into account. In most cases the reader is led by the narrator to sympathise with the magician, the priest coming across as being arrogant and ill-mannered (Williams 1933/2003: 172)[18], "intoler-

---

17   A "distinguished figure in the medical world of his day" (Williams 1933/2003: 6), brilliantly ironic and silver-tongued, Sir Bernard not only saves the novel from becoming overtly didactic a number of times, but also provides a detached vantage point from which to verify the conflicting ideas. Furthermore, as Howard aptly observes, "Sir Bernard's point of view controls the whole story, or at least hovers over the action" (Williams 1933/2003: 34).

18   Compare: "If you take the king [Inkamasi] you shall take me, Caithness cried out. "I demand that you—" / "Why demand?" Considine's laugh answered him. "I invite you, I entreat you, to come" (Williams 1933/2003: 172).

ant" (1933/2003: 180), spiritually misguided[19] (1933/2003: 207) and "supernaturally insolent" (1933/2003: 241). Last but not least, aware of the irony involved, Caithness acts like Caiaphas, promising the Prime Minister's legal protection to Mottreux, who is to sell his master as Judas once did (1933/2003: 228-230).

On the other hand, when asked by Roger why he hates Considine so much, the priest responds: "I don't hate him [...] except that he's set himself against God, like Antichrist which is to come" (Williams 1933/2003: 220). And indeed, however "attractive" Considine may seem to the narrator – and to the reader who follows the narrator's textual suggestions – he *is* an Antichrist, irrespective of what he says: "Neither Christ nor Antichrist [...] but I bring a gospel of redemption, and thus the ends of the world hear it [...]" (1933/2003: 242). Since a detailed analysis of Considine's anti-Christian utterances is proposed elsewhere (Howard 1983: 45-46; Dunning 2000: 35), suffice it to note that the magician travesties the Bible a number of times and positions himself as the other Christ. Perhaps Considine as a character *is* to be appealing so as to "demonstrate" his insidious lure on the reader, whereas the vicar *is* to look unimpressive. Or maybe the reader is supposed to choose the magician in his fight against ossified Christianity, a song of the past, and its typical/a-typical (?) minister. The final interpretation of the axiological conflict in the novel does not seem possible upon the grounds of the "predominant features" principle postulated by the autotelic-text oriented literary theory (Zgorzelski 1999: 24), unless we assume that the texts's structure is based upon *two* equally valid ideological skeletons, as it were.

In my view, however, *Shadows of Ecstasy* is a perfect instance of the text where the actual reader's involvement in the process of character-building and interpretation is evident. Contrary to Zgorzelski, who claims that the information encoded in the communicate/text "is not dependent upon the actual recipient", and that the artistic text cannot "lose its 'identity' as a meaningful structure" (1999: 21, n.18), I will follow the critical paradigm of cognitive poetics, in which the reader, understood not as a text-implied construct but rather as an actual person, plays

19 Consider Considine's words addressed to the priest: "You should have kept to your pupils, Mr. Caithness, to the morals you understand and the dogmas that you don't" (Williams 1933/2003: 207).

the pivotal role in generating meaning. Following some narratologists, Anna Kędra-Kardela observes that "only when the text evokes real experiences can the reader recognise and thus relate it to herself/himself; the text can be treated by her/him as a narrative" (2010: 122). Likewise, Magdalena Rembowska-Płuciennik highlights the fact that personal categories cannot be eliminated from the area of literary studies, since they condition communication on the most fundamental, "lower" level (2012: 112). Yet another scholar aptly states that

> Readers […] must use their own experiences of the world to bridge gaps in texts. They must bring both *facts and emotions* to bear on the construction of the world of the text. And, just like actors performing roles, they must give substance to the psychological lives of characters. (Gerrig 1993: 17; emphasis added)

Obviously, in Kędra-Kardela's words, "the picture of the fictional world as presented in a literary work is very seldom, if ever, 'given' directly to the reader" (2010: 124). The latter, therefore, "constructs the unwritten text" (Rimmon-Kenan in Kędra-Kardela 2010: 124) in the process which involves comparing the textual information with his/her knowledge of the world, organised in terms of the so called narrative cognitive frames (2010: 125)[20]. In the case of a narrative text, then, the reader determines "to what degree the picture created in the literary work coincides with the familiar model" (2010: 125). Importantly, the reader's cognitive frames include both his/her experience and knowledge of the world and the knowledge of "broadly understood traditions including literary tradition" (2010: 126).

Ralf Schneider, in turn, observes that text-understanding always involves a combination of two mechanisms: (i) the so called top-down processing, "in which the [actual] reader's pre-stored knowledge structures are directly activated to incorporate new items of information" and (ii) bottom-up processing, "in which bits of textual information are kept in working memory separately and integrated into an overall representation at a later point in time" (2001: 611).

---

20   Here, Kędra-Kardela departs from the models proposed by Monika Fludernik ("narrativization") and Peter Stockwell ("subjectivization"). While she agrees that "when reading the text the reader 'pours' her/his subjectivity into the text", she explains the underlying cognitive mechanism in terms of Ronald Langacker's theory ("comparison"). For an insightful description of the mechanism as well as its application to the literary analysis of short fiction see Kędra-Kardela 2010: 124-151.

As far as the literary character is concerned, within the cognitive paradigm it can be defined as

> [...] a coherently perceived figure existing, during the reading act, in the imaginative space produced in the reader's mind by the transmission of that figure (the text's coded instructions for perceiving it as a figure) and its reception (the reader's acting upon those instructions to imagine it as a figure). (Cohan 1983: 5)

Steven Cohan further explains that such a figure should not be identified with a psychological representation, though a degree of referentiality cannot (and should not) be avoided (1983: 7-8). Still, it must be remembered that, as Rembowska-Płuciennik argues, a literary character is *not* exclusively a function of the elements of narration and plot, a construct "devoid of psychological content" (2012: 116). As a matter of fact, the reader builds literary characters upon the basis of his/her knowledge of "living among real people", which nonetheless does *not* equal the erroneous identification of the characters with empirical beings (2012: 119).

Cognitive psychology has given ample evidence that human perception works in terms of figure-ground organisation (compare Evans 2009: 169-171). As Peter Stockwell observes, "[w]e see, hear and move in stereo three dimensions, and so the cognitive capacity for making figure and ground is clearly and literally an embodiment of this human condition" (2002: 15). This fact, however, has frequently been ignored by "objectivist" theoreticians in a number of fields, including literary studies:

> Figure and ground are aspects of human cognition. They are not features of objective, mind-independent reality. Hence, figure-ground orientation tends to be absent from studies of concepts done in the objectivist tradition, in which meaning is based on allegedly "objective" truth rather than human cognition. For human concepts, figure-ground distinctions are crucial. (Lakoff and Johnson 1999: 198)

Cognitive poetics attempts to integrate the most recent knowledge of human cognition with what has so far been achieved in literary studies, offering a unified, universal perspective from which to perceive the well-known phenomena. Thus, for instance, Stockwell observes that "the most obvious correspondence of the phenomenon of figure and ground is [the] critical notion of foregrounding" (1992: 14). The discussed figure-ground principle can also be applied to literary character analysis:

In most narrative fiction [...] characters are figures against the ground of their settings. They have boundaries summarised by their proper names ('Beowulf', 'Hamlet', 'Winnie the Pooh'), and they carry along or evolve specific psychological and personal traits. Stylistically they are likely to be the focus of the narrative, moving through different settings, and are likely to be associated with certain verbs of wilful action by contrast with the attributive or existential sorts of verbs used descriptively for the background. [...] Characters are also figures because they move across the ground, either spatially or temporally as the novel progresses, or qualitatively as they evolve and collect traits from their apparent psychological development. (Stockwell 1992: 15-16)

During the process of reading, such a figure, distinguished from its narrative background, is transported from the text "to that 'irrealised' space in [the reader's] mind, which exists beyond the realm of discourse" (Cohan 1983: 11). Importantly, "the more the discourse presents the figure as an object by not presenting its inner space as a subject through narration, the more it draws the figure into our space where we construct its identity as a subject" (1983: 20).

And this is indeed what seems to happen in the case of Ian Caithness: classified as a "minor" or "secondary" character, or else as an allegorical/figural one because in the novel he is presented as an object without a deep psychological dimension, Caithness nonetheless becomes a subject in the reader's mind opening the possibility of the more "psychological"/individualised critical readings. Depending upon the actual reader's narrative cognitive frames, which incorporate the knowledge of the empirical world (compare Schneider's "social knowledge structures" 2001: 612) as well as literary knowledge (e.g. Schneider's "genre expectations" 2001: 612), an interpretation becomes supplemented or completed, though, as Kędra-Kardela rightly puts it, "the complete closure [...] never happens, because there will always be 'facts', evoking new cognitive narrative frames, that will make it possible to interpret [...] the text in a different way still" (2010: 125). Furthermore, because the reader's own value system is essential for in his/her readings[21], it can be suspected that interpreters who identify with the Christian worldview would more likely empathise with Caithness; while those who are religiously

---

21   For details see Schneider 2001: 614.

neutral or disinclined[22] would tend to prefer unorthodox (Hermetic, Gnostic) readings.

As Stockwell notes, "certain aspects of literary texts are commonly seen as being more important or salient than others", which is usually determined by textual cues; he nonetheless also admits that "it is partly a subjective matter" (2002: 14). When the reader's attitude is not verified against the text itself, his/her reading may result in a number of highly subjective (over)interpretations to be questioned by a more careful reader (compare Kędra-Kardela 2010: 125-126). The situation becomes complex when textual cues are *all but* unambiguous, and the reader's attention is drawn to different (and even mutually exclusive) signals or aspects. Arguably, Williams's *Shadows of Ecstasy* is precisely a novel which, due to the indeterminacy of chief characters, defies black-and-white ideological classification as a Christian or Gnostic one. In the case of the considered character, it may be said that there emerges a number of Caithnesses, as it were, rather than a single, text-determined figure. It is, then, up to a particular reader – and, more technically, up to his/her narrative cognitive frames – which features of the priest will be highlighted and which will remain hidden within the dynamic figure-ground model (compare Evans 2009: 172-173). For some, Caithness could epitomise a hero who "stand[s] firm" against Anti-Christ (Williams 1933/2003: blurb); for others he might be a representative of a conservative, lifeless institution (the Church) which curbs the freedom of independent thinking under the pretext of "saving England" (1933/2003: 230); yet for others, he would remain a "functional atheist" (McLaren 2004).

In conclusion, it seems that taking into consideration the actual cognitive processes associated with text reception as well as "the dynamic aspects of narrative" (Schneider 2001: 607) in one's analytical-interpretative literary practice will, paradoxically enough, result in producing more "objective" (though, in fact, subjective) readings. While the traditional critical paradigms which postulate text-originated "objectivity" ignore the fact that "the *implied* trinity of the author, the reader and

---

22 Schneider, following Ed S. Tan, underscores the importance of the reader's "empathy" in his/her constructing literary characters, distinguishing f-emotions (fiction-based ones) and a-emotions (artefact-based ones, which originate "in response to the aesthetic qualities of a work of art") (2001: 613).

the text are *constructions* of academic critics [emphasis added]" (Blaim and Gruszewska 1994: 148)[23], cognitive poetics gives due attention to a particular reader and his/her active role in the meaning-generating process. Consequently, in opposition to the "objectivist" paradigms, it would be advisable to clearly define one's interpretative perspective. In the discussed case, it could be done, for instance, with the help of such statements as "being a Christian, I am inclined to see this character..." or "as an agnostic, I sympathise with the Hermetic ideology this character promotes", etc. to better encapsulate the reader-dependent nature of interpretation. It should also be underlined that when observed from the cognitive standpoint, some supposedly "flat", "static" or "secondary" characters turn out to be far more intricate and multidimensional, thus enabling varied readings/interpretations. After all, as Dorota Korwin-Piotrowska puts it,

> [n]one of the [interpretative] propositions pertaining to meaning can be regarded as permanent or definitive. Each of them becomes transformed; it could be undermined or specified more precisely. *The reader* is, then, in part the *co-creator of meaning*. [...] The characteristic paradox of literature consists also in the fact that texts are simultaneously completed [...] and ambiguous, i.e. unfinished or open, since they propose to the recipient a *cognitive project* which requires *realisation*. (2011: 46-47; translation mine, A.S.K.)

---

23   It is worth considering here the "deconstructive" conclusion Blaim and Gruszewska arrive at in their illuminating study of the implied "trinity" of author, reader, and text: "It would perhaps be advisable to replace the implied game of the implied author with the implied reader in the implied text with the *real game* proposed to *real readers* by *the real author* of the ultimate meanings—*the academic critic* [emphasis added]" (1994: 154). Nonetheless, the scholars believe that "it is possible to study texts in a rational manner, not their *true meanings* but the *possibilities of meaning-assignation* as defined by semiotic systems functioning in a given culture [emphasis added]" (1994: 155).

Part II

Characters in Generic Contexts

"A Jew, and circumcised":
Constructing collective and individual characters in early modern utopian fictions

ARTUR BLAIM

The traditional model of the utopian state, originally adopted in Thomas More's *Utopia*, tends to eliminate or marginalise the redundant, the shameful, and the undesirable by relocating them to the periphery. This happens to certain groups of the population such as prisoners or slaves, slaughterhouses, wars, or even bodies of those who "illegally" committed suicide[1]. The offensive, the unclean, the unhealthy, or potentially irritating is pushed to the utmost borders of the utopian space:

> We have all offensive Trades more apart scituate, as Brewers, Bakers, Chandlers, Butchers, Tanners, Dyers, Curriers, Felmongers, in some backparts in the out-skirts of the Citie, by themselves, and neer the River to carry their filth away, least their fulsome Trades should with the badness of their smells offend the more pleasant dwellings, or cause infection. All Forgemen, as Smiths, Mettlemen, Tinkers, Pewterers, and all other noise-making Artificers that deal in fire, dwell in a convenient place wholly apart by themselves also, for the better safety of the houses, as to prevent the trouble of their impetuous noises. For this cause also ringing of Bells, more than for the calling of the people to Church, is every where inhibited. (H.R. 1660: 37-38).

All "noisy, unwholesome, or disagreeable trades" are banished from the streets to special places "assigned at a distance" (Burgh 1764: 89). In New Athens, "no Trade that is offensive to the Nose, the Eyes or Ears [...] is permitted to be in the City itself: Thus Butchers, Poulterers, Smiths, Washer-women, and the like, are confin'd to little Suburbs di-

---

1   For a detailed discussion of peripheralisation in utopias see Blaim 2013.

vided from the City by a small Canal, whose Streets are every Morning wash'd by Waters from certain Engins, which throw a Stream through every Street, that carries off all the Filth that such Trades produce" (Killigrew 1720: 86). Even the cemeteries, though "spacious and beautiful" are pushed outside the city considered "to be for the living" as in *Christianopolis* (Andreae 1916: 277), or situated "without the Cities, or in the remotest places near the walls" with no tombs permitted in churches since "those holy structures being raised for the living to serve God in, and not for the dead to sleep in, by whose stench also the living might be annoyed" as in *New Atlantis* (Bacon 1999: 30).

In extreme cases, as in Sevarambia, the peripheralisation of the undesirable becomes an all-encompassing system of social and spatial organisation of the country: the state banishes "all those persons who desire to cause any alteration in their Government or Manners, or who live not according to the strict Rules which they have received from their forefathers, and which by no means they will be perswaded to change" (Veiras 2006: 77). Offenders, like thieves, robbers, and other disorderly persons are sent to the borderlands, "where they live to plague one another, but they are not suffered to abide in the middle and bowels of the Kingdom" (2006: 61). All convicted, or only potential troublemakers are expelled to "the Lonesom Islands, where he can quarrel with none but with wild beasts that inhabit there" (2006: 89). In fact, each category of offenders is assigned an appropriate location: "all the disorderly persons, the lecherous, the filthy, and base, each sort have their distinct places of abode, or Islands, from whence they are not suffered to depart till they dye naturally [...]" (2006: 68). The same applies to the physically deformed who cannot live in the central part of the kingdom. In *A Voyage to the World in the Centre of the Earth* the rebellious survivors of the earthquake in the Central World who cannot abandon their wicked ways have to inhabit the Earthly Quarter in isolation from native inhabitants (1755: 90). In the world of the Moon described in Bishop Godwin's *Man in the Moone*, any child that exhibits even a minor physical or mental imperfection is expelled to the Earth.

A similar principle applies to foreign visitors, whose stay tends to be limited or involves their "domestication", or appropriation by the utopian mode of life. Those who arrive in Bensalem are carefully watched for three days before being allowed to visit the country, in Christianopolis, they have to be subjected to a series of three examinations concerning their morals, personal qualities and culture. A similar procedure is adopted in New Athens, where visitors are permanently marked "in the Face with a most lovely and beautiful Flower" (Killigrew 1720: 83) while the Children of Love presented in *The Adventures and Surprizing Deliverances, of James Dubourdieu* make their guests undergo a long period of quarantine and purification before allowing them to enter the country. The authorities of the City of the Sun do not admit slaves or aliens into the city: "those captured in war are sold, or they are put to digging ditches or performing other fatiguing tasks outside the city, where four squadrons of soldiers are regularly dispatched to supervise them and watch over the territory" (Campanella 1981: 83).

*

In structural terms, the marginalised components of early modern utopian fiction include plot and characters. Indeed, the appearance of elaborate plot or any kind of individualised protagonist constitutes an unexpected departure from the norm of a static faceless collective emerging from the narrator's generalising comments; and even in Thomas More's *Utopia*, the foundational text of the genre, which in its frame introduces two highly nuanced "protagonists-ideologues", to use Bakhtin's terminology, the representatives of the ideal state (with the exception of its founder) remain nameless.

In most utopias, a degree of individualisation is reserved for the first-person narrator in connection with legitimising his evaluative position and with enhancing verisimilitude. In the latter case, an element of randomness may be present, as a way of constructing a pseudo-mimetic figure, whose coincidental features, unrelated to the thematic/ideological aspect of the utopian text, would possibly increase the reality effect.

In the case of secondary narrators and the characters from inset stories used to illustrate the laws governing the utopian world, their characterisation is usually subordinated to their function as elements of the overall persuasive strategy aimed at convincing the readers of the desirability and feasibility of the proposed model of the ideal state. The utopian hosts invariably embody such general values as wisdom, dignity, or nobility: the Alcaldorem – "A reverend old man he was and discreet" (Bacon's *New Atlantis*); the Master of the Society – "that Noble Gentle-

man" (L'Epy's *A Voyage into Tartary*); the Venerable Dramesco –
"struck us with a devout veneration and respect" (Barnes' *Gerania*); Jacob, a high official in Nova Solyma – "the father was of venerable appearance" (Gott's *Nova Solyma*). The characters, functioning also as typical representatives of certain occupations and offices peculiar to their
society, are often defined and characterised only in terms of their professional or social roles: e.g. Fidefendon in *Astreada*, Joabin in *New Atlantis*, or the Grand Pophar in *The Memoirs of Gaudentio di Lucca*, provide
information about their world not only by what they say, but also by
means of their social position, informing the reader that in Astreada
there is an office of the Defender of Faith, that Jews can be citizens of
Bensalem enjoying full civil rights, or that the people of Mezzorania
constitute "one great Family Govern'd by the Laws of Nature" with an
absolute ruler as its head (Berington 1737: 214). Such characters are
usually named only after their social position or described in terms of
the social group to which they belong, hence frequent use of indefinite
articles and collective nouns: "a judge", "a woman", "a certain merchant", "the Bishopes", "the Pastors" (*Siquila*); "the old men", "the children", "the teachers", "the guardians of the land" (*Civitas Solis*); "the
Talcomummi", "the Courtiers" (*Gerania*); "the attendants", "a messenger" (*New Atlantis*); "the Physicians", "the Divines", "the ministers of
state" (*Macaria*), "our Children", "our Wives", "our Clergy" (*The Island
of Content*); "every Widow", "all Parents and guardians", "every minister" (*Cessares*).

All inhabitants of the utopian land, regardless of social, age or gender distinctions seem to share the same positive characteristics. The Lu-
nars "live in such love, peace, and amitie, as it seemeth to bee another
Paradise" (Godwin 1638: 104); the Sevarambians are "free from all
those wild passions which cause so much disturbance in other Lands"
(Veiras 2006: 64); the Geranians "are all naturally healthful, streight
Bodied, all Honest and Generous, all affable and Religious" (Barnes
1675: 80); the people of New Atlantis are "loyal and peaceful [...] and
no less virtuous, rich, wise, and valiant" (Bacon 1999: 22); the inhabitants of the Island of Content "are an amicable People" (*The Island*: 20);
the natives the Central World "resemble angels rather than men" (*A
Voyage* 1755: 62); the Veritasians are "a lively cheerful people", "strictly virtuous", and "truly religious" (*A True* 1790: 19); the Children of

Love are tall, "of perfect symmetry" and their eyes carry "a perfect awe and majesty in them" (Evans 1719: 70); the Mezzoranians are "the hand-somest Race of People [...] Nature ever produced", their features "the most exact and regular imaginable" (Berington 1737: 180).

Exceptions to the general pattern are limited in scope and number. Occasionally, secondary characters from the narrator's world are given names and brief characterisation (e.g. Monsieur Cossey and Delgades in *Man in the Moone*; Demetrius, Aristides, Monthresor in *A Voyage to Tartary*; Swart, Van de Nuits, Moreton, in *The History of the Se-varambians*; Hermogenes in *A Description of New Athens*; or Othono and Euthus in *Memoirs of Planetes*. Some rudimentary psychological characterisation appears only in *Nova Solyma, The Blazing World*, and *Memoirs of Gaudentio di Lucca*, though the traits seem hardly suffi-cient to make it possible to classify the figures as mimetic characters (Phelan 1989: 2). As should be obvious now the standard classifica-tion into primary, secondary and episodic characters acquires a some-what different meaning in most early modern utopias, being based primarily on the thematic principle, i.e. the amount of information provided by a particular character about the ideal world and his/her representativeness of its dominant features. For instance, in *New At-lantis*, the Father of the Solomon's House could be regarded as a pri-mary character on account of the length and importance of his mono-logue and the position he occupies in the society, rather than because of his role in the rudimentary plot. On the other hand, in *Nova Solyma, The Blazing World*, and *Memoirs of Gaudentio di Lucca* the primary characters are granted some autonomy with regard to the thematic function, being provided with some unique features of their own that go beyond their main function of describing and representing the uto-pian world. The two protagonists in *Nova Solyma* undergo a radical internal change from two essentially decent but careless boys, who ran away from home to see the world. Their inability to control emotions, shallow religious faith, and lack of responsibility endanger their friendship and almost lead to a duel. But they are finally transformed into mature young men under the influence of long edifying conversa-tions with Joseph and the lectures they attend. The same can be said about the main character of *Memoirs of Gaudentio di Lucca* who ap-pears in at least three distinct roles: a suspected heretic extensively interrogated by the Inquisition, a protagonist of a romantic plot, and an observer and participant in the affairs of the utopian land of Mezzorania.

*

Among all possible types and varieties of characters in early modern utopian fictions in Britain, the appearance of Jews may seem somewhat surprising, considering the virtual absence of the Jewish community in England at the beginning of that period and their definitely marginal position in the English society following their readmission by Oliver Cromwell in 1655. A sudden, but relatively short-lived increase of interest in the Jews as necessary elements of the approaching Millennium (as subjects to conversion to Christianity) did little to alter the traditionally hostile anti-Semitic stereotypes functioning in popular culture and theology[2]. The latter mode of the Jewish presence in utopian fiction seems relatively more frequent, though usually limited to religious contexts, mediated via biblical references.

In Campanella's *Civitas Solis*, the inhabitants "sing the deeds of the Christian, Jewish, and Gentile heroes, and of those of all other nations, and this is very delightful to them" (1981: 105). In Gerania, Homer, the founder of the state, speaks favourably of "the Holiness and Religion of the Jews" and "the Poetical Writings of their Learned King David" (Barnes 1675: 55). In *The History of Sevarambians* there are references to "the Jewish Computation" of the age of the world being "more plausible, because it agrees better with the Progress of Sciences and Arts", and Jewish authors appear alongside other ancient authorities: "He cited the Chinese Authors, and the Brachmins; as also Jews, Greeks, and Arabians"; by which he made it appear that, "many valuable Branches of Knowledge which the Ancients had been Masters of, are now lost, but he hoped, that, in time, they would be again restored [...]" (Veiras 2006: 356). In Thomas Spence's *A Supplement to the History of Robinson Crusoe*, the Jews illustrate the possibility of being industrious in an economic system based on the common ownership of land: "Look either to us or

---

2   An extensive discussion of anti-Semitism in the early modern period in England can be found in Frank Felenstein, *Anti-Semitic Stereotypes. A Paradigm of Otherness in English Popular Culture, 1660-1830*. Baltimore and London: The Johns Hopkins University Press, 1995.

to the Jews, and see if there be any Want of Industry in acquiring Wealth as far as Law allows, though we can buy no Land; but on the contrary you will find a general Industry, not one idle" (1782: 2)

In *The Blazing World* the attitude towards "things Jewish" is somewhat more ambiguous, though still fairly neutral. The Empress, seeing no women among their religious congregations asks her newly gained subjects "Whether they were Jews, Turks, or Christians?" (Cavendish 1666: 17). She also shows keen interest in "the Jews Cabbala" upon which the spirits assisting in her enquiries "immediately disappeared out of her sight; which startled the Empress so much, that she fell into a Trance, wherein she lay for some while" (1666: 86). She is finally dissuaded from attempting to engage in it by the Duchess of Newcastle who advises her

> to let that work alone; for it will be of no advantage either to you, or your people, unless you were of the Jews Religion; nay, if you were, the vulgar interpretation of the holy Scripture would be more instructive, and more easily believed, then your mystical way of interpreting it; for had it been better and more advantagious for the Salvation of the Jews, surely Moses would have saved after-Ages that labour by his own Explanation, he being not onely a wise, but a very honest, zealous and religious Man. (Cavendish 1666: 91)

However, the predominant attitude tends to be negative. James Harrington in *Oceana* grants all citizens of his ideal commonwealth "the liberty of their own consciences, and to that way of worship which they shall choose", unless their religious creed is "Popish, Jewish, or Idolatrous" (1656: 64). In a satirical response to his project, an anonymous author ironically proclaims "That the Judaical Law will be most proper for England, since they Crucified their Master as well as the Jews" (*Decrees and Orders of the Committee of Safety of Oceana* 1659: 5). In "The Story of the Inhabitant of the Air" incorporated in *A Voyage to the Centre of the Earth*, the Comets (a kind of cosmic Hell combined with Purgatory) for "those who have been guilty of the greatest Crimes" is inhabited not just by the usual suspects, i.e. "Attorneys, Jaylors, Bailiffs and their followers", "the Royal-Exchange and the Frequenters of it", "Courtiers and Flatterers", "Beaux and Fops", but mostly by

> the immense Shoals of Jews, and their Friends and Allies, that arrive there yearly; there is hardly one of them since the Beginning of the World, but what after the leaving the Earth has become an Inhabitant of one of the

Comets, and all of them in the Shape of Swine, grovelling in the Dirt, and
feeding on the Excrements of the Filthy Inhabitants. (*A Voyage* 1755: 129)

In Joseph Glanvill's "Anti-Fanatical Religion and Free Philosophy. In a
Continuation of the New Atlantis", the theologians of Bensalem study
"the Jewish Learning, That they might be instructed in the Rites, Opinions, and Usages of that People, for the better understanding of many
things in the Scripture that relate unto them" (1676: 10). At the same
time, "Jewish Genealogies, Traditions" are characterised as "the vain
Philosophy" and "Worldly Policies" spoken against in the Scriptures
(18). Likewise, the study of "the Rabinical Learning" does not spring
"out any great esteem of the Men, or their Learning; but from a desire to
acquaint themselves by Them, with the Doctrines, Terms of speech, and
Customes of the Jews, in order to their better understanding of the Scriptures, and the defence of Christianity, against those enemies of the
Cross" (57). Indeed, a parallel is drawn between "our Separatists, and
those antient ones, the Pharisees"; and it is argued that the same spirit
"acted the Ataxites, that govern''d those Jewish Fanaticks" (27). Consequently, the imposition of limitations on particular opinions was in "no
way contrary to Gospel Liberty", but only introduced "Freedom from the
Jewish yoke, from the bondage of sin, and power of Sathan" (34) and "in
opposition to the Jews, Heathens, and some gross Hereticks, who undermined the Foundations of Faith, and Life" (55).

Gaudentio di Lucca, whose sudden arrival in Bologna and untypical,
though highly moral and decent mode of behaviour arouses the interest
of the Inquisition, is at first suspected of being "some Jew or Turkish
Spy in Masquarade" (Berington 1737: 20), which alone might occasion
his arrest, even though he has committed no offence or crime.

A very extensive treatment of Jewish history and religion appears in
The Island of Veritas. Whilst the author's deistic position makes him
somewhat sceptical towards all religions, his attitude towards the Jews
and Judaism follows the standard anti-Semitic stereotypes. The Jews are
called a "sect [...] dispersed through all the world, without king, government, or possession of territory, hated by the rest of mankind, yet
calling themselves the favoured nation of God" and a "nation, even according to their own accounts [...] impious and wicked, continually for-
getting their God", who, "[w]earied with their sins", "is said to have
pronounced a curse upon them, and to have dispersed them, a race of

vagabonds over the face of the earth, universally despised and detested by the rest of mankind" (*A True* 1790: 98-99).

However, the most peculiar project involving the Jews is Harrington's proposal to establish a quasi-utopian New Israel in Ireland, introduced in the usually ignored passage in the Introduction to *Oceana*. The native population of Ireland, appearing in the text under the assumed name of Panopea, is to be replaced by Jewish settlers, who are to function as an additional source of revenue for Oceana rather than as objects of conversion, in a way that ingeniously combines peripheralisation with an early form of racketeering, and blatant anti-Semitism with anti-Catholicism:

> *Panopea*, the soft mother of a slothful and pusillanimous people, is a neighbor Island, anciently subjected by the Arms of *Oceana*; since, almost depopulated for shaking the Yoke, and at llength replanted with a new Race. But (through what vertues of the soyl, or vice of the air soever it be) they come still to degenerate: wherefore seeing it is neither likely to yield men fit for arms, nor necessary it should; it had been the interest of *Oceana* so to have disposed of this Province, being both rich in the nature of the soyl, and full of commodious Ports for Trade, that it might have been ordered for the best in relation unto her purse: Which in my opinion (if it had been thought upon in time) might have been best done by planting it with Jewes, allowing them their own Rites and Lawes; for that would have brought them suddainly from all parts of the World, and in sufficient numbers; and though the Jewes be now altogether for merchandize, yet in the Land of *Canaan* (since their exile from whence they have not been Landlords) they were altogether for agriculture; and there is no cause why a man hould doubt, but having a fruitfull Country and excellent ports, too, they would be good at both. *Panopea* well peopled, would be worth a matter of four millions dry-rents, that is, besides the advantage of the agriculture and Trade, which, with a Nation of that industry come at least unto as much more. Wherefore *Panopea*, being farm'd out to the Jewes, and their heirs for ever, for the pay of a Provincial Army to protect them during the term of seven years, and for two millions annual revenue from that time forward; besides the Customs, which would pay the Provincial Army, would have been a bargain of such advantage, both unto them and this *Common-wealth*, as is not to be found otherwise by either. To receive the Jewes after any other manner into a Common-wealth, were to maim it: for they of all Nations never incorporate, but taking up the room of a Limb, are of no use or office unto the body, while they suck the nourishment which would sustain a natural and useful member. (Harrington 1656: B4)

*

The exceptions to this "generalised" presence of Jewish characters in early utopian fiction are few, though highly instructive. The first, and the best known, Jewish character is Joabin from Bacon's *New Atlantis*, "a Jew, and circumcised", as the narrator hastens to inform us, who, despite the obvious (for the author and his contemporary readers) disadvantages of his ethnic origins and religion, is, nonetheless, a respected and useful member of the community, a "domesticated" or "appropriated" semi-stranger/alien, a border-line figure best suited to identify with the positions of the outsiders, and so functioning as a kind of intermediary between the visitors and the society of New Atlantis[3]. We learn that the "few stirps of Jews yet remaining" in Bensalem, unlike "the Jews in other parts", do not hate the name of Christ, nor have "a secret inbred rancor against the people among whom they live" (1999: 172). They give to "our Saviour many high attributes", acknowledging that "Christ was born of a Virgin; and that he was more than a man; and he would tell how God made him ruler of the seraphim, which guard his throne; and they call him also the Milken Way, and the Eliah of the Messiah, and many other high names, which though they be inferior to his divine majesty, yet they are far from the language of other Jews" (1999: 172). Despite Joabin's belief that it was Moses, who, "by a secret cabala ordained the laws of Bensalem", and that "when the Messias should come, and sit in his throne at Hierusalem, the King of Bensalem should sit at his feet, whereas other kings should keep a great distance", which the narrator politely calls "Jewish dreams", he regards him as "a wise man and learned, and of great policy, and excellently seen in the laws and customs of that nation" (1999: 172). And yet, even though Joabin identifies himself completely with Bensalem, praising its superior institutions, manners, morals, etc (e.g. "You shall understand that there is not under the heavens so chaste a nation as this of Bensalem, nor so free from all pollution or foulness. It is the virgin of the world" [1999: 173]) and has friends in high places, as his involvement in the visit of the Father of the Solomon's house clearly demonstrates, his constant use of the pronouns "they" and "their", when referring to Bensalem, betrays his essentially

---

3   Claire Jowitt's suggestion associating Joabin with the alleged treacherousness of the
    Jews seems conjectural and unconvincing, as there are no suggestions, or hints to this
    effect in the text (2002: 143-151).

peripheral position in the society, by marking him off as an outsider. Moreover, despite the apparently friendly relations between him and the European visitors, and his status as a native guide with a superior level of awareness, he is most often referred to as "the Jew", (the mode of addressing Shylock practised by the anti-Semitic characters in Shakespeare's *Merchant of Venice*).

Nevertheless, for the anonymous author of one of the two sequels to *New Atlantis*, identifying himself only as R.H., Esquire, even this kind of attitude towards the Jewish Other seems excessively favourable. Consequently, while the "domesticated" local Jews are of necessity tolerated, since Bacon made them so, the same rules do not apply to others. There is a law "inhibiting all forein rank Jews to live in this Island, or any to have converse or commerce with them when ever they land, till they be converted & baptized" (1660: 46-47). They are sent to "a little Island" to be instructed "in the faith"; "[n]o kind of violence is used to them" as long as their "erroneous opinions strike not at the root of Christian Religion, or they do not vehemently inveigh against the professed truth, to promote strife and division". However, "if they remain obstinate, or renege, denying our Saviour, they are crucified in the same manner as they did our Saviour" (1660: 47).

The anti-Semitic sentiment proves so strong that it appears in the rather unexpected context of the demonstration of a proto-telegraph invented by a person imprisoned because of his friendship with a Jew:

> This secret was first experimented here by one *Lamoran*, who being suspected of Apostacy, because of his great intimacy with one *Alchmerin*, his friend and a Jew, and his little adhesion to some of his opinions, was sent to the Island of *Conversion*: who there to hold constant intelligence with his intimate, first found out this admirable invention. (R.H. 1660: 67-68)

In this context, the appearance of two Jewish utopias, designed by Christian authors, may come as something of a surprise. The first, Samuel Gott's *Nova Solyma*, originally published anonymously in Latin in 1648-9, depicts an ideal Jewish republic founded in the place of old Jerusalem, of which "not a vestige remained, but its glories were renewed on the same sites on a larger scale" (Gott 1902: I, 78-79). In this new ideal state, Jewishness viewed mainly in religious terms is identified with the dystopian past: "now we call none aliens from Israel, for that famous mystical separation of our fathers from all the tribes of the earth hath been done away by the communion of all the saints" (1902: I, 86). The same idea is expressed in the two poems composed by Joseph, one of the protagonists and future leaders of the Jewish republic:

> Spring's eager breath had thawed the icy showers,
> The signs that mark the winter of the Jews
> Had left the sky, and partly now had sunk
> Beneath earth's utmost edge. (1902: I, 77)

And further:

> The veil is gone from Israel's face,
> The true Light shines on Israel's race,
> Lord, grant Thine ancient people grace
> To see Thee as Thou art! (1902: I, 176)

The process of the construction of the utopian state is shown to be inseparably bound with individual search for the true religion and the divine intervention leading to the final epiphany, presented on the example of Jacob's spiritual awakening:

> We are now very close on the fiftieth year since our long and widely scattered nation was restored to its present wonderful prosperity. You do not forget, I feel sure, the terrible calamity of our nation in bygone days; it was indeed a remarkable punishment for that most awful deed of crime committed by our forefathers, and approved by the votes of every successive generation of their descendants, just as it was a most certain pledge of this future restoration and the very foundation of it. For can it be admitted that any such race of people ever was in the world before or since, who, by the space of so many years, scattered far and wide over so many countries, everywhere bowed down under the yoke of servitude, driven from place to place by all that injury and scorn could effect, and yet never, as other aliens, disappearing by intermarriage, and never subdued by the constant and continual weight of the woes that were pressing upon them now were able to rise to any position of independence even, not to speak of a republic or an empire? Certainly that condition of the Jewish race has always been an assurance that the ardent desire that Christians have so long conceived for our return was not an impossibility, and gave them firm faith in its fulfilment, long before there were any signs of it. But when indeed, by the sudden flash of divine light, that stubborn mental darkness was removed, and, prompted by a heavenly impulse, we acknowledged the true Messiah, and became His disciples with unwonted zeal, then it was that to us of that same race that had been sunk so long in the lowest depths of misery there

came, as it were, life from the dead, and our exaltation to the highest by divine mercy. (Gott 1902: I, 88-89)

The contrast between the old Jewish ways ("old daily sacrifices and later ritual" [1902: I, 104]) and the superiority of new Christian rites is constantly emphasised both explicitly ("Christian worship is of a higher grade than the Mosaic cult, with its numerous festivals and ceremonies" [1902: II, 195]) and implicitly ("No bulls or goats on altars slain, / No bloody sacrifices stain / Our Christian house of prayer" [1902: II, 192]). Moreover, "Christians have two Sacraments which seem even more important than any Mosaic rites, for these latter were only weak and beggarly elements, obscurely pointing to the Messiah that should come; the others announce Him already come, and point to yet a second coming" (1902: II, 198). Even the Christian Sabbath is superior to the traditional Jewish Sabbath, because "the commemoration of our miraculous redemption and the other mysteries of eternity is of higher import than the commemoration of the Creation, and, embracing this world and the next, is a higher incentive to religious duty" (1902: II, 192).

The new identity of the citizens of the republic of Nova Solyma is redefined in humanistic terms, with the Jewish ethnicity openly acknowledged, but implicitly deemed irrelevant in the light of the conversion to Christianity: "since you are a man by birth, you ought to consider yourself a member of the great Brotherhood of Man; since you are a Jew by nationality, you are a partaker in the civil privileges, duties, and prosperity of your countrymen" (1902: I, 132).

Jewish characters offer an interesting insight into the dialectic of centre and periphery in utopian fiction. When references to Jews, their religion, history, or system of government are made, they enter the centre of debate, only to be rejected, marginalised and pushed to the extreme periphery. On the other hand, when Jewish characters occupy the central position, as they do in *Nova Solyma*, they do so only by virtue of the radical marginalisation, or peripheralisation of their Jewishness, to the extent that it is not marked even in their names, which, at best, as in the case of the main characters (Jacob, Joseph, Anna, and Joanna) have long been appropriated by Christian culture, and at worst, simply replaced by names of Greek, or Latin origin (Appolon), with no Hebrew associations at all. And so identity replaces alterity in the paradoxical process of moving the peripheral into the centre by depriving it of the very characteristics constituting its uniqueness, which pose a threat to the centre by the mere fact of their existence[4]. At the same time, *Nova Solyma* constructs another periphery in the form of the Roman Catholic countries, as exemplified by Italy, projected in the text as a world characterised by chaos, immorality, crime, immoderation, etc, with the new centre constituted by the trade agreement between England and Nova Solyma, symbolically echoed by the two marriages of the representatives of the two countries.

---

4   This corresponds to the two seemingly contradictory tendencies of conceptualising the
     Jews in the popular culture of the period: "The two views [...] share a common mode of
     perception, each employs a particular cognitive process or habit of thinking to describe
     the Jews. Both rely on the crudely oversimplified [...] preconceptions of the distinctive
     attributes that characterise the Jews. For the one, the Jews are by their nature sadistic
     Christ-killers, blasphemers, and thieves, the irredeemable foes of the Church; for the
     other, they are the residue of God's chosen people, permitted to survive as token of his
     enduring love for the true Christian, of whose redemption their presence is covenantal.
     Each defines the Jews not for their own sake but in terms of a distinctive Christian atti-
     tude" (Felenstein 1995: 11).

Recent Secondary World Fantasy: Farewell to the hero?

GRZEGORZ TRĘBICKI

The protagonist or, perhaps, more properly, "the hero", regardless in what sort of categories we are going to speak about him/her (popular, anthropological, critical or genological), appears as one of the key elements of the modern exomimetic (Zgorzelski 2004: 32) genre convention of Secondary World Fantasy (subsequently abbreviated to SWF). This is suggested even by the very name of the genre variation of "heroic fantasy", which, actually, is frequently used by various critics and researchers to refer to rather diverse collections of fantasy texts, at times encompassing the whole of SWF. However, even if the term "heroic fantasy" is applied to only one specific genre variant of SWF, as is the case in this study, the issue of the protagonist – or the hero – very much concerns all other historical genre variants and types of SWF. In other words, the presence of the hero (howsoever described) seems to be inherent to the genre structures as such. This assumption might be supported by a large bulk of critical work partly or entirely devoted to the description of fantasy heroes. However, most of such articles take cultural or critical literary positions; they focus, for example, on anthropological significance of fantasy heroes or their similarity to various mythical figures, and analyse them in a broader cultural context[1]. What seems to be lacking, is a more theoretical discussion of the protagonist – the hero – as an integral element of the genre which entails analysing him/her in relation to all other significant elements of textual structures.

---

1   See, for example, Walker 1980, Carr, Archell-Thompson 1997, Bianga 1997, Stawicki 1997, Oziewicz 2008 and Trocha 2009.

The discussion will begin with a historical summary of the modes of the construction of SWF protagonists at different stages of the genre's evolution in search of some underlying patterns[2]. First the hero in the early heroic fantasy will be discussed and then the hero typical of "the mythological" era of SWF will be considered. The analysis will attempt to discover how and why the SWF heroes are structured as they usually are and what functions they fulfil in particular groups of texts. Subsequently, these traditional conventions will be juxtaposed with more recent developments. For the last 20 years SWF has been subjected to very profound transformations which I have described elsewhere as a peculiar "demythologisation" and "mimetisation" of fantasy[3]. These changes are especially evident in the construction of a protagonist so that it may even be justifiable to speak about the disappearance of the typical "hero" convention that seemed to prevail in SWF for such a long time. I will try, at least partly, to verify this assumption on the basis of two of the more recent texts – *Quest for the Lost Heroes* by David Gemmell and *The Steel Remains* by Richard K. Morgan.

The whole discussion should not only systematise the subject at hand but, hopefully, lead to more general conclusions concerning the evolution of SWF. The employment of the diachronic perspective may, for example, help indicate which features of the genre are relatively stable and unchangeable and thus, possibly, constitute the core markers of SWF, and which are more prone to transformations. It may also be possible to determine how flexible fantasy conventions can be and whether there are any internal limitations to this flexibility.

My interest here is more genological than interpretative, and more synthetic than analytical. In other words, I am concerned more with the

---

2   The discussion will more or less follow the chronology suggested in my dissertation *Fantasy. Ewolucja gatunku*. Though the book presents more genre variants of SWF than will be considered here, I feel that in relation to shaping of the protagonists, two major paradigms were introduced before the most recent changes have taken place as described in the following sections of the article. The present discussion develops and summarises some of my earlier observations; see, especially, Trębicki 2007 and 2011b. However, due to the relevance of the subject for the complete and coherent description of SWF, it definitely deserves a separate treatment. This analysis is completed and paralleled by the article "In the Enslavement of the Formula? – A Short Survey of Antagonists in Secondary World Fantasy", presented at the Conference "Literatura i kultura popularna w kontekście nowych i starych mediów", Wrocław, 14-15 X 2011.

3   See Trębicki 2009a and 2011a.

genre as such than with particular texts. Therefore, most typical (or seminal) works will only be discussed or mentioned. Save for the two more recent texts I will also refrain from going into more detailed analyses of works which have been quite thoroughly discussed on numerous occasions so far.

*

The patterns and conventions of the early Heroic Fantasy (subsequently abbreviated to HF) – the first historical genre variant of SWF – are relatively simple. As the emergence and subsequent establishment of HF was paralleled – or actually inspired – by "an especially rich and rapid development of the popular short story" in American pulp magazines in the 20s and 30s of the previous century (Zgorzelski 2004: 63), in many respects it relied on the conventions already introduced in other popular genres of that period, both mimetic and non-mimetic, that preceded it, such as, for example, the fantastic novel of adventure, the early space opera or – last but not least – the literary western (compare Olszański 1996: 66).

The exemplary protagonist (or more adequately "the hero") of this first genre variant, as depicted, for example, by Robert E. Howard in the seminal figure of Conan is described by Olszański as "[...] a barbarian, a mountain of muscles with brilliant instincts, lacking both intellect and psyche, not aspiring to anything save for sating his mundane lusts and desires" (1996: 66)[4]. The presentation of the hero's adventures may be regarded as the dominant of these texts. As the prevailing paragenological convention is the short story cycle, the hero is also crucial as an element that spines the whole cycle. The primary function of the protagonist is to enact adventures and supply the addressee with a proper number of engaging albeit simple intrigues and fights with other warriors, monster, sorcerers, demons or even gods. The construction of the presented world, the plot, and the predominant motifs are rather pretextual and subservient to the presentation of the hero's violent encounters.

The episodic nature of the loose superstructure of the short story cycle – which was obviously motivated by civilizational rather than artistic

---

4   „[...] barbarzyńca, góra mięśni z genialnym instynktem, pozbawiony tak intelektu jak i psychiki, nie dążący do niczego, prócz zaspokojenia swoich doraźnych żądz i zachcianek" (Transl. mine; G.T.)

mechanisms (Zgorzelski 2004: 62-65) – also resulted in shaping the protagonist as a "static" construct, unchangeable mentally and physically,
summoned in more or less the same shape in every adventurous episode.
This is not to say that the heroes do not have a sort of personal history –
we know, for example, that Conan started as a vagabond and ended as
the king of Aquilonia. The cycle about two other seminal swordsmen
and vagabonds, Fafhrd and The Grey Mouser, written by Fritz Leiber,
includes stories explaining where the two heroes came from and how
they met, but otherwise the stories and adventures are generally episodic
and – similarly to many other heroic fantasy cycles – the internal time-
line of the cycle and the chronology of particular stories is not obvious,
at least at the first sight[5].

Summing up, the protagonist of HF is invariably a mighty warrior
equipped with evidently heroic (and often exaggerated) features (Olszański 1996: 66), whose fighting prowess, physical strength and courage are always emphasised. His primary task is to act. In his later rein-
carnations he may also sometimes prove capable of intelligent (and rather cynical) comments on the textual reality, but this is relatively irrelevant for the development of his actions and the plot. He is usually depicted as a man in the prime of his life who has already achieved his full
potential although his exact age is not specified (in contradistinction to
the heroes of later epic fantasy or fantasy of initiation and maturation,
who are mostly introduced as young men/women). As it has already
been remarked, he is not subjected to any significant transformations in
the course of the action in the story/cycle (also in contradistinction to the
hero of the later genre variants of fantasy, where the process of change
and transformation of the protagonist is essential).

The conventions described above remain relatively unchanged in
subsequent works of HF, created by such authors as John Jakes, C. L.
Moore, Lin Carter, Robert Wagner or the already mentioned Fritz Leiber

---

5   It is interesting to remark that in case of the most of HF cycles, the order of writing (or
     publishing) does not reflect the internal timeline of the cycle (if it can be deduced). This
     again confirms the protagonist (and not, for example, the plot, or the model of the pre-
     sented world) as the most central element of HF's structure, around which the particular
     cycle is built and all other elements revolve.

and, interestingly, outlive the civilizational mechanisms that were to a large extent responsible for their creation[6].

*

The publication of *The Lord of the Rings* by J. R. R. Tolkien started a process of rapid transformations within SWF and the appearance of its subsequent genre variations (Trębicki 2007: 54-86). As it has been often remarked, one of the most important effects was the introduction to SWF of the elements connected "with myths, with religious beliefs, with legends, folk tales and various rituals" (Zgorzelski 2004: 152). These phenomena are especially visible in the genre variants of epic fantasy (henceforward abbreviated to EF) and the fantasy of initiation and maturation (abbreviated to FIM), which became stabilised in the 70s and 80s of the previous century[7].

It is important to understand that we deal here not merely with a more or less pronounced recurrence of certain motifs, but rather with what can be called "structural mythopeia" – "all mythic and ontological motifs constitute the core of both the presented world's and the plot's construction, frequently becoming the main dominant of the text's structure" (Trębicki 2011a: 32-33). Obviously, fantasy novels or short stories are not mere analogues of traditional myths or rites but works of literature – there is a constant tension between mythic structures on one hand and other elements and motifs on the other hand. It might be even suggested that it is this tension that often brings about the appearance of the genre's more artistic texts. The mythic elements are modified and transformed in order to suit the narrative purposes, though they still appear to constitute the core of the story and, in a way, the starting point of its construction. Thus, arguably, most of the works of SWF of the second half of the twentieth century, basically present different strategies of the adaptation of traditional mythic motifs to their individual literary purposes.

---

6   More artistic qualities, if they appear in later texts of HF, are connected primarily with a more sophisticated use of the language, and not, as in the subsequent variants of SWF, with the creation of a certain coherent and cognitive model of the textual reality.

7   Despite various structural differences between both types of SWF, the construction of the protagonists seems to be analogous.

These observations are especially relevant when it comes to the construction of protagonists. The critics have long emphasised the striking similarity of fantasy heroes to universal archetypal figures and the conformity of their adventures to archaic patterns, as for example, Campbellian wheel of adventure[8]. On the level of textual analysis, it is worth stressing that in most works of EF and FIM, the protagonist appears a much more complex construct than in the texts of early HF, but at the same time he/she is even more bound by the convention. The structuring of the hero is strictly subordinated to the dominant of the text – which, in most cases, is the creation of a certain exomimetic ontologically-explained model of the world, whose cognitive potential is, in turn, executed by the plot also inspired by various mythic scenarios.

Thus, the protagonist "is usually a young man (or woman), often predestined by his/her birth, providence or some transcendental forces to enact great deeds" (Trębicki 2010a). He/she is presented as a young and inexperienced person also because of his/her other function in the text. It is usually through his/her eyes that the model of the world is gradually deployed to the reader. Thus, the protagonist and the reader are simultaneously initiated into the textual reality.

The protagonist's story "dramatize[s] the passage from childhood [...] to a new social status – manhood (or in some cases, womanhood)" (Walker 1980: 189). The core of the story is the hero's quest during which

> the protagonist is often confronted with the conflict between the forces of good and evil (or harmony and chaos) and is forced to make crucial ethical choices, at the same time discovering his/her identity [...] The quest itself follows more or less closely the structure of "the circle of adventures" as described by Campbell or the rites of passages as described by Van Gennep and Mieletinski, and includes such obligatory elements as: a call to adventure which wrestles the protagonists from his mundane reality; various tests which he/she has to pass, sometimes with the assistance of unusual or magical helpers; crucial decisions of ethical nature he/she has to take in order to complete his maturation; a separation from the society and – in many cases – a symbolic temporary death (or a near-death experience) and an encounter with spirits which enables a personal renewal and achieving new powers (Mieletinski 1981: 281); a final spiritual transformation (often dramatized in a single act) and an acquisition of a "treasure" or "boon"

---

8   See, for example, Walker 1980 and Archell-Thomson 1997.

which he/she "can bestow on his fellow man" (Campbell 1968: 30) at the same time contributing to the victory of the forces of good or harmony (and a renewal of a protagonist's world – on a grander or lesser scale) in which protagonist's participation proves instrumental. This is usually followed by the protagonist's rise to a new, ultimately noble (and at the same time ultimately demanding) status. (Trębicki 2010a)

The first and the third volumes in the seminal Earthsea cycle provide an exemplary, and, perhaps, best known case here. It is not necessary to analyse texts that have already been thoroughly discussed on numerous occasions, so let me only remind at this point that

> A Wizard of Earthsea recounts the story of the initiation and the coming to maturity and power of a young sorcerer apprentice Ged, whereas The Farthest Shore relates the final quest of the same Ged as an old mage and his symbolic "passing away" and parting with power, and the simultaneous initiation of his young companion, Arren/Lebannen who is destined to become the king of the whole Earthsea. [...] not only the events but also the very structure of the novels closely reflects the structure of the rites of passage. [...] Major events in the novel have a deeper symbolic meaning and mark subsequent steps in Ged's initiation and maturation. All crucial elements of the traditional rites of passage have been included and both the plot and the construction of the protagonists (Ged and Arren) are subordinated to the function of composing [...] an inspiring model of a rite of passage, capable of generalizing human experience creatively (Trębicki 2009b).

The characters basically function here as "signs in the symbolic, myth-related system" (Trębicki 2009b) – all their acts and speeches are subordinated to the texts' dominants – the presentation of a cognitive and metaphorical world model.

The protagonists in other notable fantasy works may appear less restricted by myth-inspired narrative structures, as those are often permeated and counterbalanced by other, sometimes culturally distant elements[9]. However, they still remain within the confines of convention described above. The patterns inspired by the heroic myth of initiation or the heroic epic – no matter how they get distorted and transformed in the

---

9   For example, in some fantasy texts archaic patterns seem to be breached by such modern cultural motifs as feminism or humanistic or third force psychologies. See my discussion of Tanith Lee's *Volkhavaar* and Andre Norton's *Year of the Unicorn* in Trębicki 2005. Compare Archell-Thompson 1997: 28.

artistic process[10] – nearly always constitute the starting point of the protagonist's construction.

In comparison to HF, the protagonist of the later genre variants does not exhibit any obviously heroic features, though he/she ultimately proves a hero in a more sophisticated, Campbellian meaning. He/she is a hero *in statu nascendi* and the narration focuses on his/her transformation. What is also important, his/her heroism is not completely "self-contained" (or egotic) as it is in the case of the protagonists of early heroic fantasy. He/she acts as a mere agent, no matter how instrumental, of some higher power, and through his acts he/she achieves some external, transcendental values. Unlike the protagonist of HF whose world is fragmented and not ordered by any coherent ontological system, he/she ultimately acts in conformity with natural harmony in a universe that is marked ethically (compare Zgorzelski 2004: 39). This unity exists even in texts which emphasise individualistic nature of the protagonist's quest. It might be said that, in a manner of speaking, the structuring of the protagonist as well as of the whole narration is determined by the ontological assumptions of the presented world and the myth-inspired scenarios of cosmic or personal revival that are played out there. The universe of SWF is meaningful and ordered – not unlike the universe of medieval romances or allegories – and the protagonist has to accept his/her role as a sign in its semantic system.

*

As I argue in a different place (Trębicki 2009a: 63-70), SWF has been undergoing very profound changes for the last 20 years, probably comparable in scope and significance with those that transformed it into a truly syncretic and complex genre convention in the 50s and 60s of the twentieth century. At the same time, the changes seem to be pointing in the exactly opposite direction than those inspired by the seminal works of Tolkien, Le Guin and other writers at the beginning of the "mythic" era of SWF. However strange such discrepant directions of development may seem, this is the way the literary conventions often evolve – by breaching and counterposing existing paradigms.

---

10   I discuss several such strategies of transformation of the traditional patterns in Trębicki 2010.

Though I have described these phenomena as "the mimetisation of SWF" (Trębicki 2009a: 63-70), obviously I do not mean a sudden change of the mode of the construction of the presented world – in fact, placing the action in an exomimetic, quasi-medieval secondary world with a low level of technology but with magic present, seems to be the most diachronically constant and defining element of SWF. I rather refer here to the gradual but wide-reaching process of the ousting of the conventions rooted in the broadly understood non-mimetic tradition and deriving primarily from the myth, the heroic epic or the fairy tale, by the conventions characteristic of modern mimetic fiction, such as, for example, the contemporary historical fiction, the military novel, the techno-military thriller or the political thriller. In other words recent SWF seems to be marked by a peculiar "escape from the marvellous" (Trębicki 2009a: 64). Another change, which I refer to as "demythologisation", can be defined as the replacement of myth-inspired scenarios that have traditionally shaped the plots and protagonists of SWF, by those motivated by the fascination with history or, more precisely, historiosophic issues (2009a: 68-69).

As I suggest in the beginning of this study, these changes are especially visible when it comes to the shaping of protagonists. This latest stage of the genre's evolution can be presented by means of preliminary analyses of SWF's heroes in two texts: David Gemmell's *Quest for the Lost Heroes* from 1990 and Richard K. Morgan *The Steel Remains,* published in 2008.

David Gemmell is usually regarded by reviewers as the follower of the tradition of heroic fantasy, but his novels usually include also elements of other genre variants such as EF or FIM[11]. *Quest for Lost Heroes,* as its very title signals, reveals affinity to traditional HF by its emphasis on the motif of the warrior/warriors. However, the motif of character's initiation and maturation is also present (primarily connected with the character of Kiall), and additionally the book includes some elements traditionally associated with epic fantasy in its classic shape, such as the team of brave characters supporting the protagonist on his quest (vide Frodo and the Fellowship of the Ring). Yet all these elements are reinterpreted and reworked very considerably.

---

11   See my discussion of another novel by Gemmell, *The Dark Moon* in Trębicki 2007: 115-117.

The whole plot revolves around the story of Kiall, a young peasant from a tiny state of Gothir, whose village is attacked by a band of slavers. They kidnap several women, including the girl Kiall loves, Ravenna (who does not return his love). The youth resolves to find and rescue Ravenna despite not receiving any help from other villagers or from the local Lord. Rather accidentally he wins the support of an ex-hero and eminent swordsman Chareos and his former companions, Beltzer the Axeman, and the bowmen Finn and Maggrig.

However, in contradistinction to a typical FIM or EF plot, it is difficult to perceive Kiall as the central protagonist, although he can be seen as initiating the action. His story does not develop in conformity with any mythic scenarios and he is obviously no hero *in statu nascendi* as he does not possess any hidden qualities. The fact that in the course of the action he slightly develops his initially non-existent fencing skills definitely does not make him a classic hero. Even when – in the culminating moment of the plot – he manages to defeat Junghir, the Khan of Nadirs, in a duel, it is only because he agrees that his body be temporarily possessed by the soul of the former Khan and Junghir's father, the legendary Tanaka. His quest cannot possibly be judged as successful by the standards of the fairy tale conventions prevailing in earlier SWF. Although Ravenna (now pregnant with the child of Junghir to whom she has been sold) is finally regained, she still does not return Kiall's feelings. Unlike the protagonist in a typical FIM or EF plot, Kiall does not rise to a new, noble status and no extraordinary destiny awaits for him – it is suggested at the end of the book that his future fate is completely insignificant for any oncoming events save his own personal happiness. His maturation focuses more on the process of disillusionment and acquiring new, often painful experiences, than on achieving any supernatural powers. Yet, from a strictly personal perspective, he does not fail. He matures in the sense that he is able to perceive life and himself more realistically, and in the epilogue he happily marries another woman – the Nadir Princess Tanaki, although, initially, they both seem very improbable candidates for each other's loves.

It is also questionable whether Kiall can be regarded as the central protagonist. The narration devotes even more space to Chareos, the once famous hero of the siege of Bel-Azar and eminent blademaster, now a poor, disillusioned and lonely man, slowly starting to age. He is as different from a conventional HF protagonist as Kiall is different from young protagonists of EF or FIM. Although, on one hand, the narration appreciates his bravery, nobleness and martial skills, on the other hand he is definitely not invincible; his human weaknesses and limitations to his strength are clearly shown. He is presented as a reflexive and slightly sentimental man, continuously contemplating his past, and the narration is frequently interrupted by his reminiscences. What is interesting, they are largely devoted to his unhappy marriage with Tura. In fact, Chareos – as a complex but essentially noble man, disappointed with life and other people, and hurt by the woman he loved – is presented in a way more typical of modern mimetic novel than classical SWF[12].

Although at first sight Kiall and Chareos seem to be the main protagonists, the narration also follows quite closely some other characters, notably the Kiatze envoy to Junghir's court, Chien-Tsu, the Nadir princess Tanaki and the three companions of Chareos. The difference in the treatment of these characters is quantitative rather than qualitative. They are introduced later in the book, they appear less frequently than Kiall and Chareos, but their feelings, memories and actions are described as thoroughly and with equal care and sympathy on the part of the narrator. It may be justifiable to view them not as secondary characters but rather as supplementary protagonists.

Thus, instead of a simple, superhuman construct of a hero, or another incarnation of a Campbellian "hero with a thousand faces", Gemmell's novel features a cluster of various characters, major and minor, brought together not by destiny or providence but by accident. This way of structuring protagonists seems to be a direct consequence of shaping the model of the presented world. Although the action still takes place in a quasi-medieval, secondary world, and magic plays a prominent role, ontologically this is a very different reality from the models described in FIM, and, especially EF. This world is no longer ordered; it is constructed to be as chaotic and ruled by accident as the realities of many of the contemporary mimetic novels. The events are not governed by some discernible, myth-inspired scenario but are made to appear as resulting from actions of different groups and individuals with their respective

---

12   Along with many other heroes of recent SWF, he strongly resembles, for example, the protagonists of the modern detective story, much in the vein of Raymond Chandler's Philip Marlowe and other innumerable incarnations of the hardboiled detective.

motivations and interests – not unlike in the contemporary political thriller.

Although the world is not marked ethically, and the transcendental forces of good and evil (or their non-deistic, non-transcendental and im-personalised but ontologically rooted equivalents such as Equilibrium in Earthsea cycle), signposting characters' choices are basically absent from the narration, this does not mean that the ethical issues are not vital for the construction of the protagonists. The characters do not act as agents of transcendental forces guiding them more or less openly, and their role is not to restore the natural order because it does not exist in the text. To behave ethically they have to construct some moral order for themselves in a chaotic world surrounding them, relying on their con-science, intuition and past experiences. If they are heroic, it is neither because it is their inherent feature (as it is in the case of HF Conan-like protagonists) nor because they act out some mythic scenarios, but be-cause they are able to show courage in the face of obstacles that surpass them – without any transcendental help. All of this, obviously, makes them constructs more complex and less restricted by conventions than the protagonists of all earlier genre variations of SWF; they are also much more prone to defy reader's expectations.

The Steel Remains, the first volume in a cycle by Richard Morgan, a prominent British SF and cyberpunk writer, exhibits quite similar tendencies. What is especially interesting here, is the permeation of the text with conventions characteristic rather of cyberpunk[13] than traditional SWF (which is, by no means, surprising in view of the writer's previous output). This, again, is most visible in the construction of the world model and in the shaping of the protagonists[14]. The world of *The Steel Remains* is, similarly as the world of Gemmell's novel, chaotic and even more cruel and ruthless. It is also, in a way quite analogous to many cy-berpunk texts, a place of political intrigue and hidden shifts of power

---

13 The status of cyberpunk seems a little vague; personally I am inclined to see it as a the-matic variant within SF, or, simply "a certain set of motifs which surface – in various proportions - in contemporary works of SF and postmodernism" (Trębicki 2010b).

14 And also in the use of language. While the language of *Quest for Lost Heroes* still to a large extent resembles the language of a traditional SWF narration, the language of *The Steel Remains*, with its use of slang, vulgarisms and short aggressive dialogues, ostenta-tiously mimics the language of cyberpunk.

(where the powerful and villainous corporations of Cyberpunk have been replaced by the equally powerful and villainous Cabal).

The text, apparently more conventionally than *Quest for Lost Heroes*, features three clear protagonists, former brothers-in-arms: Ringil Eskiath – ex-commander and ex-hero, once aristocrat of the merchant city-state of Trelayne and now a common mercenary; Egar – the clan leader of a Majak tribe; and Archeth – the court sorcerer of the Yhelteth emperor. Although Ringil proves most central and definitely most instrumental for the development of the plot, the narration regularly follows all three characters. What is notable, their respective stories are for the most of the book developed as parallel and independent plot lines, initially with only slight hints suggesting that they have something in common. The characters meet only as the plot is heading towards its culmination. Such construction of the narration is again more typical of SF and cyberpunk (vide, for example, William Gibson's *Neuromancer* or Neil Stevenson's *Snowcrash*)[15].

As the most central protagonist, Ringil is also in many respects the most unconventional of the three main characters. Once a hero of the war with the Scale Folk, at the beginning of the story he lives a rather miserable life in his voluntary exile. Rather reluctantly he sets out, at his mother's request, in order to find and save his enslaved and kidnapped cousin Sherin. This initial quest – the dangerous investigation Ringil starts, with obstacles from all possible sides, his ventures into the underworld of Trelayne, his discovery of subtle mechanisms connecting the local crime with the ruling class – all this is highly reminiscent of the hardboiled detective story conventions (or cyberpunk, which also relies on them quite extensively).

In Morgan's novel the changes in the presentation of the protagonist are even more far-reaching than in *Quest for Lost Heroes*. A lot of emphasis is put on the description of Ringil's complex personal problems:

---

15 The parallel protagonists narrations, obviously, do take place in more traditional SWF, however, they usually have a common starting point; in other words, the narration simply forks at some point, and it diverges and converges again (see, for example, *The Lord of the Rings*, or almost any EF cycle). In contradistinction, the three narrations in *The Steel Remains* develop completely independently and clearly present three quite separate stories which – to some extent accidentally – converge only at the very end of the book.

his homosexuality[16] (which makes him a pariah in his own town), his difficult relationship with his father and brothers, and his being a social misfit. These modern psychological and social motifs form a very radical breach in the traditional SWF conventions. The breach becomes even wider with the appearance of the text's central antagonist, Seethlaw of the half-mythical and dangerous dwenda race. The ambiguous and constantly shifting relationship between Ringil and Seethlaw is one of the most important and dynamising plots in the novel. At first

> the dwenda is for Ringil only a gossip, an indefinite but fatal threat. Then, he appears in person and defeats the protagonist in combat; however, instead of killing Ringil, Seethlaw decides to take the wounded enemy to his hideout and nurses him. The man and the dwenda quickly become homosexual lovers, fascinated by each other. After Ringil's recovery, Seethlaw takes him on a long journey through the realms inaccessible to men and acts as his guide into the unknown. At the end, however, the roles turn again; Ringil, appalled by the plans of the dwenda, chooses the loyalty to other humans and his own moral attitudes over the loyalty to his lover. He decides to abandon Seethlaw and oppose him. In the final confrontation, determined Ringil kills Seethlaw, without showing much regret. (Trębicki 2011b)

The actions of the protagonists of Gemmell's novel and their ethical code, although no longer related to the ontology of the presented world or restricted by traditional scenarios, refer to some discernible patterns of honour, bravery and loyalty, deeply rooted in the whole non-mimetic tradition and reaching back to such literary conventions as the chivalric romance or the heroic epic. Ringil's actions are complex and ambiguous, often aimed at confusing the reader, and as chaotic as the world he lives in. Thus, the protagonist himself becomes one of the most puzzling constructs SWF has created so far.

*

The present discussion hopefully demonstrates the necessity for a distinction between generic features which remain relatively stable and unchangeable in the diachronic development of a genre, and thus, may be regarded as the core or defining ones (we might call them, for example,

---

16   What is interesting, another of the protagonists, Archeth is a lesbian, although in her case the problems of sexuality are less pronounced and are counterbalanced by her affiliation to an ancient Kiriath race.

"primary" generic features) and those that are subjected to sometimes very profound changes (we might call them, in turn, "secondary" generic features). In the case of SWF, specifying the set of primary features seems to be relatively simple: they include, as already observed, placing the plot in a secondary exomimetic quasi-medieval world of relatively closed spatial and temporal parameters[17] at a low level of technological development but with magic openly present and functioning within the presented model of the universe[18]. Almost all other elements – the use of particular conventions in shaping the plot, characters and language, the text's axiology, the ontology of the fictional universe, the appearance of various literary and cultural motifs – all those traits belong to the sphere of secondary features, subjected to very significant transformations with the evolution of consecutive genre variants over the years.

As I try to show, these changes significantly influence the shaping of the protagonist. The protagonists of the more recent texts seem to be very different constructs, fulfilling different literary purposes, than those present in the previous SWF. This shift can be viewed as a way of redynamising of the genre's structures, otherwise quite strictly regulated by the set of primary features. It is interesting that SWF ultimately proves a rather conservative genre – any vital changes seem to be restricted to the already mentioned sphere of secondary features whereas the core aspects of the presented world, defined by the primary features, remains relatively intact[19].

In this context, it might be also argued that – in respect to the structuring of the protagonist in SWF – some things never change. Due to certain patterns apparently inherent to the genre structures as such and determined by the set of primary features, the protagonist of SWF, no matter how exactly he/she is described and what literary purposes he/she serves, is bound to be a man or a woman of action: a skilled warrior (or a wizard), someone ready to face any set of impossible odds and bravely fight with most formidable opponents, in other words – a hero.

---

17 For the comparison of the description of spatial and temporal parameters in SF and SWF see Zgorzelski 2004: 37.
18 See also Trębicki 2009a: 63-64.
19 I do not take into consideration different hybrid forms of SWF and other genres such as, for example so called science fantasy or models of multiverses (see Trębicki 2007: 118-155) as in my opinion they do not constitute the main branch of SWF's current evolution nor its statistical mainstream.

The realistic novel and the creation
of literary characters:
William Faulkner's *The Sound and the Fury*

ŻANETA NALEWAJK

In an exemplary nineteenth-century realistic novel[1], the creation of a literary character – understood as an integral, fictional component of the presented world expressed in the text – involves the use of the following rules of construction:

The first rule: A literary character has to be anthropomorphic (Markiewicz 1984), and not a plant, an animal or a thing. Even if a literary character undergoes a metamorphosis, it has to take place in the background and under the influence of social realities in the world presented in a novel. This metamorphosis must therefore be probable (not fantastic), well-motivated, and logical within the cause-effect sequence of events[2]. Even when events are not presented in the chronological order, its reconstruction should not cause any problem for the reader. Moreover, the metamorphosis should not have ontological nature – in this regard, the status of the character remains clear from the beginning to the end. In the presented literary convention of the novel there is no place for the metamorphosis of a character into a cockroach or an electric bell, for example, which is entirely possible in grotesque or satirical texts. In the realistic novel we deal with the change of the fate of a character, whose identity is relatively stable and possible to recognise despite

---

1 For the discussion of the realistic novel compare: Brodzka (1964 and 1967), Markiewicz (1995), Lukács (1968), Auerbach (1968), Stanzel (1980), Kolb (1969), Barrish (2001), and Ludwig (2002).

2 Literary characters are discussed, among others, by Markiewicz (1976 and 1984) Labuda (1979), Okopień-Sławińska (1967), and Kasperski (1993, 1998 and 2006).

the passage of time, but we do not encounter radical transformations from one form of existence into another.

The second rule: A literary character should have his name and surname. If these anthroponyms are significant, their significance indicates the nationality of a character and his membership in a particular social group. However, the main function of the anthroponyms is not an allegorical reduction of the character to one trait – as it is in fables, or grotesque and satirical texts. Names and surnames are not parabolic either, as this could induce the reader to treat the character as a medium of symbolic meanings, which might turn out to be fundamental for the interpretation of the presented world as an allegorical example of the universal truth.

The third rule: The age, the appearance and the mental dispositions of a character presented in this kind of novel must be precisely described and defined through characterization. Moreover, such information could not be relativised – which occurs, for instance, when the features of a literary character are mediated by the narrator who is unconscious or suffers from disturbances of perception, and so his point of view cannot be treated as reliable by the reader. Usually the realistic novel does not allow such relativisation though the story of one literary character may be told from the perspective of another. It forces the audience to keep redefining all the information about the character, which they gain during the continuous process of reading.

The fourth rule of the presented convention of the novel – linked closely to the three principles defined above – consists in the fact that the protagonist (unambiguously distinctive from other beings), must be rational and, therefore, able to exercise authority over his own body and the sphere of instinct. The ability of self-control testifies to strong will. Moreover, a literary character in the realistic novel is constructed in such a way that the virtual recipient has no doubts about the main purpose of his existence (expressed in the worldview and system of values accepted by the character), even if this character encounters obstacles or is defeated while achieving his goals.

The fifth rule: The protagonist of a realistic novel is an acting literary character. He is presented not only as a co-creator of verbal events (which are included in dialogues), but also as a co-creator of occurrences, which take place in the fictional reality and are usually related by an omniscient, third-person narrator, who hides behind the presented world of the novel. The use of such a literary convention excludes the construction of literary characters who are extremely reified and whose actions are reduced to a few monotonously repeated gestures while their utterances are completely eliminated from the text and replaced by verbal expressions of other persons or limited to some incoherent or internally contradictory phrases.

The sixth rule: the creation of a literary character should allow the reader to become acquainted with broader social background and the family in which the protagonist grew and with relationships prevailing in his house. In accordance with the conventions of the realistic novel the reader is often granted the knowledge about the education of the main character. This kind of prose also provides the recipient with an insight into the process of initiation of the protagonist into the social life presented in the novel, indicates the location of the literary character in the fictional time and makes his/her aspirations understandable.

The seventh rule is closely connected to the previous principle. It the assumes that a literary character – as an anthropomorphic creature – exists in the image and likeness of the human social existence involving the ability to stand up against determinisms resulting from implacable laws of nature. In addition, the literary character shows a tendency to self-recognition and, making use of chance, seeks for personal development and self-reflection.

The eighth rule: The realistic novel often aspires to create a social panorama of a given time; the characters then serve as representatives of social classes – and in this sense the characters may become typical. However, this typicality should not result from the moralistic intentions of the author. A literary character does not need to be constructed as a role model for the reader to be recognised by him/her as imitation-worthy, which was popular as a principle of character creation, for example, in the Middle Ages.

The ninth rule: Even though the third-person omniscient narration in the realistic novel implies the dominance of linguistic presentation of a literary character as an object, the same convention, paradoxically, determines his/her subjective existence in the presented world of a novel. This happens because the authors of realistic novels tend to portray a literary character as someone who feels that he has a continuous identity ensuring his/her being the same person despite the passage of the time and the dynamics of events, which influence the fate and behaviour of an individual character. This is due to the fact that a literary character is responsible for his own actions, regardless of their nature and their ethical evaluation made by the reader.

The tenth rule: The convention of the realistic novel determines the shape of the presented world, which does not need to be and – generally – is not friendly to the protagonist. The virtual recipient, however, being allowed a deeper insight into the context of the fictional events by the narrator, perceives the presented world as understandable and rationally explicable even if it poses complications in the fate of the fictional character. The intelligibility, which results from the writer's striving to endow his/her text with the cognitive function, is to a large extent responsible for the mechanism of the reader's identification with the protagonist, which in this way appear during the process of reading. The identification is made possible because the reader is given a chance to understand the origins, motivations and circumstances of the literary character's actions.

It is worth pointing out, that the rules reconstructed above and treated as a model of the creation of a literary character in the nineteenth-century realistic novel, are subjected to modifications in the historical processes of change, as evidenced, for instance, by alterations in the conventions of the novel in the twentieth century. Possible transformations of the construction of literary characters may be genologically significant. If these modifications are not radical, then the changes remain within the area of genre. But when the alterations become far-reaching – whether in relation to one constructional rule or to several, whether by overemphasising one rule and thus decreasing the importance of or even eliminating one or more rules – then we may speak of the emergence of new genres or at least of the contamination of the existing ones.

All the tendencies important for the convention of the novel in the first half of the twentieth century seem possible to observe and analyse on the example of William Faulkner *The Sound and the Fury* published in 1929[3]. The novel consists of five parts – I treat the last part entitled

---

3   Compare: Cowan, M.H. (1968) *Twentieth century interpretations of* The sound and the fury: *a collection of critical essays*; Matthews, J.T. (1982). *The Play of Faulkner's Lan-*

"Appendix" (added some years after the original publication of the novel) as an integral component of this literary work. The titles of the other four parts – which are dates – suggest to the reader who starts perusing the book by looking at the table of contents, that the novel employs diary convention with a strong subjective orientation[4].

The table of contents may also erroneously suggest that Faulkner's novel will operate with only one narrator constituting both the protagonist and the narrator or the textual author (the problem of the empirical author is purposefully put aside). One can also mistakenly assume that other literary characters who appear in the novel, will be presented from the narrator's point of view, so that their views and actions in the presented world of the novel will be shown as an object of perception, interpretation and eventually evaluation. What is more, the convention of a diary suggested in the chapter titles requires the reader to expect that the rules of the text's composition will not be very rigorous and consequently its various components will not be thematically related. The reader may also wrongly assume that the only instance uniting the various elements of the literary work and determining its semantics will be the literary character, identical to the narrator and the textual author.

Nothing could be further from the truth. The novel seems characterised by polyphony and an extraordinary precision of composition. Its main literary characters, such as Maury/Benjy, Quentin, Jason (i.e. the members of the Compson family whose collapse is presented in Faulkner's text) are simultaneously narrators. It should be added that their status – defined by their contribution to the narrative, and the manner in which they shape their utterances – is not equivalent. It is from their point of view that we get to know both themselves and other characters. The reader gains the insight into their psyche through the stream of con-

---

guage; Hoffman, F.J., Vickery, O.W., Lansing E. (eds.). (1960). *William Faulkner. Three Decades of Criticism.*

4   The literary convention of the diary posed a big problem for literary researchers because it is related to autobiography and thus requires distinguishing autobiographical components from elements of fiction. Without any exaggeration one can talk about its popularity in the literary studies in the second half of the twentieth century also connected with defining the phenomenon of autofiction; see Gasparini, F. (2008). *Autofiction – Une aventure de langage*, Paris: Le Seuil.

sciousness technique[5] and gets acquainted with their systems of values, dispositions, their position in the social hierarchy and in the family.

It should be added that the stream of consciousness utterances of the narrators contain dialogic responses of the other characters, which are recollected by the narrators. The narrative is conducted by the voices of several characters, which constitutes an important strategy in the novel. As a result the points of view in narration are multiplied. Thanks to this strategy, the characters, who occupy certain places in the social hierarchy of the presented world (in which racial divisions play a significant role), gain situational and contextual identity when they are presented from the perspective of other characters or indirectly characterised though dialogic responses connected with the family matters. Their identity, depending on who talks about them and how, appears as contingent on the situation and context for the reader, especially when he/she has not read the fourth part of the novel yet and the "Appendix".

Moreover, when the characters formulate utterances directed to other characters, independent what or who they talk about, they characterise themselves indirectly by their way of speaking and their use of language. Consequently, it is always doubtful whether the characters, who are simultaneously narrators, ever speak of the same things even if their utterances relate to the same events. The one thing that the reader cannot doubt after reading the first three parts, is that the strategy of employing multiple narrative perspectives in the text results in a multidimensional relativisation of the literary characters in the novel.

This is a significant change in the construction of characters in comparison to the techniques of the character creation in the realistic novel described earlier in this study. Faulkner's approach to the construction of characters forces the reader to confront several crucial issues. For example, the reader has to face the important problem of trustworthiness of the characters-narrators – the issue which appears crucial for the analysis of modernist transformations of novelistic techniques. Another important question concerns the identity of the characters-narrators in terms of their motivations and their own interpretations projected into the presented world of the novel. Equally significant is the matter of the

---

5   Compare Humphrey, R.R. (1970). The term" stream of consciousness" is not entirely adequate with regard to Maury/Benjy – but this problem will be discussed later in this study.

character's identity defined as dependent on situational parameters and contextual data. The character's identity is not essentialist and independent, existing in itself and for itself, but is strictly relational and thus possible only with reference to the other – both in the micro- and macro-social sphere of the presented world. Another crucial problem is posed by the limited nature of individual cognitive efforts: the knowledge about the presented world, which the characters themselves communicate, concerns only some aspects and can never achieve completeness.

The constructional techniques employed for the creation of literary characters in the first three parts of Faulkner's novel substantially differ from the nineteenth-century rules as defined above. They changes are most fully manifested in the creation of Maury/Benjy. This character appears to involve radical transformations of almost all the rules of a typical character creation assumed in the nineteenth-century realistic novel (with the exception of the sixth rule).

The modification of convention is suggested, for example, even by anthroponyms: by the change of the name of the mentally handicapped Maury who is called – depending on who is talking about him – Benjy or Benjamin. This transformation has several important motivations and functions. The new name is a sign of a new social identity – the change is demanded by the mother as she wants to forget about her wasteful brother who is the namesake of her youngest child. The anthroponym chosen by Quentin has biblical origins (Benjamin was the youngest son of Jacob and Rachel who – before her death almost immediately after giving birth – with her last breath named him Benoni, "son of my sorrow". This name was later changed by the loving father to Benjamin which is translated as the "son of luck" or the "son of the South". The latter meaning seems to be particularly important because of the social significance of Faulkner's novel with its construction of the South. Thus Benjy's name can be interpreted as a suggestion of the parabolic nature of the character in *The Sound and the Fury* and, possibly, of the parabolisation of the novel as a whole. The parabolic interpretation seems to be borne out by the novel's focus on the collapse of a particular family, as well as on the decline of the model of society based on racial discrimination.

Moreover, it is highly significant that Maury/Benjamin, though he is presented against the social background of the South, is entirely deprived of self-determination. He is an example of a character who is extremely reified and treated by the others as an un-human being, which means in inhumane ways, worse than a slave. There are only a few exceptions to this rule in the novel: the first one concerns his relationship with Caddy, the second is his contact with Dilsey. Additionally, Maury/Benjy is a literary character who does not have self-awareness. His mental development, his childish behaviour and his psychological predispositions are conspicuously incongruent with manhood. Maury/Benjy does not exercise volitional control over himself as he is unable to rule his own body and emotions. It is worth mentioning that Maury/Benjamin's perception is not intellectual but sensual and emotional, which is clearly manifested in the language of the first part of the novel with its high incidence of vocabulary associated with the senses of hearing, sight, smell and touch.

The discussion of how the techniques of the realistic novel are transformed in Faulkner's text should also involve the consideration of the character's actions. If we perceive Benjamin as an acting literary character, we have to notice that his activities are to a large extent reduced to physiological or emotional reactions involving, for example, uncontrolled salivation or sobbing. The limitation of the character's activity to such reactions forcefully suggests that the presented world is beyond the grasp of this literary character, both in the intellectual and physical sense. It should also be noted that Benjamin is not the only character who has no control over himself. Lack of control also applies to the other family members, as evidenced by the motif of incestuous love between Quentin and Caddy. Thus, the presence of Benjy in the Compson family can be interpreted as a clear signal of its progressive collapse.

The described departures from the rules of literary character creation characteristic for a novel written within the convention of realism, do not necessary imply that the construction of characters and the narration in Faulkner's novel are not rooted in the memory of the compositional patterns of a nineteenth-century realistic novel. Quite the opposite – as testified by the fourth part of the novel where the third-person omniscient narrator returns. The fourth part features the character of Dilsey, whose utterances are quoted by the omniscient narrator and whose thoughts are presented in reported speech. Moreover, the "Appendix" can be treated as a form of a sketchy dossier usually constructed by realist writers in the initial stages of the novel creation. If we read *The Sound and the Fury* from the end to the beginning, the novel might be taken to illustrate all the historically conditioned crucial changes of the novelistic techniques contingent on the cultural transformations of the vision of the world and understanding of the human being.

These modifications were related to the epistemological crisis and the increasing awareness of the progressive disintegration of a particular model of society. This model – eventually perceived as unfair – was for ages considered as the only possible and appropriate one, and its rules – if properly respected – seemed effective and durable, because they introduced hierarchically structured order in human relationships and defined the limits within which human desires could be fulfilled. Such re-evaluations were definitely essential for the art of the novel. The conventions of objective, realistic presentation of literary characters – typical of the nineteenth-century realistic novel – gave way to more a personal type of narration and then to the display of a whole gamut of narrative points of view, or else to the stream-of-consciousness technique. One of the results of the change of the narrative techniques is the relativisation of the literary character. But the new techniques of narration and of character creation also suggested the possibility of cognitive processes occurring on the sensory, pre-rational stages before the imposition of the ordering structures of the worldview. The category of the literary character and principles of its construction turn out to be crucial for the changes of genre patterns – as even the present short analysis suggests.

Character sketch and its fantastic transformations: H. G. Wells's "The Crystal Egg"

HALSZKA LELEŃ

The aim of this study is to discuss the applications of the supra-generic convention of fantastic fiction to redynamise the structuring of character in the short story by H. G. Wells entitled "The Crystal Egg" (1897). The text falls into the category of fantastic fiction understood as the fiction which assumes the implied reader's "knowledge of the empirical reality" derived from his presupposed linguistic competence, and which describes the confrontation of a quasi-empirical model of reality with a different, strange model of reality (Zgorzelski 1984: 302)[1]. The discussion developed here aims to consider the artistic techniques used by Wells to represent characters in his short fiction.

The literary character is defined following Henryk Markiewicz: as a particular human subject of description endowed with some features, actions, and internal and external states (1996: 166-167). In my analysis, I assume that in the process of structuring the literary character, the important factors are both his/her directly expressed as well as implied features. The conventional strategies which determine the selection and organisation of a character's internal and external attributes are also crucial (Markiewicz 1996: 171-72). Wells's fictional protagonists are revealed not only through direct description but also indirectly through presenting their relationships with other characters and their attitudes to the elements of the fictional world. In the latter factor, the structure of the fictional world is of vital importance. It is therefore interesting to see

---

1   The terms "mimetic fiction" and "antimimetic fiction" are used in this paper in the senses also defined by Zgorzelski (1984).

how Wells uses the "two-world structure" constitutive for fantastic fiction to enhance the semantic and artistic potential of his human figures (Huntington 1979: 35). As in any type of fiction, Wells's characters are defined not only though the linguistic choices applied to them but also through narrative strategies and the principles underlying the complex semantic units derived from particular combinations of features.

In the context of our analysis, it is interesting to note that Wells was severely criticised as an author precisely for his techniques of characterization. Although he was seen as an author of minor fiction containing brilliant ideas, his ill fame as an artist was initiated with the modernist attack on his prose style and on his character structure in particular. Wells's characters were denounced for their simplicity and the lack of artistic strategies applied to endow them with the effect of quasi-real complexity. E. M. Forster in *Aspects of the Novel* declares Wells's characters "flat as a photograph". The critic notices some positive traits but undermines his argument at the same time, when he describes them as "influenced with such a vigour that we forget their complexities lie on the surface" (1974: 9-10). The weakness in Wells's prose style was also directly pinpointed by Virginia Woolf who blamed him for his construction of characters, plots as well as for what she identified as an unrefined style. Her unambiguous criticism of Wells published in *Modern Fiction* (1919) is indeed directed not only to the author of "The Crystal Egg" but also to other Edwardian prose writers, like Arnold Bennett (1867 – 1931) and John Galsworthy (1867 – 1933). It seems that it is Woolf's voice that has ever since become the prism for the critical underestimation of the literary qualities in Wells's works (Hardy 1993: 2; Brown 1989: 55; Head 1992: 82). Woolf finds fault in the Edwardian external approach to characters and criticises Wells's focus on plausibility, which she contrasts with her own objectives: representing the "spirit of life itself" (Hewitt 1988: 111). Although Wells did not directly address the criticism from Woolf and Forster, he is known to have discussed his art with Joseph Conrad (1857 – 1924) and Henry James (1843 – 1916), with whom he developed a kind of literary friendships, though they ended in some divergences and quarrels.

I would like to suggest that Wells's debate with the Modernists should also be understood in the context of what Markiewicz identifies as the changes in the shaping of the literary character in the nineteenth-century fiction, which led to application of such devices as reduction, relativism, disintegration and degradation (1996: 160). What I aim to demonstrate is the way Wells disintegrates his character by introducing an artistically potent strategy of applying contradictory attitudes and incongruous features into the depiction of standard generic contrasts and conflicts. A close analysis of descriptive techniques in the short story "The Crystal Egg" reveals that Wells's approach to the shaping of the character is indeed deliberately schematic and patterned in the way which foregrounds textuality. Wells's discrepancy with the Modernists derives from his different concept of art rather than from any artistic deficiency on his part.

In the structuring of human figures in "The Crystal Egg" one can see a common Wellsian strategy employed in his short stories – the author orchestrates the common principle of contrasting features. Multiple juxtapositions are built between individuals as well as within major protagonists. In the development of action in most of his short stories Wells follows the conventional patterns of genre-determined types of conflict. However, he is also markedly oriented towards transgressing and destabilising the traditional ways of structuring characters.

"The Crystal Egg" is very typical of Wells's fantastic short stories with the quasi-scientific motivation of the confrontation with the fantastic world. It seeks to use the insight from the reality shaped as mimetic into the fantastic reality so as to redynamise the conventions of social fiction. One of the main generic influences is that of the character sketch, often used in Wells's mimetic fiction, for example, in "A Catastrophe" (1895) or "The Purple Pileus" (1896), and to be found also in his antimimetic fiction, as in "The Flowering of the Strange Orchid" (1894) or "The Wild Asses of the Devil" (1915).

Wells's reverting to the seventeenth-century genre of character sketch, sometimes called "the character" (Cuddon 1982: 110-12) or the "story of character" (Abrams 1981: 286) implies coming back to its standard function of "charactery," namely "expression of thought by symbols or characters" ("character" sub-entry "charactery" in *New Shorter* 1973; Cuddon 1982: 110-12). Wells's human figures seem to follow the ancient idea "that man in little was an embodiment of the universe". There may also be a trace of Francis Bacon's reshaping of the above thought to be found in *Advancement of Learning* (1605), where he stated that "man was *microcosmus*, an abstract or model of the world". Moreover, Wells's short stories might be taken as reshaping the ideas of Sir Walter Raleigh who stated "[...] because in the little frame of man's body there is a representation of the Universal; and (by allusion) a kind of participation of all the parts there, therefore was man called *Microcosmos*, or the little World" (the above passages quoted after Cuddon 1982: 111).

In "The Crystal Egg", the convention of the confrontation with the other world, typical of fantastic fiction, is functionalised within the convention of character sketch to redynamise the traditional presentation of internal and external limitations of the individual's life. In this way, the short story reveals the application of Wells's staple artistic construct based on the juxtaposition between the inherently incongruent pattern of the so called Wells's "little man" (shaped in much the same way as in the mimetic fiction) and the grandness of what happens to him. Wells's character type is named so by the critics after the quotation from "The Purple Pileus" describing the unexpectedly successful Mr Coombes as an "absurd little man" (Wells 1998: 215). Some scholars see it as heavily influenced by Wells's novelistic character Mr Kipps (Colmer 1983: 17). It is worth noting that what the criticism started to call Wells's "little man" (Parrinder 1977: 58), came to be used to define a whole type of Edwardian characters (Colmer 1983: 17). The short stories of that period are linked by the common tendency to present outsider figures at the moment of their characteristic isolated experience (Harris 1979: 109) in the way which is represented by Mr Cave of "The Crystal Egg".

The predominant role of Wells's conflicted character pattern can be seen in the foregrounded plots of character's social conflict in the quasi-documentary world of the short story, the perspective on which is modified by the vision they get. Before the description of Cave's confrontation with the alien world, "The Crystal Egg" builds suggestive details of the protagonist's emotional domestic situation, reminiscent of the cases of protagonists in "The Purple Pileus" and "A Catastrophe". The suspenseful opening is built round the suggestive plot of a tussle over the potential sale of the titular crystal egg. This is combined with the plot of domestic drama involving typical characters like the henpecked husband, the overbearing wife and displeased step-children who squabble over money and social ambitions. The plot clearly deploys tragic overtones tinged with the conventional element of humour (Frye 1969: 225). The text constructs the situation of implicit pressure, sketching the conflict between the spouses by means of foregrounding Cave's emotional reactions. The pressure for the crystal egg to be sold, which Mr Cave tries to prevent and thus assert his mastery of the house, leaves him "greatly perturbed", "without excessive assurance asserting his right" to decide about it (Wells 1998: 268).

The individualising approach to character structure can be seen in the focus on the central character's state, which makes his portrait idiosyncratic. The text precisely names his physical and psychological reactions: "his agitation" becomes "painful" and "the poor little man [is] quivering with emotion". The emotional disturbance of the character is expressed by ample mimetic details like the lost control over his speech: he "muddle[s] himself between his stories", gives "wretched" answers and he can only "mumble weak assertions that he [knows] his business best" (Wells 1998: 268-269).

The two-sided plot of family-business conflict is realised against the background suggestive of family privacy, which foregrounds the conventionally realised narrator's omniscience. The third-person narrator demonstrates full insight into the situation, as indicated by the description of minute details. Thus he specifies the stage of eating the meal, the colour of the ears and the position of the tears: "[t]hey drove him from his half-eaten supper into the shop, to close it for the night, his ears aflame and tears of vexation behind his spectacles" (Wells 1998: 269). All these techniques of verifying the conflict by detailed description work to build the story of Cave as an individual. This unique quality of the situation is yet used as the tensional counterpoint to the technique for generalisation. Cave's conflict is universalised by the principle of analogy and contrast attained by the confrontation of the world of domesticity (represented as mimetic) with the Martian reality. Cave gains insight into this strange world precisely by means of the unassuming, yet fantastic, object: the crystal egg.

The structuring of Mr Cave as a character is also strongly rooted in the principle of incongruence of features. The generalised perspective on this initially individualised man is introduced within the framework of apparently consistent verisimilitude, which is gradually fractured by the elements implying inconsistency in composition. An example of such a strategy is the principle of incongruence applied to the shaping of the dubious scientist figure of Mr Wace who is shaped as Mr Cave's counterpart. The pattern of contradiction applied on the level of characterisation of the two scientists becomes here a self-referential marker of textuality. The nature of the quasi-scientific discourse in Wells's text is deliberately undermined by the imperfectly asserted professional profile of the scientist characters. It is precisely through the figure of a scientist, conventionally used for *vreisemblance*, that Wells manages to fracture the quasi-documentary framework of the short story. For all the apparent consistency attained by the generic techniques of verisimilitude, it is the inconsistent combination of character features which becomes the means of advertising the nature of a literary construct in Wells's works.

In "The Crystal Egg", the technique of verisimilitude, applied in order to authenticate the text as a report of a scientific experiment, is deliberately destabilised through the principle of incongruence. The major factor of this self-referential aspect of the text is the system of parallelisms and contrasts which reorients the short story's focus from the picture of the fantastic world, onto the picture of Cave's domestic situation. The convention of the report of a scientific discovery is clearly built in juxtaposition to the plot of domestic drama concerning Mr Cave's persecution. The conflict developed within the formula of a character sketch, and redynamised by the plot of fantastic-fiction discovery of the unknown world, is the dominant one as indicated by the short story's resolution focused on Cave's mysterious disappearance. However, both the assurance of the quasi-scientific discovery and the techniques of authenticating the report also reveal their nature of rhetorical devices by their inherent flaws which reveal the meta-conventional orientation.

The suggestion of Cave's quasi-scientific background, which is signalled by the information of his deliveries of live creatures for some other experiments, creates the reader's expectation for reliability of his procedures. However, typically of Wells's tensional style, this aspect of Cave's characterisation is undermined by commenting on his lack of competence. The figure of the other pseudo-scientist, Mr Wace, is seemingly introduced with the primary function of authenticating the procedures. His professional stance is amply characterised with the apparent intention to guarantee the reliability of the scientific procedures undertaken in the observation of the Martian reality. The style adopted for the relation also reinforces the understanding that Mr Wace is a proper scientific figure. However, while Wace's professional attitude is repeatedly stressed in the text, it is clearly established as such only by means of contrasting it with the approach of Mr Cave which is described as that of a layman. Along with suggesting the reliability of the characters, the short story simultaneously undermines this principle. The two men's scientific capacity as a team of investigators is weakened where it seems to be reinforced through the meticulous focus on their procedures. The incongruities in the semantics of descriptions are functional in activating the characters' dubious stance in the text.

Wells's technique of undermining operates on many levels, including the syntactic level of the text. Mr Cave's interest is declared to be just "a transient revival of the scientific curiosity" (Wells 1998: 272), with the word "transient" working to challenge the implication of the phrase it modifies. Wace's characterisation is likewise strung between the directly argued reliability of his stance and the meagreness of his post. The pattern of semantic and syntactic juxtapositions is a central technique in destabilising senses. Adopting the inherently undermined motif of expertise functions here as a marker of the "tall story" which foregrounds its artistic pattern through the principle of incongruence (Bayley 1987: 317; Baldick 2001: 247). Wace's formalised lengthy introduction as "Mr Jacoby Wace, Assistant Demonstrator at St Catherine's Hospital, Westbourne Street" (Wells 1998: 271) is tensionally strung between the surface argument of the grandness of his post and the undercurrent implication of the meagreness of his position as not even an independent demonstrator.

The tensional twisting of character roles is particularly vivid as it is Wace who coordinates Mr Cave's observation, while the latter, despite being the one who sees everything, is treated as though he was an assistant who is guided in his actions. Such a structure of inter-dependence belies the narrator's surface argument of the team's systematic approach and reveals the quality of textual manipulation. Evidently the "trick" which is mentioned in the context of the experiment description works as the self-referential hint of the textual trick on the reader (Wells 1998: 275).

Wells's techniques of destabilising the character structure are applied to the figures of scientists so as to work as self-reflexive elements of Wells's short story. They transpose the function of these characters from the mimetic element of the fictional world into the thematic sphere suggesting the figure of an artist. This technique is not restricted to the fantastic short stories with the quasi-scientific motivation like "The Crystal Egg". Such equivalence can also be demonstrated in the case of the professional profile of the protagonist in "The Triumphs of a Taxidermist" (1894). The same technique is applied in shaping the central characters of inventors whose creative acts become the means of contact with the fantastic worlds, such as the Time Traveller in "The Time Machine" (1895) and Dr Nebogipfel in "The Chronic Argonauts" (1888).

Wells's technique of accumulating incongruent details draws attention to the central role of the pattern which dominates the individualised presentation. The system of congruence and incongruence of motifs is reinforced through the two-world structure. Cave's involvement in the visions of Mars offered by the egg is made psychologically plausible by his need for escaping from the family pressure. However, in spite of idealisation of Martian reality, which is realised through its contrast with the space of the shop, the fantastic world is also implied to be the space of oppressiveness. The fantastic world is incongruent, being first patterned as a paradise-like space, only to become the alter-image of Cave's oppressive domestic situation. This becomes apparent when the salesman observes what is represented as the Martian creatures' attack upon the ape-like creatures – in a scene reminiscent of the wife's attack upon Mr Cave. It is noticeable that the text attains a balance between the juxtaposed and mutually-complementary conventions of characterisation proper for fantastic fiction (character's wonder at the fantastic world) and domestic drama (characterisation through domestic conflict), which are used so as to reciprocally redynamise one another and attain the distinctive Wellsian combination of tensional elements in the world and character structure.

In "The Crystal Egg", the plot of Mr Cave's engagement with the vision of Martian reality is featured by the principle of contrast with that of domestic subjugation, while it is also built on the principle of parallelism with the conflict in the world presented as mimetic. This is attained by the prominent patterning of descriptive detail. What is readily apparent is the dual application of motifs connected with looking and with aggression both in the mimetic and fantastic realities. Wells applies here the horror-fiction device of suggesting the quality of "supernatural powers and threatening malice" through the focus on the face (Grixti 1989: 13). In Wells's case it is reinforced by the principle of parallelism. In both realities, the text suggests the interconnection of some scenes through similar lexical choices. One cannot fail to notice the parallelism in the description of Mrs Cave's spying on Mr Cave and the description of the Martian creature peering into his domestic situation.

The motifs of aggression are suggestive enough for certain expectations to be raised, while the resolution is made indefinite. This technique foregrounds the schematic features of Wells's plot patterns. The short stories typically signal some incongruent generic plot patterns, which become juxtaposed to suggest some new qualities emerging from the juxtaposition, while the resolutions typically remain inconclusive. It is not entirely clear what happens to the Time Traveller in "The Time Machine" or to Elstead, the protagonist of "In the Abyss", on their last journeys. What Cave saw through the egg is likewise left unresolved, just as his ultimate fate is left uncertain. Ambiguity is thus foregrounded though the tensional use of motifs which are suggestive but inconclusive in the poetically opalescent way, in the sense identified by Roman Jakobson in "Closing Statement: Linguistics and Poetics" (1986: 69).

Wells's unique artistic construct in his fantastic short stories with quasi-scientific motivation, as represented by "The Crystal Egg", is clearly the tensional composition of seemingly discrepant elements. The belittled character structure of the protagonist from the mimetic world clashes with the incommensurable features of the fantastic world he faces. Wells's character patterns should indeed be seen as the reflection of the mood of decadence of his times, which found expression in questioning the fixed perspective on reality through the principles of rhetoric. They are also marked by the way the flawed and belittled character profile is used to underlie the mood of "discontinuity and isolation" emblematic of the 1890s (Harris 1979: 108-9). Wells's tensional character structure can be thus treated as the typical turn-of-the-century tendency for "working out reasoned typologies of structures and trying to account for 'deviations from the norm'" (Brooke-Rose 1981: 3).

Wells's emphasis on structure over characterisation can also be viewed as the feature of the turn-of-the century writers (Scheick 1994: 28). William J. Scheick makes an important observation of the common duality in the approach to character in the nineteenth-century fiction, strung between individuality and typicality. This duality is present not only in Wells's fiction but also in texts separated from his by a literary epoch, such as George Eliot's *Adam Bede* (1859) or Thomas Hardy's *Tess of the d'Urbervilles* and *Jude the Obscure* (1895). The critic indicates its presence in Robert Louis Stevenson, Oscar Wilde, Galsworthy and Bennett. The scholar yet observes that the particular objective of such duality is slightly different for each author. He also notes that through applying characterisation in terms of a type the authors achieve an enlarged perspective on characters, which becomes a premise for ambiguity (Scheick 1990: 36-37).

The artistic quality of Wells's texts, as representative of the general artistic tendencies in the whole turn-of-the-century fiction, can also be seen through this technique of ambiguity which projects an active role for the reader in Wells's fantastic short fiction. Such a role of the reader is necessitated by the open quality of the fantastic world and the techniques of narrative instability (Rimmon-Kenan 1983: 118-20). Scheick makes a point that with the subordination of the typical characters to the structure of a fictional work, the text invites the implied reader to complete the character's "open" quality expressed through the character's "representativeness" and simultaneous "incompleteness". Scheick quotes a remark by Woolf who stated that the reader must "finish them [turn-of-the-century characters], actively and practically, for himself". The scholar also relates such techniques to the methods of allegory (Scheick 1990: 38). Wells's approach consists in showing the individualised character in terms of some schematised features of a type. It is enhanced by applying the principles of incoherence, spatio-temporal patterning of fantastic type and repetition in characterisation. All these techniques are employed within the genre of the character sketch. They are the features defining the author's literary objectives. While these traits of Wells's writing are the reason why Woolf included him in the observation that "The Edwardians were never interested in character itself" (1966: 328), it seems that this critically influential judgement needs a reservation. As we have seen on the example of "The Crystal Egg", the convention of the character sketch applied within the precepts of fantastic fiction enables Wells to use character as an artistic constituent of the literary work of art. He shapes his characters in the way which implicitly advertises his literary goals.

Reconstructing the Gothic villain:
Shirley Jackson's *The Haunting of Hill House*[1]

MARTA KOMSTA

> I am like a small creature swallowed whole by a
> monster, she thought, and the monster feels my tiny
> little movements inside.
>
> Shirley Jackson, *The Haunting of Hill House*

Regarded as one of the staple twentieth century ghost fictions, Shirley Jackson's 1959 novel *The Haunting of Hill House* recounts the tragic fate of Eleanor Vance, a young woman who takes part in a disastrous research project of an ill-reputed mansion[2]. The narrative's central plot revolves around a field study of the eponymous Hill House led by one doctor John Montague, an academic and a stern believer in the existence of the supernatural, who embarks upon an in-depth investigation aided by a group of individuals he has invited to the endeavour on account of their more or less subdued psychic abilities[3]. One of them is Eleanor

---

1   The research for this contribution was financed by Maria Curie-Skłodowska University/Faculty of Humanities grant no. MPK: BS-05-0000-D012, ZFIN: 000 000 40.
2   Interestingly, the novel was filmed twice: the first adaptation, *The Haunting* (dir. Robert Wise, 1963, starring Julie Harris and Claire Bloom) was universally praised by the viewers and critics (including Shirley Jackson herself). The other film of the same title (dir. Jan de Bont, 1999, starring Lily Taylor and Catherine Zeta Jones) met scathing reception mainly due its action-oriented screenplay and the overblown use of the CGI effects.
3   The exception being here Luke Sanders, who joins the team because of this familial situation: he is the legal heir to Hill House. Apart from that, Theodora/Theo (no surname of this character is given in the novel) has confirmed telepathic abilities and Eleanor was involved in a telekinetic incident in the form of a shower of stones that fell upon her family home when she was only twelve. Doctor Montague suspects that Eleanor is responsible for the supernatural occurrence. The inclusion of the incident in the novel

Vance who sees doctor Montague's offer as a chance for changing her drab urban existence. For Eleanor, Hill House becomes something more than just a site of supernatural phenomena – it becomes a promise of a new life altogether. "During the whole underside of her life, ever since her first memory, Eleanor had been waiting for something like Hill House", we learn at the beginning of the novel (Jackson 2006: 7). Intriguingly, as the text makes clear soon enough, Hill House seems to have been waiting for Eleanor as well. At the generic level, Jackson's narrative employs numerous Gothic conventions: its very plot is focused upon the fate of a hapless heroine imprisoned within a haunted house, here a rendition of a Gothic castle. In her struggle to uphold sanity, the female protagonist (Eleanor) succumbs to the machinations of the narrative's villain (Hill House), despite the attempts of the quasi-detective character of a ghost hunter (doctor John Montague) who eventually fails to rescue the heroine from the clutches of the evil-infested mansion. Unsurprisingly, such conflation of the formulaic premises invites some major plot- and character-related perturbations, infusing the classic tale of a haunted house with implications of a psychological nature. As a result, the reader's attention is drawn to the relationship developed between the novel's anguished heroine and the eponymous Hill House that functions in the novel in the double role of both the setting and the main villain.

The precarious bond poses multiple questions, particularly in the department of "hows" and "whys", yielding to a multitude of critical interpretations as well as instigating discussions as to the generic status of Jackson's novel. Darryl Hattenhauer, for instance, sees the novel as Jackson's "fullest development of the house as a metaphor for the disunified subject" (2003:155) with Eleanor being an innately "disintegrated protagonist" (2003: 159) – the features perceived by the critic as typical of proto-postmodernism[4]. For Stephen King, an ardent fan of Jack-

---

led some critics to assume that Eleanor herself is responsible for all the phenomena taking place in Hill House. However intriguing, such a possibility is never explicitly confirmed in the text, the suggestion being rather that Eleanor heightened preternatural abilities combined with her fragile mental state make her an easy prey for the evil that dwells within the House.

4   Hattenhauer defines proto-postmodernism as "late modernist writing that shows traits of what will become postmodernism", the mode including themes such as "divided subject, the seeming chaos of events, the incongruity of institutions, the undecidability of current epistemes, and the intertextuality of signification" (2003: 2).

son's fiction, Eleanor Vance is "surely the finest character to come out of [the] new American gothic tradition" (King 2006: 297-298) in which "the psyche is given priority over the society" as "the weakling characters struggle with narcissism, which often destroys others as well as themselves" (Parks 2005: 240)[5]. Still, the label that has been most steadfastly attached to Jackson's classic is that of a stellar representative of the Female Gothic, a term originally coined by Ellen Moers in her study *Literary Women* (1976) signifying works that "women writers have done in the literary mode that [...] we have called 'the Gothic'" (quoted in Smith and Wallace 2009: 1). Over the years, the term has been considerably nuanced, and eventually associated with texts that deal with "the central character's troubled identification with her good/bad/dead/mad mother, whom she ambivalently seeks to kill or merge with; and her imprisonment in a house, that, mirroring her disturbed imagination, expresses her ambivalent experience of entrapment and longing for protection" (Rubinstein 2005: 130). As it happens, the said definition accounts for the prevalent psychoanalytical interpretation of the novel, according to which the relationship between Eleanor and Hill House reflects the one the protagonist had with her dead mother[6].

---

5   The generic umbrella of the new American gothic was put forward by Irving Malin and later, John G. Parks as a literary convention that, apart from the features mentioned in the main text, "employs a microcosm, with love as a primary concern", the said microcosm being in most cases family. Traditional Gothic elements such as the castle/house, the double etc. "function now as images of narcissistic love and antagonism". "Nearly all journeys end in failure of disaster", Parks writes, "[t]he narcissism of the character intensifies their isolation and loneliness, creating a kind of vicious self-destructive cycle" (2005: 240). Stephen King perceives Malin and Parks' approach as a change from the usual interpretation of the so-called Bad Place (the castle vel the haunted house) as a womb symbolizing sexual insecurity to the more general category of fear. The haunted house then would indicate here "not [...] sexual interests and fear of sex but interests in the self and fear of the self" (King 2006: 297).

6   Rubinstein's extensive psychoanalytical examination of Jackson's novels is based upon Claire Kahane's influential analysis of the Female Gothic, *The Gothic Mirror*, in which she approaches Jackson's novel as the staple representative of the genre. "What I see repeatedly locked into the forbidden center of the Gothic [...] is the spectral presence of a dead-undead mother", Kahane writes, "archaic and all-encompassing, a ghost signifying the problematic of femininity which the heroine must confront" (1985: 336). According to her interpretation, the major antagonist to the Female Gothic heroine is "the spectral mother" (343) and the protagonist's "active exploration of the Gothic house in which she is trapped is also an exploration of her relation to the maternal body that she

Yet, the heavy metaphorical load invested in the figure of the House seems somewhat to obscure the basic assumption that might be derived from Jackson's work: that Hill House is first and foremost a character in a contemporary re-appropriation of a Gothic romance, a villain extraordinaire endowed with powers of scheming that allow it to manipulate the protagonist into submission and ultimately, to consume her[7]. Appropriately, what underpins Jackson's text is the generic subversion of the Gothic schemata that tends to be overlooked by the majority of critics writing about the novel. It is all too common to approach Eleanor solely in psychological terms since this protagonist, although remarkably pliable in such a context, has much more to offer in terms of character complexity that comes into the limelight as a result of Eleanor's relationship with Hill House. This particular case of character interdependence is correlated with the overall approach adopted in this analysis, a rhetorical examination of the intra-character parasitism that lies at the core of Jackson's novel.

James Phelan's rhetorical approach, as outlined in the Introduction, defines the literary character in terms of three components: mimetic, thematic and synthetic (Phelan 1989: 3). It is the synthetic function – defining the character as a construct – which seems of primary importance

---

shares […]" (Kahane 1985: 338). Also, Judith Newman makes a piercing assertion when she states that Jackson's novel is based upon "the dynamics of mother-daughter relation with its attendant motifs of psychic annihilation, reabsorption by the mother, vexed individuation, dissolution of individual ego boundaries, terror of separation and the attempted reproduction of the symbiotic bond through close female friendship" (Newman 2005: 171-172).

7   Hattenhauer, for instance, writes that "[i]n the modern fantastic, the referent is not a ghost but the unconscious. The mode is, then, allegorical. There is no haunted house; Eleanor haunts herself, or rather the traces of history make one part of herself haunt the Other part – the conscious being Other to the real home of the subject: the unconscious". For Hattenhauer, the existence of a ghost within Hill House is disputable as it is Eleanor who "frightens the other characters with her pounding and giggling" (2003: 172). Bernice M. Murphy also seems to share the view stating that "this is a ghost story in which no ghosts actually appear" (2005:11). Such interpretations, while stimulating and opening new vents for discussion on Jackson's novel, seem however to misread the narrative which rather straightforwardly points to the existence of the supernatural within Hill House. Depriving Hill House of a ghost would deny the entire catalyst for Eleanor's transformation as well as necessitate omitting certain valid clues as to the supernatural, such as doctor Montague's statement that "the evil is the house itself" which "has enchained and destroyed people and their lives […]" (Jackson 2006: 82).

here. By consistently uncovering the thematic foundations of the main female protagonist, the House is responsible for the synthetic shift occurring at the end of the novel in which Eleanor is revealed to be the actual Other in the House, finally devoured by her tormentor. Therefore, I want to argue that the synthetic/thematic resonance within the character of Eleanor Vance constitutes the driving force of the novel's progression as Eleanor's thematic transformation is furthered by the synthetic metamorphosis (a heroine turned into a villain). The conflux of generic and interpretative ambiguities associated with Eleanor Vance marks Jackson's novel as one of the most disturbing examples of the Female Gothic in which the character's gradual self-awareness is made possible through the recognition of her own failings. In other words, by accommodating the monster that dwells in the haunted house, the female protagonist accommodates the monster within herself[8].

*

The first stage of the novel's progression functions as mimetic-cum-synthetic overture to the story to follow: the Gothic heroine (Eleanor Vance), the villain (Hill House) and the supporting cast of characters are introduced to the authorial audience, which, according to Phelan's definition accepted here, is able to "pick up on all the signals in the appropriate way" (1989: 5). The mimetic dimensions of the characters are foregrounded in the first two chapters[9]. Along with the two main protagonists, we thus have doctor Montague, the leader of the group ("careful and conscientious") (Jackson 2006: 5); Theo, the narrative's tongue-in-cheek take on *femme fatale* (passionate, but also irresponsible and egoistic) and Luke Sanders, the supposed rascal ("a liar" and "a thief") (Jackson 2006: 9). At the same time, the chapters in question draw the readers' attention to mimetic and thematic correspondences between Eleanor and Hill House that highlight the narrative's ambiguous generic status. The opening act of mimetic transposition in which the building is en-

---

8   Hattenhauer also notices that Eleanor is not "pure innocence" despite the fact that as a character she "recuperates the victimized heroines of eighteenth-century sentimental novels" (Hattenhauer 2003: 157).

9   Mimetic dimensions are "a character's attributes considered as traits" while "mimetic functions result from the way these traits are used together in creating the illusion of a plausible person and [...] in making particular traits relevant to later actions, including of course the development of new traits" (Phelan 1989: 11).

dowed with character-like qualities is introduced through tension developed in the first two sentences of the narrative. The house, although "not sane", comprises of elements which nevertheless highlight its apparent 'saneness'. We have then "upright" walls, "neatly" structured bricks, "firm" floors, doors which are "sensibly shut and "steadily" present silence (Jackson 2006: 3). The discrepancy occurring in the very first paragraph of the novel is an important indication of the overriding quality of the house: by infusing the place with human (and therefore often conflicted) attributes, we are given to understand that the house possesses human features. The discord between the description of the house ("not sane") and the following elements that accentuate exactly the opposite, constitutes a powerful introductory suggestion of its characteristics: by a series of contrasting mimetic attributes we are led to believe that Hill House is actually what Phelan terms as "a meeting place of many predicates" (Phelan 1989: 4), indicating its plausibility as a person of rather shaky psychological foundations who nevertheless strives to uphold a guise of sanity.

The second section in Chapter 1 begins with an equally complex description of the novel's central human protagonist, Eleanor Vance, whose mimetic attributes immediately dismantle any assumptions of generic conventionality as well as allow for some interesting conclusions about the implied affinity between this particular character and Hill House:

> Eleanor Vance was thirty-two years old when she came to Hill House. The only person in the world she genuinely hated, now that her mother was dead, was her sister. She disliked her brother-in-law and her five-year-old niece, and she had no friends. This was owing largely to the eleven years she had spent caring for her invalid mother, which had left her with some proficiency as a nurse and an inability to face strong sunlight without blinking. She could not remember ever being truly happy in her adult life; her years with her mother had been built up devotedly around small guilts and small reproaches, constant weariness, and unending despair. Without ever wanting to become reserved and shy, she had spent so long alone, with no one to love, that it was difficult for her to talk, even casually, to another person without self-consciousness and an awkward inability to find words. (Jackson 2006: 5-6)

Eleanor's mimetic dimensions are based here almost exclusively on the protagonist's mental faculties: she is plagued by "constant weariness" and "unending despair", which leads to the protagonist being "reserved and shy". Also emphasised here is Eleanor's strong feeling of hatred towards the members of her own family (mother and sister), a mimetic-thematic dimension that accentuates the connection between Eleanor's hostility towards her family and her role of a child exploited as a giver[10]. The resulting tension between the protagonist's preordained function of the Gothic damsel in distress and the intensely negative emotions that torment her alerts the authorial audience to the complexity of this particular protagonist and her uncertain synthetic function with relation to the Gothic convention recognizable in the narrative. In effect, we cannot be entirely certain whether we are dealing with a miserable heroine or perhaps a character of far greater (and more sinister) complexity.

Thus, the purpose of juxtaposing the two opening paragraphs is to make the authorial audience aware of two things: that there is definitely *something* inherently wrong with Hill House and that *something* is not entirely right about Eleanor Vance either. Bearing in mind the high level of generic self-reflexivity of Jackson's novel, it should be apparent that these particular passages are intended to introduce the villain and the heroine, though not without a question mark in the case of Eleanor. The mimetic-thematic affinity established between Eleanor and Hill House (since both are presented as devastatingly lonely and incapable of sustaining any relationship with the outside world) is also a vital clue for the authorial audience to follow. Apparently, there is much more to be expected from the relationship between Eleanor and the House than the conventional victim-villain distinction.

It becomes clear then that the novel's progression is initially fuelled by the tension between the authorial audience's assumption as to the generic status of the female protagonist and her actual behaviour that effectively counteracts the synthetic presuppositions. What follows, the hints pointing to Eleanor's problematic synthetic status appear at the beginning of the novel through a series of instabilities that seem to pave the character's way towards Hill House[11]: she quarrels with her sister over

---

10   The thematic dimensions are "attributes [...] viewed as vehicles to express ideas" (Phelan 1989: 12).

11   Instabilities are defined by Phelan as "occurring within the story [...] between the characters, created by situations, and complicated and resolved through actions" while tensions are "created by the discourse [...] between authors and/or narrators, on the one hand, and the authorial audience on the other" (1989: 15).

the ownership of the car (which she later steals in order to get to the House upon the invitation from doctor Montague), she bumps into an elderly lady who first scolds Eleanor and then half-mockingly promises to pray for her, which is followed by a rather awkward exchange of information with the locals at the town of Hillsdale where the House is situated and ends with a confrontation with the guardian at the gate, old servant Dudley, who initially refuses to let her in[12]. In the meantime we observe Eleanor indulging in a trance-like daydreaming during her journey to Hill House, her fantasies of domestic bliss next to prince charming ("[c]oming down from the hills there will be a prince riding, bright in green and silver with a hundred bowmen riding before him, pennants stirring, horses tossing, jewels flashing") disclosing the protagonist's interrelated feelings of solitude and homelessness (Jackson 2006: 20)[13]. In result, Eleanor's continuous clashes with other people on her fantasy-filled journey towards the House are supposed to alert the authorial audience to some of her mimetic and thematic dimensions that appear to contradict her supposed synthetic dimension. Jackson's Gothic heroine-to-be comes across as surprisingly whimsical and self-conscious, prone to self-delusion and not devoid of narcissism, eliciting our ambiguous reaction of pity and empathy[14]. Thematic-wise, Eleanor is an implied victim of her upbringing, an isolated and unhappy child forced to enact the role of a guardian.

---

12 Darryl Hattenhauer argues that the novel's plot can be related to Joseph Campbell's convention of the monomyth in what becomes a parody of "the archetypical hero journey" (Hattenhauer 2003: 172).

13 Laura Miller observes that "Eleanor's fantasies serve as a bulwark against the actuality of her life, the grim years she spent at the beck and call of a failing, miserable mother and later, at her sister's house, the sad cot in the baby's room. Even after her mother's death, Eleanor has been relegated to the nursery, bossed around and kept on a short leash. Her identification with the likes of Cinderella and Sleeping Beauty makes a certain sense; she's had an unloving family who consigned her to menial labor and refused to let her grow up. Eleanor is drifting in and out of a dream state even before she arrives at Hill House, endlessly taking apart and reassembling bits of fantasy and experience to fashion the imagined life she hopes eventually to live" (Miller 2006: 2)

14 Some critics suggest that narcissism is the defining mimetic attribute of Eleanor (Stephen King and Laura Miller, for example). I may add that Eleanor's self-obsession is based upon the protagonist's self-consciousness and sense of inadequacy. Eleanor focuses upon herself because she herself has never been the focus of anyone else.

However, the novel's core instability is established between Eleanor and Hill House, its all-encompassing aspect highlighted during the protagonist's first encounter with the House in Chapter 2. It is a dramatic moment ("an atavistic turn in the pit of the stomach") which furthers the authorial audience's ambivalent approach towards Eleanor as the victim-type of a character (Jackson 2006: 35). Especially that the House is described as a quasi-human monstrosity: there is "evil in the face of a house" emphasised by "a watchfulness from the blank windows and a touch of glee in the eyebrow of a cornice" (Jackson 2006: 34) – the mimetic make-up pointing here to the synthetic function of the character as the novel's villain. In the light of such suggestions, Eleanor's reaction after the initial shock seems puzzling, to say the least, indicating another important tension emerging between the protagonist and the authorial audience:

> It was an act of moral strength to lift her foot and set it on the bottom step, and she thought that her deep unwillingness to touch Hill House for the first time came directly from the vivid feeling that it was waiting for her, evil, but patient. Journeys end in lovers meeting, she thought, remembering her song at last, and laughed, standing on the steps of Hill House, journeys end in lovers meeting, and she put her feet down firmly and went up to the veranda and the door. Hill House came around her in a rush; she was enshadowed, and the sound of her feet on the wood of the veranda was an outrage in the utter silence, as though it had been a very long time since feet stamped across the boards of Hill House. She brought her hand up to the heavy iron knocker that had a child's face, determined to make more noise and yet more, so that Hill House might be very sure she was there. (Jackson 2006: 34-35)

As Eleanor bursts out laughing when she crosses the threshold, the tension, accentuated by the reverberating Shakespearean line ("Journeys end in lovers meeting"), suggests a blossoming intimacy between the heroine and the villain, an uneasy relationship that will have its impact upon the synthetic function of the female protagonist. Thus, although Eleanor is aware of the malign personality of the House, she remains oblivious to what the authorial audience is now made fully cognizant of: that her stay in Hill House will irrevocably change the protagonist, and, most certainly, it will be a change for the worse.

The protagonist's strange behaviour at the threshold of the haunted mansion heralds the change in the narrative's development. Henceforth, the progression is going to be propelled by Eleanor's futile attempts to maintain the disguise of an independent, will-do type of a character, the ensuing events demonstrating the gradual foregrounding of her thematic component (the tension resulting from the synthetic discrepancy being at that time relegated into the background). With the arrival of the other characters in Chapter 3, Eleanor decides to reconstruct herself by inventing an entirely fictitious autobiography with the purpose of maintaining an intricately woven illusion of her very own self.[15] The characters begin a parlour game by playfully adopting different roles as a 'cast' in a horror story; for Eleanor it is the role of "an artist's model" who lives "a mad abandoned life, draped in a shawl and going from garret to garret" (Jackson 2006: 61). During her later conversation with Theodora, despite providing some facts (such as recounting her role as a carer for her mother), she quickly turns to confabulation, inventing an entirely new home for herself[16]. "I have a little place of my own", she tells Theodora, "[a]n apartment, like yours, only I live alone. I'm still furnishing it [...] to make sure I get everything absolutely right. [...] Everything has to be exactly the way I want it, because there's only me to use it [...]" (Jackson 2006: 88). And since we know that Eleanor lives with her sister's family (her domestic situation is described in Chapter 1), her lie functions as the protagonist's attempt to create new mimetic and thematic dimensions: Eleanor wants to be perceived as a confident woman living independently on her own. The tension appearing as a result of the rift

---

15   As Andrew Smith observes, "Eleanor is enthralled by the prospect of fashioning an identity which is free from her mother's influence" (2009: 154) providing as an example a scene that appears later in the same Chapter in which Eleanor admires her own feet stating that she is "a complete and separate thing [...], individually an I, possessed of attributes belonging only to me". However, soon enough, "[t]he promised freedoms of the house are ultimately challenged by her unconscious projection of her mother which suggests that she is unable to free herself from the past" (Smith 2009: 154).

16   Tricia Lootens argues that the research group attempts to "play at being a family" (2005: 150) with Hill House offering only "delusions of family" for those who are brave enough to become its guests (2005: 159). Indeed, the novel abounds in details pointing to the innately subversive approach to the notions of domesticity. There is a child's face on the main doors and the Hill House phantom frequently disguises itself as a child, including the ghastly picnic with "the children [...] and a puppy" that Theo and Eleanor see during their stroll around the House (Jackson 2006: 177). On the other hand, Luke Sanders, for instance, describes the House as "motherly," unaware of the ominous aspect such a description has for Eleanor (Jackson 2006: 209). For further information, see Lootens and Newman.

between her 'new' and 'old' life points again to the self-delusory aspect of her personality: Eleanor wants to restructure herself, believing that she is capable of changing her life at will.

Soon enough, Eleanor's domestic fantasy is countered with the biography of the novel's major antagonist as doctor Montague gives his companions a detailed account of the history behind Hill House. The juxtaposition of Eleanor's fake reminiscences and the story behind Hill House foregrounds the House's synthetic function of the protagonist's *doppelganger*: despite Eleanor's attempt at reconstruction, the biography of Hill House immediately reveals to the audience the *real* story of Eleanor Vance by allowing the audience to make associations between Eleanor and the hapless women that were destroyed by the ominous mansion. As doctor Montague explains, Hill House was erected eighty years earlier by one Hugh Crain, a man whose company proved to be as ill-boding as that of his house: his three wives met premature death while his two daughters, raised in the mansion, eventually clashed over the ownership of the House. The quarrel was decided in favour of the elder sibling who came to live and die within Hill House. Doctor Montague recounts that "the older sister died of pneumonia […] in the house, with only the little companion to help her – there were stories later of a doctor called too late, of the old lady lying neglected upstairs while the younger woman dallied in the garden with some village lout" (Jackson 2006: 78). The following lawsuit between the maid and the younger Crain sister concerning the ownership of the House was resolved in favour of the former. The court victory did not, however, bring any good fortune to the winning party: the new proprietor of Hill House committed suicide by hanging herself in the turret of the House.

Significantly, the story of the conflict between the Crain sisters reflects Eleanor's animosity towards her own sibling: just like the dispossessed younger daughter of Hugh Crain, she too is essentially homeless. The fate of the unwary guardian, on the other hand, functions as a premonition of Eleanor's fate, as the authorial audience is asked to draw informed predictions concerning Eleanor's immediate future in the haunted house.

The similarities between Eleanor and the former inhabitants of Hill House function then as the set-up of the events to follow, emphasising those elements that will become particularly significant in the protago-

nist's thematic make-up. Therefore, when the group decides to explore
the mansion in Chapter 4, the two specific areas within Hill House – the
library and the nursery – activate Eleanor's thematic dimensions connected with her mother[17]. The library carries powerful thematic potential
as it is the place where the negligent servant girl to the older Crain sister
committed suicide, the tragic event triggering the malodorous repute of
the House. Eleanor refuses to enter the library, repelled by the smell of
"mold and earth" that pervades the room (she is the only member of the
group to sense it) and utters the words "My mother" before she steps
away from the entrance (Jackson 2006: 103). The smell of the room, indicative of a tomb, as well as Eleanor's exclamation signal the psychological strain associated with the death of the protagonist's parent. The
nursery, on the other hand, hailed by doctor Montague as "the heart of
the house", points to the corresponding thematic dimension associated
with Eleanor: her role of a mistreated child (Jackson 2006: 117). The
room adorned with macabre ornaments, has "an indefinable air of neglect found nowhere else in Hill House" (Jackson 2006: 119), emphasised by a cold spot at its threshold that Theo compares to "the doorway
of a tomb" (Jackson 2006: 117). These synthetic cues – the stench permeating the library, the cold spot and the gruesome decorations in the
nursery – enable the authorial audience to notice the thematic similarities between Eleanor's life outside the mansion (apart from being her
mother's guardian, she also sleeps in the nursery at her sister's place)
and the *unnatural* existence within the Hill House. Still, although visibly
alarmed of the mansion's unsettling features, Eleanor is not yet ready to
face the image unfolding in front of her. The distinctly funereal qualities
of both the nursery and library leave, however, little room for doubt as to
the fate of the heroine: at the end of the journey through the haunted
house, death awaits the distressed protagonist.

---

17   Critics have argued that it is entirely plausible to interpret the spatial intricacies of Hill
     House as a reflection of Eleanor's personality. Thus, it is no accident that her room has
     "an unbelievably faulty design" (Jackson 2006: 40) since the whole "clashing dishar-
     mony" of the House's architecture is correlated with Eleanor's twisted psyche as the
     confirmation the House's synthetic function (Jackson 2006: 38). In many ways, the
     House enacts the role of a carnival mirror (itself being compared by Theo to a "[c]razy
     house at the carnival"), highlighting, but, most importantly, distorting the mimetic-
     thematic dimensions of the protagonist (Jackson 2006: 105). For further information,
     see, for example, Hattenhauer.

As a coda to the first stage of thematic development, the intricacies of Eleanor's thematic component receive a dramatic emphasis in the last section of Chapter 4 in which the House openly attacks the researchers for the first time. At night the villain announces its presence with thunderous knocking upon the doors followed by a peal of "a little mad rising laugh" as the spectre walks down the mansion's corridors (Jackson 2006: 131). Eleanor wakes up to the sound of knocking convinced at first that it is her mother who requires assistance:

> "Coming, mother, coming," Eleanor said, fumbling for the light. "It's all right, I'm coming." *Eleanor*, she heard, *Eleanor*. "Coming, coming," she shouted irritably, "just a *minute*, I'm *coming*." [...]
> Then she thought, with a crashing shock which brought her awake, cold and shivering, out of bed and awake: *I am in Hill House.* [...]
> It is only a noise, and terribly cold, terribly, terribly cold. It is a noise down the hall, far down at the end, near the nursery door, and terribly cold, *not* my mother knocking on the wall. (Jackson 2006: 127)

Eleanor's frantic reaction to the supernatural presence succinctly encapsulates the major thematic dimension connected with the protagonist: a parasitic relationship between the parent and the child (the knocking on the wall that is supposed to remind us that Eleanor's mother used to knock on the wall of her room in order to get her daughter's attention) that irrevocably harms the daughter who is left defenceless (the cold) when faced with the volatile parent figure (the mocking laughter)[18]. Subsequently, the House begins to exploit Eleanor's weaknesses connected with yet unspecified psychological wound related to the protagonist's relationship with the dead mother. The abuse commences with the inexplicably appearing inscriptions that establish Eleanor as the villain's focus of interest. The first writing, "HELP ELEANOR COME HOME" appears in chalk upon the wall in one of mansion's corridors. The second one – written in blood – "HELP ELEANOR COME HOME ELEANOR" is found by Theo in her room, the gruesome liquid covering not only the wall but also the clothes of Eleanor's next-room neighbour. Eleanor's reaction is understandably that of shock and bewilderment ("It knows my name, doesn't it?") that is clearly related to the fact that Hill

---

18   "We've been clutching each other like a couple of lost children", Theo remarks after the ordeal, accentuating poignantly the thematic aspect linked to the first visitation of the Hill House phantom (Jackson 2006: 131).

House has successfully established a bond with the protagonist (Jackson 2006: 146).

Most importantly, however, the supernatural intrusions are supposed to draw the authorial audience's attention to the next stage of the novel's progression in which Eleanor's synthetic dimension of the Gothic heroine is gradually transformed into the function of the Female Gothic 'villain', a process which is actualised by the ensuing instabilities between the protagonist and the other members of the research group[19]. The notion of the heroine becoming the Other is accentuated by highlighting Eleanor's self-absorption, a mimetic trait that is largely responsible for the ruptures between the participants. When confronted with the writings on the wall, Eleanor's hysterical reaction to the implication of being somewhat responsible for the occurrence ("You think I *want* to see my name scribbled all over this foul house? You think *I* like the idea that I'm the center of attention? *I'm* not the spoiled baby, after all – *I* don't like being singled out –") exposes her wilful blindness as to the real enemy: Hill House itself (Jackson 2006: 147). Theo's direct accusation of Eleanor being the culprit provokes a surge of hatred on the part of the protagonist: "she had never felt such uncontrollable loathing for any person before" (Jackson 2006: 157). Eleanor's concealed aggression towards Theo seems to escalate almost preternaturally, as if the personality of the protagonist has undergone a radical refashioning when she expresses a desire to "hit [Theo] with a stick [...], to batter her with rocks [...]". "I hate her," the protagonist announces in her thoughts, "she sickens me [...]. I would like to watch her dying" (Jackson 2006: 158-159)[20].

---

19   I should make clear at this point that I use the inverted commas as an indication of the profound ambivalence pertaining to Eleanor's presupposed 'villainous' status. She is not therefore the villain sensu stricto (such as Hill House), but rather a character whose function is that of the inevitable Other, the transgressor of the fixed conventions.

20   It is, in fact, one of the most effectively established instabilities in the narrative in which the protagonist's mimetic attributes (hatred and resentment towards Theodora) begin to resemble those of the House's (which was, after all, described in Chapter 1 as "arrogant" and "hating"), contributing to the mistrust towards the protagonist among other group members. The relationship between Eleanor and Theodora also bears all the markings of a passive-dominant type of a bond in which Eleanor is from the outset placed as the 'weaker' personality, a 'child' continuously patronised by the more assertive partner. Hattenhauer sees Theodora as "the projection of Eleanor's denied self", embodying her "repressed eroticism and assertiveness" (2003: 163). Tricia Lootens also perceives Theo as "Eleanor's mirror image, an image of the kind of woman Eleanor is

Later, when Luke confesses to Eleanor that he never had a mother, the heroine's reaction is that of scorn and spite as she interprets his admittance as a way of stealing her spot in the limelight: "Is *that* all he thinks of me, his estimate of what I want to hear of him; will I enlarge this into a confidence making me worthy of great confidences?" (Jackson 2006: 165)[21].

What is triggered by the violent outburst towards Theo in Chapter 4 is then a process of *possession*: Eleanor's personality is changed under the influence of the House. Hill House, it would seem, maliciously aggravates Eleanor in order to separate the protagonist from the fellow researchers as well as to prey on her overpowering sense of inadequacy that is directly related to Eleanor's past. The synthetic transformation ('victim' to 'villain') is therefore paralleled with the deepening of the protagonist's thematic component (Eleanor as an ill-treated child). It is an interlocking process in which the synthetic aspect complements the thematic one. The scene which most convincingly reflects the establishment of the thematic foregrounding occurs at the end of Chapter 5 in which Eleanor falls asleep holding Theo's hand only to be woken up by the sound of laughter followed by a child's cry somewhere within the House:

> It is a child, she thought with disbelief, a child is crying somewhere, and then, upon that thought, came the wild shrieking voice she had never heard before and yet knew she had heard always in her nightmares. "Go away!"

---

afraid even to dream of becoming" (2005: 162). The peculiar familial-erotic connection between these two characters (at one point Theo states that Eleanor and she "are practically twins") constitutes one of the major instabilities in the text, second only to the one established between Eleanor and Hill House (Jackson 2006: 158).

21   Eleanor's egotism is clearly noticed by her companions; in Chapter 6, when the researchers discover a grisly scrapbook on Seven Deadly Sins made by Hugh Crain for his daughter, Luke immediately (albeit half-jokingly) associates Pride with Eleanor (Jackson 2006: 170). Hugh Crain's moral teachings function here as a warning and a premonition for Eleanor's fate as the daughter is never to free herself from the bond she shares with the parent: "Daughter: sacred pacts are signed in blood, and I have here taken from my own wrist the vital fluid with which I bind you" (Jackson 2006: 171). The appearance of Hugh Crain's scrapbook seems also an intentional wink at the authorial audience, another intimation that we are reading a self-reflexive narrative that makes a very precise use of the Gothic formula, its paradigm being refashioned as the heroine turns out to be less virtuous than required. See also Hattenhauer's discussion of *The Haunting of Hill House* as a heteroglossic narrative.

it screamed. "Go away, go away, don't hurt me," and, after, sobbing, "Please don't hurt me. Please let me go home," and then the little sad crying again. (Jackson 2006: 162)

As Eleanor stands in defence of the harmed babe, Theo suddenly wakes up and, in what becomes one of the narrative's most climactic moments (Shirley Jackson herself considered it to be the crucial passage in her novel), Eleanor discovers that her friend has been sleeping in her own bed for the whole time (Hattenhauer 2003: 163). "God God – whose hand was I holding?" mutters frightened Eleanor, while the authorial audience knows all too well by now that the spectral hand the protagonist was clutching in a gesture of bonding belonged to the villain (Jackson 2006: 162). The synthetic act of communion (the 'victim' holding hands with the 'villain') is coupled with the expansion of Eleanor's thematic dimension: the phantom child reactivates Eleanor's suppressed memory ("the wild shrieking voice she had never heard before and yet she had heard always in her nightmares"), pointing to the undisclosed trauma from the protagonist's past[22].

In Chapter 7, with the appearance of Mrs Montague, doctor Montague's wife and a self-professed medium, and her assistant, Arthur Parker, the process of synthetic convolution between Eleanor and Hill House gains momentum. The comic duo of paranormal investigators succeeds in establishing contact with the haunted mansion by means of a planchette (a kind of an Ouija board). With the answer to the medium's first question "Who are you?" being "Eleanor Nellie Nell Nell", the further inquiries receive answers that point directly to Eleanor being *claimed* by the House:

"What do you want?" Arthur read.
"Mother," Mrs. Montague read back.
"Why?"
"Child."
"Where is your mother?"
"Home."
"Where is your home?"
"Lost. Lost. Lost. [...]" (Jackson 2006: 191-193)

---

22   Hattenhauer concludes that the described scene suggests the abuse that Eleanor must have experienced as a child (2003: 158).

The follow-up occurs during the next attack of the House upon its guests occurring the first night after Mrs Montague's arrival. During a particularly violent manifestation, Eleanor is depicted as possessing an eerie kinship with the villain. While the protagonist observes that she is "disappearing inch by inch into this house" (Jackson 2006: 201), the final assault becomes the moment of her definite surrender when the victim is finally giving in to her persecutor:

> She heard the laughter over all, coming thin and lunatic, rising in its little crazy tune, and thought, No; it is over for me. It is too much, she thought, *I will relinquish my possession of self of mine*, abdicate, give over willingly what I never wanted at all; whatever it wants of me it can have. (Jackson 2006: 204)

The dispossession of identity points to the final stage of a generic *salto mortale* as the heroine's synthetic function of the 'villain' is confirmed and Eleanor actually *becomes* Hill House. What is more, by possessing the main protagonist, the House succeeds in isolating Eleanor from the group. The penultimate Chapter 8 highlights the irreversible rift that has occurred between Eleanor and the research team: the protagonist, now the monstrous Other, is almost unanimously rejected by her colleagues, once again *outside* any kind of meaningful relationships. In a delusional attempt to regain her place within the community, Eleanor tries to impose herself upon Theodora by announcing that they will be living together (obviously she is flatly refused) and later, while taking a stroll in the vicinity of the House, she is abandoned by Theodora and Luke who decide to avoid her company, considering Eleanor to be demented. At the same time, Eleanor's growing isolation corresponds with the increased identification with the House: Eleanor's senses are preternaturally heightened (she can hear everything that happens within Hill House), and the protagonist experiences a series of visual and auditory hallucinations that she interprets (ecstatically, it should be noted) as the sign of her status as the chosen one. "None of them heard it", she remarks about a song she hears inside the House, "Nobody heard it but me" (Jackson 2006: 226). In the very same chapter, facilitated by the synthetic upturn into an outcast, Eleanor's fundamental thematic dimension (the neglected child) receives significant exposure when the ambiguity connected with Eleanor's relationship with her mother is finally delineated, pointing to the causes of the protagonist's vulnerability to the House's psychological manipulations:

> "It was my fault my mother died," Eleanor said. "She knocked on the wall and called me and called me and I never woke up. I ought to have brought her the medicine; I always did before. But this time she called me and I never woke up." [...] "I've wondered ever since if I did wake up. If I did wake up and hear her, and if I just went back to sleep. It would have been easy, and I've wondered about it." [...] "It was going to happen sooner or later, in any case," Eleanor said. "But of course no matter when it happened it was going to be my fault." (Jackson 2006: 212)

Propelled by Eleanor's impending derangement, the confession of the ostensible transgression furthers the authorial audience's understanding of Eleanor's susceptibility to Hill House's manipulative tactics. We are never to learn what has actually happened on that fateful night, but the narrative itself provides certain clues that Eleanor, the tormented child, might have subconsciously resisted the good-daughter impulse to aid the elderly woman, the resulting pangs of conscience making the protagonist susceptible to the malevolent scheming of Hill House[23]. The ensuing madness stems therefore from Eleanor's inability to cope with the conflicting emotions of guilt and relief after her mother's death. The thematic correlates of the child's guilt and abuse function then as the prime reasons of Eleanor's descent into insanity due to the manipulations of Hill House that correctly recognises her as a maltreated child[24].

---

23   Judith Newman rightly observes that Eleanor "has been both mother and child" as she "detests the mother's dominance, resenting the loss of her own youth in the forced assumption of the mothering role" and simultaneously she "feels guilt at not having mothered adequately". In short, Newman concludes, Eleanor "is haunted by guilt as a mother over the neglected child within herself" (Newman 2005: 175).

24   In his compelling analysis, Dale Bailey draws a comparison between Jackson's novel and Charlotte Perkins Gilman's *Yellow Wallpaper* as "[b]oth tales employ the haunted house as a metaphor for patriarchal systems which confine women in the home" (Bailey 1999: 43). The House therefore becomes the embodiment of masculine oppression that thwarts the women that are somehow connected to it. From this point of view, Eleanor's 'villainy' is based precisely upon her unsuccessful struggle to break away from the constraints of the image of the woman dominant in the 1950s according to which a woman "functioned largely in a domestic capacity, a role impressed upon her by countless cultural forces" (Bailey 1999: 43). Hence, the implication of neglect would come to symbolise Eleanor's unconscious attempt to liberate herself from the societal expectations.

The progressive foregrounding of the protagonist's thematic dimension (the forlorn mistreated daughter) concomitantly facilitates the resolution of the initial tension caused by the synthetic incongruence (Eleanor, the supposed innocent victim, revealed to be the Other). In what becomes a final spin on the Gothic convention, the female protagonist, now the exposed 'villain', is to be punished for her offence of violating the typically ascribed role of a daughter – a punishment more severe since it is to be conveyed upon herself. In the novel's last chapter Eleanor, running around the House and knocking upon the doors as the Hill House phantom embodied, returns to the ominous library of the House, the place where the servant girl (the caregiver) committed suicide in the final act of unity with the villain[25]. Eleanor strives towards the same goal as she begins climbing the staircase leading to the fatal turret attempting to merge with the House through death. "I have broken the spell of Hill House and somehow come inside. [...] I am home," she concludes (Jackson 2006: 232). Rescued at the last possible moment by Luke, Eleanor, now a threat and a liability to the rest of the group, is expelled from the project and asked to leave. However, the separation is impossible: "The house wants me to stay" she tells doctor Montague (Jackson 2006: 240). Eleanor's suicide committed in an act of defiance against the expulsion reveals the extent of the protagonist's identification with Hill House, pointing yet again to her key mimetic attribute, self-absorption:

> Journeys end in lovers meeting. But I *won't* go, she thought, and laughed aloud to herself; Hill House is not as easy as *they* are; just by telling me to go away they can't make me leave, not if Hill House means me to stay. "Go away, Eleanor," she chanted aloud, "go away, Eleanor, we don't want you any more, not in *our* Hill House, go away, Eleanor, you can't stay *here*; but I can," she sang, "but I can; they don't make the rules around *here. They* can't turn me out or shut me out or laugh at me or hide from me; I won't go, and Hill House belongs to *me.*" [...]
> In the unending, crashing second before the car hurled into the tree she thought clearly, *Why* am I doing this? Why am I doing this? Why don't they stop me?[26] (Jackson 2006: 246)

25   At one point Eleanor remarks about the rest of the research team: "what fools they are [...]; we trick them so easily", the "we" being an indication of the heroine's identification with Hill House (Jackson 2006: 229). See also Newman.

26   King states that "[Eleanor]'s last thought before her death is not of Hill House, but of herself", something entirely generic for a representative of the new American gothic, which, as we remember, is peopled with egotistic characters (King 2006: 311).

In the moment right before Eleanor crashes into the tree, the protagonist's mimetic dimensions change into functions as it is the heroine's almost monstrous self-indulgence and narcissism that prevent her from seeing the House for what it really is, a mistake that leads her to the tragic end. Eleanor's death is at the same time an unavoidable outcome of a series of profound transformations effected by the novel's progression that produce a character whose demise is the culminating point in the development of all three functions: mimetic (death as a result of self-deception and loss of identity), synthetic (death of the Gothic villain) and ultimately, thematic (the lonely death of an abandoned mistreated child). Eleanor's thematic component is arguably the most developed of the three as the protagonist's mimetic and synthetic clues inevitably turn our attention towards her central thematic function emerging throughout Jackson's work: the disastrous effects of prolonged abuse upon forlorn, alienated individuals such as Eleanor Vance who ultimately turn to violence first against the world around them and then against themselves.

Consequently, through tensions and instabilities that indicate the deepening connection between Eleanor and Hill House, the readers can observe how synthetic and mimetic attributes function as springboards for the thematic aspects while the gradually unravelled thematic dimensions of the protagonist (the neglected daughter, the dispossessed younger sister, the exploited caregiver) facilitate the novel's progression. Eventually, the character of Eleanor Vance becomes inexorably intertwined with Hill House in a process of synthetic convolution in which the heroine has been deformed into a 'monster', an outcast shunned by the group. It is then through the final metamorphosis that the narrative's achieves completeness[27]:

> Hill House [...], not sane, stood against its hills, holding darkness within; it had stood so for eighty years and might stand for eighty more. Within, its walls continued upright, bricks met neatly, floors were firm, and doors were sensibly shut; silence lay steadily against the wood and stone of Hill House, and whatever walked there, walked alone. (Jackson 2006: 246)

---

27   Phelan makes a distinction between *closure* and *completeness*. "Closure [...] refers to the way in which a narrative signals its end, whereas completeness refers to the degree of resolution accompanying the closure. Closure need not be tied to the resolution of instabilities and tensions but completeness always is" (1989: 17-18).

The last paragraph in the novel – the *doppelganger* of the opening passage – makes no mention of Eleanor Vance and it is my contention that it is not needed. After all, Eleanor and Hill House have become united in their solitary existence of the Other, their merging emphasised by the appearance of identical paragraphs at the beginning and at the end of the novel[28]. Jackson's narrative, based upon synthetic and thematic parallelisms, can be seen a multilayered exercise in character creation in which the synthetic fusion of the main protagonists provides us with the broadest thematic vistas. It is an effort abounding in paradoxes since only through the acknowledgment of their inherent loneliness can Eleanor and Hill House recognise themselves in each other.

---

28   Interestingly, in view of Eleanor's identification with Hill House, the fact that the mansion remains unchanged might be considered somewhat ironic as the protagonist's anguished existence and violent death leave no trace upon the structure of the House.

Character in the academic mystery novel: Joanne Dobson's *The Raven and the Nightingale*

ELŻBIETA PERKOWSKA-GAWLIK

Literary characters are constructs bound to a fictional world they inhabit. Influenced by situations they encounter and actions they perform, witness, or simply refer to, fictional characters are also inseparable from the plot. James Phelan admits that while working out his rhetorical methodology he felt a strong temptation to analyse a literary character in isolation, yet eventually he "ended by mixing up the study of character with the study of the [progression]" (Phelan 1989: ix). The term progression that Phelan introduces in his theses on character is found preferable and more telling than 'plot', as it foregrounds "a narrative as a dynamic event" (1989: 15). Character and progression are, in his opinion, so closely interrelated that any attempt to separate one from the other in the analysis of fictional characters would inevitably lead to simplification of the multiple roles played by protagonists. Whereas the traditional, separatist analysis of character is usually limited to enumeration of the character's significant traits and skills, or at best to classifying it/him/her as dynamic or static, Phelan's rhetorical analysis allows us to observe and comment on the interplay of various dimensions and functions that fluctuate and metamorphose, which exerts a dynamising effect on the progression in the work of fiction. Phelan applies his rhetorical approach to elucidate how in the course of narrative progression different dimensions of character turn or fail to turn into functions. The taxonomy of character's dimensions and functions in reference to the three components of a literary character he distinguishes, namely, synthetic, mimetic and thematic, is the focal point of Phelan's theory. Moreover, the scholar perceives most literary characters as multichromatic, that is, displaying all three components mentioned above; nevertheless, he notices that their foregrounding may differ considerably depending on the shape and direction of progression.

The aim of the present article is to analyse Joanne Dobson's *The Raven and the Nightingale* investigating the multichromatic nature of selected characters whose impact upon progression and setting understood in terms of social context seems crucial. The mutual relations between their mimetic, thematic and synthetic components contribute to the development of different functions. Bearing in mind that the academic mystery novel blends two different sets of literary conventions – the novel of manners (academic novel) and the detective novel – I will attempt to pinpoint and juxtapose the most prominent dimensions and functions of particular characters within the narrative progression aiming to find the dominant responsible for the production of meanings in the text.

The Raven and the Nightingale by Joanne Dobson is an academic mystery novel which employs a postmodern technique of interlacing different literary conventions formerly classified as either elitist or popular. The academic mystery novel is highly conventionalised: it usually intermingles a traditional plot of the formulaic detective novel with a university campus setting (Cuddon 1992: 107) and characters representing academic circles. *The Raven and the Nightingale* is a part of Dobson's academic mystery cycle, which forms a complex sequence of *Professor-romane* presenting several crime investigations not only leading to the capture of the perpetrators but also to illuminating the issues that contemporary university is haunted by, namely, "rationalization", gender, class, university career, etc.

The Raven and the Nightingale is structured around two plot lines set in two different chronotopoi and involving two women characters acutely aware of their role in patriarchal society: Karen Pelletier, an untenured literature professor, and Emmeline Foster, an unknown poetess. Karen Pelletier's narration focuses on the criminal investigation that takes place in the "small world" of the twentieth-century academia, whereas Emmeline Foster's journal entries recount the life of the nineteenth-century New York boheme. Long excerpts from Emmeline's journal are interwoven into the main narrative line in chapters 21 and 22. The thematic interrelation of the two worlds is conveyed through the motif of plagiarism which provides the scaffolding for the novel. The common, 'tangible' object of desire present in both worlds and plots is Emmeline Foster's poem entitled "Bird of the Dream", an alleged proto-type of Poe's "The Raven". Her poem plays a crucial role in both plots since the pursuit of it can be perceived as the initial cause of two deaths: Emmeline's and a twentieth-century professor's who wrote a monograph on Edgar Allan Poe.

Dobson's characters fall within the categories typical of both aca-demic and detective fiction. Karen Pelletier, the main protagonist of the novel, is an academic who simultaneously plays the role of amateur sleuth. She is juxtaposed to the police investigator, lieutenant Charles Piotrowski, whom she helped to untangle a few crime puzzles before. From the way they talk and care about one another the reader gets an impression that some kind of infatuation on both sides cannot be exclud-ed. The potentiality of romance draws the police investigator – one of the very few characters who are not insiders of the academic world – closer to the private life of the university professor. Unlike the lieuten-ant, other characters crucial to making the detective story complete, namely, the victim, the criminal and suspects, come from different levels of academic hierarchy. Karen's fellow scholar Elliot Corbin, a specialist in Poe, is stubbed to death. All suspects – Jane Birdfort, a poet and visit-ing professor at Enfield, Monica Cassale, the English department secre-tary, Harriet Person, a declared feminist and college fellow, and finally Amber Nichols, a young adjunct professor working on her dissertation and trying hard to obtain a tenured position at Enfield – represent aca-demic circles. Also the culprit turns out to be the insider. The homicide is Amber Nichols, whose unbridled ambition to become a member of tenured university staff gets confronted with exploitative and unscrupu-lous Elliot Corbin, her former teacher and mentor.

Campus, an obvious setting for academic novels, perfectly satisfies W.H. Auden's demand: "a detective story requires a 'closed society'" tightly knit by geography or occupation (Rollyson 2005). Thus, in *The Raven and the Nightingale* the reader is presented with typical temporal and spatial dimensions of the campus novel: the action takes place dur-ing the winter term at the English Department at Enfield, the elite New England College with students busy writing their papers and scholars exhausted by the endless process of correcting them. However, Dob-son's way of depicting Academia by no means gives an impression of "an innocent society in a state of grace" (Rollyson 2008: 2005) whose only aim is to fulfil its educational mission. On the contrary, Dobson shows academics fighting over "curriculum reform, course scheduling, and tenure decisions" (Showalter 2005: 96). Frequent visits of the police, following the homicide, make the usual atmosphere of anxiety even denser, at times hardly bearable. Nobody feels safe, for he/she may either become a suspect or, since the culprit has not been caught, another victim.

Although the novel's mystery plot seems to comprise motifs of typical 'whodunit' story, with the prevailing question "who killed Elliot Corbin?", from the start its development gets academically potent due to Karen's conviction that mysterious manuscripts by the nineteenth-century poetess Emmeline Foster, she has unexpectedly received in a parcel sent to her name, will prove invaluable in solving the criminal puzzle and as such require an academic interpreter who can read between the lines. In *The Raven and the Nightingale*, Dobson invents journals and poems by Emmeline Foster, whose works are said to have sunk into oblivion, and whose name is dimly remembered by Dobson's characters only because there were rumours that she had committed suicide for her spurned love to Edgar Allan Poe. All the journals – apart from the one Karen absent-mindedly slipped into her bag – together with a blue notebook containing Emmeline's unpublished poems are stolen from Karen's office. The theft at the academy, which appears as irregular an event as the murder, is immediately linked by Professor Pelletier to the world of crime and investigation. And the two events form a base from which she starts to reconstruct possible versions of the past.

Unsurprisingly, the investigation conducted by the literature professor opens with acts of close reading and preliminary interpretation of the poetess' autobiographical material as well as her literary output, that is, with the texts which seem both professionally challenging and simultaneously relevant for the criminal investigation. In this initial stage of progression, the mimetic dimension of amateur sleuth is thereby strongly linked to that of literary interpreter and critic. To Pelletier's (and the reader's) surprise, Emmeline Foster's last journal reveals that Emmeline blamed Poe for having stolen her poem entitled "Bird of the Dream". Having re-written and published it as his own, Poe is acclaimed as the author of the famous "The Raven". The issue of plagiarism that Poe's case touches upon turns out to be a recurrent motif in Dobson's novel. Actually it does not start with the motif of Poe's theft – it is encountered at the beginning of the novel, in the description of the unfair behaviour of Karen's student, Fredderica Whitby, who cribbed her final paper from Amber Nichols's (the culprit's) essay found in the Net. The motif of plagiarism returns when Professor Pelletier finds out that also Elliot (the victim) made (unfair) use of Amber's work, for he based his famous, well-received Poe monograph on the main theses put forward in Amber's unpublished paper without a single reference to their authoress.

To sum up, the impression that the reader of Dobson's novel obtains is that the worlds of the academics and the literatti are peopled with characters reading and preying on (re-writing) texts produced by others. The motif of plagiarism linking most characters in Dobson's novel makes the reader acutely aware of the constructedness of the novel and the characters whose synthetic aspect is thus underlined: Emmeline Foster, Amber Nichols, Fredderica Whitby, Elliot Corbin are neat literary constructs caught in a network of dependencies investigated by the protagonist – who herself is a figure that migrates from one text of the cycle to another like Agatha Christie's Miss Marple or Amanda Cross's Kate Fensler before her.

Professor-detective Karen Pelletier is not only the first person narrator but also the main character in the novel. The reader who knows Karen from other novels of the cycle approaches the text with well-grounded expectations concerning her synthetic function in the progression[1]. In other words, it is assumed that she is going to face some mysterious crime committed for reasons that we can call 'literary' and eventually manage to solve it using her analytical and interpretative skills, associative thinking and literary erudition. However, as in all the previous novels of the cycle, also here Dobson goes to great lengths to focus the reader's attention on Pelletier's mimetic-thematic dimension[2]. Paradoxi-

---

1   Phelan points out that "synthetic dimensions will always be synthetic functions because they will always have some role in the construction of the work" and although their presence may be more or less foregrounded in the progression or even hidden because of frequently expansive character of mimetic-thematic components, the "[synthetic] function cannot be eliminated" (Phelan 1989:14).

2   According to Phelan's definition "a dimension is any attribute a character may be said to possess when the character is considered in isolation from the work in which he or she appears" (Phelan 1989:9). If a character seems to be not only plausible, but can be

cally, the author herself expresses some reservations about her main character's plausibility.

> [Karen] is [...] an unlikely professor, born working class into the hard-scrabble factory-town life of Lowell, Massachusetts, pregnant at eighteen, married at nineteen, by the age of 22 a single mother on her own with only a high school diploma as an academic credential. [...] By her late thirties, through a daunting application of hard work, persistence, and sheer inborn intellect, Karen has managed to earn a Ph.D. in English and make a rewarding academic career for herself. (Dobson in Peters 2002: 10).

Karen's mimetic-thematic attributes, which are introduced in the form of external analepses, realise the Cinderella myth: if observed from a particular angle, Karen can be perceived not as a mimetic, highly individualised protagonist in the story, but rather as a typical character with a thematic potential – a twentieth-century academic Cinderella who "unexpectedly achieves recognition or success after a period of obscurity and neglect" (Newfields). Like in all other texts with Cinderella in the narrative centre, also in Dobson's novel the delineation of Pelletier's character makes the reader wish that all the impediments, such as her disadvantaged background or early motherhood, would not settle the matter of her personal and professional life. And indeed they do not, for Karen becomes both a model, if not perfect, mother and a successful scholar.

Karen's roles of a loving mother, estranged daughter and ex-wife, enhancing her mimetic aspect, find their textual justification (continuation or juxtaposition) in the character of her daughter Amanda. As Lindsay notices, "the relationships between Karen Pelletier and her daughter [Amanda] and between her own mother [...] are strikingly different and provide insight into characters" (Lindsay 2007: 70). Amanda, already a student in another city and a secondary character who is not directly involved in the criminal plot, is a rare guest at home, yet she and Karen often call each other. Karen, who unlike her own mother, deeply cares about her child, always envisages the worst things that can happen to her "Sweetie", which exemplifies the caring mother-daughter relationship. When Amanda "[drops] a daughterly bombshell" that she has decided to look for her estranged father, who "had completely disavowed her since

---

also perceived as a representative entity, he or she is said to possess mimetic-thematic dimension.

[Karen] had walked out on him after three-and-a half years of calamitous marriage" (Dobson 1999:73), Karen is completely devastated. She knows that she cannot stop Amanda, yet she "can't bear to see [her] get hurt" (Dobson 1999: 74). Amanda's determination to search for her father, Karen's abusive ex-husband, as well as her fascination and reunion with Karen's estranged mother and sisters contribute immensely to Karen's distress throughout the novel, however, neither her motherly apprehension nor love is converted into corresponding mimetic function by the progression of the narrative[3]. They are not there to provide us with a deep psychological study of a mother-figure who happens to be an academic; they are there to make the reader trust and sympathise with the main protagonist who is to provide the answer by solving the murder case mysteriously linked with Poe and plagiarism.

The way Emmeline Foster's character is introduced into the narrative differs substantially from that of Karen's, despite the fact that Emmeline's mimetic-thematic dimensions also inscribe her into a group of lonely female characters who have to struggle to achieve their professional position, independence and stability. The delineation of Emmeline as a character is scattered in the narrative and thus the process of collecting basic facts about her and her life is protracted. The verisimilitude is strengthened by an entry from *Encyclopedia of American Women Authors* on Emmeline Foster, a nineteenth-century poetess. The reader gets acquainted with her mimetic-thematic components indirectly: through 'listening' to other characters who digress about her and through reading selected entries in her journal quoted in the main narrative.

In Chapter One, during her literature class, Karen makes a digression from the main subject and tells her students a gloomy story of Emmeline Foster's death in the Hudson, close to Edgar Allan Poe's New York home. At this point in the novel, the digression by no means signals the importance of Emmeline for the development of the criminal plot – she seems to serve as an element building Karen's mimetic reliability as a literature professor. Also the narrator herself does not overtly draw the

---

3   Phelan underlines the relation between mimetic-thematic dimensions and corresponding functions focusing his attention on the fact that "every function depends upon a dimension but not every dimension will necessarily correspond to a function" (Phelan 1989:9). Hence, any conversion of dimension into function is to contribute to the development of narrative progression, otherwise "the text achieves closure before it develops the [mimetic-thematic] potentiality of these dimensions" (Phelan 1989:9).

readers' full attention to the unknown (fictional) poetess, on the contrary, she undermines Emmeline's role by redirecting her students' (and the reader's) attention to pondering the nickname given to Poe by Manhattan newspapers – "the Demon Lover" – the result of his numerous "romantic involvements with such women poets as Frances Osgood and Sarah Helen Whitman" (Dobson 1999: 4). Simultaneously, by Karen's joining Emmeline's name to Poe and the famous women from Baltimore society, the author provides Emmeline with an effective mimetic dimension allowing thereby for the reader's emotional reactions to misfortunes that happened to the wronged woman.

The reader has to wait till Chapter 6 to find out that Emmeline is not merely a part of the context against which Karen acts her academic role. In Chapter 6 Karen finally finds time to open the parcel with Emmeline's manuscripts only to learn that Emmeline Foster was Poe's significant rival, not just an insignificant lover. In the following chapters of the novel additional information is added to strengthen the poetess' position in the narrative. A clearer picture of Emmeline's miserable situation emerges from the consecutive entries of her journal which narrate the inset story. The reader of her journal is informed, for example, that after the death of her father, Emmeline's fairly stable financial existence was endangered by her greedy stepfather, who not only separated her from her mother, but also tried to reclaim Emmeline's inherited property. Again members of the family serve to sustain the mimetic illusion.

Karen, the first-person narrator, feels stronger and stronger empathy with Emmeline, as she herself, together with little Amanda, was left without any support from her own family and had to work hard to make ends meet. Karen's compassion and identification with Emmeline's struggle exemplify the audience's affective response to the mimetic component of the character read about in the text. Karen's sympathy toward the nineteenth-century poetess and her objections to the nineteenth-century legal regulations, which '[put] *all property in husbands' hands*' (Dobson 1999: 227), contribute to evoking similar emotions in the narrative audience. This in turn enhances the plausibility of both characters, or to put it differently, foregrounds their mimetic dimensions.

Emmeline's mimetic attributes are entwined with the thematic ones, for she comes across as a representative of creative women of the past doomed to failure in the patriarchal society. Since time immemorial, the

lack of connections or family support, together with consciously or subconsciously conceptualised belief that only men can come up with original ideas have contributed immensely to female artists' alienation and
failure as published authors. As the reader learns from Emmeline's journal, when she fell prey to plagiarism she had nobody to fall back on.

> *31 January 1845*
> *He has stolen my poem! The treacherous Man! He has taken my "Bird of*
> *the Dream" and rewritten it as a ghastly vision of a Raven, retaining the*
> *somber Bird, the unhallowed Love – even the refrain of "Nevermore'! But*
> *he has twisted them, and darkened them – and given them his name. Oh,*
> *what shall I do? I am surrounded by perfidy! I must see him! I must plead*
> *with him to retract the Poem! All my work depends on it! [...] And I will*
> *get acknowledgment of my Poem, or I will expose his theft to the World!*
> (Dobson 1999: 233)

Despite her decision to fight for her rights, Emmeline died or was killed
before she managed to bring any accusation against Poe. On February 1,
her "dead body had been found floating among the ice floes around the
filthy New York City docks" (Dobson 1999: 233).

Karen's and Emmeline's inferior positions in patriarchal societies as
well as their involvement in the issue of plagiarism demonstrate their
twofold thematic dimension. Their dependence on men is exposed by
different kinds of relations, such as Emmeline vs. stepfather, Emmeline
vs. fellow poet (Poe), Karen vs. father, Karen vs. ex-husband, Karen vs.
fellow scholar (Elliot). In none of these relations the woman figure is
treated as an equal: she is rather victimised and humiliated. However,
although interesting in itself, neither Karen's nor Emmeline's struggle
for the position in the patriarchal world develops into a corresponding
thematic function that could advance the progression of the main narrative in Dobson's novel. Similarly, despite Karen's and Emmeline's involvement in the issue of multi-layered plagiarism, neither of them has
their thematic dimension developed into a respective function: it is not
plagiarism that makes both characters act and participate in the action
but rather their creative and/or interpretative skills that are revealed in
the progression[4].

---

4   Emmeline's dimension linked to the issue of plagiarism is changed into the correspond-
     ing function by the narrative progression of her journal. She could not come to terms
     with the theft of her poem and planned to blackmail Poe in order to regain the right to
     her "Bird of the Dream". Even if her determination to stand for her property does not

In order to observe how a thematic dimension concerning the problem of plagiarism transforms into a corresponding function in the course of the progression, we should focus the analysis on Freddie Whitby, an episodic character, and Amber Nichols, Elliot's murderer. Freddie is one of Karen's students who usually gets D or C for her papers, not to mention "numerous x's to indicate her numerous absences" (Dobson 1999: 15). Being a daughter of the Enfield College's benefactor, she demonstrates irreverent attitude towards academics as well as to her student duties. If it were not for the family background and attitude, her mimetic component would be reduced to a few frowns, grimaces and snarls which both represent "the impervious mass of Freddie intellect" and best depict her reaction to Karen's remarks on her poor achievement. No matter how vestigial Freddie's mimetic dimension seems to be, it plays an immense part in the development of her thematic function. As Freddie is unable or unwilling to write her own analysis of Poe's "The Raven", she resorts to cribbing it from the Net. This seemingly trivial act of plagiarism produces the initial instability in the narrative progression, which is resolved when Karen, fulfilling her academic duty, locates the source of Freddie's paper. The style and sophisticated academic jargon of the cribbed paper that Freddie has submitted as her own incites the associative thinking in Karen's mind. The essay reminds Karen of Amber Nichols's unpublished article which she came across after Elliot's death, while sifting through his files and folders. The association between two, supposedly independent academic texts inspires Karen to follow the lead and ultimately enables her to solve the academic and criminal mystery.

> 'You see, Lieutenant [Karen is talking about her suspicions to Piotrowski], I think Elliot Corbin used this essay of Amber's as the basis for the book on Poe that made him famous. The title of her paper is "Poe in a Dress". It's dated four years ago. Elliot's book was called *The Transvestite Poe*. It was published [...] eighteen months ago. Plenty of time for him to rewrite'. (Dobson 1999: 275)

Amber's mimetic dimension is also underdeveloped, produced in a few analeptic sentences elucidating her disadvantaged background and her tough road to Academia. Similarly to Freddie, her mimetic and thematic

---

fully explain the mystery of her death, it, at least, puts an end to the rumours of her alleged love affair with the famous Edgar Allan Poe.

dimensions contribute to the development of her thematic function, which is also linked to plagiarism. However, unlike Freddie, Amber is the consenting victim of plagiarism, not the perpetrator. Having once sold her ideas to Elliot, her mentor, she harbours a deep grudge against him which is like the fuse of a bomb. Strengthened by another theft on the part of Elliot that she witnesses – this time the theft of Foster's blue notebook constituting a potentially invaluable source for the critic interested in Poe – the grudge eventually leads to Amber's bloody revenge. Until the murderer has been discovered, however, the reader is not aware that the instability introduced by the eavesdropped altercation between Elliot and some woman is in fact the very first trace of the perpetrator observable in the narrative and progression.

> 'Why, you double-crossing, scheming, careerist bitch! ...You are going to do WHAT?... We had an agreement, and you damn well know it!' Elliot blared. An unintelligible female voice mumbled in response, and I [Karen] could hear Elliot choke in muffled rage. (Dobson 1999: 9)

The woman Elliot had the agreement with was Amber, yet the reader and Karen learn about it at the very end of the novel, where the narrative comes to a close. The fact that she takes a deferred revenge by murdering Elliot not only foregrounds the thematic component of the progression, but also illuminates the complex network of other cases of plagiarism introduced in the novel, namely Freddie's cribbed essay, Poe's "The Raven" developed from Emmeline's poem, and more importantly... the novel itself. A detailed analysis of *The Raven and the Nightingale* would prove that it happens to be a crafty collage of different intertexts, such as Poe's "The Fall of the House of the Usher," "The Cask of Amontillado," "The Black Cat" or "Purloined Letter". In other words, the process of untangling the mystery of Elliot's death is accompanied by the identification of sources as well as the close reading of numerous texts (including Dobson's novel) and thus raises the question of intertextuality in literature.

In the course of the novel, Dobson ponders about different attitudes of academics towards the issue of plagiarism. Elliot's folder labelled "Current Professional Correspondence" familiarises Karen with his views on such notions as originality and plagiarism. The leftist discourse used by Eliot enables him to shun responsibility for the intellectual theft he has committed: *"All texts circulate within a prior textual matrix, and aside from meretricious capitalist claims of "ownership" of "intellectu-al property," no such act as "plagiarism" can be seen to exist, for, plainly, who can "own" or hold "property" in language"* (Dobson 1999:155). Paradoxically the authorial audience may feel a strong temp-tation to believe that Dobson herself shares Elliot's opinion since *The Raven and the Nightingale* deploys numerous literary motifs – disguised, but easily recognizable – borrowed without acknowledgment and intro-duced as plausible events belonging to the current action. It is enough to compare Poe's "The Cask of Amontillado" to the way Karen, in her nightmare, gets rid of her assailant.

> I soon uncovered a quantity of building stone and mortar. With these mate-rials and with the aid of my trowel, I began vigorously to wall up the en-trance of the niche. (Poe 1962: 15)

> I retrieved a Penguin paperback edition of *The Scarlet Letter* from the wheelbarrow of books placed so conveniently close to my hand, laid my hand on a convenient trowel, slid it into the mortar, and began to brick up the archway, book by book by book. (Dobson 1999: 263)

The two excerpts quoted above demonstrate how Dobson draws on Poe's well-known motif of burying people alive. Obviously, by chang-ing "a quantity of building stone" into "the wheelbarrow of books", she makes the material for bricking up "the archway" or "the niche" differ-ent. Nevertheless, the situation remains strikingly similar, which broad-ens the discussion on the phenomenon of plagiarism to so that it trans-cends the borders of the presented world and crosses into the world of the flesh-and-blood author.

The last issue to be discussed is the synthetic function of Dobson's characters and the ways in which mimetic-thematic components influ-ence its development within the main narrative progression. As stated earlier, Karen and Emmeline are both narrators, yet they operate at dif-ferent narrative levels. Their synthetic function is in a sense inscribed into the role they play in the narrative. The synthetic function of charac-ters is also prominent within the conventions of mystery and crime nov-el: the constructedness of the figures of the victim, perpetrator, witness, and detective is unquestionable.

"Literary critics [and scholars] make natural detectives", for they have been trained in numerous kinds of textual analysis and they display "narrative curiosity" which helps them to untangle different mysteries of

a text (Byatt 1987: 257, 259). Professor Karen Pelletier's ability of associative thinking, which could otherwise be perceived as a necessary mimetic attribute of an academic scholar and amateur detective affecting
the development of the mimetic-thematic function, is ascribed by Dobson a crucial synthetic function which organises the narrative. Karen,
with all her expertise in stylistic registers and experience in literary studies, turns out to be the right figure in the right place who can solve
'modern mysteries' by arranging data and missing links into a neat
whole prompted by the structure of literary texts she is acquainted with.
The dimension of associative thinking is overtly changed into function
when Lieutenant Piotrowski classifies Elliot's homicide as "another one
of [Karen's] literary mysteries" (Dobson 1999: 93). From that point on,
the narrative audience may be confident that Karen's literary discoveries
and findings will be treated seriously by the police, whereas the authorial audience will perceive them as plausible instabilities and tensions of
the narrative, which are likely to have a great impact on the progression.

Emmeline's 'second degree' presence in the main narrative (she 'exists' in the text-within-the text) results in her synthetic function being in
fact the synthetic function of her inset story within the main narrative
progression. Emmeline's defeat foreshadows and generalises Karen's
and Amber's difficulties in winning acclaim in the patriarchal society.
Untenured and trapped within the academic maze, neither Karen nor
Amber feel safe and free to voice their discontent. Emmeline's unequal
fight against the famous writer and her premature death influence the
reader and ease his/her affective response to Amber's revenge. It does
not mean that Amber as a murderer is fully justified by the text, yet
Emmeline's victimization foregrounds the inferior position and help-
lessness of women in the world ruled by men and thereby makes it easier
to see Amber as a "victim-victimiser" figure. Emmeline's delineation of
the nineteenth-century social order mirrors Karen's description of university in terms of a rigidly defined class structure. When Amber reveals
that she killed Elliot because of the nineteenth-century poetess, Emmeline's synthetic function is finally confirmed. Last but not least, the
synthetic function of Emmeline's misfortunes is implied in her suggestive surname. "To foster" means to help something develop over a period of time. The authorial audience is tempted to suspect that Dobson

carefully planned Emmeline's surname to leave a trace of her *fostering* both in the mystery and its investigation.

In the narrative progression of Dobson's *The Raven and the Nightingale*, viewed as a mystery novel, the synthetic component of the main characters seems to prevail, which confirms its formulaic character. The fact that academic mysteries operate on the border-line between conventions of the detective novel and the campus novel might invalidate the above conclusion. For when analysed in terms of academic fiction, *The Raven and the Nightingale* features characters whose thematic function as if overshadows the synthetic one, in other words, the heated debate over intertextuality versus plagiarism, or 'borrowers' versus plagiarists, makes the reader downplay the synthetic component of the characters involved in the progression. Yet even if we find this perspective rewarding, the text itself reminds us that we are first and foremost among the constructs which are allowed to voice their creators' opinions. Performing her synthetic function metafictionally, Karen comments on the genre she herself is produced by when she classifies mystery fiction as literature aiming at relaxation. Apart from a steamy bath, a glass of red wine, and her favourite Emmylou CD, what she needs to complement a perfectly peaceful evening at home is "a paperback mystery novel" selected "from [her] pleasure-reading pile" (Dobson 1999: 134).

Possible men and women of science:
Constru(ct)ing characters in academic fictions

LUDMIŁA GRUSZEWSKA-BLAIM

> The first property of light we consider is reflection
> from a surface, such as that of a mirror.

For obvious reasons a density of scholars, scientists and geniuses per square mile in the mainstream *college novel*, together with its *science in fiction* and *lab literature* sub-genres, is high and provides an interesting research material exemplifying techniques of introducing science as well as possible (wo)men of science into the literary discourse. As Peter J. Rabinovitz asserts, we may choose between different lines of inquiry concerning the use of science in literary texts: first, we can focus on the mutual influence of science and literature; second, we may deal with their shared premises or epistemological differences exploring the ways in which fiction refracts science; third, we can analyze the representation of science and scientists as thematic content and scrutinize narrative commentary on science, pursuing thereby issues of scientific truth in literature; and forth, we can focus on the *rhetorical* use of science, that is, on *how science is used* in texts in order to mould the *reader's* experience. Rabinovitz distinguishes three axes along which science operates rhetorically: Plot Requirements, Positional Reinforcement, and Possible People (2011: 202).

In what will follow I intend to focus on selected aspects of constructing and construing *possible scientists* and outline some of the methods which enable readers to assume that they know 'what it is like' to be a scientist and a genius. My point of departure is that, unless *de*constructed, scientist as a literary or cinematic figure is one of the most opaque figural signs – intellectually and emotionally more distant from the narratorial and authorial audience than, for example, a king, saint or artist figure. In order to make it operative in constructing *a possible self* (or *qualia* to use the term used by philosophers of mind; see Rabinovitz 2011: 208), the figure of the learned (wo)man is often subject to multiple intra- and intertextual reinterpretations – not all of them as sophisticated as one might expect.

With the exception of science in fiction novels – where longer parts of texts are specifically devoted to lecture on factual knowledge – science/scholarship and scientists/scholars are most frequently introduced in fiction by an equivalent (*sensu* Zgorzelski 1984b). A frequent mention of a given domain (e.g. math, philosophy), more or less comprehensible concepts scattered here and there in narrative (e.g. "prime numbers", "Feit-Thompson theorem", "the Copenhagen interpretation", "the mind-body problem"), references to leading scientists in the field (e.g. Bohm, Bohr, Einstein or Nash, Descartes, Spinoza, Leibniz), real or fictitious titles of seminal works (e.g. "On the Properties of Supernatural Numbers", *Discourse on Method*)[1], names of departments at fictitious or factual universities and other similar markers of a given branch of science are sufficient to build an aura enveloping a mathematician, quantum physicist or philosopher. The markers may be intensified when woven into the very construction of the fictional world, which is the case in Rebecca Goldstein's academic novels. In *The Mind-Body Problem* (1983), Goldstein, a philosopher herself, not only introduces Cartesian dualism in debates between Renee Feuer, a philosophy graduate student drop-out and wife of a world-renown mathematical genius Noam Himmel, and her interlocutors, but also imposes the dilemma onto the construction of Renee, the protagonist-narrator, Noam, and other *possible people*, who tend to view, yet simultaneously rebel against perceiving themselves and/or others as either beautiful minds or beautiful bodies.

> "[…] I knew you loved the genius. I know that all I've ever been to anyone, including you, including myself, for that matter, has been defined by my mathematical gifts. It was all anyone ever asked of me. It was my justification."
> The urge to comfort overwhelmed me, in spite of myself. "You always talk about people's justifications," I said. "People don't need justifications. They're people. That's enough". (Goldstein 1983: 267)

---

1   Examples are taken from the novels of Rebecca Goldstein: *The Mind-Body Problem* (1983) and *Properties of Light* (2000).

Fictional figures of scholars, scientists, professors and geniuses are characterised by a prominent thematic dimension that obfuscates their mimeticism. Regardless of an impact factor produced by a novel's exposition, once the academic status of some possible professor is pronounced, a thematic dimension of the figure turns automatically into a thematic function (*sensu* Phelan), which often renders attempts on the part of the author to present the protagonist mimetically, i.e. as a human person, unsuccessful. Scholars and scientists rarely turn out equal to other literary or cinematic constructs in their physical and socio-emotional fictional existence. Involved in some complex mental activity – as any diegetic or extradiegetic observer assumes – that propels their quest for knowledge, the fictional learned seem to occupy a precarious position even in the spatio-temporal dimension of the world: they are viewed and described as if they simultaneously *were* and *were not* there.

> Noam in action, in the grip of mathematical intuition, is an awesome sight, like some natural wonder, expending vast amounts of energy. [...] Oblivious as he is at such times to his surroundings, I used to watch for his crashing into walls. But he never does. Just before hitting, he executes a neat little pirouette and continues on his way.
> Then sometimes he'll halt quite suddenly and stand there motionless, his REMming eyes now off the floor and on God knows what. (Goldstein 1983: 91-92)

Literary, cinematic, TV or other mass media representations of the scientific mind imply that unlike other humanoid constructs, scholars, scientists and geniuses – either individually or in small research groups – subside in some lighter and brighter *chronotopos*, which is not fully constrained by the laws of clock-and-garden time or gravitation. As they are not supposed to think or feel like ordinary people, the ordinary time and space often prove inadequate to contain their physical bodies. The more abstract (formal) science they deal with, the more estranged they become: the *floating effect*, supposedly exerted by what they research, may take them literally off the ground.

> It had seemed to her as if the entire table of mathematicians was lifting itself off the ground, wordlessly acquiescing in their collective transcendence, they were levitating upward toward the ceiling of the faculty club; while beneath them, over at the other tables, occupied by the wretchedly earthbound empiricists, the plodding art historians and chemists, literary

theorists and linguists had continued to talk and chew their food... (Goldstein 1993: 250)

The floating effect appears to concern also those who remain in close proximity to the exceptional mind. Melted in brilliance and intensity of his/her thought ("'Wife of the genius' does not in itself define a distinct personality"; Goldstein 1983: 5), the genius's spouse, children and friends craft their own fluid identities by responding to expectations of the others.

> I'm often asked what it's like to be married to a genius. [...] I could never even decide how I should arrange my face when I answered. Should I radiate the faintly dazed glow of one who stands within sweating distance of the raging fires of creativity? Or should my features exhibit the sharp practicality capable of managing the mundane affairs of an intellectual demigod? (Goldstein 1983: 55)

Undoubtedly the figure of "intellectual demigod" that surpasses its natural environment – regardless of whether it is real or fictitious – imperils egalitarian world pictures to a greater extent than any Miss World character. Advocating the idea that every human person is equal in fundamental worth or moral status to another human person, egalitarian doctrines encourage us to acquire a sense of distributive justice also in other domains. From an egalitarian stance, one expects all people to "get the same, or be treated the same, or be treated as equals, in some respect"[2]. Our dream of equality shapes various artistic visions that either utopianise or satirise a process of equalising.

> The year was 2081, and everybody was finally equal. They weren't only equal before God and the law. They were equal every which way. Nobody was smarter than anybody else. Nobody was better looking than anybody else. Nobody was stronger or quicker than anybody else. (Kurt Vonnegut 1961)

Distributive injustice concerning not only wealth and income, but also mind and body, has been remedied differently in different areas of human activity. Effective means of restoring the social equilibrium, shattered by nature, God or rules of economy, are provided by popular culture and the mass media which have learned how to steal from the rich, the handsome and the learned in order to satisfy and comfort the poor, the ugly and the uneducated. Long-lasting defamation of scientists in all

---

2   http://plato.stanford.edu/entries/ egalitarianism/ 1 Dec 2012.

kinds of popular culture production exemplifies the phenomenon best. Caricatures of naïve, absent-minded, pompous scholars and scientists proliferate, compensating the drastic inequality of the intelligence quotient (IQ) distribution. "For almost a century the professor figured as the most available target of every onslaught of American anti-intellectualism", asserts DeMott (quoted in Moseley 2007: 65). Terry Eagleton makes a parallel observation while discussing the English attitude to the intelligentsia:

> Ever since Burke and Coleridge's testy polemics against the Jacobins, the English attitude to the intelligentsia has been one of profound ambivalence. Intellectuals are seen as faintly sinister figures, bohemian and nonconformist, treasonable clerks whose heartless celebrations pose a threat to the unreflective pieties of ordinary life. But they are also pathetically ineffectual characters – crumpled figures of fun pursuing their ludicrous abstractions at a remote distance from the bustle of daily life. (Eagleton in Moseley 2007: 15)

Considering this pop culture remedial policy, the four presentational types of professor and scholar/scientist figure distinguished by Richard Sheppard – none of them strikingly positive – do not come as a surprise: 1/ a comic fool (impotent half-man); 2/ a hypocrite; 3/ a fraud; 4/ a diabolic (quasi-)magician (Sheppard 1990: 12).

In light of Sheppard's typology revealing a strikingly negative attitude of society to "intellectual demigods", it can hardly be considered unexpected that two other categories we should add to professorial types have long been regarded as inferior and/or alien (viz. unacceptable): 5/ a female; 6/ an ethnic minority figure.[3]

The vilification of the learned in popular culture resorts to modification of their typical thematic dimension and function. Instead of accentuating assets of their exceptional minds and creative potential, society often subjects them to a critique that, paradoxically, focuses on other social roles they play, or to be exact, fail to play. Apart from standard equalisation-defamation technique, i.e. re-thematisation – owing to which the

---

3   In his 2002 study on scientists in film Matthew C. Nisbet distinguishes four types of figures: scientists as Dr. Frankenstein, scientists as powerless pawns, scientists as eccentric and anti-social geeks, scientists as heroes (http://scienceblogs.com/fra ming-science/2010/05/05/reconsidering-the-image-of-sci/). I argue elsewhere that the American college novel of the last decades presents a wider variety of academic types that reflect newer trends in contemporary culture (see Gruszewska-Blaim 2012a: 31).

reader or viewer can at least partly identify with a whole array of brainy, yet henpecked husbands, lousy fathers, impractical weirdoes – fiction writers tend to enrich the characterisation of the professor-scientist figure with other tendentiously selected mimetic (humanising) traits developed later into functions. Attributes that never fail to bring the reader or viewer closer to the egalitarian ideal are related to: 1/ sex, 2/ misdemeanours, 3/ hobbies and ambitions, 4/ gender and/or ethnicity – their main objective being a reduction of an emotional, if not intellectual, distance between a given "intellectual demigod" and the reader.

The techniques of thematisation, re-thematisation and mimetisation are extensively deployed by college fiction writers. The floating effect and 'anchoring' are the two poles between which fictionists suspend their professor figures.

The most popular leveller among various techniques familiarising the ethereal figure of genius or professor, i.e. reducing or nullifying the floating effect, is sex. Love-making scenes show that even a Harvard professor is 'typical' and earthly when it comes to sexual preferences and practices.

> He wanted to weep: the breasts he had longed to see were flat as any man's. He shut his eyes against the sight and got into bed. [...] [S]oon he felt limpness being replaced by energy. He worked very hard. (Bernays 1989: 39)

Numerous college novels describe passions and sexual encounters that violate a standard Western ethical code; a sexual harassment motif – like alcoholism in Kingsley Amis's times – has apparently become a must in contemporary academic fiction. Jacob Barker, a professor of psychology from Anne Bernays's novel *Professor Romeo* (1989), officially accused of and punished for committing serial sexual harassment, can so skillfully manipulate his discourse and outlook that his unrestrained sexual cravings find justification, at least in his own eyes. By appealing to his manly nature "Professor Romeo", unredeemable womaniser, cannot help thinking that his right to seduce female students (his campus Julias) results from natural law. Regardless of whether Barker's argumentation convinces the reader or not, his behaviour places him among 'ordinary' sex-offenders, which nullifies sophistication of the floating effect.

> He might, for a time, be able to keep his hands off the sophomore in the front row, gazing up at him with wet and wondrous eyes, but to forgo for-

ever the ardent chase, the quickening pulse, the verbal foreplay, the heightened fantasies—how could he promise such a thing? He might as well promise to have his gonads removed. (Bernays 1989: 275)

The sex-life of some 61-year-old professor of sociology – a participant in a group sex encounter from Carol Bergé's scandalous roman à clef *Secrets, Gossip and Slander* (1984) – blooms where it should not, that is *within* rather than outside the walls of academe. A self-described "Derrida" style of prose, that blurs the boundary between fact and fiction, paradoxically succeeds in *de*constructing the professor figure as a creature of mind. Among many academic sex-offenders, Bing Owen from *The Cosmology of Bing* (2001) by Mitchell Cullin looms large. Owen, a professor of astronomy and a married, bisexual, paranoiac alcoholic, gets infatuated with a male student. None of the mentioned figures, however, can equal Hal Kizer, a professor of psychiatry and sadomasochist from John L'Heureux's *Having Everything* (1999). "The man's entire inner life existed 12 inches south of his belt" (169). And so did his death: Professor Kilzer dies on New Year's Eve "in some sort of compromising position" (216), during the act of autoeroticism.

Fictional scientists from the mainstream academic novel[4] get into trouble with ethics or law. In order to live ordinary people's lives and feel what other people feel, they sporadically get involved in other lawbreaking activities, which equally well impair the floating effect. Brian Kelly, a political science professor from *Intimate Enemies* (1987) by Caryl Rivers, takes over a local bank in the name of and with the help of a homeless woman. Philip Tate, a professor of psychiatry from *Having Everything*, is driven by an irrepressible urge to break into other people's houses. Professor Hartke from Kurt Vonnegut's *Hocus Pocus* (1990), a physicist, is unjustly accused of and incarcerated in prison for masterminding the prison breakout. In all cases a spatio-temporal 'bubble', in which the scholar subsists due to his/her superior IQ, crashes in confrontation with the materiality of court-rooms or prison cells.

Not all hobbies and ambitions ascribed to main characters in college novels serve as attributes of the eccentric learned. Some preferences or interests lead professors *out* of their floating reality, where the body serves as a dispensable cocoon of the mind, *into* the real world, where

---

4   The mainstream academic novel is differentiated by John Kramer from the academic mystery and crime novel.

more often than not the body is served by the mind. For example, due to his writing a pornographic novel, the figure of Professor Wheelwright, a philosopher lecturing on phenomenology in *Philip's Girl* (1985) by Lucy Ferriss, is anchored in a more familiar world of sex, drugs and money making. Porn fiction ties Wheelwright to a stable and sufficiently degrading reality to make the reader forget about the intellectual distance between the academic and her-/himself. Likewise, when we learn that the biggest ambition of the Moo U. professors from *Moo* (1995) by Jane Smiley is to grow the world's largest pig, the elegant architecture of the ideological and spatio-temporal 'bubble' as if falls down under the weight of the enterprise (i.e. the weight of the largest pig) and its mundane connotations.

Despite all niceties of political correctness, the presence of women and other minorities among white *men* of science is still considered an intrusion into the order of things. Professor Coleman Silk, an Afro-American dean accused of racism in *The Human Stain* (2000) by Philip Roth; Benjamin "Chappie" Puttbutt III, a neo-conservative black junior professor of literature supporting the new Japanese authorities in *Japanese by Spring* (1993) by Ishmael Reed; dr. Alice Coombs, a physicist in love with Void (Lack) from *As She Crossed Across the Table* (1997) by Jonathan Lethem; Ava and Dana, quantum physicists, from *The Mind-Body Problem* (1983) and *Properties of Light* (2000) by Rebecca Goldstein; Lucinda, "the goddess of game theory" from *36 Arguments for the Existence of God* (2010) by the same author; Catherine, a mathematician from *Proof*, directed by John Madden (2005); Einstein's niece, a mathematician from *IQ*, directed by Fred Schepisi; Thérèse, a child prodigy from *Antonia's Line*, directed by Marleen Gorris (1995, Dutch); and many other literary and cinematic fictional figures indicate that contemporary white male Faustuses and Frankensteins are made to share the world of the mind with their lesser brothers and sisters.[5] However the

---

5   "In a survey of 60 films containing scientists between 1929 and 2003, Eva Flicker from the University of Vienna reported that eleven (18%) included female scientists. But a survey of more recent films (1991-2001) by Jocelyn Steinke at Western Michigan University found 23 female scientists in 74 science-related films (31%). My own keyword searches on the Internet Movie Database (IMDB) identified 84 women scientists out of 382 films containing scientists (22%). So female scientists on film are in the minority, but there are more of them in recent films" (Sidney Perkowitz, http://www.the-scientist.com/?articles.view/articleNo/24170/title/Female-scientists-on-the-big-screen/).

latter – women and the ethnic Other – tie the world of academy to this side of the mind-body problem which seems responsible for re-thematisation of the professor figure. The body of woman of science, like that of her Afro-American or Japanese colleague, attracts sufficiently big attention to anchor the academic 'bubble' in feminist or other cultural causes and contexts.

Dana Mallach, a quantum physicist from Goldstein's novel *Properties of Light*, and Catherine, a mathematician from Madden's film *Proof*, based on David Auburn's acclaimed 2000 play of the same title, find themselves in an intertextually similar situation. Born as the world famous scientists' only daughters and brought up under the dome of academicity, Dana and Catherine are expected to remain young and beautiful Mirandas. The role of loving, supportive, 'naturally' inferior females, taking good care of aging Prosperos, is all they can count on. Two young Ferdinands from the novel and the film sustain the model: the budding academic geniuses who appear in the houses of the burnt-out professors fall in love with their weird daughters at first sight. A sense of kinship with the fathers' beautiful minds as well as desire for the beautiful female bodies make the contemporary Ferdinands disregard Mirandas' inherited brilliance of the mind. Even to them (most of all to them?), Mirandas replacing aged Prosperos would unpleasantly shatter the natural order of things.

The novel and the film have different endings, yet apparently allude to the same cultural paradigm. Goldstein's novel leaves the reader with uncertainty as to the daughter's science talent – it gives no definite answer to the question whether Dana could ever be her father's or young Justin's peer. The play and the film show Hal cautiously taking into consideration that his Catherine may have inherited not only her father's weaknesses, but also his mathematical talents. Hal gradually starts to believe that a brilliant mathematical proof found in Professor Mallach's desk may not have been done by the once genius father but rather by his genius daughter. To put it differently, the Ferdinand from *Proof* at least considers himself for a position of a little brother learning from his weird bigger sister. However, uncertainty about Catherine's future sanity – like Dana Mallach's depression and her suicide attempt that kills Justin and turns him into a ghost haunting the campus, leaves the question about the role of Mirandas in the male academic world open. On the other hand, the havoc that both women produce in the world of *men* of learning only adds to the portrayal of women scientists as spoilers of the traditional 'bubble of the mind'.

*

In the 1980s, George Gerbner's study concerning figures of scientists on US primetime television proved a high ratio of negative stereotypes. Having completed his research undertaken in the mid-1990s, Gerbner concluded that changes had occurred in Hollywood since the time of his "initial study, which found scientists to be typically evil, disturbed, sexually dysfunctional villains". "[T]here is no basis to claim that any kind of systematic negative portrayal of scientists exists. [...] [T]his is no longer the case" (Gerbner in Nisbet). The analysis of TV content, updated at the turn of the centuries and later, shows that over the last decades the portrayal of scientists in film and television has gradually changed from negative to positive: at present scientists are shown as increasingly fragile but basically positive heroes, whose turbulent careers raise sympathising interest, if not admiration.

Considering a compensative role of popular culture and the mass media, we can argue that this present tendency to make scientists and university professors feel better may result from the unprecedented commercialisation of science and the idiocy of the so-called "rationalisation" in the higher education system which have succeeded in lowering the status of the scientist and academic to that of a busy supplier in an efficiently (corporations) or poorly (universities) run businesses. The levelling process that stripped a fictional scientist figure of its status and familiarised it partly through defamation, partly through enhancing the role of private lives and hobbies, either substituted a satirising mimetic function for a thematic one or considerably re-thematised the figure by placing it within other cultural contexts. What we observe in the academic mainstream novels and films of the last two decades or so is an attempt at a positive re-mystification of characters in question. Fictional professors (even women scholars) get as if a second chance to feel empowered.

> She felt better than confident, she decided. For the first time in months she felt, well, empowered. She smiled to herself and passed into the welcoming shadows under the live oaks beyond the plaza. A chill winter wind began to

blow from behind her, urging her along, but Virginia did not mind, because the wind was going in her direction, and the shadows reminded her of her gloomy childhood [...]. Indeed the wind was like a mischievous old friend who teased her as she walked, plying about her ankles, tugging at her scarf, and whispering in her ear, all the way home. (Hynes 1997: 334-5)

Neo-gothic forms that boldly encroached upon the terrain of postmodernist academic fictions in literature or film have been deployed ever since, mainly to restore the mystique of *possible scientist*,[6] whose opaqueness and syntheticity (constructedness) are the sine qua non of the reality torn by the body-mind problem.

---

6   For a discussion of various forms of faculty gothic in contemporary academic fiction see Gruszewska-Blaim 2012b, 2014a, 2014b. See also Sherry R. Truffin.

Part III

Characters in Extra-Textual Contexts

Terry Pratchett's Lord Vetinari
as a transtextual character

KAMIL KARAŚ

This study is devoted to the transtextual character of Lord Havelock Vet-inari, the Patrician of Ankh-Morpork, from Terry Pratchett's domain of the Discworld[1]. Rarely does it happen that a literary character, though not a protagonist, focuses the reader's attention, and yet this is the case with the Pratchettian leader of the most recognisable Discworld city-state. Lord Vetinari's importance in the novelistic series, partly due to the author's crafty use of language and humour, invites questions about the functions of this outstanding character as well as his status in Pratch-ett's oeuvre.

Lord Vetinari can be seen as an example of a transtextual character, since he appears in several Discworld novels[2] and his individual identity persists from text to text (compare Richardson 2010: 527). Actually, he also appears in some TV and BBC Radio productions, e.g. *Colour of Magic* (2008) or *Going Postal* (2010), so that he can be also considered a transmedial character, but this issue, involving the problems of adaptation, is beyond the scope of this article.

---

1   Discworld – the fictional world of a novel series by Terry Pratchett – consists of a flat shield lying on the backs of four elephants standing on a huge turtle, the Great A'Tuin. It is a fantasy world with different races – humans as well as fantastic creatures – coex-isting and interacting with one another. The biggest and the most important city on Disc is Ankh-Morpork – ruled by Lord Havelock Vetinari. The whole city is a strange com-bination of many cultures and races. In spite of the presence of advanced technology, trolls, dwarfs, werewolves, banshees, witches, wizards and the undead mingle with hu-mans on the streets of Ankh-Morpork.

2   In 2013 *Raising Steam*, another book featuring Vetinari, was published, but since its appearance took place after the completion of this article the novel is not discussed here.

It should be added that Lord Havelock Vetinari is by no means the only transtextual character to appear in Pratchett's novels. The recurrence of characters seems to constitute an important unifying strategy in the series. Quite a few characters seem to play important roles in many books, for instance: Samuel Vimes, Carrot Ironfoundersson, Nobby Nobbs, Sgt Colon, the Monks of Time, Death (and the Death of Rats), Mustrum Ridcully, the Archchancellor of the Unseen University, Susan Sto Helit (the granddaughter of Death), Detritus the Troll, Ponder Stibbons the Wizard, or Rincewind the Wizard. However, Lord Havelock Vetinari appears to be the most important and the most interesting figure among them in terms of his role in the fictional world of the Discworld as well as his function in the textual semantics.

Brian Richardson explains that a transtextual character has to appear in more than one text, preferably by one author, set in one fictional world. He or she should also have the same mimetic attributes throughout the whole series or sequels he/she appears in (though some degree of change within the story is possible) and at the same time perform the same roles within the narrative (Richardson 2010: 538-540). This clearly matches with Maria E. Reicher's claims that, ontologically, characters may change and yet retain their identity in the course of the plot. The characters can, for instance, grow up and change their personal attributes with the course of fictional time – both in the chapters of one text or in a series of books treated as if they were chapters (Reicher 2010: 131-132). Richardson also emphasises that in the case of transtextuality "information from the later works will add to our knowledge of the character" (2010: 539).

The character of Lord Havelock Vetinari is only gradually revealed in the Discworld series. Since the first book, *The Colour of Magic* (1983), the author tends to dose small pieces of data concerning the leader of Ankh-Morpork. Lord Vetinari appears in twenty-two Discworld novels so far, especially in those belonging to the so-called City Watch subseries. Until now the most plentiful amount of data appeared probably in *Unseen Academicals* (2009). The character inhabits the same fictional world of the Disc, which sails through the interstellar space on the back of a turtle. Within the Discworld, a more limited spatial area with which the fictional life of Havelock Vetinari is connected (the city-state Ankh-Morpork) remains the same through all the books in which he appears.

An important aspect of the character's unity within the series is the name[3]. In the case of Havelock Vetinari, his name and surname are constant all through the Discworld series. Under his own name Lord Vetinari starts to appear regularly in novels published since the late 1980s[4]. The character's appearance does not seem to alter either: he is tall and slim, with a goatee and a small black cap always on the top of his head. He uniformly wears black and does not devote much attention to his clothes – he wears pragmatic, clean, and comfortable robes.

In the sphere of "the psychological makeup", Lord Vetinari's character seems to have several principles of composition. First of all, his character features seem to be invariable – he never succumbs to anger and is very stable emotionally. Even when threatening someone with death (for example Moist von Lipwig), he always speaks in a calm, indirect way, with a witty comment[5]. He is a shrewd observer of his reality, which can be deduced from his reading a book about camouflage and concealment, written by the late Lord Winstanleigh Greville-Pipe. He wants to learn how to blend into the shadows to such an extent he cannot be seen, which goal he achieves, as confirmed by the fact that Vetinari's teacher of stealth has not seen him even once during lectures (Pratchett 2020: 234). In the future, being unnoticeable will be one of the most useful skills for Vetinari as a Patrician.

However, in some books the reader may actually be unsure whether the author describes the same character or not. One example of such a situation presents itself in the *Colour of Magic*, where a character called the Patrician appears but no proper name is given, so that the recipient of the series cannot be sure whether the Patrician described is Vetinari him-

---

3   Compare Richardson's discussion on various problems connected with proper names and transtextuality (2010: 528-9).

4   The name Vetinari appears in *Sourcery* (1988), *Guards! Guards!* (1989), *Moving Pictures* (1990), *Reaper Man* (1991), *Men at Arms* (1993), *Interesting Times* (1994), *Soul Music* (1994), *Feet of Clay* (1996), *Jingo* (1997), *The Fifth Elephant* (1999), *The Truth* (2000), *The Last Hero* (2001), *Night Watch* (2002), *Going Postal* (2004), *Thud!* (2005), *Making Money* (2007), *Unseen Academicals* (2009), *Snuff* (2011) and *Raising Steam* (2013).

5   For example, in *Reaper Man* one can find a threat towards the mages: "If per capita was a problem, decapita could be arranged".

self or rather his predecessor, the Mad Lord Snapcase. The Patrician is witty enough to be Vetinari (Lord Snapcase was known to be utterly mad and genocidal) but in the book he has "chins" and rather fat fingers, whereas Vetinari is slim (and therefore has only one chin). Additionally, the unnamed Patrician is wearing rings while Vetinari wears only one ring with his coat of arms. All in all, it is doubtful whether the Patrician character in *Colour of Magic* can be identified with Havelock Vetinari.

A different example of an identity problem appears in *Night Watch*. The novel features a character called Havelock Vetinari, but the plot takes place about thirty years before he becomes the Patrician, partly in the past of Samuel Vimes, the protagonist, when Havelock Vetinari is only a student of the Assassins' School and not a lord yet. In the book Sir Samuel Vimes accidentally goes back in time to Ankh-Morpork from the years of his own adolescence, where and when he has to act as his younger self's mentor – John Keel (actually the "real" John Keel is killed in an accident at the same time). Young Havelock Vetinari kills a thug who intends to assassinate Vimes-Keel, and therefore enables the story to proceed. It is assumed that if Vimes had been killed, there would have been no future Ankh-Morpork the way it was before the time-jump. In comparison with the other Vetinari novels, the setting of *Night Watch* is different – though only temporally, since spatially it is still Ankh-Morpork. Also the person called Vetinari is not exactly the one later called the Patrician – he is younger and does not seem to have the same sense of humour; he has much worse insight into the surrounding reality and does not play the plot roles typical of the character Lord Vetinari. All these differences, however, may be accounted for by the admissible change of the character's time relative properties (Reicher 2010: 131).

*

Considering the roles and functions of Lord Vetinari in the Pratchettian series I will first focus on his role within the fictional world and then proceed to discuss his functions on the textual level with the help of categories proposed by Vladimir Propp. In the former sphere Vetinari plays, first of all, the role of the ruler which is essential for the consideration of this character.

Edward James says that the name Vetinari "is obviously meant to recall the consummate cynical politicians of the Italian Renaissance, the

Medici rulers of Florence. The name 'medici' derives from 'doctor'; Vetinari, obviously, from 'veterinary doctor'" (James 2010: 209). James's claim is evidently based on Pratchett's own explanation of the name provided in an interview given to Brendan Wignall:

> I always think of the Patrician as a vaguely Florentine prince, a sort of Machiavelli and Robespierre rolled into one. And of course there was Medici. So I thought if you had the Medici then you would have the Dentistri and the Vetinari. The Discworld is full of things which don't look like gags but are gags if only you can work out what the intervening step is which I haven't given. (Wignall 1991)

Havelock Vetinari as the Patrician, or the ruler, of the city-state Ankh-Morpork, the biggest and the most powerful city on the Disc, is at the first glance ruthless and cruel, but in fact, he is not very bloodthirsty. He does not even believe in unnecessary violence[6]. Giorgio Agamben writes in his book *Homo sacer – sovereign power and bare life* about the notion of *homo sacer* – a scapegoat – or a man that can be killed or sacrificed in order to save the rest of the country/society/people. That kind of thinking seems to be what constitutes the character of the Patrician whose main aim is the good of his people (his city), and who will not falter while pursuing his ideas.

Vetinari really cares for Ankh-Morpork. All the guilds (with the only exception of Beggars and Assassins, which are said to be ancient) have been either set up by him (like Seamstresses' Guild) or encouraged to become legal (like the Thieves' Guild). He reactivates the City Post Office and the Royal Mint, and changes the city for the better by altering the rules of a dangerous game, called foot-the-ball. He protects his people from being robbed by the Trunk clacks company. He also tries to prevent rich people from becoming too powerful and from oppressing the poor – like when he makes Vimes work against smuggling goods from the countryside[7]. Lord Vetinari may be identified with the city it-

---

6   He does, however, believe in the necessary violence – which means he would do everything that is needed to protect the city. As he says, "dismantling a person is sometimes necessary" (Pratchett 1993: 60).

7   To quote Vetinari: "[…] a certain amount of harmless banditry [smuggling in this case] amongst the lower classes is to be smiled upon if not actively encouraged, for the health of the city, but what should we do when the highborn and wealthy take to crime? Indeed, […] how high would the gallows need to be to hang the rich man who breaks the law out of greed?" (Pratchett 2011:19).

self. When he comes to kill one of his predecessors, Lord Winder, he says: "I come from the city [...]", and then "think of me as [...] your future" (Pratchett 2002: 410). He is the punishing arm of the city as well as the future of the city, the Patrician-to-be after the Mad Lord Snapcase. He does what he can to protect Ankh-Morpork – to fix what is broken, as his motto suggests.

In view of his features as a ruler of Ankh-Morpork, Lord Vetinari may be perceived in the context of yearning for a powerful leader, despotic yet caring, who knows the world he lives in, knows what the ailments of his world are and how to alleviate them. Such a ruler, knowing how to help his people and willing to do so not for his/her own profit, but *pro bono publico* – sometimes killing certain individuals in order to save others – would fit perfectly with the character Lord Vetinari. In fact, Havelock Vetinari seems to be a personification of an ideal ruler, a model of politics and politicians – whose existence is possible only in the fictional world. However, this conclusion should be modified by the constant association of the character with humour. It is not that Vetinari is a funny character, but he is amusingly cynical and witty. The addition of humour seems to add an ironic quality to Vetinari-as-the-ideal-ruler.

A very interesting aspect of Havelock Vetinari is that – in spite of appearing in numerous texts – he has never been a protagonist yet. Numerous transtextual and multimedial characters (like Sherlock Holmes or Conan the Barbarian) are always (or often enough to constitute a rule) protagonists, i.e. leading characters on which the plot and the fictional world often depend. They are needed for the main events to take place and for separate stories to be consistent. One cannot imagine a Sherlock Holmes or a Conan the Barbarian story without these two as protagonists. Although the latter aspect is not applicable to Lord Vetinari, it may be surprising that his functions may be in some respects similar to those fulfilled by the protagonists, while he is just a secondary character, supporting or legitimising the hero.

In order to discuss several different functions[8] Lord Vetinari has on the textual level in the Discworld series, I will make use of Vladimir Propp's model of character's roles, which, although created to describe the genre of the Russian magic folktale, to some extent seems also appli-

---

8   I use the term function in its usual sense (of role, purpose) and not in the way Propp
     proposed in his analysis of the event sequences in the magic folktale.

cable to the genre fantasy. In his book *Morphology of the Folktale*, Propp distinguishes seven main roles the character can play (or character types): the *villain*, the *donor*, the *helper*, the *sought-for-person / the Princess and her father*, the *dispatcher*, the *hero* and the *false hero*. It seems that Lord Havelock Vetinari mainly fulfills three roles distinguished by Vladimir Propp, namely the role of the dispatcher, helper and donor[9]. I am going to present these roles on the examples from *Guards!Guards!*, *Jingo*, *Unseen Academicals*, *Snuff* and *Night Watch*, beginning with the role of the dispatcher, i.e. a character who sends the hero on a quest or mission. One can claim Lord Vetinari fulfils this role in all but one book he appears in, namely the *Night Watch*.

For example, in *Jingo*, he organises an underground expedition to the island of Leshp in order to prevent a war. His role of the dispatcher, which concerns sending his more or less willing subordinates on the mission, is slightly modified when he surprisingly joins them in the submarine. Even as a participant of the mission, however, he does not become a protagonist, but maintains his function of a secondary character.

Snuff in turn presents the reader with a story in which the Patrician makes Sam Vimes take a two-weeks leave and go with his family to their summer residence. As it turns out, this is a plot conceived by Lord Vetinari (together with Sir Vimes's wife, Sybil Ramkin) in order to probably suppress the smuggle of goods undertaken by wealthy people, even though the official reason is to allow Vimes to rest before he overworks himself.

When Moist von Lipwig (better known as Albert Spangler), the protagonist of three novels, is caught by the Watch and sentenced to die for a fraud in *Going Postal*, he is given a chance by Lord Vetinari. Moist can choose working for the city as a Postmaster – or die. Vetinari gives him clear orders and sends him to deal with the Post Office. His function can therefore be seen as that of the dispatcher. The situation is repeated in *Making Money* and *Raising Steam*.

---

9 In *Guards!Guards!* there is a joke about Vetinari playing the role of the father of the Princess. When the summoned dragon slayers appear, they want to receive the hand of the Princess and half of the kingdom as a reward. When they learn that Vetinari does not have daughters (only an aunt and a dog) and rules only a Patrimony, not a kingdom, they leave in distaste.

In *Unseen Academicals,* the Patrician gives certain orders to the protagonist (this time the main character is a collective of mages from the Unseen University) – their task is to create a team which is to play against the best players from the city. The reader is also faced with the obvious fact that the fate of the protagonist depends on Vetinari's will – namely, should they fail to let the University foot-the-ball team play, they would lose a huge amount of possessions. Vetinari also changes the rules of the game – a very brutal and chaotic version of street football – into something much more player- and audience-friendly and then he sends the protagonist to fulfil the task.

In *Guards!Guards!,* facing the crisis situation of a dragon burning his city and devouring his people, Lord Vetinari gives the Captain of the City Watch, Samuel Vimes, a strange order, which can look as if he did not care for Ankh-Morpork or its citizens. Namely, he forbids Vimes to continue his search for the dragon. The Patrician knows Captain Vimes well enough to use forbidding in order to cause the exactly opposite reaction, i.e. to push Vimes deeper into action so that the dragon is soon found and defeated. Also here Vetinari clearly performs the function of the dispatcher, though the role is changed in a rather original way.

Another role Havelock Vetinari can be perceived to perform in the action is that of a helper, which embraces a broad category of both people and objects that help the hero. This role may also be played by an animal (often talking one). The role of helper is also connected with the notion of returning the equilibrium to the world of the protagonist (Propp 1968: 135). Vetinari is a helper every time he makes the quest easier for the protagonist or provides support. In *Jingo,* he helps neutralise difficulties the protagonists encounter and in this way ensures an almost bloodless and peaceful outcome of a conflict evidently leading to war. In this way he also restores equilibrium to the world. In *Unseen Academicals,* Lord Vetinari supports the aspirations of the protagonist and brings back equilibrium to the city torn by fights between supporters of the foot-the-ball teams, when he changes the rules of the game in order to make Ankh-Morpork a better place. It can be seen that the role of the helper, although it appears less often than the role of the dispatcher, is clearly connected with the latter. This is not a rare occurrence in a folktale or even in modern fantasy, that these two roles are performed by one character.

A minor role which can be ascribed to Vetinari is that of a donor, i.e. someone who gives the hero something of importance, like a magic weapon or some object of great power, necessary for the success in the quest. This role often merges with that of the helper. In fact, Lord Vetinari plays this role actively only once, when he participates in the feast for the foot-the-ball players and provides the prize for the winner – a magical, bottomless vase with never-ending beer. The gift seals the agreement between the players and makes the new, better game possible (which will, in time, change the whole city).

It is easy to notice that though the aforementioned roles often merge, the most frequent and hence the most important one for Lord Vetinari is the role of the dispatcher. Among the analysed books, only *Night Watch* does not have Vetinari as the dispatcher, mainly because he is not yet the Patrician, which suggests a significant connection between his role as a ruler and that of the dispatcher. His plot role of allotting tasks and sending characters on missions results in Vetinari's being able – to a considerable extent – to determine the course of events, which seems significant for a character who is not a protagonist.

Vetinari seems almost godlike in his ability to create and destroy characters and places within his domain (directly in Ankh-Morpork and its closest vicinity, indirectly – via politics – in nearly the whole Disc and even outside it[10]). For instance, he elevates Samuel Vimes from a mere drunk Captain of the Night Watch to the title of the Duke of Ankh, while a conman, Moist von Lipwig, is raised to the status of the Postmaster General and the master of the Royal Mint. He often gives no alternative (except for death) and does whatever he thinks is good for the city. As he seems to be behind all important acts in the fictional world, he may be taken to be the *spiritus movens* and the main cause of action, the equivalent of the Great Architect – with the only difference that the Deistic God does not care for the world he created, while Lord Vetinari certainly does.

Moreover, Vetinari's role of the ruler makes him able to perceive things at a different level than the other characters and to use both objects and people to realise his plans. In fact, Lord Vetinari seems to represent a higher level of consciousness since he observes and knows more

---

10   For example, in *The Last Hero*.

than any other characters in the fictional world. Addressing the City
Guilds' Presidents he says:

> 'I know who you are [...]. I know where you live. I know what kind of
> horse you ride. I know where your wife has her hair done. I know where
> your lovely children, how old are they now, my, doesn't time fly, I know
> where they play. So you won't forget about what we agreed, will you? And
> he smiled. So did they, after a fashion'. (Pratchett 1990: 59)

Vetinari consistently appears to know more not only in comparison with
other characters but also with the reader. In other words, from the perspective of characters and the reader, he is almost omniscient. It seems
entirely possible to conclude that the character of Lord Vetinari performs the metafictional function of the authorial figure inside the fictional world.

Lord Havelock Vetinari, a secondary character from a popular fantasy series, is definitely not meant to be a complex psychological creation.
As a transtextual character, he is gradually revealed to the recipient of
the Pratchettian series while his attributes and roles suggest important
semantic functions as a humorous, perhaps even slightly ironic, figure of
an ideal ruler and as a god-like authorial figure suggesting a metafictional dimension of the character.

Breaking Out and Speaking: Old Myths and Narrative Tensions in Ursula Le Guin's *Lavinia*[1]

KATARZYNA PISARSKA

> Women cannot write—using old myths.
> But using new ones—?
>
> Joanna Russ, *To Write Like a Woman*

In recent years there have appeared numerous novels by women writers which offer retellings of the grand narratives of our culture or of some perennial works of European literature. In these novels a well-known story is related through the eyes of a previously marginalised female character who is either the subject of focalisation or "breaks her silence" in order to show the woman's true experience in a patriarchal society as well as her place in the literature written by men. Suffice it to mention *The Red Tent* (1997), Anita Diamant's much acclaimed and best-selling midrash version of the biblical story of Jacob and his wives, told from the perspective of his only daughter Dinah. Or Jenny Diski's *Only Human. A Comedy* (2000), which centres on Sarah, Abraham's wife, caught in a love triangle with the only God, struggling for her husband's heart and the control of both her destiny and her narrative. Another strand of female recyclings comprises mythological narratives, probably most famously exemplified by Margaret Atwood's *The Penelopiad* (2005), a feminist retake on Homer's *Odyssey* which explores the combined issues

---

1   The research for this contribution was financed by Maria Curie-Skłodowska University of Lublin/ Faculty of Humanities grant no. MPK: BS-05-0000-D012, ZFIN: 000 000 40.

of gender and story-telling[2]. Such works testify to the exploration of the literary tradition by female writers in search of *lacunae*, i.e. missing elements, whose reconstruction or rewriting would allow them to (re)assert the female presence in the history of letters and culture.

Ursula Le Guin's novel *Lavinia* (2008) continues this trend, as it gives voice to a Latin princess from Vergil's *Aeneid* to whom the Roman poet devoted only a few lines in his great epic. Rewriting the last six books of Vergil's poem, Le Guin imbues the lifeless and silent character of Lavinia with courage, determination and passionate nature, and makes her the protagonist, narrator and also, frequently, the prime mover behind the well-known epic events. Such a redirecting of perspective and function gives precedence to the experience of the young woman, previously ignored by the men-oriented epic, and turns Lavinia into a fully-fledged character, with a well-developed and foregrounded mimetic component (as defined by James Phelan[3]). At the same time, Le Guin's character reveals the awareness of her own fictionality (the synthetic status, according to Phelan's analytical framework), of her existence being contingent on the words of the poet but also on her own act of writing. Thus, her role as narrator and character becomes intertwined with the alleged authorship of the text:

> I know who I was, I can tell you who I may have been, but I am, now, only in this line of words I write. I'm not sure of the nature of my existence, and wonder to find myself writing. I speak Latin, of course, but did I ever learn

---

2   A comparison of *The Penelopiad* and *Lavinia* is drawn by T. S. Miller who claims that despite the apparent similarity, there is a significant difference between Le Guin's and Atwood's mythological retellings: "Unlike Atwood's contrarian Penelope, [...] Lavinia very much sings in the same key as Vergil, even if she chooses to take for her primary subjects, in place of arms and the man, her own domestic life and indeed the poet himself. In a sense, for all her tinkering with Vergil's mythology and narrative arc, Le Guin delivers a fairly orthodox reading of the great Latin epic; [...]. Lavinia's measured piety remains many Roman miles away from Atwood's penchant for the 'subversive,' for lack of a better term" (2010: 29, 31). Although *Lavinia* clearly offers a less revisionist re-reading of the epic than *The Penelopiad*, being, as Le Guin states in the Afterword to the novel, "an act of gratitude to the poet, a love offering" (2010: 289) rather than an attempt to "improve or reprove him" (291), the writer's feminist agenda still makes itself felt in the construction of Lavinia's character, which I intend to explore in my analysis.

3   The notion of three major components for the analysis of character in literature – the mimetic, the thematic and the synthetic – as distinguished by James Phelan in his study *Reading People, Reading Plots* (1989), is discussed in more detail in the Introduction.

to write it? That seems unlikely. No doubt someone with my name, Lavinia, did exist, but she may have been so different from my own idea of myself, or my poet's idea of me, that it only confuses me to think about her. As far as I know, it was my poet who gave me any reality at all. Before he wrote, I was the mistiest of figures, scarcely more than a name in a genealogy. It was he who brought me to life, to myself, and so made me able to remember my life and myself, which I do, vividly, with all kinds of emotions, emotions I feel strongly as I write, perhaps because the events I remember only come to exist as I write them, or as he wrote them. (Le Guin 2010: 3)

This self-reflexive passage introduces a tension between the narrator and the authorial audience[4], as it immediately follows the opening section in which we become acquainted with the character in her mimetic aspect, while the synthetic one is still kept in the background. Such a juxtaposition signals the demand put on the authorial audience to read the narrative at once mimetically and synthetically-thematically. In the first scene of the novel, the first-person narrator recounts her visit at the age of nineteen to the mouth of the river Tiber. The authorial audience is placed in the midst of the character's world and made to read as if they were familiar with it. Every successive bit of information deepens the tension between us and the narrator: the apparently regular activity on the part of the character – digging up salt from the salt pans for the sacred meal, the matter-of-fact introduction of her companions ("Tita and Maruna came with me" [2010: 1]), as if the narrator took for granted our familiarity with them, or her revelation of the secret names of Father Tiber. The narrator's mention of the old house slave and a donkey as a means of transport, as well as her subsequent description of the war-ships coming into the river's mouth (manned with oarsmen, with "long, arched, triple beaks" of bronze [2010: 2]), serves to foreground the temporal distance between the authorial audience and the character's world.

The arrival of the strange ships builds up a new tension, as the narrator-character's knowledge is shown as greater than that of the authorial audience. She claims she knows who their leader is; however, this information is withheld from the reader for some time. The coming of the ships also signals the event which will be only later – halfway through

---

4   In Phelan's sense authorial audience "will pick up on all the signals in the appropriate way"; it is contrasted with narrative audience treating the narrative situation as real (1989: 5).

the novel – explained as the arrival of Aeneas and his Trojan warriors. The opening section therefore allows the audience to become partly familiar with the character's mimetic attributes: we may speculate that she is a woman (judging by her closest female company), a king's child, familiar with sacred rites, religious and responsible for making salt for the royal household. We also start developing certain expectations and interest in the character's fate in relation with her mimetic qualities. However, the following section (i.e. Lavinia's confession of her own constructedness quoted above), redirects the authorial audience's attention to the character's synthetic component and, by implication, to her thematic importance. This foregrounding of the synthetic component occurs early at the beginning of the novel, so the authorial audience has an opportunity to allow for the consequent tensions in their response to the progression of the narrative. At the same time, we are made aware that the character's enhanced mimeticisation will be effected in the service of her thematisation.

The authorial audience's disbelief is again put to the test when the character/narrator/presumed author muses over her knowledge of Latin in speech but doubts her ability to write in this language, while maintaining that she is indeed writing at the moment. All we get in the passage and the whole text is after all English, which is only metaphorically the Latin of the modern world. Lavinia's further musings about her communication with the reader, as well as her recollection of the Trojans speaking perfect Latin to her people, convince us that there must be some superior entity responsible for the words she "writes" just as there apparently was someone to enable the Trojan-Latin understanding in the *Aeneid*:

> After all, how can it be that we can all talk to one another? I remember the foreigners from the other side of the world, sailing up the Tiber into a country they knew nothing of: their envoy came to my father's house, explained that he was a Trojan, and made polite speeches in fluent Latin. Now how could that be? Do we all know all the languages? That can be true only of the dead, whose land lies under all the other lands. How is it that you understand me, who lived twenty-five or thirty centuries ago? Do you know Latin?
> But then I think no, it has nothing to do with being dead, it's not death that allows us to understand one another, but poetry. (Le Guin 2010: 5)

The synthetic component of Lavinia's character is foregrounded again, first, as Vergil's creation and second, as a construct in a new narrative whose authorship she at once professes and questions. At the same time, Lavinia's synthetic aspect serves the novel's thematic agenda, namely challenging the patriarchal representation of femininity as silent and submissive, and using literature, which in the past marginalised a woman, to assert her presence and agency in narratives previously written by men about men. Although Lavinia acknowledges Vergil's role in bringing her to life in the first place (resuscitating her historical person and giving her a literary life), she also accuses her male creator of his "slighting" and "scanting" of her character in the *Aeneid*:

> And yet [...] the life he gave me in his poem, is so dull, except for the one moment when my hair catches fire – so colourless, except when my maiden cheeks blush like ivory stained with crimson dye – so conventional, I can't bear it any longer. If I must go on existing century after century, then once at least I must break out and speak. He didn't let me say a word. I have to take the word from him. He gave me a long life but a small one. I need room, I need air. My soul reaches out into the old forests of my Italy, up to the sunlit hills, up to the winds of the swan and the truth-speaking crow. My mother was mad, but I was not. My father was old, but I was young. Like Spartan Helen, I caused a war. She caused hers by letting men who wanted her take her. I caused mine because I wouldn't be given, wouldn't be taken, but chose my man and my fate. (Le Guin 2010: 4)

The passage is important because it contains a set of postulates linked with the construction of Lavinia's character on the synthetic, the mimetic and the thematic levels in the course of the novel. The narrator/protagonist resists the conventionality of her character's presentation by Vergil and, by implication, also the representation of femininity in patriarchal literature. She refuses to remain silent: challenging the meekness and voicelessness of Vergil's Lavinia, and her submission to male politics and desire, the narrator/protagonist questions both the gender relationships and the heroic ideal upheld by the culture of the time. The narrator of Le Guin's novel claims that in contrast to Spartan Helen, whose life was decided by men's whims and passions, Lavinia "caused" a war in Latium because she would not be a pawn in men's game, which emphasises her thematic freedom as a woman and individual. One last important assumption communicated in the passage is the character's need for "room" and "air", that is the necessity to endow her underdeveloped character with mimetic substance, which will be accomplished through her connection with a particular space, namely Latium.

Accordingly, the aim of the present analysis is to examine the ways in which the synthetic component of Lavinia's character (the fact that she is a poetic/literary construct) is foregrounded in the novel. Moreover, it will be shown how the transformations of this component (Lavinia's awareness of her own literariness and the need to re-construct herself mimetically, i.e. to present more of her traits and motivations, etc.) serve the thematic functions of Le Guin's work: a woman's stand for her personal freedom and independence, her struggle against oppressive relationships in a patriarchal society, and, what follows, her resistance to the patriarchal representation of femininity in literature, here exemplified by Vergil's *Aeneid* and the epic convention as such.

At this point, it is worth recalling the character of Lavinia in Vergil's *Aeneid*, whose mimetic component (apart from her oft-emphasised virginity, emotionality, golden hair and rosy cheeks) relies to a considerable extent on her distinguishing mimetic dimension of being of marriageable age – she is described as "iam matura viro, iam plenis nubilis annis" [already ripe for a husband and of full age for marriage] (Vergil 1996: 2; Book VII, l. 53), and so pursued as a potential match by young princes from the neighbouring kingdoms with Turnus, king of Rutulia, among them. Although she is considered "causa mali tanti," [the cause of all that evil/woe] in Vergil's poem (1996: 121; Book XI, l. 480), she is a rather passive "cause," as neither her feelings for Turnus, Aeneas or any other suitor, nor any active behaviour to determine the choice of her husband play a part in provoking the war[5]. The suitors are indeed "[f]ired with her love" but also "with ambition led" (Vergil 1997: 195; Book VII, l. 80), which means that however lovely the princess is, her pulling power depends considerably on her political value. Moreover, the Fury Allecto, sent by Juno to spur Turnus to war, appeals more to his sense of warrior's pride than to his lover's heart, and reminds him of his blood right to the crown of Latium. When he derides her warmongering, the Fury pierces his chest with a "smouldering torch, impressed/ With

---

5   Despite the fact that Lavinia's feelings in the *Aeneid* are never made explicit, some critics write about love between the princess and Turnus. For example, J. W. Mackail calls the Rutulian king Lavinia's "lover" (1922: 107), while W. Y. Sellar writes about "the wrong done to [Lavinia] and Turnus by the enforced severance of their affections" (1965: 400).

her full force" (1997: 211; Book VII, ll. 638-9), so that when in Book XII Turnus will not be persuaded to stop bleeding the country in the war and putting his royal life in danger, it is as much due to Lavinia's "beauteous face" and "crimson blush" as to his own Fury-fuelled wrathful character, which makes "[r]evenge, and jealous rage, and secret spite,/ Roll in his breast and rouse him to the fight" (1997: 364; Book XII, ll. 110-111).

It seems therefore that Lavinia's most important mimetic attribute in Vergil, apart from her captivating beauty, is her position in the political tapestry of Italy. She is the only heir of Latinus, the king's daughter who cannot rule on her own but whose hand in marriage would legitimise her husband's claim to the throne of Latium[6]. Given that Aeneas' rule in Italy has been foretold and promised by Jove to Aeneas' mother, Venus, all the human characters in the epic are simply playing out their predestined roles. However, without Lavinia as his wife, promised by her father and rightful king, Aeneas, in spite of the divine license, would have been nothing more than an invader and usurper, and the ideological function of Vergil's national epic would have been lost. After all, Aeneas represents the virtue of *pietas*, as opposed to Turnus' *furor*, and, as foretold by Aeneas' father in the underworld, Aeneas' rule will lead to the establishment of Rome, which will exercise the "worthy" and "Imperial Arts" "to tame the Proud, the fettered Slave to free" (Vergil 1997: 189; Book

---

6   A. M. Keith postulates that Lavinia in the *Aeneid* becomes inscribed in her father's territory of Latium and metonymically represents her father's realm – being "located at the centre of her father's household (*domus*), she defines the extent of her father's territory (*sedes*) in Latium, so that she too is in some sense constitutive of the topography of Italy" (2000: 49). According to Keith, in Latinus' response to the Trojans' request to be given a portion of land in his kingdom, Lavinia, whom Latinus promises to Aeneas in marriage, and the land become united through the metaphor of fertility – the land is rich and the princess is "ripe for a husband", which "guarantees the fertility of the ground of the state" (49-50). Keith further observes: "The opening lines of the poem define Aeneas' goal in Italy as 'Lavinian shores', in a phrase that collapses the twin political goals of marriage alliance and city foundation into one. Although Lavinia herself never speaks in the *Aeneid*, the city of Lavinium (XII.194), traditionally the home of the very Penates which Hector entrusts to Aeneas (II.293–5) and the goal of Aeneas' journey, the *telos* of his epic *labores* (1.1–3), will take its name from her. [...] Lavinium in the *Aeneid* is an idealised site founded on political marriage with Lavinia, 'a representation of' Lavinia, as Lavinia is 'the ground of that representation' [...]" (50).

VI, ll. 1175-6)[7]. By legitimising and making pious Aeneas' claim to the throne of Latium and his role of the founder of Rome and forefather of Romans, Vergil is also giving righteousness to the deeds of Aeneas' progenitors, and especially to the rule of Augustus and his right of emperorship. Thus, Lavinia's mimetic dimension of being a marriageable royal heir not only turns into a mimetic function, as it leads – indirectly – to the main instability of the epic plot, i.e. the war among the Latins and Trojans, but it also serves the thematic function reverberating through the poem, as the match between her and the Trojan is a matter of piety understood as duty, filial obedience, religiosity and mindfulness of the welfare of her city and the future city of Rome.

Here lies the difference between Lavinia and Dido in the *Aeneid*. It is Dido's personal qualities of beauty, goodness, being passionate and entirely devoted to love which influence the course of the epic plot – Aeneas' fate as the founder of Rome foretold by the gods is thwarted for a while because the Trojan warrior falls in love with the queen of Carthage. Dido's mimetic attributes responsible for her female charm turn into functions and affect the gods' plot which was going to lead Aeneas to Latium. However, she must pay dearly for her freedom in choosing her lover and "husband" in the world ruled by men and patriarchal morality. Her overwhelming passion makes her forget about her duties towards her nation and city – all works in Carthage are stopped and her government is failing because she subordinates everything to the matters of her heart. Abandoned by Aeneas, who, reprimanded by Mercury and obedient to his Italian fate, has set sail for Latium, Dido kills herself in despair, having lost her honour, queenly authority among her people and bellicose neighbours, as well as self-respect for betraying her late husband's memory. The instability between the characters of Dido and Aeneas is therefore rooted not only in the thematic conflict between the life

---

7   In his discussion of Aeneas' claim to the throne of Latium, S. E. Stout notices: "Vergil has been careful to leave in his reader's mind the feeling that Aeneas enters without injustice to any one upon his destined task of laying the foundations of the empire that was to rule the world. The charge of *iniuria* shall not lie against the power of Rome even at its far beginnings". At the same time, Stout thus comments on Latinus' offer of marrying his daughter off to the Trojan leader: "We see that if this marriage is consummated Aeneas will soon succeed in good right to the lands and to the throne of Latinus. We are pleased, for we know that through this union the two peoples are entering upon their destiny" (1924: 154-155).

of piety and the life of fury. It also involves a thematic juxtaposition of individual freedom set against slavish obedience to destiny and to mechanisms beyond man's real control, and, as a result, the relinquishment of the freedom of choice[8].

Lavinia in Vergil has little choice – she is a prize in the male struggle for power and a leaf in the historical whirlwind, unable to decide about her own future. She is all obedience and innocence, never voicing what she wants. The scene in which she sheds tears hearing her mother implore Turnus to save his own life and give up the duel with Aeneas is thus interpreted by James Morwood:

> Is she in love with Turnus, whom we imagine she knows? Does she love the hero Aeneas whom she has never met? Virgil has resolved not to tell us. We are suddenly taken by a poet with a supreme understanding of the workings of the human heart into the inner being of a young girl who is pawn in a brutal dynastic conflict and whose feelings nobody is willing to pause to discover. The method is characteristic of the poet, who brilliantly evokes the emotions of those who are to be eliminated or altogether transformed by the juggernaut of the Roman mission. (1997: XV)[9]

---

8   My point here is supported by the observations of Louise E. Matthaei, who claims that the governing force in Vergil's universe is not the standard epic machinery of the Olympian pantheon but morally-charged fate (1917: 14-17). In this context, whereas Aeneas is obedient to the tyranny of fate, Dido defies it through suicide, displaying a unique and laudable example of human freedom of will, on which Matthaei comments: "My impression is that Vergil, who clearly conceived the passion of Dido as a sin, was impelled to glorify her suicide, simply as an act of rebellion to an intolerable state of things. [...] Through long and laborious vistas of thought, Vergil has faithfully toiled at his vision of a moral world; fate, the great ruler, is the power of god and the conscience of man: it is the rule of justice and the working of nature: it is the life of the universe and the meaning of good. But in the episode of Dido he throws the whole splendour of his worship away. He rises to the greatest artistic power of all, the power to criticize himself while he continues to create, the power to follow a great idea by a matchless criticism. The conduct and faith of Aeneas are splendid achievements; but as the passion of Dido unerringly exposes his conduct, so does her suicide as unerringly challenge the whole system of the world and lay it in the dust" (25).

9   In his study "Hero and Theme in the *Aeneid*," L. A. MacKay postulates that Vergil's Aeneas in fact prefigures Julius Caesar, one of the Julii and Augustus' adopted father, the war in Latium being "the mythical counterpart of the civil war in which Caesar decided the fate of Rome" (1963: 159). Lavinia, in this context, is, according to MacKay, "simply *basileia*; Vergil's awareness of this explains why he, not incapable of depicting a feminine character, left her such a shadowy figure" (159).

Morwood's doubts are resolved in Le Guin's novel, where Lavinia's mimetic component is enhanced by such attributes as strong will, self-assertiveness, fear and simultaneously defiance of her mother, as well as her antipathy towards her Rutulian suitor, Turnus. The progression of the narrative in the novel is determined by personal traits and preferences of Lavinia, as opposed to the external circumstances in the *Aeneid*: her features are shown as leading to major instabilities in Le Guin's text and thus change into thematic functions[10].

Having forewarned the authorial audience of the novel that her character's story would transcend the one told in Vergil, Lavinia-the narrator does a volte face and informs us that if they had met her character as a girl, they would have accepted Vergil's perfunctory portrait of her: "a girl, a king's daughter, a marriageable virgin, chaste, silent, obedient, ready to a man's will as a field in spring is ready for the plow" (Le Guin 2010: 5). However, she also immediately makes clear that this limited mimetic (and thus thematic) model of submissive and will-less femininity resulted from her status of a daughter in a household where priority was given to the sons. The above quotation highlights Lavinia's thematic function and signals her later progression from traditional womanhood towards freedom and self-awareness, as she will repeatedly try to avoid the social and political constraints put on her sex and women in her position.

Misinterpreting her mother's terms of endearment addressed to her two younger brothers, whom Amata calls her "warriors", Lavinia extends the name to herself, as it is clearly connected with Amata's love and pride she takes in her children. The importance granted to masculinity and heroism results in the girl's subconscious yearning for those ideals in childhood, which reveals the marginalisation of womanhood as a prerequisite for a child's appreciation in the domestic sphere. Amata's suffering after her sons die of fever reveals its strong cultural basis: boys become kings and warriors and are unquestionable heirs, while the girl's role in the dynastic politics is to "marry well" and give birth to male children[11]. Amata's pain and frustration are vented upon her only surviv-

---

10 Phelan's notion of instability applies to unstable situations within the story, in contrast to tensions which take place on the level of discourse (1989: 15). For more details, see Introduction.

11 According to Sandra J. Lindow, Le Guin's novel traces the development of Lavinia's inner voice which guides the character on her way to achieving moral maturity and be-

ing child, on which Lavinia reflects: "I was silent and meek because if I spoke up, if I showed my will, she might remember that I was not my brothers, and I'd suffer for it" (Le Guin 2010: 5). The passage therefore introduces the first major instability in the novel – the conflict between Lavinia and her mother, Amata – and signals the thematic potential to be fully explored through the subsequent instabilities, i.e. the novel's critique of the masculine ideal and the suppression of the female principle.

The dysfunctional relationship with her mother is juxtaposed with Lavinia's close and loving relationship with her father, king Latinus, who suffers the same derision from his wife as Lavinia. By reason of his years, long-gone heroic glory and conciliatory nature, Latinus is called "old eunuch" by Amata, his alleged infirmity being to blame for the death of her royal sons. He therefore lacks the manliness which Amata finds so attractive in her nephew Turnus, king of Rutulia, and which presupposes such attributes as youth, virility, physical beauty and fitness, uncompromising nature, violence, vanity and wilfulness which borders on madness. Instead, Latinus' mimetic attributes include: wisdom, calm, emotional stability, diplomacy, responsibility, patience, devotion to gods and obedience to their decrees, which his wife usually perceives in terms of effeminacy[12].

The instability between Amata and Lavinia, on the one hand, and Lavinia's rapport with Latinus, on the other, which determine the family

---

coming "a woman who deserves to be queen". Amata's moral development, in contrast, is thwarted by the trauma following the death of her sons, as, in Lindow's view, Amata perceives her own worth in terms of "her ability to produce male heirs" (Lindow 2010: web). The latter observation gives credence to the opinion that it is Amata, and not Latinus, who represents the ideological agenda of patriarchy.

12   Amata's opinion of her older husband in Le Guin's novel may, in fact, correspond to the image of Latinus as presented by Vergil. Richard F. Moorton claims that despite his level-headedness and piety, Latinus in the *Aeneid* is the embodiment of the calm, innocent, passive and "quasi-feminine" nature of Latium, further observing: "First Vergil tells us with pointed significance just after his account of Latinus' genealogy that the gentle Latinus has been unable to produce a male heir hardy enough to survive to maturity [...]. However, in accordance with his nature he has begotten a daughter, Lavinia, who has reached marriageable age, and the necessity to seek a son-in-law, a surrogate for the son Latinus does not have, leads to a tragic contention between more vigorous men. The second sign of Latinus' deficiency is his inability to control what are in part the consequences of the first. When Latium, with Lavinia's suitor Turnus in the vanguard, demands an unnecessary and unjust war, Latinus knows that this conflict is wrong but lacks the strength to prevent it" (1989: 122-123).

dynamics in the royal house in Laurentum, translate into the thematic conflict between two models of conduct (out of which eventually arise different approaches to masculinity and femininity). One model, represented by Amata (and her nephew Turnus), is shown as monstrous and disruptive, both for the household and eventually the kingdom, as it involves the subjection of other people, be it one's own daughter, a young woman, or a nation, to one's personal whims and desires. The other, represented by Lavinia (and Latinus), is only allegedly submissive, because constructed on a different principle. Le Guin, just like Vergil before her, seems to link the thematic context of her novel with the Roman concept of *pietas* (piety) – being pious is understood here as being "responsible, faithful to duty, open to awe" (Le Guin 2010: 13). Although *furor* in Le Guin's novel is never called by its Roman name, it is synonymous with lack of piety (or with madness), which Lavinia often observes in Turnus or her own mother. It is the mimetic-thematic attribute of piety that prevents Lavinia's father from excessive mourning for his dead sons and thus also from insanity which afflicts Amata, as Latinus finds relief in "his duties as king, […] the rites to perform, […] the reassurance of the ancient family spirits of his house" (2010: 7). He teaches his daughter to behave with the same piety and recognise it in others, which in the end makes Lavinia reject her cousin Turnus and welcome Aeneas as her future husband.

As can be noticed, despite the fact that Lavinia's parents are well-devised in terms of their mimetic components (traits of personality and appearance), each of them also seems to possess an important synthetic component, as they constitute moral poles with reference to which Lavinia's mimetic and thematic progress takes place. Amata's and Latinus' respective attitudes towards their only daughter – unfeeling and injurious mother vs. patient and doting father – influence the authorial audience's affective response to Lavinia's mimetic function, as we positively judge and applaud her decisions and actions which lead to the fulfilment of the Latin-Trojan union and the eventual ruin of Amata's plans to marry her daughter off to Turnus. At the same time, the polarity between the values incarnated respectively in Lavinia's parents, i.e. fury, leading to oppression and disorder, which Lavinia resists, and piety, which brings peace and liberation, and whose precepts she follows, influences our thematic understanding of Lavinia's predicament as a young woman and princess who must show extraordinary courage and determination to achieve the life and love of her own choice.

The thematic fusion of womanhood and piety in Le Guin's reinterpretation of the *Aeneid* serves yet another purpose, namely the one of foregrounding Lavinia's status as the protagonist of her narrative in contrast to the marginal role she is given by Vergil. According to Miller, to give Lavinia her voice, Le Guin needs to silence two most important female characters from the epic, Dido and Camilla, who are "united in their defiance of the quality of *pietas*" (2010: 39-40). Although Le Guin's character, very much in Dido's vein, frequently questions the decrees of fate foretold to her by Vergil, or disapproves of the model of bloodthirsty heroism promoted by his epic, "the emphasis on [her] commensurate *pietas* elevates her from the position of inferior female counterpart to equal status with Aeneas" (Miller 2010: 41-42). The vindication of femininity and its domestic responsibilities, which are no less important than those reserved for men, will later be contrasted with the notion of piety as virtue which reveals itself in battle, advocated by Lavinia's misogynist warlike stepson, Ascanius. The difference in their respective approaches to piety will lie at the root of the last major instability in the progression of the narrative; however, the theme of piety will also prove determinant for the previous instabilities and character development in the novel.

The second instability in the narrative is introduced along with Turnus' first visit in Laurentum to ask for the hand of fifteen-year-old Lavinia in marriage, and it is then that the protagonist for the first time realises the vulnerability of her position as a young woman, princess and potential bride:

> No man in the house, in the city, in all the country, could look at me as Turnus was looking. My realm was virginity and I was at home in it, unthreatened and at ease. No man had ever made me blush.
> Now I felt myself burning red from the roots of my hair clear down to my breasts, to my knees. I cowered with shame. I couldn't eat. The besieging army was at the walls. (2010: 20)

The metaphor of the virginal realm and the besieging army underscores the character's personal crisis, being important for the underlying theme of the woman's struggle for independence in the world of men. The relationship with Turnus, who lacks piety and subdues everyone to his will, means capitulation and threatens Lavinia's "territorial" integrity because she will have to relinquish her home, understood here as both the state of innocence and her father's house at the Regia.

Lavinia's reluctance to leave her house and land as a result of marriage is consistently prepared by the narrator through the mimetic reconstruction of Lavinia's character as closely connected with her father's country and its nature from early childhood. Her friendship with Sylvia, a daughter of the cattleman Thyrrus, and their childlike games in the forests and meadows of Laurentum, foreground Lavinia's mimetic attributes of independence, love of the Laurentian countryside and her sense of affinity with its inhabitants. Lavinia's meetings with Sylvia allow her to escape the ceremonial and everyday duties of a princess, whose life is shown as more strictly subjected to outside rules and circumstances than the life of common women. The space of the country with its nature (as opposed to the urban space of public affairs and politics run by men) allows Lavinia to play unchaperoned outside her own social circle, which again contributes to Lavinia's thematic function of the woman's pursuit of freedom. The instability caused by Turnus' proposal, which endangers the peace and relative liberty of Lavinia's adolescent existence, is eventually resolved by Latinus, who considers his daughter too young for marriage. However, the resolution is only partial, as we are informed that Turnus will return in three years to renew his advances, and so we expect further complications.

The thematic function of Lavinia emerges again in the third major instability of the novel, namely the arrival of her suitors. Although aware of her position and the inevitability of marriage, Lavinia grows reluctant to the courtship, observing her own marginalisation as a woman and individual. Despite the appearances of vying for Lavinia's love, it is her father whom the suitors need to win over to get the princess as their bride[13]. The presence of the suitors and the tension they bring into the

---

13   Moreover, Lavinia becomes unwillingly involved in a game in which she is forced to play her own mother's rival to Turnus' heart, which is an insult to her father (and herself) and a breach of propriety. Amata transfers both her maternal and erotic feelings onto her young nephew, and her open favouritism of Turnus runs counter to Latinus' politic intention to retain peace and good relations with all the noble suitors, and thus undermines Latinus' authority both as her husband and the king. On the other hand, Turnus' own vanity and greed for power make him pursue an ambition to become Latinus' son-in-law and his successor, even if it means his public acceptance of Amata's

Regia is shown as difficult to bear for Lavinia because her mimetic component is constructed in connection with its space, and especially with the female part of the palace in Laurentum, where she is loved and cared for by devoted servants and guardians, and which she will have to leave after marriage. Her hesitation and reluctance to be married to imposing Turnus (or anyone), as well as her rebellious thoughts which emphasise her connectedness with Laurentum and its people, again encourage the thematic reading, pointing to the oppressiveness of the norms which bind a young woman in Lavinia's culture:

> How I loved this house! How could I ever leave it, leave the spirits of the tree, of the spring, of my storerooms, of the hearth, of my people, leave the beloved familiar powers and go serve those of a stranger in a strange place? That would be slavery. (Le Guin 2010: 37)

Lavinia's stand for independence and freedom is paradoxically connected with the mimetic dimension which eventually puts pressure upon her, i.e. her being the only daughter of the king. Laying all his love on his first-born child, Latinus makes her the chief guardian of his household, the one who keeps the fire of Vesta, prepares the holy salt dug up from the bed of the father Tiber, and whom he also acquaints with the matters of Latin politics and thus teaches her to think for herself. Moreover, she becomes Latinus' acolyte in the rites at Albunea, the place of the oracle, where "he praised and propitiated [their] ancestors and the powers of the woods and springs" (2010: 18). Her special position is additionally reinforced by her own responsiveness to the call of the spirits, the gift which she shares with her father, and of which her mother remains resentful and scornful, because it gives Lavinia some "uncanny importance" (2010: 38). Last but not least, Lavinia's position at the Regia, and thus her independence, depends on the position of her father: "[W]omen's side or men's side –", says the narrator, "it was my father's house, and I was my father's daughter" (2010: 14). Therefore, she cannot understand why a woman has to follow her husband, as for her freedom and independence can only be enjoyed in the family home: "Where can a man take me that is better than my father's house? What do I want with a lesser king? Why should I serve Lares that are not my family's Lares,

---

advances. This combination of inappropriateness (lack of piety) as well as the pressure exerted on Lavinia to become a wife, and Turnus' wife for that matter, repulses the princess, and causes her avoidance of Turnus and the suitors altogether.

the Penates of some other woman's storerooms, the fire of a foreign hearth? Why, why is a girl brought up at home to be a woman in exile the rest of her life?" (2010: 44-5).

The arrival of the young men at the Regia is preceded by and thus placed in the context of Lavinia's reflections on the god Mars and men's worship of his warlike figure, which also contributes to the thematisation of Lavinia's character with reference to two distinct gender-related spaces. The part of the house which belongs to Lavinia and which gives her the feeling of homeliness and safety is the space devoted to Vesta and her ever-burning hearth. The activities traditionally performed in this space by "the king's daughter, the camilla, the novice" (Le Guin 2010: 32) are concerned with the keeping of the holy fire, taking care of food and the sacred salt to bless it. This typically female space is contrasted with the space governed by Mars, represented here by a small room which houses weapons – swords, spears, and shields – brought out by men (the Leapers) on the first day of March to worship their deity. Mars is described by the character as "the one who walks the boundary, the one who sets the ram on the ewe, and the bull on the heifer, and the sword in the farmer's hand" (2010: 32). His qualities are therefore connected with unpredictability, sexual desire, a drive for domination and violence, which are threatening to the space of Vesta, associated with stability, warmth and protection. As a woman and a virgin, Lavinia fears Mars and cannot worship him but she honours the boundary between their adjoining spaces, never trespassing on Mars' domain. However, Mars invades her own space embodied in the suitors who bring to the Regia their young boastful manhood, volatile tempers and a desire to prove themselves in competition. Therefore, the resultant instability, represented here in spatial terms, serves the purpose of the thematic exploration of the aggressive nature of masculinity, and its oppressive influence on the woman and her world[14]. No wonder the only place where

---

14   The suitors' arrival is also preceded by a section in which Lavinia contemplates the scenes depicted on Aeneas' shield, which show women's place in the history written and carried out by men – a history of heroism which is in fact one of violence and death. She can see "a few women here and there" but the actors are mostly "men, men fighting, endless battle scenes, men torn apart, men disemboweled, bridges torn down, walls torn down, slaughter" (Le Guin 2010: 25). Women are shown as victims of male desire for power and domination, as Lavinia can see "a mass rape, women screaming and fighting as they are dragged off by warriors" 2010: (26). In the end she can also see

Lavinia can find refuge and regain her peace of mind is Albunea, the sacred place in the forest, close to nature and haunted by the spirits of the forefathers, where strangers (and Mars) have no entry[15].

Lavinia's visit to the oracle at Albunea where she meets with Vergil's ghost serves as a focal point of the narrative, as it results in her realisation that she is a literary/poetic construct of Vergil's invention. Moreover, it also introduces another instability of the novel between two important persons each of whom carries a particular thematic function. One of them is Vergil, the male author who reaffirms the patriarchal worldview in his *Aeneid*, by glorifying the mythical male ancestor (Aeneas) and his descendant – a contemporary male emperor (Augustus), and who can thus be perceived as a spokesman of men, not women, in relating history and representing gender relationships in literature. The other is Lavinia, who turns out to be both a woman in a patriarchal society and a character in a poem written by a man, and who interrogates and challenges the ideals and stereotypes upheld by patriarchal culture and reasserted by the epic.

During their several meetings at Albunea, Lavinia takes on the role of the authorial audience for Vergil's story-telling, while the resultant tensions point to the discrepancies in their respective worldviews and foreground various thematic preoccupations of the narrative. Firstly, on "hearing" the *Aeneid*, Lavinia questions Vergil's male perspective in the representation of women and gender relationships, which sentence a woman to certain conventional roles: a commodity or a prize over which men can fight and pit themselves against each other (herself and Helen of Troy); a passing fancy to be used and abandoned (Dido); or a sacrifice

---

in the shield a vision of the future ravaged by carnage and destruction, which culminates in the nuclear blast. In this way, the hero's shield – a usual epic emblem of his greatness and valour – turns into a symbol of aggression and bloodshed, underscoring the thematic conflict between peace-loving womanhood and destructive masculinity.

15 It is worth noting that the characters of Lavinia's suitors, Turnus included, are rather poorly developed in terms of their mimetic components. Messapus is too weak to rule independently, Aventinus is "a fine lad" but "hasn't much sense" (Le Guin 2010: 78), Ufens is dressed in wolfskins and wild, Clausus belongs to the "shifty Sabines" (2010: 72), some of them are "good fellows" and "easy to laugh at" (2010: 34). However, it is not their independent traits which matter but their collective thematic function of being male intruders in Vesta's realm.

for a man's mission (Creusa)[16]. On this occasion, Lavinia also provokes Vergil's re-evaluation of herself as a character who has undergone a conventional depiction and marginalisation for the sake of bringing to light preoccupations which are more typically in accord with the ideological concerns of epic poetry. While admitting his "injustice" to her, i.e. the mimetic impoverishment of her character in his epic, Vergil also verbalises his own role in glorifying the exploits of men at the expense of representing the private lives of women:

> 'She came to Albunea by herself,' he said, speaking into the darkness, 'and knew the sacred names of the river, and had no wish to be married. And I knew nothing of all that! I never looked at her. I had to tell what the men were doing [...]' (Le Guin 2010: 42)

Vergil's acknowledgement of his conservative portrait of Lavinia gives rise to emphasising the difference in expectations between male and female readers, and thus also thematises the role of the epic as a mouthpiece of patriarchalism:

> 'You know everything, don't you?'
> 'No. I know very little. And what I thought I knew of you – what little I thought of at all – was stupid, conventional, unimagined. I thought you were a blonde! [...] But you can't have two love stories in an epic. Where would the battles fit? In any case, how could one possibly end a story with a marriage?'
> 'It does seem more like a beginning than an end,' I said. (2010: 61)

Lavinia's acquaintance with the events depicted in Vergil's poem – and thus also the overriding pattern of her own life in the foreseeable future – leads to another thematic conflict (previously suggested by the suitors' presence at the Regia), namely that between the woman's yearning for peace and stability and men's drive for domination resulting in the besti-

---

16   Helen, whose infidelity was the reason for war, must be retrieved by Menelaus, which cost many men their lives in the siege of Troy. Dido, an anguished heroine of romance, is to suffer from a broken heart, then undergo hours of agony before her death from a self-inflicted wound, and, in the end, to prophesy the coming of the avenger (Hannibal, a male warrior) as opposed to taking her own revenge on the unfaithful lover. Aeneas' first wife, Creusa, sacrifices herself and dies in the slaughter effected by the Greeks in Troy so that Aeneas can be the founder of Rome and have children with another woman. Significantly, when he descends into the underworld, he does not even look for her there, which Lavinia resents and cannot comprehend.

ality and violence of war which lays waste the world created by women, the world of Vesta:

> 'Why must there be war?'
> 'Oh, Lavinia, what a woman's question that is! Because men are men. [...] And there will be war. Battles, sieges, slaughter, slave taking, town burning, rape. And men who rant and boast, and then kill sleeping men. And men who kill young boys. And the growing crops laid waste. All the wrong that men can do is done. Justice, mercy, does Mars care for them?' (2010: 91)

The ensuing account of the war in Latium, describing scenes of atrocity and carnage, make Lavinia challenge the ideal of heroism which turns out to be little more than a manifestation of aggressive masculinity in the service of the political agenda of conquest and domination. For her, the hero in Vergil's poem "kills like a butcher", and to her question why he kills a helpless man Vergil replies: "Because that is how empires are founded" (Le Guin 2010: 94).

However, the most important aspect of the instability is a tension resulting from the clash of Lavinia's sense of being a living person, whose freedom is limited only by the existing social and gender relationships, and her awareness of becoming a literary character in a poem, and thus forced to conform to the limits of Vergil's creation. The blurring of the boundary between life and literature, as a result of which Lavinia's life becomes a text, involves the subordination of her mimetic component to the synthetic one, bringing together the destiny of a person and the sphere of literature, and making literature her destiny[17]. Therefore, paradoxically, Lavinia's path is determined by the future, not by the past – first, because Vergil and his poem come from the future, several centuries after Lavinia's historical existence, and second, because her person plays a part in the larger scheme which should result in Augustus' reign

---

17   Miller claims Lavinia is "*made* of words" and, in fact, she is a book, which is emphasised by the fact that the name of the character and that of the novel are the same. "In her channelling of Vergil and her (auto-)po(i)etic self-creation", writes Miller, "Lavinia becomes a synecdoche for the epic and its legacy: on one figurative level, the true heroine of the novel becomes Vergil's *Carmen*. [...] Lavinia/*Lavinia* stands in for the enduring literary tradition stretching from Vergil to Le Guin and beyond, but simultaneously serves as a link in that chain, a particular reimagining in which the daughter of Latinus is more than a blushing maiden [...]" (2010: 37-38).

as depicted in the *Aeneid*, which is reflected in the following conversation:

> 'I am searching for my duty here. How much is it right for me to tell you?
> Do you want to know your future, Lavinia?'
> 'No,' I said at once. Then I sought in my own mind for my duty, or my
> will, and finally said, 'I want to know what's right to do, but I don't want
> to know what's to come of it.'
> 'It's enough to know what ought to come of it,' he said, gravely agreeing.
> (Le Guin 2010: 43)

As shown in the passage, in order for the epic to have its effect ("what ought to come of it"), Lavinia must conform to the scenario written for her, i.e. resist Turnus (and her mother's pressure) and marry Aeneas, so her concession to do "what's right to do," that is, to piously play her part, is at once indispensable and indicative of her paradoxical freedom within the narrative. Lavinia thus escapes from the plot of her historical life determined by political factors and social constraints, and instead, subordinates her existence to the plot devised by the poet.

It is also during Lavinia and Vergil's meetings – in which the character and the author engage in discussions, explain their motivations and verify their opinions – that the synthetic component of the whole narrative fully comes to the fore and serves the thematic function of the woman's role in literature, along with such issues as her self-fashioning as a character and her claim to authorship. Interestingly, Vergil is a figure of the future, however, Lavinia's presence at Albunea invokes him (or his ghost), which gives rise to narrative entanglements and ontological disturbances, and thus presents us with a clear case of metalepsis[18]. If it is Lavinia who invokes Vergil, then it is she who determines his existence in her story, and therefore may be said to invent him as much as he claims to have invented her. In narratological terms, Vergil is reduced from the extradiegetic level of authorship/narration (of the *Aeneid*) to the diegetic level of the narrative in which he becomes a character, which can be seen in his musings that he can "still live in [his] poem" (2010: 54), or when he compares himself to a "dream that has flown into a dream", i.e. into his poem (2010: 41). Lavinia, on the other hand, is a character, narrator and the presumed author of the story presented to the audience, which makes her operate on at least two narrative levels – die-

---

18   For a discussion of metalepsis see, for example, McHale 1987: 119-121.

getic and extradiegetic[19]. Whatever she hears from Vergil, whatever she is "instructed" to do, seems to be filtered and determined by her narrato-rial-authorial position, and thus the synthetic contributes to the thematic, as it foregrounds the woman's freedom and authority in rewriting his-story as her-story.

Lavinia's compliance with her synthetic status (or maybe her own vision of the future) gives her freedom to pursue her own happiness by asserting her right to choose her life mate. The knowledge that a pious Trojan warrior is coming from afar and that her Grandfather will talk to Latinus in sleep and warn him against marrying his daughter off to a man from Latium, gives Lavinia the strength to pursue her own goals and do what she deems right for herself as a woman, manipulating the circumstances or actively opposing any attempts to prevent her union with Aeneas[20]. The reality of Lavinia undergoes textualisation, or rather synthetisation, while the existence of her father, her people and herself become dependent on the poetry of Vergil, which can be noticed during the meeting of Latinus and Aeneas' envoys, when Lavinia can hear Ver-gil's voice: "the high house of the king and all of us in it had being only in those words" (2010: 105). Her existential freedom is possible only upon her subordination to the text, which results in the resolution of the previous instability:

---

19   For the distinction between the diegetic and extradiegetic levels see Fludernik 2009: 36-
     38, 100.
20   It is at her request that Latinus visits Albunea and receives the warning in dream, which
     he announces to his subjects and which makes him promise his daughter's hand to the
     leader of the recently arrived Trojans. The same knowledge and determination to do
     what is right and will make her happy makes Lavinia resist her mother's plans and dom-
     ination. First, she plots an escape when her mother and her trusted female servants or-
     chestrate a Goat Feast attended only by women high in the mountains to transfer Lavin-
     ia into Turnus' hands. Second, she moves out of the female part into the male part of the
     house, on the one hand, seeking there refuge and the protection of her father's guards,
     while on the other hand, displaying a decisiveness and courage denied women in patri-
     archal culture. Her decision to move to the male part of the house alienates her from the
     female part but also underscores her thematic function, as it shows her as an independ-
     ent woman whose femininity transcends her own times. Turnus has everything a young
     princess should see in her mate, i.e. good looks, courage, male charm, position of a
     king, and he is an Italian. However, Lavinia's expectations go beyond the traditional
     romantic yearnings of her sex. For her, the choice of Turnus means slavery, oppression,
     exile, submission to male ambition, while in choosing Aeneas she will get freedom and
     personal happiness in piety.

To hear myself promised as part of a treaty, exchanged like a cup or a piece of clothing, might seem as deep an insult as could be offered to a human soul. But slaves and unmarried girls expect such insult, even those of us who have been allowed liberty enough to pretend we are free. My liberty had been great, and so I had dreaded its end. So long as it could end only with Turnus or the other suitors, I had felt that insult, that bondage awaiting me, the only possible outcome. I had been the dove tied to the pole, flapping its silly wings as if it could fly, while the boys below shouted and pointed and shot at it till at last an arrow struck.

I felt nothing of that entrapment now, that helpless shame. I felt the same certainty I had seen in my father's eyes. Things were going as they should go, and in going with them I was free. The string that tied me to the pole had been cut. For the first time I knew what it would be to fly, to take to my wings across the air, across the years to come, to go, to go on. (Le Guin 2010: 107)

The resolution of Lavinia's personal crisis, however, leads to the exacerbation of the global instability, i.e. the war in Latium, which ends only with the death of Turnus, but which also marks the closure of Vergil's *Aeneid*. In his study, Phelan distinguishes between closure and completeness, defining the former as "the way in which narrative signals its end", and the latter as "the degree of resolution [of instabilities and tensions] accompanying the closure" (1989: 18). In the *Aeneid*, which was left unfinished by Vergil, Turnus' death in a duel with Aeneas lets us presume that the political crisis will be automatically resolved and that Aeneas will eventually become the king of Latium, Lavinia's husband and Silvius' father, as prophesied by Anchises in the underworld. Le Guin's novel allows us to actually see this completeness in the progression of the narrative beyond the point of the epic's closure, which coincides with Lavinia's marriage to Aeneas and the foundation of the city of Lavinium, which spatially reflects her thematic yearning for independence and self-assertion and her already discussed connection with the land and its people. However, the end of the poem means that the voice of the poet can no longer be heard and Lavinia's narrative loses its synthetic underpinnings provided by the *Aeneid*:

But what am I to do now? I have lost my guide, my Vergil. I must go on by myself through all that is left after the end, all the rest of the immense, pathless, unreadable world. [...]

I have found my way so far, even though the poet did not tell me the way. I guessed it right, without mistake, from things he said, the clues he gave

me. I came to the center of the maze following him. Now I must find my
way back out alone. It will be longer and slower in the living, but not so
long, I think, to tell. (Le Guin 2010: 182)

The death of Aeneas (the last thing foretold by Vergil) three years after
their wedding is followed by Ascanius' taking over the throne of Latium. This introduces an instability between Lavinia and her stepson,
which translates into the thematic conflict between the life of Vesta and
the life of Mars, the former being constantly marginalised for the sake of
the latter. Lacking his father's longing for peace and stability, Ascanius
displays such mimetic attributes as arrogance, vanity, desire for domination as well as distrust of women and appreciation of aggressive masculinity. The conflict between bellicose manhood and peace-loving womanhood is again (like in the case of the suitors' "invasion") played out in
spatial terms: Ascanius forces Lavinia to leave her city and takes her to
Alba Longa, the royal city in the north, where Lavinia feels imprisoned
and where her freedom as a woman and the queen is limited by the un-
familiarity of the land, by the atmosphere of the ongoing war as well as
by her stepson's chauvinist prejudices towards herself and women in
general. It is only when Ascanius challenges Lavinia's rights as mother
to raise her only son, Silvius, that she realises the full extent of her subjection ("Ascanius had ruled my life for nearly ten years. I had done his
will not my own, and he had taken that for granted, as if I were a slave"
[2010: 252]), as well as an unbridgeable gulf between their worldviews:
"I was a woman, therefore never to be trusted, never obeyed. I must be
disregarded, or defeated" 2010: (252).

The conflict over Silvius' upbringing is thus decisive for Lavinia's
awakening after years of submissiveness and for her renewed struggle
for independence from the constraints of patriarchalism. The instability
is aggravated by Lavinia's escape with her trusted women servants and
Silvius to Lavinium. However, it is only resolved as a result of Lavinia's
visit to Albunea, where she once again invokes the ghost of her "dear
poet", who using the words of the *Aeneid*, foretells that Lavinia will
bring Silvius up in the woods to be "a king, a father of kings" (2010:
267), the prophecy that she imparts to her people. Lavinia's compliance
with the words of the poem, i.e. her reliance on the synthetic aspect,
once again enables her to break free from the political constraints and
dynastic feuds, which resulting in her son being educated and brought up

in accordance with the standards set by his father (and Vergil) so as to make him worthy of the foretold future. The novel ends with Lavinia receiving her completeness as a mimetically enriched character (a mother, grandmother, queen dowager etc.), just as the plot reaches its completeness by the resolution of major instabilities through Silvius' coronation[21].

To sum up the present analysis, it is worth recalling a passage which throws more light on the interaction of the mimetic and the synthetic components in the development of the character's thematic function:

> I was fated, it seems, to live among people who suffered beyond measure from grief, who were driven mad by it. Though I suffered grief, I was doomed to sanity. This was no doing of the poet's. I know that he gave me nothing but modest blushes, and no character at all. I know that he said I raved and tore my golden tresses at my mother's death. He simply was not paying attention: I was silent then, tearless, and only intent on making her poor soiled body decent. And my hair has always been dark. In truth he gave me nothing but a name, and I have filled it with myself. Yet without him would I even have a name? I have never blamed him. Even a poet cannot get everything right.
>
> It is strange, though, that he gave me no voice. I never spoke to him till we met that night by the altar under the oaks. Where is my voice from, I wonder? the voice that cries on the wind in the heights of Albunea, the voice that speaks with no tongue a language not its own? (Le Guin 2010: 277)

As has already been stated, Lavinia's life conforms to Vergil's text, being conditioned by (her awareness of) the future. At the same time, however, Vergil's poem itself becomes subordinated to the text of the future (Le Guin's novel), which refocuses the perspective from men to women, and which, in a way, pays literary homage to Lavinia's life as it

---

21   In his review of the novel, Adam Roberts thus sums up this completeness as reflected in Lavinia's life narrative: "Lavinia is surrounded by people, from Virgil, to her father, to her suitor Turnus and her stepson Ascanius, who trace out their lives in spiral tangles of ego. Lavinia herself sails through, always conscious of the fact that the key salient for life is not that it coalesces around particular moments, or particular subjectivities, but that *it goes on*. It is this that makes narrative the key mode of art for apprehending life. That's why Le Guin's story rolls smoothly not only past the death of Turnus (where the *Aeneid* stops), but also the death of Lavinia's loved husband Aeneas – very touchingly understated, here – and onward. [...] Le Guin is capable of very affecting poetry, but she is a storyteller first. Her novel is a narrative, and is about narrative: about the fact that life goes on after setback, disaster, and death" (2009: web).

could/should have been[22]. Lavinia is frustrated with the "life" that Vergil gave her, because in his presentation he failed to overcome the mimetic constraints involved in patriarchal ideology. "[H]e did not sing me enough life to die," says the protagonist, "He only gave me immortality" (2010: 286). So she yearns to be given a literary life which will do justice to all that she aspired to be. Lavinia claims to have filled her name with herself; however, her voice depends on "a language not her own". This points to her synthetic status as Le Guin's creation, and thus her subordination to the worldview of the modern author, who mimeticises Lavinia's character, giving her a probability which transcends Vergil's patriarchal fantasy, and foregrounds Lavinia's thematic function as a woman of the future who in her search for independence goes beyond the limitations and conventions of her culture. The same quality of Lavinia's character was apparently noticed by Charlotte Higgins in her *Guardian* review of the novel, when she observed that "Virgil would never have written her: she is a modern projection of a modern intelligence and sensibility" (2009: web).

---

22 According to Miller, when Lavinia says "One must be changed, to be immortal" (286), she means as much herself (i.e. changed into an owl living in the trees of Rome and changed by Le Guin's rewriting) as Vergil's tradition – by retelling the *Aeneid* in the form of a contemporary narrative, Le Guin will preserve the epic for posterity even when Vergil's own voice has been silenced along with the death of its ancient language, Latin (see Miller 2010: 46-47). In the same vein, Vergil, undergoing textualisation as Le Guin's verbal creation, will be immortalised as Lavinia's guide through the narrative of her life, just as he was immortalised by Dante as a guide through the narrative of his *Inferno*.

Transtextual characters in literary adaptations: E.M. Forster's *Howards End* and Zadie Smith's *On Beauty*

PATRYCJA PODGAJNA

The question of how a continuous identity is established between the initial presentation of a character and the subsequent occurrences in a given literary work constitutes an intricate issue, considering the fact that in most texts characters are presented in separate narrative sequences. Obviously, linguistic referents, mimetic markers, and characterisation play a pivotal role in sustaining a coherent identification. However, the complexity of the process increases when introduced in an intertextual context, in which characters transgress ontological borders of fictional realms and exist in more than one text. This propensity is acutely encapsulated in the concept of "transworld identity" defined broadly by Umberto Eco as characters' "transmigration from one fictional universe to another" (Eco in Kundu 2008: 11). The term specifies the criteria of correspondence between a given fictional character and its intertextual variant: "If an entity in one world differs from its 'prototype' in another world only in accidental properties, not in essentials, and if there is a one-to-one correspondence between the prototype and its other-world variant, then the two entities can be considered identical even though they exist in distinct worlds" (Eco in McHale 1987: 37). The question of characters' transmigration is also addressed by Brian Richardson who in his essay "Transtextual Characters" establishes the criteria of characters' transportability claiming that it is the mimetic component encompassing a set of internal properties and psychological makeup which conditions transtextual compatibility between characters (2010: 539-540). Theoretically speaking, apart from foregrounding the continuity of essential properties as a requisite for characters' correspondence, the true implication of these theoretical concepts hinges on the 'overlapping of worlds', when the same fictional individual can recur in different possible worlds. Such ontological crossover is characteristic of a literary adaptation, which particularly problematises the criteria for establishing the persistence of a character's identity across texts.

Associated largely with cinematic and theatrical context, the process of adaptation defined by Linda Hutcheon as "an announced and extensive transposition of a particular work or works, a creative appropriation, and an extended intertextual engagement with the adapted work" (Hutcheon 2006: 7) constitutes an interesting case for tracing the criteria of recognisability between intertextual characters raising such compelling questions as: How is the link between the source character and its adapted counterpart established? How are these transtextual representations related to each other? And finally on what textual or paratextual grounds does the reader cognitively map the attributes of the prototype to its intertextual variant? By analysing *On Beauty* the aim of this paper is to demonstrate that in Zadie Smith's literary adaptation transtextual recognisability of *hypertextual* characters with their *hypotextual* prototypes is propelled by progression (as defined by James Phelan) rather than by mimetic, psychological or linguistic attributes.

Within a vast array of postmodernist rewritings, Zadie Smith's novel *On Beauty* published in 2005, particularly highlights the complexities of literary indebtedness. Appropriating the motif of two ideologically conflicted families: the liberal Belseys and conservative Kippses, the novel emulates the compositional and thematic framework of E. M. Forster's canonical text *Howards End,* with enlightened Schlegels and capitalist Wilcoxes as the literary prototypes. In both novels the families are intertwined through a series of unexpected events: an undesired romantic infatuation, a tentative friendship between the members of the opposing families, and the resultant legacy propel dramatic as well as ideological collision. The intertextual relationality between both texts is accentuated in Smith's introductory acknowledgement in which she explicitly states her *homage* to the canonical predecessor. Given Zadie Smith's outward acknowledgement that "It should be obvious from the first line that this is the novel inspired by a love of E.M. Forster" (*On Beauty*: acknowledgements), an axiomatic primacy of Forster's novel as a source text is firmly established. Serving as an inspiration, *Howards End* functions as an *intertext,* or in Gerard Genette's terms as a *hypotext*[1]. Differentiating between the earlier text (*hypotext*) upon which a later text (*hypertext*) is based, Genette's model of *hypertextuality* formally highlights the external literary framework of cross-references and allusions, in which texts are in the constant state of referral. In Smith's novel its realisation operates extensively on the level of characters as most of the main protagonists in *On Beauty* have their counterparts in Forster's novel – as represented by Margaret Schlegel and Kiki Belsey. Despite emulating Forster's thematic thread of female friendship and bequeathed legacy, the characters' construction departs significantly from clear-cut mimetic identification, and entails a certain contextual and cognitive differentiation between the *hypotextual* prototype and its *hypertextual* embodiment.

Considering the reader's imaginative propensity for ascribing mimetic attributes to characters, it seems reasonable to assume that in tandem with anaphoric referents the mimetic component[2] holds prominence in supporting continuous identity of a given character or characters. Its importance is grounded in the dual perception of characters as on the one hand more or less realistic images of people and on the other hand as textual artefacts. This inherent duality translates into opposing theoretical models which vacillate between stressing primarily the mimetic sphere in the reception of characters as individuals in the fictional world and considering them primarily in terms of semantics and pragmatics[3]. Some critics, like Jens Eder, advocate that it is the perception of characters as fictional beings, rather than artefacts, symbols or symptoms, that propels the construction of their continuous identity.

Surprisingly, in *On Beauty* rather than facilitating the identification of intertextual characters, the mimetic component defers a direct connection between the source character and its *hypertextual* equivalent. This is because Zadie Smith re-contextualises Forster's leading protagonist by defamiliarising situational framework and physical properties of the *hy-*

---

1   What Genette terms the hypotext is often used by critics as intertext (see Allen 2000: 108).

2   James Phelan's idea of analysing literary characters from the perspective of their mimetic, thematic and synthetic components, as employed in the present study, is outlined in the Introduction.

3   For the elaboration of this model see Uri Margolin's essay "Characters in Literary Narrative: Representation and Signification".

potextual prototype. This camouflaging propensity is signalled right from the opening line of Smith's novel. "One may as well begin with Jerome's e-mails to his father" (Smith 2005: 3) while obviously emulating the opening of *Howards End*: "One may as well begin with Helen's letters to her sister" (Forster 2006: 3), not only accentuates the transposition in the temporal framework but, more importantly, changes the role of the actants in the opening sequence. In Forster's text, the role of the recipient of Helen's letters announcing her infatuation with Paul Wilcox is allotted to her sister – Margaret Schlegel, in Smith's intertextual reworking, the female addressee is substituted with Howard Belsey, Kiki's husband who learns about their son's romance with Victoria Kipps. Thus, the focal point in resolving the initiated narrative tension is Howard and his trip to London to dissuade his son from an irrational marriage, while Kiki's role in the narrative denouement moves to a secondary position of a mother concerned about her adolescent son. Consequently, this transformation affects not only the line of progression but, more importantly, the degree of the reader's initial ability to identify transtextual similarity between both heroines. By modifying the roles of the actants in the opening sequences and introducing alteration in their family status, Smith initiates a set of new assumptions towards the narrative dynamics involving both protagonists, which in turn defers right from the onset clear-cut correspondences between them.

The narrative sequences in which Margaret Schlegel and Kiki Belsey are presented exacerbates the discontinuity between textual identities. In the complex network of identification, the contextual cues determining the social as well as cultural status of both protagonists serve more as a detaching rather than binding factor in the course of narrative. This is partly determined by disparity between spatiotemporal frameworks of both novels, which are set respectively in the Edwardian England and contemporary America. Clearly, this diegetic transposition[4], which by means of proximisation moves the text closer to contemporary readers, necessitates pragmatic shifts in the social status of the characters. These shifts are observable in substituting Margaret's upper-class position fortified by unearned income as a member of financially privileged class with a more contemporary profession of Kiki Belsey as a hospital nurse.

---

4   Defined by Genette: "When the hypertext transposes the diegesis of its hypotext to bring it up to date and closer to its audience" (1997: 304).

The divergence in the social and cultural dimensions of characters hinges not only on the quantitative and qualitative properties but also on the linguistic mode of their articulation. In Forster's novel, the account of Margaret's mixed English and German background is mediated by the extradiegetic narrator by means of the collective pronoun 'they', which inevitably refers also to her sister Helen: "They were not 'English to the backbone' [...] But on the other hand, they were not 'Germans of the dreadful sort'" (Forster 2006: 42). Although Smith retains a certain degree of hybridity inherent in *hypotextual* prototype's identity, she makes her *hypertextual* character variant a vehicle for commenting on contemporary multicultural issues of Afro-Americans in the predominantly white society: "Everywhere we go, I'm alone in this... this sea of white. [...] My whole life is white" (Smith 2005: 57).

Obviously, the dissimilarity of contextual frames necessarily triggers discontinuity in the textual identity of characters as established by mimetic properties. Following Eco's criteria, the process of transworld identification/differentiation is structured along the essential properties axis. This view is also shared by Brian Richardson, who advocates that it is durability of independent essence that is a prerequisite for character's transportability between different texts (Richardson 2010: 539). Clearly, the problem lies in the nominal relation and mimetic symmetry between the *hypotextual* and *hypertextual* variant, which presuppose some level of character's continuity. Adhering to this principle, the comparison of Margaret's mimetic characterisation as: "Not beautiful, not supremely brilliant, but filled with something that took the place of both qualities – something best described as a profound vivacity, a continual and sincere response to all that she encountered in her path through life" (Forster 2006: 33), to Kiki's depiction as: "a solid two hundred and fifty pounds. Her skin had that famous ethnic advantage of not wrinkling much [...]. At fifty-two her face was still a girl's face. A beautiful tough girl's face" (Smith 2005: 15) reveals a considerable level of inconsistency rather than symmetry. The disparities in their physicality notably serve as a differentiating quality in sustaining the idea of motherhood inscribed in the roles of Margaret and Kiki as caretakers of their families. Even though the nurturing aspect of Margaret, who raises her brother and sister at a young age and takes care of Helen during her pregnancy, is thematically delineated, it lacks correspondence in the mimetic sphere. Contrastingly, even on a superficial level, Kiki's appearance makes her seem motherly from the start: "Her enormous spell-binding bosom gave off a mass of signals beyond her direct control: sassy, sisterly, predatory, motherly, threatening, comforting... a strong fabulation of the person she thought she was" (Smith 2005: 47). Thus, given the discontinuity in the mimetic component, the cognitive mapping between Margaret, portrayed as not a particularly attractive woman of caring nature, and a motherly figure of Kiki, described as a "goddess" of "unspeakable" beauty who invites comments that "[she] should be in a fountain in Rome" (Smith 2005: 121) proves impossible.

Undeniably in all literary texts, the depiction of character's behavioural and emotional construction constitutes an essential aspect in the process of transworld identification. The construction and exploration of compatibility of psychological profiles is inscribed in the process of characterisation. Defined broadly as the ascription of mimetic, social, and psychological traits to a particular character (Eder, Jannidis, and Schneider 2010: 32), the process of characterisation empowers readers to understand via verbal signs and textual cues the motives and behaviour of a fictive individual. The source of this textual knowledge is equally important, as the information about the character may be provided by the character him/herself or by the agencies such as the narrator or other characters within the same textual world. In the case of the characters considered here the change in the psychological and emotive disposition of both heroines is communicated by the extradiegetic narrator. Overtly opposed to patriarchal hegemony, Margaret Schlegel is characterised as a woman of strong self-awareness, intellectual mindset, and cosmopolitan sensibility: "temperance, tolerance, and sexual equality were intelligible cries to her" (Forster 2006: 41). Within the world of Wellington Kiki Belsey is striking because of her emotional intelligence in lieu of academic intellectualism: "Where Kiki had felt her way instinctively through her problem, Jerome had written his out [...] not for the first time, Kiki felt grateful she was not an intellectual" (Smith 2005: 43). As James Lasdun acutely observes: "Kiki Belsey seems intended to embody a kind of feelingful alternative to Howard's hyper-intellectuality but never quite comes out from behind the enormous bosom" (Lasdun 2006). This internal dissonance translates into an overtly altered trajectory of personal formation and development. Although the same conven-

tion of *Bildungsroman* is preserved, its realisation entails several coun-
terpoints in the narrative progression. The dissonance between Kiki's
acknowledgement of emotional intelligence and aesthetics of truth in
place of Howard's over-intellectual cynicism and focus on the physicality of a beautiful object leads to the crisis in their marriage sparked by
Howard's continuous infidelities.

However, Kiki's reliance on emotions instead of reason enables her
to create more enduring relationships so that each family member can
thrive in a healthy supportive environment. Kiki becomes a stronger
woman for facing adversity and prioritising her family; after all, "it was
just Kiki being Kiki, offering the empathy her children were used to"
(Smith 2005: 290). Contrastingly, Margaret is less successful in realising
her motto "only connect", observed in her marriage with Henry Wilcox,
which aims on the abstract level at reconciling the "great outer life" of
the Wilcoxes "where telegrams and anger count" with Schlegels' cul-
tured and intimate world of personal relations. Though the marriage that
the novel works towards has the potential to unify the Schlegels and the
Wilcoxes despite their differing outlooks, instead of presenting the characters in a harmonious union, the novel's conclusion leaves Henry Wilcox entirely "broken up", while Margaret has had to abandon many of
her former values by forgiving, or appearing to forgive, all of Henry's
failures. As Lesile White has noted, the novel's conclusion emphasises
the great cost suffered by both the Schlegels and the Wilcoxes (White
2005: 56).

Ultimately, although the *Bildungsroman* in both novels is structured
on the same thematic thread of unsuccessful marriage, the line of psychological development diverges most notably in the ending of the novel. The initial juxtaposition of self-awareness and insecurity embodied
respectively by the *hypotextual* prototype (Margaret Schlegel) and its
hypertextual variant (Kiki Belsey) is underscored in the course of the
narrative with the effect that it is Kiki Belsey rather than Margaret
Schlegel who appears as a stronger and more unified character. On the
abstract level, this transformation also highlights the role of thematic
component in the characters' identification. Although the theme of personal development is explicitly incorporated from the *hypotext*, its reworking impedes direct associations between the discussed characters,
as its realisation is supported by different psychological properties.

The presented delineation of disparities between Forster's and Smith's novels proves that the role of physical markers and personality traits in identifying intertextual links between the considered characters is definitely problematic. Although some references and textual cues contribute to identifying correspondences between transtextual identities, the information provided in the process of characterisation proves contingent in tracing intertextual interconnectedness between the *hypotextual* prototype and its *hypertextual* variant, as the characters differ in their essential properties. Contrastingly, as observable in the narrative sequences involving both characters, the main operating mode of identification is concerned with progression, the aspect widely recognised as crucial in the analysis of literary characters[5].

Tracing the entanglement of Forster's and Smith's characters in narrative dynamics reveals that the sequences in which they appear share a considerable degree of correspondence. The same contextual framework of a tentative friendship between Margaret Schlegel and Ruth Wilcox is preserved in Smith's novel in the relationship between Kiki Belsey and Carlene Kipps. In both cases the result of this female bond is a valuable legacy in the form of the property or a painting bequeathed respectively by Ruth Wilcox and Carlene Kipps, which is returned to its rightful owners (Margaret Schlegel/Kiki Belsey) at the end of the novels. Particularly significant for the narrative dynamics is the description of Margaret Schlegel's and Ruth Wilcox's shopping spree when they look for Christmas presents, which is followed by Margaret being invited to spend a night at the Wilcox country house Howards End. Correspondingly, in *On Beauty*, Kiki Belsey and Carlene Kipps's shopping trip culminates in an invitation to Amherst which Kiki, like Margaret, first refuses only to rush off to the train station at the last minute in the hope of meeting Carlene. Both chapters begin with strikingly similar reflections on the puzzling nature of the older women. Margaret ponders on Mrs Wilcox: "Was Mrs Wilcox one of the unsatisfactory people – there are many of them – who dangle intimacy and then withdraw it?" (Forster 2006: 95). The same tone reverberates in questions about Mrs Kipps: "Was Carlene Kipps one of these women who promises friendship but never truly delivers it? A friendship flirt?" (Smith 2005: 264). Clearly, the degree of similitude between the passages imposes the juxtaposition

---

5   A double focus on character and progression is elaborated by James Phelan (1989).

of the characters of Mrs Wilcox and Carlene Kipps, and also of the events following the parallel scenes in the two novels. The rest of the chapter in both novels presents Margaret and Mrs Wilcox, as well as Kiki and Carlene, on their shopping tour and abortive visit to the country. While the subsequent pages of the respective chapters offer less precise similarities than the above excerpt, later scenes are nevertheless played out with recognisable correspondences to the very end of both chapters. At the end, the intended country visit is foiled by the arrival of the Kipps family: "They were just walking arm in arm up the platform when they heard Carlene's name cried out several times: 'Mum! Hey, Mum!'" (Smith 2005: 270). Smith, although more concise, follows in Forster's footsteps:

> They began to walk up the long platform. Far at its end stood the train, breasting the darkness without. They never reached it. Before imagination could triumph, there were cries of 'Mother! Mother!' and a heavy-browed girl darted out of the cloakroom and seized Mrs Wilcox by the arm. (Forster 2006: 94)

As can be seen, although Forster's version is clearly more elaborate and poetic, Smith nevertheless crafts hers with precise regard to detail. 'Mother' becomes 'Mum' and the gentle narration peculiar to Forster is swept away by Smith's concise equivalent. Despite this stylistic divergence, Smith's passage as well as the following sections explicitly emulate the progression of *Howards End*, with Kiki being left on the station like Margaret Schlegel:

> The voices of the happy family rose high. Margaret was left alone. No one wanted her. Mrs Wilcox walked out of King's Cross between her husband and her daughter, listening to both of them. (Forster 2006: 97)

> The happy clan bustled away back down the platform, laughing and speaking over each other, as the Amherst train pulled away and Kiki stood with Carlene's hot chocolate in her hand. (Smith 2005: 271)

As illustrated in the above passages, the narrative convergence relies predominantly on the emulation of the core linguistic structures, rhetorical style, and thematic overtones taken from the source text. Inevitably, the degree of correspondence between the sequences is obscured by the temporal and cultural frameworks, as the lines from Smith's novel explicitly defamiliarise Forster's world in a postmodern vein in terms of contemporary discourse and context. The effect of this process is two-fold: on the one hand, the recontextualisation hinders the recognition of *intertextual* correspondences, but on the other hand, it establishes proximity with the contemporary audience. By extension, the intersection of two different narrative trajectories within one text activates the act of cognitive mapping, in which the reader reconstructs mentally the whole pattern of intradiegetic and extradiegetic correspondences between the *hypo-* and *hypertext*. The oscillation between two fictional worlds results simultaneously in ontological crossovers and, more importantly, in the recognition of intertextual components, among which characters as act-ants hold prominence.

Obviously, the process of identifying continuities in the presentation of intertextual characters hinges on different criteria. While the mimetic, psychological, thematic, and linguistic aspects constitute a backbone in the reception of a character presented in a single fictional work, their potential for identifying *hypertextual* variants with their *hypotextual* proto-types is questionable: intertextual characters in Smith's novel may differ in their essential properties. However, the lack of external or psychological symmetry of characters can be compensated by progression, which, by providing contextual frames, allows the reader not only to trace convergent thematic lines and relationships between two fictional worlds but also to cognitively conceptualise and identify intertextual links between characters located in different fictional realms. This cognitive reconstruction unavoidably involves boundary-crossing, as the reader is induced to actively refer *hypotextual* prototypes to their *hypertextual* variants.

Irony as the principle of constructing a character: *Young Adolf* by Beryl Bainbridge

BARBARA KLONOWSKA

> What is character but the determination of incident?
> What is incident but the illustration of character?
> What is either a picture or a novel that is *not* of
> character? What else do we seek in it and find in it?
>
> Henry James, *The Art of Fiction*

Character is one of the most notorious concepts in literary theory; indispensable on the one hand, contested and almost abandoned on the other, it creates problems for most theoretical formulations, especially those derived from structuralism. As Jonathan Culler observes, "[it] is the major aspect of the novel to which structuralism has paid least attention and has been least successful in treating" (1975: 230). Among the reasons of this theoretical failure Culler mentions the general "ethos" of structuralism which favours the role of the discourse, conventions and language over individuality, and makes a character a site of forces rather than a psychologically plausible individual (1975: 230). Yet, despite this discourse-oriented turn in literary theory, what the Jamesian motto to this article emphasises is that in the simple everyday practice of reading, character remains probably the single most important novelistic element and thus produces a constant challenge to any literary school. As Aleid Fokkema points out,

> traditionally, 'character' is a term that both nourishes and feeds on approaches to literature which operate on mimetic premises [...] for a long time nothing seemed more natural than to take it for granted that characters represented human beings, that novels were about people, and that psychological motives sustained plots. (Fokkema 1991: 18)

This traditional view seems to inform most of the reading habits and underlie numerous critical interpretations. Yet, according to Fokkema, this traditional concept is "not only inadequate in the face of postmodern literature, but in the face of practically any literary text, because representation is understood [in it] to be a natural process rather than a matter of literary conventions" (1991: 18). What this formulation implies, then, is that each literary character, however plausible or fantastic he or she might seem, is by necessity always a literary construct generated according to specific literary conventions employed in fiction, and thus treating it in psychological or mimetic terms makes little sense. Consequently, contemporary literary theory prefers to speak of characters as signs, constructs or subjects rather than protagonists or heroes. Many novels published during the last half of the twentieth century might illustrate precisely this 'constructedness' of characters, their ostensibly artificial qualities, and their departure from the premises of the mimetic representation of human beings. Accordingly, they often tend to be critically described as 'flat' or 'badly' characterised (compare Fokkema 1991: 14), as they depart from the traditional concept of 'round' or 'dynamic' literary characters. Yet, in the light of poststructuralist theories, their function in the novel is quite simply different: openly manifesting their constructedness, they draw attention to universal mechanisms of novel writing and the rules that generate literary representation.

The aim of this article is to analyse one of such characters, the young Adolf Hitler from the novel by Beryl Bainbridge *Young Adolf*, which on the one hand is modelled on the historical German dictator, and on the other is a manifestly literary construct. I will argue that the interplay between these two understandings of the character (as a mimetic representation of a real-life historical figure vs. a purely literary construct) – very much reminiscent of the tensions present in literary theory itself – is the chief factor responsible for both the aesthetic effects of the novel and its subversive turn, taken not merely on the particular historical figure but on the very premises of historical fiction.

*

Published in 1978, *Young Adolf* is a historical farce presenting a seemingly unknown episode in the life of Adolf Hitler: his visit and stay in Liverpool, at the house of his half-brother Alois and his sister-in-law

Bridget. Hitler is 23 at the time, and the visit falls at the moment of his personal crisis: rejected several times by the Vienna Academy of Fine Arts, a failed artist, destitute, penniless, homeless, lonely and miserable, Hitler apparently seeks refuge and opportunity with his older brother. His stay in Liverpool lasts a few months and finishes with his disappointment with England, failure to find a job, and the decision to come back to Europe (for the lack of funds, South America is out of the question) and to settle down in Munich.

The episode is a made-up story, thriving on the legend cherished by many Liverpudlians, that Hitler indeed stayed with his brother's family in Liverpool between November 1912 and April 1913. The still controversial legend is based on the memoirs of Bridget Dowling, Alois Hitler's first wife, written with their son William Patrick in the 1940s and published in the 1970s, which are the only source of this alleged episode[1]. Both the memoirs and the novel (and then a two-part play by Bainbridge, *The Journal of Bridget Hitler*, produced by the BBC in 1981) capitalise on the relatively little known period of the real Adolf Hitler's life before his moving to Munich. As Mike Royden observes,

> At the time the memoir was written, it was common knowledge that there was a 'lost year' in Hitler's life. Hitler had never alluded to it, it wasn't in *Mein Kampf* or any other of his writings. Hitler had conveniently glossed over the period, or rewritten it, to provide a more acceptable version for a public figure he now was. His failure to enter the Academy, living rough, the doss houses, and draft dodging, was a phase he felt was not for public consumption. Bridget and William may have been only too ready to fill the 'missing months' with an alternative story. Those close to him say apart from brief trips to Italy and Paris, he had made no visit to any other country, although this is still not conclusive enough. (Royden)

Thus, the novel accurately recreates facts from the life of both the historical Adolf Hitler and his family, while the research done and events mentioned generally abide by the publicly known and accepted versions of his biography.

Yet already at this preliminary factual stage, small inconsistencies are inserted, which might signal to the reader that the novel is not to be taken quite seriously, and suggest that it should be read as a literary joke

---

1 Compare the informative article by Mike Royden discussing historical research and controversies surrounding the memoirs of Bridget Dowling-Hitler, Adolf Hitler's sister-in-law, and the following 'myth' of Hitler's stay in Liverpool.

rather than a historical novel. One of such hints is the imprecision of names: in the novel, Hitler comes to Liverpool with the forged documents made out in the name of Edwin, his dead brother; yet, the real-life Hitler had no brother of that name. Similarly, there are inconsistencies surrounding the family life of the beloved sister of Alois, Angela. Moreover, the very title, although precise and accurate, due to its lack of the protagonist's last name and the inevitable associations with the title of James Joyce's *A Portrait of the Artist as a Young Man*, suggests not only and not so much a historical novel, as a novel that will play with historical material and use it for its own fictitious story. It seems, then, that despite its care and precision with the facts, the novel simultaneously makes it clear that it is not to be read and interpreted as historical fiction, and that certain liberties are going to be taken with the events and characters portrayed. Nowhere is this liberty better seen than in the construction of the main character, the young Adolf Hitler.

*

Fictional writing introducing historical figures as characters is always based on the distance between the generally known historical character represented by historical accounts, whose image and deeds are well-known, and the fictional character bearing his or her name that the novel seeks to portray. This distance can be either minimal, with the author trying to portray the literary character as close to the historical one as possible, aiming perhaps to fill the gaps in knowledge, show little-known contexts and facts, or explain the historical figure better, yet without distorting or abusing the generally agreed-upon profile of the 'great person'. Conversely, this distance may be vast, and deliberately so, to emphasise the difference, show the historical figure from an unusual perspective, or cut a new angle at the old story. The latter strategy in particular is characteristic of recent historical fiction, with its unusual presentations of such figures as Napoleon or Samuel Johnson, whose aim is frequently to question and complicate the sometimes naive authority invested in historical fiction and, more generally, in history writing[2]. In contrast to the so-called "Great-Men model of history" (compare Holmes 1997: 41), some contemporary novels tend to represent either

---

2   Compare such novels as Jeanette Winterson's *The Passion* or Beryl Bainbridge's *According to Queeney* which treat historical characters in an openly non-historical way.

marginal figures and unexceptional lives, in keeping with the socially oriented model of history, or to present the 'great' figures from unusual perspectives, illustrating Brian McHale's thesis about "the postmodernist revisionist historical novel" (1987: 90).

Thus, a literary character modelled on a historical figure is always a complex construction: a sign which is not empty from the beginning to be only gradually filled with meaning and interpreted by the reader, but already meaningful and read in relation to the extra-textual historical reality with its interpretation revealed, not just by the text, but by the interplay between this text and the prior historical and cultural accounts. Obviously, no sign is ever absolutely empty; the difference, however, between an ordinary sign and that denoting a historical figure lies in the degree of its concretisation: in the case of a historical character, his or her very name already may be a very significant piece of information immediately activating the process of semiosis.[3] What generates the meaning of a historical character in fiction, then, is not merely the fictional text itself but also the extra-textual context and knowledge, and this meaning is produced at the intersection of these two factors. In the case of well-known historical figures, and Adolf Hitler is undoubtedly one of them, this game is inevitable and constitutes the main source of the aesthetic effect of a text.

In novels like *Young Adolf*, then, two characters, or in this case two Hitlers, are imposed upon each other: the literary fictional one, admittedly little interesting or appealing, and the historical one, a failed artist and architect, known to every European reader, however scant their historical knowledge might be. The character, then, is produced both by textual strategies (description, dialogue, narration, comments, presentation of thoughts and other literary techniques of characterisation employed normally in the novel), and by the prior knowledge and images brought into the text by the reader, and, perhaps most importantly, by the relationship or distance between these two sources.

---

3   In the case of this novel such a signal is indeed provided by the very name: after Hitler, the name Adolf seems to have gone out of use, increasingly rarely given to boys because of negative historical associations; thus the phrase 'young Adolf' will quite probably not be interpreted neutrally, as designating an ordinary young boy, but rather will automatically bring connotations with the historical figure – a similarity shared e.g. with the name Napoleon, although for different reasons.

Thus, in the case of literary characters modelled on historical figures, no purely and exclusively textual interpretation, in the New Criticism fashion, is actually available: the extra-textual reality, the knowledge and experience brought inevitably into the reading process, cannot be eliminated; on the contrary, they provide the background against which the literary character operates, and from which it derives much of its effect. The character and its implied meaning or function within the narrative may fail if the reader's knowledge, for example, is not up to the task and he or she will simply not recognise the connections or allusions; a huge part of the character's role is ruined then. The role of the extra-textual context, then, is a part of the complex mechanism of the construction of the literary historical characters, always involving a subtle interplay between the assumed cultural image of the character and that constructed in the novel. The distance between the two is more often than not a source of interesting aesthetic and ideological effects.

Despite its factual accuracy and general reliability, in Beryl Bainbridge's novel the distance is vast and based on implied ironic discrepancy between the generally accepted cultural image of the historical character of Hitler and its literary 'incarnation'. In so doing, the novel produces comic effects that both deflate the vast and monstrous historical character and present a not quite serious version of the deadly serious history. More importantly, however, irony and humour thus employed in *Young Adolf* work to de-naturalise and defamiliarise the traditionally accepted vision of the past and draw attention to its always already constructed nature.

In the chapter of *The Art of Fiction* devoted to irony, David Lodge defines it in the following way:

> In rhetoric, irony consists of saying the opposite of what you mean, or inviting an interpretation different from the surface meaning of your words. Unlike other figures of speech – metaphor, simile, metonymy, synecdoche etc. – irony is not distinguished from literal statement by any peculiarity of verbal form. An ironic statement is recognised as such in the act of interpretation. (Lodge 1992: 179)

Irony, thus, is not produced by any peculiar verbal manoeuvres but by the distance between the meaning stated and that implied. In the case of character construction this ironic distance is produced between the projected and implied reading of the protagonist. And while it is true that it is the act of interpretation that ultimately produces irony, it is also the case that it is the distance between two readings that is essential for irony to be produced. In the case of a literary character modelled on a historical figure, this is the distance that separates the officially accepted image of a character and its representation in the text.

It is the ironic distance between the historically and culturally established figure and its textual representation that lies at the core of *Young Adolf*, in which the sinister figure of the historical Adolf Hitler, with his characteristic image, looks and views, is juxtaposed with an entirely less intimidating and less serious literary character. Thus, the first and perhaps main mechanism producing ironic effects in the novel is based on the exploration of the distance between the narrative and the extra-textual knowledge. It is perhaps most striking in the general picture of the fictional young Adolf produced by the novel: instead of a self-confident future dictator, the novel presents a moody, neurotic and immature young man. Most of the time the protagonist is either irritated or angry; easily unnerved, he either reacts violently to other characters, or withdraws, unable to stand even the smallest frustrations. Over-sensitive and over-ambitious, he is unable to like and to be liked, although to be loved and accepted are perhaps his greatest desires. He spends his days mostly doing nothing, either sleeping endlessly, or idly walking about, while his only occupation, forced upon him by his brother, is being an errand boy. The contrast between his idleness and his grand ambitions makes him ridiculous, even more so due to his clear delusions of grandeur.

Equally diminishing is young Adolf's persecution mania, ever-present in the plot. Although the mania turns out to be not entirely invented, as he indeed is being followed, his paranoid thoughts and fears suggest an unstable mind. Combined with a weak body (thin and smallish) and weak constitution (easily exhausted, unable to drink and hold alcohol), constantly sick and frustrated, the protagonist cuts a figure of a weakling, both mental and physical. Thus, the principle of characterisation here seems to be that of ridicule: the literary character is systematically portrayed as miserable, pitiful and over-proud at the same time. Juxtaposed with the formidable historical figure, this portrayal creates an ironic contrast. Nowhere near is it as pronounced as in the conclusion of the novel: seen off by his family at the station, young Adolf departs for

Munich, while Meyer the neighbour comments: "Such a strong-willed young man. It is a pity he will never amount to anything" (Bainbridge 2003: 218). In the light of the knowledge about the historical 'young man' and his career, this statement produces 'dramatic irony' of sorts: the historical figure definitely did amount to something. As Victoria Glendinning observes in her review of the novel, "it is on this irony that the novel gallantly hangs" (1979). Thus, one of the techniques employed to generate the ironic contrast between Hitler's public image and that constructed in the novel serves to create a literary protagonist presented as a reduced and ridiculed version of the historical figure.

Another mechanism responsible for the ironic contrast in the construction of the character consists in providing simplistic, down-to-earth circumstances to explain numerous features characteristic of Hitler's image. Some of them are connected with his appearance: for example, the novel explains young Adolf's hair style with his wish to hide a cut injury, rather than with any kind of conscious or intentional stylisation. Similarly, he decides to grow his moustache so as to avoid being ever again taken for a woman. His characteristic brown shirt, a uniform and an ideological statement, allegedly springs from equally pragmatic reasons. Poor and destitute, he has but one shirt, and out of compassion his sister-in-law makes him another one from a piece of brown linen she manages to find among old rags. Apparently, as the following passage demonstrates, the fictional young Adolf does not seem to mind:

> Alois, seeing him strutting about the front room, eying himself in the mirror above the fireplace, couldn't help smiling.
> 'It's a queer colour,' he said.
> Adolf took no notice. The brown shirt meant he needn't sit wrapped in a blanket while his other one was in the wash. He hadn't been so well-dressed for years. (Bainbridge 2003: 67)

No particular ideology, then, but sheer poverty stands behind the emblem of the future German Nazis, just as equally pragmatic reasons underlie the fictional Hitler's personal image. The contrast between the iconic status they acquired later in culture and the pitiful conditions they spring from in the novel is yet another mechanism generating the ironic distance in the construction of the character.

Even the mysterious historical silence surrounding young Adolf's stay in Liverpool is humorously explained in the text. The 'lost year' that still puzzles historians and biographers is apparently little known due to the character's resolution; tired and disappointed he decides:

> Never in all my life, thought Adolf, under torture or interrogation, will I mention that I have been to this accursed city, visited this lunatic island. (Bainbridge 2003: 216)

The myth of the real-life Hitler's stay in England, then, is another episode which is 'explained' away in the novel in a down-to-earth, pragmatic way, and the mystery or importance of the secret period in the life of the historical figure is once again reduced to a trivial and banal matter.

Yet another method of generating the ironic contrast consists of the introducing of funny or pathetic scenes which undermine the serious profile of the historical figure. In the last scenes of the novel the protagonist, afraid of being watched and followed, runs into a theatre and changes into female clothes so successfully that he is indeed taken for a woman. This slapstick comedy-like episode, contrasted with the stern and manly cultural image of Hitler and indirectly implying his effeminate qualities, again becomes a source of ironic distance in the interpretation of the character. Playing on the image of triumphant masculinity propagated by the cultural representations of Hitler, and suggesting its 'weaker' and less prestigious features, the novel undermines both the commonly accepted representation of the dictator and the gender stereotypes usually associated with it.

Finally, similarly not-quite-serious circumstances explaining the character's decisions, views and ideas are another way to produce irony. Hitler's decision to settle down in Munich is presented in the novel as entirely accidental and not even his at all:

> South America being out of the question, Alois said he would buy a ticket to Linz. Meyer suggested that Munich might be better: he had some contacts in the city that could prove useful to Adolf – certain political organisations, certain persons of note and influence.
> Certain trouble, thought Adolf, but he kept his thoughts to himself. (Bainbridge 2003: 218)

In effect, the decision that in the life of the historical character was of utmost importance, is presented in the novel as coincidence and chance, and the character emerges not as an individual consciously shaping his life but as a passive figure moved about by other figures. The cultural image of Hitler as a decisive or even ruthless man who does not refrain even from unpopular decisions, is juxtaposed with the novelistic character seemingly portraying the historical personage, and yet drastically different in this respect. The discrepancy between the character constructed by culture and that produced by the novel is once again one of the possible mechanisms generating irony.

Similarly, the novelistic Adolf's views and ideas do not seem to spring from any deep reflection or reading; on the contrary, they seem to be formed under the spur of the moment, as emotional reactions to some more or less imaginary injuries inflicted upon him. Generally in the novel, for a future dictator and ideologue, the fictional young Adolf presents or forms his views surprisingly infrequently: his mind seems preoccupied with much more mundane matters. On rare occasions when he does express them, however, they resemble a rant of a hurt and vengeful boy who desperately wants to hurt someone back rather than a systematised and consistent ideology. His largest exposition of political ideas is provoked by his conversation with Meyer:

> 'It is my belief,' Adolf told him, in a voice querulous with despair, 'that European history is merely the history of racial struggle. The decline of the Roman Empire is a classic example of historical decadence resulting from contaminated blood. Like Rome, Europe is sinking under the burden of bastard peoples. [...] Impure blood spawns impure ideas and creeds. We've not only the Jews to contend with but the Slavs, the Socialists, the Hapsburg Monarchists, the Roman Catholics, the Croats...'
> 'There would seem to be no one left,' Meyer observed mildly.
> 'Europe is rotten at the core,' spluttered Adolf. 'Rotten.' He couldn't repeat the word often enough. That small adjective contained all the wretchedness he felt at Meyer's rejection of him. (Bainbridge 2003: 74-75)

Feeling rejected and unwanted, the protagonist reacts with aggression directed indiscriminately towards the whole world. In the novel, this is clearly the passage showing the character as an immature and childish egotist. It casts ironic light on the historical Hitler, although, as Victoria Glendinning points out, it does in fact introduce some of the features that are indeed believed to make up the latter's psychological profile:

> It is by the characterisation of Adolf that the book must be judged. Even at this early stage in his life, Miss Bainbridge gives him those traits that historians have ascribed to him: inability to establish ordinary friendships, in-

tolerance and hatred of non-Germans, a tendency to live in a fantasy world
and to erupt into passionate outbursts. (Glendinning 1979)

Yet, despite the psychological similarity of the historical and fictional
Adolf, it is rather the discrepancy between these two representations that
is chiefly responsible for the comic effects of the novel. The novelistic
portrayal combined and juxtaposed with the extra-textual knowledge
produces an ironic distance between the cultural image and the literary
one.

Thus, it seems that in *Young Adolf* it is irony which is responsible for
both the construction of the main protagonist, and the general effect of
the novel. The aim of all the trivialities and banalities humorously revealed in the treatment of the character of Hitler appears to be to imagi-
natively play with the established historical stereotypes. As Rachel Redford observes, "Bainbridge revels in the bizarre and grotesque, but the
real interest here is in the twisting plot of her idiosyncratic imagination,
and the constant tension between the reader's knowledge of the future
and novel's teasing ironies" (Redford 2001). Irony, then, is both the chief
aesthetic effect produced by the novel, and the main mechanism of prob-
lematising the seemingly agreed-upon vision of the past.

*

The example of Beryl Bainbridge's novel demonstrates a certain strategy
of constructing a literary character in fiction by employing historical material. Fictional characters which are modelled on historical figures tend
to either imitate their real-life models, or to differ from them. In the latter case, the difference both serves as a source of specific aesthetic effects, and may have certain ideological implications. In *Young Adolf*, the
aesthetic effect produced is that of irony and humour: the fictional young
Hitler is a deflated and ridiculed version of the historical *über-Mensch*,
and the contrast between the protagonist of the novel and the image derived from the reader's extra-textual historical knowledge inevitably
brought into the reading, creates a complex character made up of the
two.

This combination, however, has far-reaching effects for the interpretation of the character, going far beyond a simple comic joke. First of
all, in a truly revisionist fashion, the ironic character of Bainbridge's
novel reveals its own fictional status: the contrast between the cultural

image of Hitler and that projected on the pages of the novel suggests that the latter is a sort of fantasy, a variation on the historical figure, produced by the intellectual game of 'what if'. Irony and humour additionally strengthen this effect, implying the not-quite-serious treatment of the character and signalling clearly that it should not be interpreted historically. Thus employed, the character becomes a strong metafictional element which prevents a straightforward interpretation of the text as a historical novel supposed to present 'true facts'. Instead, the text's fictional status is clearly indicated which suggests its interpretation as fiction rather than history.

More importantly, however, the character's manifested fictionality invites reflection on the possible fictionality and constructedness of the historical figure itself. While the historical real-life Adolf Hitler undoubtedly existed, his public image, produced and proliferated by various media, with its iconic features, characteristic looks, and infamous ideology, was a deliberate and conscious construction. In the historical Hitler's case this image was founded on seriousness, sternness, leadership and will; his fictional 'image' in Bainbridge's story is based on exactly opposite features. The contrast between these two images, then, shows not only the principles of construction of the literary character within the novel but also, paradoxically, of the historical one. The ironic contrast employed in *Young Adolf* works, on the one hand, to create a comic fictional character, and on the other to undermine and problematise the accepted cultural image of the historical figure, showing its equally, though differently, constructed nature. Irony becomes one of the tools employed to question the seemingly natural and accepted version of history; following Frederick M. Holmes we may observe that it "permits [...] a contesting or even rewriting of standard or orthodox accounts of, or ways of thinking about, the past" (Holmes 1997: 41). Thus, in so doing, Bainbridge's novel seems to imply, in the fashion of Hayden White, that each and every historical character, and all history writing as such, no matter how fictional or factual, is at its core a constructed narrative with equally constructed characters.

Characters in mythical and historical contexts: William Golding's "The Scorpion God"

JADWIGA WĘGRODZKA

It seems unquestionable that in the understanding of characters in fictional worlds the reader's "knowledge that comes from outside the text plays a crucial role" (Eder, Jannidis, Schneider 2010: 12). In order to understand characters in a literary text the reader must not only pick up relevant information provided therein but also make use of several different types of cultural knowledge, including social knowledge, media knowledge and narrative knowledge (2010: 14). The most obvious illustration of the essential necessity of cultural knowledge is provided by fictional historical narratives. To a greater or lesser extent all historical fictions rely on the reader's awareness of the assumed time distance to the events related and his/her knowledge of the period described. In some historical narratives the understanding of a spatiotemporally distant setting is facilitated for the reader by the narrator's comments or by the introduction of the character of a stranger who receives explanations about puzzling features of the presented world[1]. However, there are many different ways in which the reader's historical knowledge may be prompted, activated and utilised by fictional narratives.

A very interesting case of historical knowledge as an important element in the interpretation of characters, and the text as whole, is provided by William Golding's novella "The Scorpion God". It belongs to a collection of the same title published in 1971 and featuring two other texts: "Clonk, Clonk" and "Envoy Extraordinary". All three stories,

---

1   The device of a stranger to whom various aspects of the fictional reality need to be explained often appears in utopia and dystopia, science fiction or in many different variants of fantastic fiction.

called "short novels" in the subtitle, are set in ancient or even pre-historic times. Neither story facilitates the reader's understanding of the distant time and space setting through the narrator's or characters' explanations. "The Scorpion God" does not provide the reader with any dates or any place names helpful for the temporal and spatial localisation of events. The reader can identify the setting as ancient Egypt only by interpreting textual hints such as customs, emblematic colours, or some details of the space setting, but the exact time or the identity of characters appear to remain unspecified – at least until the final part of the novella.

As is often the case in literary texts, also in "The Scorpion God" the insight into the text's semantics crucially depends on the reader's understanding of the character's social roles and relations as well as on the grasp of the characters' personalities, which constitute the mimetic aspect in James Phelan's terminology (1989: 2). Equally important, though contingent on the former aspect, is the understanding of the juxtaposed world models dependent on the characters' spatial and temporal attributes, which in Phelan's terms represents the thematic component. It has to be emphasised that both mimetic and thematic aspects involve various kinds of the reader's cultural knowledge, such as, for example, psychological or anthropological. However, in Golding's novella the activation of the reader's historical knowledge seems to significantly modify the understanding of the protagonist and, consequently, the whole text.

*

The characters in "The Scorpion God" are introduced by the descriptions of the third person narrator who mostly focuses on the exteriors, often takes note of minute details and occasionally draws conclusions concerning the internal qualities of the figures. The first important character introduced in this way is the runner who is first presented from a distance, with the help of the perspective of a group of people watching him:

> These people were all looking away down the river, away from the sun [...]. There was a faint noise down the river. The waiting men looked at each other, rubbed their sweaty palms on their linen kilts, then held them up [...]. A man came into sight on the track [...]. (Golding 1977: 9-10)

After establishing the perspective the narrator goes on to depict the elements which become visible as the runner comes near the watching group: his jerky movements, his white "costume" with gleams of gold and blue, his sweat shining on dark skin (1977: 10). Having provided a general view from a distance, the narrator says: "Now the runner was so near he could be seen in detail" and proceeds: "His face had been oval once, but good living and authority had slabbed it to a rectangle in keeping with his stocky body" (1977: 10). The sentence not only reveals the physical appearance of the runner but also establishes him as a figure of authority and defines him as a man advanced in years without actually divulging his exact age. Subsequently the narrator goes on to interpret the character's external appearance as indicative of his personality traits and current mental state:

> He looked like a man who had few ideas but held those he had without examining them; and just now, his idea was to run and keep running. But there were outliers to this central idea, outliers of astonishment and indignation. (1977: 10)

Thus, the runner is characterised as a narrow-minded and determined person. Presently the narrator explains the apparent external reasons of his indignation connected with the difficulties of running, but abstains from providing the explanation for astonishment, which, presumably, is not caused by external problems. Only after two long paragraphs of descriptive details the runner's name is revealed through the utterance of another character who cries: "Run, Great House!" (Golding 1977: 11).

The pattern of initial description from the external perspective – with different degrees of distance – is regularly applied to major characters. The third person objective narrator seems to limit the information about the fictional reality and its elements (including characters) mostly to their physical aspects. Only once – in the passage quoted above – does the narrator supply a more direct characterisation of a figure by providing interpretation of external features. It seems that this single instance serves to suggest an interpretative procedure of drawing conclusions from external details which further on the reader should apply on his/her own.

Also the characters' utterances serve as an important method of characterisation, both direct and indirect. Even though it is the narrator who describes the character's external appearance, the utterances may reveal less obvious physical aspects, such as the state of health. For example, in the conversation with the blind man, the Prince – a boy about ten years old who is another individualised character introduced in the novella – supplies self-characterisation by mentioning his breathing difficulties, tiredness, and progressive loss of eyesight. However, just as in the example above when the narrator provides an interpretation of the runner's external features, so in this instance the information revealed by the Prince about himself is immediately interpreted by the blind man as indicating disaster for his people. Though this interpretation is not connected with the boy's personality, the pattern of drawing conclusions from information provided in the text is reinforced here in relation to characters' utterances.

Because the narrator does not generally venture inside the characters' minds, the utterances are also functional in revealing the character's intentions, fears, desires, convictions and beliefs – sometimes through voicing their thoughts aloud, and sometimes in conversation with, or in reply to, other figures. An example of a character directly revealing their own mental state can be found when a humiliated girl, Pretty Flower, moans: "Oh, the shame, the burning shame of it!" (1977: 36). Yet such direct expressions of emotions are rare. Usually the characters' utterances, similarly to actions, provide indirect self-characterisation from which the reader, and sometimes other characters, have to draw their own conclusions.

The expository parts of the novella serve to reveal character constellations which define the relationships between the main figures (Eder, Jannidis Schneider 2010: 26). The cast of major characters in "The Scorpion God" is not numerous. Almost all of them belong to the court of Great House (the runner), who is in fact the ruler. Three figures are additionally linked by family relationships: Great House is the father of the Prince, who, as his heir, will be expected to marry his "Royal Sister [...] Pretty Flower" (Golding 1977: 14). The Head Man and the Liar, who belong to the court, and the blind man whose position is ambiguous, are not related to the royal family but all have important contacts with its members, especially with Great House. In the opening sections of the text essential features of the major characters (in their mimetic aspect as defined by James Phelan) are all established in their relation to Great House. The young Prince is frightened of the necessity of performing royal duties. Blind man is anxious about the Prince's state of health and tries to inform Great House immediately. Pretty Flower is conscious of her own beauty and feels devastated when her erotic dance fails to arouse her father's sexual desire. The Great Man is competent and clam in his assurance about what has to be done in the face of the crisis. The Liar is nervous, voluble and uncertain; his evidently subservient position of a jester does not prevent him from trying to manipulate the other characters to his own advantage.

However, it is the Liar who seems increasingly differentiated from other characters. He is first introduced as a character who energetically encourages Great House in his run, and emerges as a secondary flanking character similar to the villagers who also cheer the ruler in his run. Gradually it becomes clear to the reader that the Liar has a strong personal motivation in trying to ensure Great House's success and then in attempting to diminish his failure: the old king has to die, and his demise will entail the death of all the servants – including the Liar – who he might find useful in the afterlife. Unlike the others, the Liar does not want to drink poison during the funeral and enter Great House's grave. According to the notions of the other characters, he refuses "the gift of eternal life" (Golding 1977: 58), claiming that "this one [life] is good enough" (1977: 40). The latter pronouncement is so shocking in the context of the funeral rites that his "words silenced every sound [...]. The dancing stopped and the Liar was surrounded by a ring of shocked and contemptuous faces" (1977: 40).

The characters' relation to space also confirms a significant division between the Liar and the remaining figures. All the characters (except the Liar) regard the world as limited to their immediate surroundings. The sky above the world is believed to be supported owing to the ritual daily performed by Great House, who is also the God. The world cannot be too large because then the weight of the sky would be enormous and, consequently, impossible to support; such a view is logically defended by the Head Man in conversation with Pretty Flower (1977: 55). The Liar is the only character who claims that there are other lands, other peoples and other customs, but his words are taken by the remaining characters to be just humorous stories or lies – hence his name[2]:

---

2   The Liar's stories may be also considered from the perspective of their metaliterary function, which, however, is beyond our immediate concern here.

The God tapped the Liar on the shoulder.
'Tell me some lies. [...] Tell me about the white men. [...] Tell me what their skin's like!'.
'They look like a peeled onion', said the Liar dutifully. 'Only not shiny. They're like that all over [...]. They don't wash – '
'Because if they did, the paint would come off!' Great House roared with laughter [...].
'And they smell', said the Liar, 'like I told you they smell. Their river runs round their land in a ring and rises up in great lumps and is salt [...]'.
Great House laughed again [...]. (Golding 1977: 25-26)

It is obvious to the contemporary reader, to whom Golding's text is addressed, that the Liar describes white skinned people living on an island surrounded by the sea. It is later revealed that the "lies" are based on the character's past experiences when he was repeatedly sold as a slave, which can be inferred from the Liar's conversation with the Prince (1977: 46-47). The Liar's journeys in his role of a slave have evidently given him broader knowledge about the world, and make him despise the narrow-minded people among whom he lives. In a desperate outburst he succinctly expresses this contempt for them not only through derogatory words but also by significant spatial suggestions:

'A patch of land no bigger than a farm – a handful of apes left high and dry by the tide of men – too ignorant, too complacent, too dimwitted to believe the world is more than ten miles of river – '. (1977: 59)

The Liar's words juxtapose "the patch of land" and "the world" which for the other characters in the novella are identical, while for the Liar – completely different. In the climax, when the Liar is about to be killed as a sacrifice to the dead king, he manages to save his life by convincing Pretty Flower, who will be the wife of the next ruler, to accept the enlarged view of space, which also involves a different concept of time, and actually introduces a new world model.

The limited spatial dimensions of the fictional world are inextricably linked with the circumscribed notion of time. One of the opening descriptions of the fictional world emphasises its motionlessness:

Between the cliffs and the river, the black earth was burnt up. The stubble seemed as little like life as the feathers caught everywhere among separate stubs. The few trees, palms, acacias, hung down their foliage as if they had given up. The houses of limewashed mud seemed as alive as they and not more motionless; not more motionless than the men and women and chil-

dren who stood on either side of a beaten track that lay parallel with the
river [...]. (Golding 1977: 9)

The trees, the houses and the people are all linked by their immobility,
which indicates their metaphorical unity. Spatially, the immobility is
soon dispelled by the arrival of the runner, but the sense of temporal sta-
sis will be strengthened when the reader learns that the run is in fact a
part of a ritual cyclically performed to prove the virility of the king. The
understanding of the world by all the characters, except the Liar, involves a circular concept of time. They seem to live in a static world not
only radically limited in space but also defined by cyclic repetitions of
unchanging patterns of activities: for example, the God/Great House has
to perform rites for holding up the sky every day and has to run the race
(with which the story opens) every seven years. The characters live in
what is defined as "now", which after death and burial rituals becomes
eternal and unchanging – and that is treated as extremely desirable. The
Liar, however, is desperate to hold on to his present life: he wants to
survive at all cost and does not hesitate to kill for it. Evidently, he is not
a great believer either in the eternal Now or in the essential changeless-
ness of existence both in this life and the next.

    In his determination to save his life, the Liar not only opens to Pretty
Flower a vision of unlimited (or at least extensive) space, but also introduces a revolutionary notion of change: the possibility of doing something that has never been done before. He says to Pretty Flower:

    'You have soldiers – you, one of a dozen petty chieftains that line this river
    – you have the beginnings of an army – [...] What could you not do? [...]
    The man who holds the high seat in this country [...] could burn up the
    banks of this river from one end to the other, until all men living by it were
    bowing to your beauty'. (1977: 59-60)

Characteristically, the Head Man replies to the Liar's (rhetorical) question: "What could you not do?" with "We know what to do" (1977: 60).
The Head Man's view of the world does not require, or admit, any
change of established patterns: he knows what is always done. The Liar's idea of conquest, however, points out to the possibility of initiating
a chain of unprecedented events which will not just modify the current
pattern but in fact remove it.

    The spatial and temporal dimensions of the presented world, which
we have considered in connection with the characters, confirm the sug-

gestion that particular figures are representative of certain attitudes or even world models. Within this area of functionality, called thematic by Phelan and symbolic by Eder, the role of characters may be seen as emblematic or exemplary[3]. Such a view of characters seems to be supported by their names. None of the characters bears a proper name in our usual understanding of the term. Most of them are named for their social functions: Great House (his name refers to his superior position as the chief inhabitant of the palace, i.e. the Great House); the Prince, and the Head Man. Also the Liar's name refers to his role of a story-teller/jester at the court. Perhaps only the name of Pretty Flower derives from her personal trait (beauty) and not her social role[4]. This way of naming accords with the predominantly exterior presentation of characters and puts emphasis on generalising rather than more personalising functions of their attributes.

The exemplary function of characters as representatives of distinct world models seems to suggest the understanding of Golding's novella as a parable about the shift of paradigms in the course of human cultural evolution[5]. The mythical understanding of the world defined by endless repetitive patterns closely intertwining natural processes and human activities is static in what the characters describe as "now". This world model offers stability and security by barring anything unexpected and offering answers to all possible questions – not only concerning the physical world but also the metaphysical one, which actually is just an eternal version of the present one. The new world model, suggested by the Liar's proposal of conquest is evidently based on different spatio-

---

3   The term "symbol" is used to refer to the characters in "the context of themes and network of signification" (Eder, Jannidis and Schneider 2010: 45); I would prefer to reserve the term symbol for more particular semantic strategies of meaning multiplication. The term "exemplary" is employed in connection with characters in Golding's fiction by Usha George: "Since Golding proposes to embody general truths, he is committed to select those human experiences that can be viewed as *exemplary* and not merely *typical*. [...] Consequently the novels tend to be short and densely textured, and the characters function as exemplars of facets of human nature" (2008: 24).

4   The blind man is also consistently referred to by this noun phrase focusing on his physical attribute but in his case the phrase is printed in low case and so does not function as a proper name. It is significant, however, that in its construction, the phrase designating this character does not differ from the names of some other characters.

5   The theme of paradigm change links all three stories in *The Scorpion God* collection (Redpath 1986: 100-101).

temporal coordinates: the space is not limited by the well-known and plainly visible borderlines but extends into unfamiliar and unexplored areas; time will lose its repetitive and cyclic nature of endless reiteration to embrace new events in linear progression determined by the advancing conquest. The extensive space and linear time are manifestly correlated with the notion of change which in the story is defined as war, establishment of belligerent power, and subjugation of others by force.

Summed up in this way, the juxtaposition of the two paradigms seems to leave little doubt as to how they should be evaluated by the reader. Especially that the characters appear to be crucially involved in determining possible evaluations of these paradigms. Two characters: the Liar and Pretty Flower, are particularly significant as they are the ones who embrace the new world model at the end of the story. Even more crucially, they are the only major characters who survive the crisis initiated by Great House's failure – while all the other major characters find their deaths. The mimetic features of the Liar and Pretty Flower are essential in suggesting the evaluation of the new paradigm. The girl is a self-absorbed beauty who seems to have no concern for anything or anybody save herself. She even breaks the sexual taboo of her people by making the Liar her lover (even if he is not her brother) though it has to be added that this act seems caused by genuine passion. She is not a character who evokes the reader's sympathy since she is presented as cruel to her servants and to her young brother. The Liar is depicted as an over-active, nervous character who never ceases to talk – it may be inferred that speech has always been a tool of survival for him. He is very good at manipulating people. For example, he easily persuades the Prince to help him escape from the pit (i.e. the prison). The Liar's statement (quoted above) that the proposed conquest will result in all men admiring Pretty Flower's beauty, is an obvious case of manipulation, playing on the girl's central preoccupation with herself, in order to achieve the Liar's own, quite different, aims. Survival is the Liar's top value: his attempt to gain the highest power available in the world where he lives (by marrying Pretty Flower) is essentially motivated by trying to protect his life. In order to survive he even kills other characters in the course of the action: the Head Man in the final fight with the soldiers and the blind man by depriving him of food and water which he takes for himself in the pit. In his conversation with the Prince, the Liar reveals his matter-of-fact attitude to the blind man's agony:

'He is dying', said the Liar. 'Taking a long time'. [...]
'I think he's thirsty" [the Prince said].
'Of course he is,' said the Liar impatiently. 'That's why he's dying.'
'Why didn't he have any water?'
'Because I needed it,' shouted the Liar. 'Have you any more silly questions?' (Golding 1977: 47)

Neither the Liar nor Pretty Flower are presented as positive characters and though their motivations are psychologically comprehensible, they do not evoke the reader's sympathy. The presentation of the two characters as completely self-centred and ruthless strongly suggests a negative evaluation of the new cultural paradigm they initiate.

The critic Philip Redpath confirms the condemnation of the new pattern of "aggression, power and murder" in the novella, but this leads him to conclude that the old paradigm, as defined by "art, vision, faith and harmony", is therefore obviously positive (1986: 106). Redpath claims that "[t]he Liar destroys the mystery by which the Egyptians live", and adds that "Golding sympathises with the Egyptians who accept mystery and hold religious beliefs" (1986: 106).

Indeed, it seems possible to argue that the characters who, in contrast to the Liar and Pretty Flower, have unwavering belief in the mythical world order, are presented as more positive, while the surviving pair are selfish and cynical. Neither the Liar nor Pretty Flower are able to recognise any metaphysical dimension beyond the sphere of their immediate self-interest, which indeed characterises the new paradigm as deprived of any transcendental values. The representatives of the mythical paradigm – especially Great House and the Head Man – seem to have dignity and integrity rooted in their unwavering belief in the transcendental dimension of reality. Great House joyfully accepts the necessity of death and calmly drinks the poison. His understanding of death as being "born into perpetual Now" (Redpath 1986: 102) is radically different from anything conceivable in the contemporary western culture (to which the personal author and the book's target audience belong). Great House's belief is firmly shared by numerous minor characters of servants who drink poison and enter his grave to continue serving him after death. Also the Head Man appears steadfast in his beliefs and, as a person of powerful intellect, can justify them with irrefutable logic.

However, contrary to Redpath's positive assessment of "the mystery by which the Egyptians live", some aspects of the mythical world model may also evoke reservations. The idea of sacrificing people's lives to a religious belief does not seem appealing, if we take into account the perspective of the contemporary western reader. From this viewpoint the Liar's desperate struggle for survival seems much more comprehensible than the attitude of Great House and the other characters who willingly accompany him into death. Moreover, the strategies of dealing with the crisis of power and with the destructive flood, implemented by the characters representing the mythical paradigm appear inefficient and even misguided from the perspective of the contemporary reader: the Prince does not want to take up his father's duties because he believes himself unable to hold up the sky, while the Head Man staunchly believes that the disastrous rising of the river will stop if the Liar finally agrees to enter Great House's grave and join him in death. The contemporary reader cannot but see these attitudes as completely misguided even if they testify to the characters' firm belief in the mythical view of reality. It is certainly significant that these characters all die in the course of the action: Great House drinks poison provided by the Head Man, the blind man and the Head Man are killed by the Liar, the Prince is about to drink poison at the end of the novella. No major character survives to continue the mythical paradigm.

While the reader is evidently expected to recognise that the world order based on military conquest has little to recommend itself, neither is the mythical paradigm unequivocally commended in the text. Firstly, its most positive exponents, Great House and the Head Man are occasionally presented as rather humorous characters. For example, the tall white hat falling over Great House's eyes while he is running makes him a rather comical figure. Secondly, in a conversation with Pretty Flower – highly amusing to the contemporary reader – the Head Man appeals to rationality and logic, which ironically emphasises that the mythical world model is simply and evidently untrue:

> 'What distinguishes man from the rest of creation? [...] His capacity to look at facts – and draw from them a conclusion. [...] First,' he [the Head Man] said, 'we must establish the facts. [...] Who kept the sky up? Mm?'
> 'Well – He [Great House] did.' [said Pretty Flower]

'Who, year after year in His – paternal generosity – made the river rise?'
'He did, of course.'
'*This* time – is there another God yet?
'No', said Pretty Flower heavily. 'Not yet'.
'Therefore – who makes the river rise now?'
'He does'. (Golding 1977: 50)

In the mythical paradigm the duties of the king-god involve the responsibility for all the aspects of the natural world: the position of the sky, and the flooding which ensures the harvest. Even after his death Great House is believed to make the river rise: when the flood does not subside, it must be caused by the dead ruler's displeasure – a situation definitely calling for a sacrifice. The stern logic applied by the Head Man does not make the mythical view any more credible for the contemporary reader, though it definitely adds a strong humorous touch to the conversation. When Pretty Flower expresses doubt as to some point in the logical chain of the Head Man's reasoning, he clinches the argument with: "Your woman's heart must not struggle against the granite durability of rational demonstration" (1977: 50), and translates in view of her perplexity: "The words are difficult admittedly; but they mean that I am right and you are wrong" (1977: 51), which ironically underscores his self-satisfied narrow-mindedness.

The evident falsity of the mythical convictions is juxtaposed with the Liar's stories about people with white skin, about the sea, about sexual customs allowing relationships with unrelated strangers – which the contemporary reader must recognise as true, while for the ancient Egyptian characters in the novella they are hilariously absurd fictions. Additionally, the reader's extra-textual knowledge may suggest that the Prince's health problems could be related to genetic disorders caused by incestuous marriages – which again does not seem to recommend the ancient Egyptian culture to the contemporary reader's admiration.

The evaluation of the two paradigms – mythical and historical – is definitely ambiguous. The manipulative cynicism and ruthlessness of the Liar definitely suggest a negative evaluation of the latter. But the former is not deprived of negative features and – from the perspective of the reader's extra-textual knowledge – appears as emphatically false. The ambiguity of the relative evaluation of the two world models juxtaposed in the novella is rooted in the rich and many sided presentation of characters who are impossible to ascribe to a simple

good vs. bad opposition. The characters are equipped with interesting
personality traits which turn out to be functional in the evaluation of
the conflicting world models, associated with particular figures in
their thematic functions.

*

Even though the characters' mimetic and thematic aspects are eminently
significant for the understanding of "The Scorpion God" as a parabolic and
philosophical tale about the change of cultural paradigms, Golding's novella
appears to suggest still another semantic layer whose presence is also crucially connected with the characters. The phrase used as the title, by virtue
of its strong similarity to other anthroponyms, appears to refer to a character.
Moreover, since the phrase the "Scorpion God" is used in the title, it could
(should?) be the name of the protagonist but in the course of the text several
characters seem to be temporarily foregrounded and then replaced by other
figures, so that the role of the protagonist is rather difficult to determine.
Additionaly, it is a remarkable feature of Golding's text that its cast of characters does not include a figure called the Scorpion God. The noun God is
used to signify Great House, but he is definitely not called the Scorpion
God. The motif of a scorpion appears only once in the whole text – at the
very end of the novella – not in a name but in a sentence containing a comparison: "He stings like a scorpion", used by the Head Man about the Liar
(Golding 1977: 62). Earlier in the same scene the Liar suggests that he
might become the next Great House, i.e. the God. Thus, the final scene may
be taken as an indication that the title phrase should be linked with the character of the Liar. This requires a retrogressive re-assessment of the Liar's
importance, especially since his initial role seems to be one of the minor
characters flanking Great House. The name Scorpion God does not refer to
the Liar's fictional present (in which the character is consistently called the
Liar) but to the possible fictional future – after the cessation of the narrative.
In this way the title serves to extend the narrative beyond the limit of the
textual ending. This manner of using the title additionally functions to emphasise the idea of change and the linear notion of time as well as to indicate
to the reader the importance of the extra-textual sphere.
     The novella actually contains many details which link the text with
the reader's extra-textual knowledge. As has been already pointed out,
the reader is never provided with definite identification of the setting as

ancient Egypt but has to draw his/her own conclusions on the basis of textual information and extra-textual knowledge. Thus the hot climate, the emphasis on gold and blue in the descriptions of the landscape and of the characters' clothes, the importance of the river and its periodical rising, as well as some of the customs, such as endogamous, or even incestuous, marriages treated as a norm – all point to ancient Egypt as the place of action in Golding's novella. A well-informed (or curious) reader may also know (or find out) that Great House is the literal sense of the word "pharaoh" (from the Egyptian *pr-'o*, through Hebrew *par'oh* and Late Greek *Pharao* as *Webster's New World Dictionary* informs), which definitely confirms the Egyptian setting. It is the novella's title, however, which discloses (or hides?) the most important extra-textual reference: historians of ancient Egypt mention King Scorpion, whose image was found on what is now known as Scorpion Macehead – discovered in 1897-98 by archaeologists James E. Quibell and Frederick W. Green in a temple near Hierakonpolis[6].

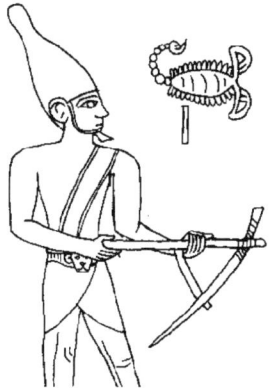

The image from the Scorpion Macehead; the original artefact on view in Ashmolean Museum, Oxford (Source: Wikipedia)

---

6   Compare *Encyclopedia of Ancient Egypt*. MobileReference. http://books.google.pl. 20.01.2012. On the excavations in Hierakonpolis compare Kathryn A. Bard's (ed.) *Encyclopedia of the archaeology of ancient Egypt* (1999: 445-448), where information on the area can be found: "Hierakonpolis is the Greek name for the ancient site of Nekhen [...] located on the west bank of the Nile [...]. Hierakonpolis was the Predynastic capital of Upper Egypt, and possibly the southern limit of Egypt in late Predynastic times. [...] The site owns its fame to the legendary prehistoric conquest of Lower Egypt and subsequent unification [...] (1999: 445).

Even if little is factually known about historical King Scorpion, he (or his son) is generally linked with the unification of the Upper and Lower Egypt under one rule, which entails the transition from Predynastic Egypt to the Dynastic period with its famous pharaohs, wonderful temples and awe-inspiring pyramids. The dim historical figure of King Scorpion seems to stand between the little-known semi-mythical era and the historical period in which time is measured by records of consecutive dynasties.

The historical reference contained in the novella's title redefines the character of the Liar[7]: from an apparently minor character he rises to the semantically crucial role as a fictional representation of a historical personage whose existence is confirmed by archaeological evidence even if factual information is scant. Consequently, the novella "The Scorpion God" is revealed to be an imaginative rendering of a decisive moment in the history of Egypt, the country with which William Golding was fascinated (Redpath 1986: 106).

The open ending of the story, which seems to suggest its possible continuation in the reader's imagination, turns out also to refer to the historical records which, however fragmentary, unmistakably confirm the fact of Egypt's unification under a strong and efficient ruler. While "The Scorpion God" as a philosophical parable certainly dramatizes a clash of the mythical, circular and static concept of time with its linear, dynamic and historical notion involving unpredictable change, the activation of the reader's historical knowledge allows to place this change in the concrete historical context, providing the novella with a generic dimension of a historical tale. Moreover, the title reference to the historical King Scorpion places the character of the Liar in the order of history and thus makes it possible for the reader to perceive the end of the novella as the beginning of the paradigm in which we live – still defined by change, conquest and bloodshed, and cut off from any metaphysical dimension.

Owning to their descriptive names and to the stress on external characterisation techniques, the characters in William Golding's "The Scorpion God" may be viewed as dominated by their thematic functions as representatives of two contrasting cultural paradigms or world models.

---

7   As Willem G. Weststeijn observes "the reader's (historical) knowledge may add important connotations or reveal hidden meaningful relations" (2007).

Such a role of characters is correlated with the possible generic qualification of the novella as a philosophical tale or even a parable about a shift of cultural patterns. The mimetic aspect of the fictional figures, who also emerge as interesting personalities owing to their plausible psychological qualities, appears functional in evaluating the juxtaposed paradigms and is thus subordinated to the thematic function. However, the application of the reader's historical knowledge redefines one of the characters as not only an interesting fictional personality and one of the emblems of the new paradigm, but also as an imaginary representation of a historical, though shadowy, figure – which changes the generic qualification of the novella and also appears to invite reflection on the personal qualities needed to make history. It seems typical of Golding that it is not a cheerful vision.

Counterfactual model of the self in J.M. Coetzee's *Summertime*

DOMINIKA SZWAJEWSKA

> As an exercise, let's imagine a character who is a
> contemporary writer.
>
> Max Apple, *Post-Modernism*

It should be noted that *Summertime* is not the first novel in J.M. Coetzee's ouvre in which he romances with the notion of autofiction. Firstly, the novel's subtitle, "Scenes from Provincial Life", establishes an unmistakable connection with *Boyhood* and *Youth*, two previous works fitted with the very same referencing device. These novels recreate real-world Coetzee through fiction, albeit under a much younger guise. What follows, one of the impending results was their equivocal branding – both texts were posited at one time under the category of memoir/nonfiction and then under the label of fiction. To a large extent, all of this is true for *Summertime* as well. Secondly, *Diary of a Bad Year* from 2007 can also be considered from the perspective of autofiction being a novel in many ways much more extensive and important to the present consideration, built on Señor C's – an ageing Sydney resident – musings upon real-world events and their implications. In fact, even Coetzee's first novel, *Dusklands*, exhibits inklings of historiography in the figure of Jacobus Coetzee and his narrative, particularly since the story is structured by means of authentic and fabricated documents.

However, *Summertime* is much more radical and discontinuous in its marriage of facts and fiction than any of its predecessors. The novel refers directly to the writer, by means of a full name, and there is no doubt it is *the* J.M. Coetzee. The name association is thus one marker which attests to the transworld identification. What is more, facts taken directly from real-world Coetzee's life are also introduced into the fictional context, and they are presented accurately even with regard to their temporal ordering. Yet, unlike real-world Coetzee, his fictional counterpart is dead. It is thus mostly owing to the narratives in the second or third degree – of those who knew him and the biographer who did not – that any light is shed on the persona of fictional Coetzee. The insertion of a few passages – of Coetzee's fabricated autobiography – may be said to further undermine the already feeble fact/fiction distinction. The result of this narrative practice is a relentless flickering effect between the fictum of the novel – a reconstruction of a stage in the life of the late J. M. Coetzee – and the story itself as a construct (fictio) – ushered in by a writer who passes under the very same name. These notions – the multifold hybridisation of fact and fiction as a source of narrative dynamics and the ontological opalescence effected by such transformative practices – outline the scope of the following analysis of Coetzee's *Summertime*.

The dichotomy of presence/absence[1], discernible even at this level of generalisation, when coupled with cognitive concretisation, are of course notions common to the process of semiosis whereby a sign, such as a fictional character, an initially vacant category, acquires attributes and meaning. Coetzee's *Summertime*, however, in a self-reflexive mode, reverses this pattern. In the novel, Vincent, an almost anonymous character referred to more often as Mr Biographer, attempts to write a factual account of life and times of a writer. It is no easy feat given that the writer is no longer alive and left behind little valuable biographical material – his private notebooks contain only studs of topics he wanted to elaborate on but never did. And even this meagre factual record is soon discredited by the biographer as a foray into the imaginative at the expense of the historically verifiable. As a result, Vincent's work must be based on interviews with people who were close to the departed. Having narrowed down the list of interviewees to Julia, Adriana, Margot and

---

1 Presence/absence is established by Leszek Kolek, who analyses the semiotic nature of clothes, as one of the primary oppositions, a force majore behind the generation of the first sign – the biblical fig leaf as a symbol of knowing, a newly acquired awareness. Kolek makes an important point, which will be valid also for the consideration of Coetzee's fiction: "the very first sign manifests its ambiguous nature: intended to cover, it exposes. There is no innocent use of any sign, for the very fact of using it demonstrates one's intentions and, on a deeper level, one's motivation" (Kolek 1996: 126).

Sophie, all in one way or another emotionally involved with the writer, as well as one male interlocutor – Martin, the biographer begins to assemble a body of work in the hope of synthesising from these miscellaneous tales one unified story. In fact, the novel as a whole can actually be seen as a draft of the work Vincent is to publish – "a serious book, a seriously intended biography" (Coetzee 2009: 225)

Nonetheless, the elusive presence which the biographer wants to pinpoint is nobody else than the persona of J.M. Coetzee, a writer of South African descent and Nobel Prize laureate. Thus, we soon learn that the inclusion of a culturally well-established name is not a case of mere homonymy but an intended reality-distorting device. In other words, the mode of existence of Coetzee as a fictional character, even at the level of mere name association[2], is that of a sign within already semiotically constructed context – external to the diegetic level of the novel. As such, it constitutes a dramatic break with what Uri Margolin terms one of the constitutive conditions for individuals in a narrated state of affairs, i.e. unity of traits (Margolin 1990: 865). By performing the simple gesture of incorporating himself in the work of fiction Coetzee may be said not only to carry out an assault on the mimetic level of the narrative, but also ostentatiously defy the thematic dimension such a unity of traits seems to serve. Hence the question who this textual Coetzee is remains open, for the type or category into which this fictional individual could be fitted cannot be readily established.

Thus in order to be able to analyse the fictional persona of J.M. Coetzee as a characterological counterfactual of the real-world writer, we first have to assess the degree to which the two overlap. As in the debate between historical and fictional discourses, here too one of the key concepts will be that of narrative framing. While describing postmodernist historiographic metafiction, Linda Hutcheon speaks of frames that are first established and then crossed (1998: 110). A similar strategy can be observed in *Summertime*. The novel opens with a very precise deictic expression – an entry from 22 August 1972 about a violent incident in Botswana, which is one of several entries in the fictional Coet-

---

2   "Mere name association" is used here in opposition to the entire scope of the narrative
     practice of structuring Coetzee as a fictional character. It is clear that the use of any referencing device that belongs to an ontological level different from the one that the novel
     (pretends to) represent(s) is always a source of ontological scandal.

zee's notebooks from years 1972–75 he plans to elaborate upon in future. Chronologically speaking, the novel deals with the time span that corresponds to the real Coetzee's return to South Africa after being forced to leave the US. However, more importantly, it covers the time when the writer creates *Dusklands* and (however critically the real-world Coetzee may now look upon it[3]) moves into the literary limelight. Although these biographical 'facts' are not dealt with explicitly in the novel, they are at least alluded to, establishing a frame of reference rooted in historical evidence, or actuality.

What is more, the parallels between the two Coetzees are established even with regard to physical aspect both personages – factual and fictional – may be said to share. This shows particularly well during a chance encounter of Julia with Coetzee in the supermarket. Studying his physique, she notes several traits as particularly distinctive of the man. For instance, she notices Coetzee's slight built, his beard and his horn-rimmed glasses. Julia also mentions his aura of an "abstracted scientist", a feature she in part attributes to his apparent loneliness. General as this description may seem, it is difficult to overlook even a certain degree of similarity to the real-world author. To sum up, the observation of this type of nomic and taxonomic regularities of the actual Coetzee and his life story enables us to conceive of his fictional counterpart as an actuality-variant individual performing its definitional function by which "all surrogates must retain a foothold in the original history" (Margolin 1990: 868)[4].

However, postmodern poetics also involves a break with the practice of tightly patrolling the borders of fact and fiction. In the metafictional play of the author the 'real' comes to exist only as a point of reference for the narratively recontextualised subject though it has no grounding, no centre, and no organising principle per se. Thus, we may only speak of 'versioning' of the real in postmodern narratives. This point has been well summarised by Smethurst who states that in the metafictional play "grounding is always sought and withdrawn, as the real is always turned

---

3   In "Voice and Trajectory" Coetzee states that "there are 'experiments' in *Dusklands* that are gestured at but not carried through productively" (Coetzee 1997: 87).

4   Hilary P. Dannenberg, in a similar tone, retorts that it is only by perceiving those two input spaces – based on similarity and difference – that we can appreciate the emergent structure of the counterfactual world which is the sum of a binary pair of events, the factual and its hypothetical other – the counter-factual (Dannenberg 2008: 60).

into a construction of the 'real'" (2000: 86). When applied to Coetzee as a characterological counterfactual of the actual-world writer, it may be said that this narrative recontextualisation takes two forms: radical reinterpretation of the prototype and altered ending of a life history[5].

When Max Apple, in the opening quotation, invites the reader to imagine a character who is a contemporary writer, the image one may envisage cannot be further from the fictional version of Coetzee as presented in the novel. For the fictional Coetzee emerges not as a character convinced of the strength of his artistic voice, not even as a struggling artist assured of the message but uncertain of the means for expressing it, but rather as a confused idler, little more than an embarrassment and irritation. "He was nothing and his words were nothing. [...] To me he really was a fool" (2009: 193) attests Adriana Nascimento whose open lack of interest relates to both Coetzee's literary endeavours and to him as a possible object of romantic love. Somewhere later in the narrative, Sophie Denoël, Coetzee's former colleague, in a similar tone states that

> his work lacks ambition [...] nowhere do you get a feeling of a writer deforming his medium in order to say what has never been said before, which to me is a mark of great writing. Too cool, too neat, I would say. Too easy. Too lacking in passion. (Coetzee 2009: 242)

One by one, fictional Coetzee's world mates pass a crushing critique of his literary endeavours. At best, he is seen as a skilled craftsman, fluent with words, but never as a true artist.

Even more interestingly, however, it seems that this perspective is shared by Coetzee himself. In one of the conversations with his cousin he swears to his alleged inadequacy to become an established artist: "I wasn't destined for that fate [...] the fate of being a rich and successful writer" (2009: 149). When such self-conscious statements are considered in terms of prototype-surrogate relation, it is clear that the reinterpretation of Coetzee as a counterfactual to the real-world author involves a strong dose of irony. While questions of alleged wealth are not of interest to the literary study, considering real-world Coetzee as an established figure of the literary world, one may safely say that he is little else than a successful writer. Actually, what we find in *Summertime* can be treated as an exemplification of a general attitude Alan Wilde terms suspensive irony. Postmodernist suspensive irony, he writes, takes for granted "the

---

5   For other procedures of counterpart creation see Margolin (1990).

ironist's immanence in the world he describes" (Wilde 1987: 166). And, one may ask, is there a bigger degree of immanence of the ironist in the world he creates than incorporating a version of himself in the fictional world and subjecting it to a meticulous scrutiny under the reversed optics of irony?

Moreover, in *Summertime* Coetzee emerges from the fictional tale not only as a failed writer, unworthy pretender to the public sphere, but also as a failed human, unable to shape his private reality. A case in point for this argument, as well as for the ironical turn in the presentation of the counterfactual version of Coetzee, may be the French translation of the novel's title. Whereas in many languages the title is translated literally, as summer or summertime[6,] the French translator rendered it as "L'eté de la vie", the summer of life. Even if this phrase does not invoke any immediate references, at the level of basic association we may agree to classify it under the category of opulence and plenty rather than scarcity, austerity or lack. But the associations with plenty do not feature in *Summertime*. The descriptions of Coetzee's everyday life verge on McHale's contrastive banality. In the "important yet neglected" period of his life Coetzee is living with his widowed father in a dilapidated house he unsuccessfully attempts to renovate, trying to make ends meet by taking up part-time jobs that offer no self-fulfilment and pay starvation wages. His emotional life does not offer much solace either, for he is constantly rejected by all women towards whom he feels any semblance of romantic attachment. In fact, such is the degree of ineptitude the character demonstrates in all his endeavours that his reality becomes exaggeratedly normal, normal to the point of boredom, making thus the confrontation between factual and fictional Coetzee even more flamboyant. Whether it is brick laying or never-ending repairs around the house, forging meaningful relationships with other people or just love making described at best as having an "autistic quality", the result is always deception and disappointment.

The imprint of such a conceptualisation of fictional Coetzee is visible even in people who are most partial towards the writer, such as his cousin Margot. Her expectations of him – not excessive, just "slight hopes" that he would break away and achieve something – are challenged in the light of his forced return to South Africa and the limbo of

---

6   See, for example, Spanish, Italian and Portuguese translations.

existence he comes to lead there. Her dispirited claim becomes thus an echo of a general attitude expressed in the novel:

> Even the one member for whom she had had some slight hopes [...] turns out to be a lightweight. Who ran away to the big world and now comes creeping back to the little world with his tail between his legs. Failed runaway, failed car mechanic too. [...] Failed son. (Coetzee 2009: 120)

Coetzee's life story is thus repeatedly presented as a true reflection of its protagonist – local, flawed, unsatisfactory.

The notion of locality becomes useful also while analysing the marginal position Coetzee is said to occupy in the narrative of his own life. This peripheral position he is willy-nilly ascribed to is defined most clearly by Julia, Coetzee's former lover, who at one point of the novel contends: "I *really* was the main character. John really was a minor character" (2009: 44; emphasis original). Quite interestingly, such policy of effacement is also replicated at the metatextual level. In *Summertime*, the writer's memoirs constitute only a minor part in terms of both importance and the novel's scope. Yet even this feeble semblance of authority Coetzee may execute in this sphere is further put into doubt by the biographer who warns that the memoirs are not to be trusted, at least not as a factual record. Coetzee is a fictioneer, the biographer says, "in his letters he is making up a fiction of himself for his correspondents; in his diaries he is doing much the same for his own eyes, or perhaps for posterity" (2009: 225). Thus, the writer's insubstantiality as a lead in the story of his own life becomes once more accentuated both at the narrative and paratextual level.

Finally, the character's local allegiance, his belonging to a "little world", may be seen through the larger prism of Africa as a sign of a place expressing a general crisis of representation. If we assume that setting can be treated to some extent as an extension of a character[7], then the contradictory nature of fictional Coetzee has to be reflected in his surroundings. This inference seems to be confirmed by David Attwell who defines place as a site of paradoxes, the result of a struggle of antagonistic forces. He writes: "Place in J.M. Coetzee's writing is seldom just *home*, in any comfortable sense [...]. On the contrary, place in Coet-

---

7   This claim is validated, for instance, by David Herman who observes that "spatial reference [is] not an optional or peripheral feature of stories, but rather a core property that helps constitute narrative domains" (Herman 2002: 296).

zee is a site of epistemological dualisms, of failed self/other relationships, of incommensurability, of aesthetic destruction" (Attwell 2008:
229, emphasis original).

The macroscopic scale of this phenomenon is easily translated into
particular represented sites. A case in point may be the house Coetzee
plans to buy. On the one hand, its general condition leaves a lot to be desired. The house is old, dilapidated and remotely located – so that even a
low selling price does not help attract any potential buyers. Nonetheless,
the fictional Coetzee sets his mind on it. For him, the technical state of
the house is only secondary. More importantly, the house is to become a
place in which he can surrender himself solely to the regimes of writing.
What follows, he often returns to it in his thoughts and conversations,
and it is with pride that he shows it to his cousin Margot. There is, however, one issue. Coetzee never actually buys the house and the novel
makes it clear he is not likely to ever relinquish the responsibility for
taking care of his aged father. The house thus becomes little more than
an idealised representation of a place in which the dream of a better life
could be attained. In the meantime, the opposed forces – of responsibility and habit – tie the writer to quite another abode. As can be seen,
Coetzee's would-be artistic Mecca constitutes precisely the site of dualisms Attwell writes about.

To return to the discussion of the types of narrative recontextualisa-
tions which can be traced in Coetzee's novel, it has been stated that the
second technique employed by the author takes the form of the altered
ending of the life history. As such, this technique cannot stand by itself –
depending on the narrative variant, out of necessity it will entail procedures of addition/subtraction. In other words, supplementing/detracting
constitute a sine qua non for the modification of the ending to take place.
Quite naturally so: any change we introduce to the original sequence of
the last stage of the life's career – happy end instead of misery, life instead of death – will as a consequence leave an imprint on the character's situation and his/her pattern of interrelations.

In *Summertime*, the death of Coetzee may be regarded as one of the
most obvious arguments in favour of the existence of the counterfactual
model. As a literary device, it works on several levels. When looked at
from the perspective of those who take part in the discussion on the departed, i.e. from the ontological level of the story proper, it constitutes

an enabling factor. The fact that Coetzee is dead allows his world mates to deliver judgments upon him, an opportunity they do not let pass by easily. While talking about their affair, for instance, Julia mentions: "since he is dead, it can make no difference to him, any indiscreetness on my part" (2009: 37). The same kind of logic seems to be operating in the case of Adriana, very likely the harshest judge of all, when she states "pardon me for saying this, but he is dead, so I cannot hurt his feelings" (2009: 193).

However, taking the argument one step further, we may assert that Coetzee's death also functions in terms of a narrative technique. Although the novel cannot be termed futuristic, the proleptic jump effected by the demise of the author's counterfactual makes it in a sense future-oriented, unveiling a secret history of when a writer ceases to be his own master and instead is treated as public property. In *Summertime*, in analogy to the norms of historiographic metafiction, there is no sense of a-historicity or a-temporality. On the contrary, the subject is rooted in history, albeit in a manner specific to postmodernist discourse. The imaginative stylisation of Coetzee-the character seems a self-reflexive echo of a claim put forward in the novel that "our life-stories are ours to construct as we wish, within or even against the constraints imposed by the real world" (2009: 227). Such a treatment of the past defies easy ideological affiliation, for history, whether private or public, is understood neither as a totalising narrative nor as a notion that has to be done away with altogether. Indeed, this way of conceptualising time seems to be in agreement with the real-world Coetzee's theoretical call for new forms of representation of the past: "decentering strikes me as a rather negative move. There ought to be other ways of thinking about it" (Coetzee 2004: 101)

Finally, climbing yet one step higher in the ladder of generalisations, the figure of feigned death of Coetzee-the character metafictionally points us in the direction of Coetzee-the author, the *strategist* behind the literary work. By a short-circuit we thus come back to the dichotomy of presence and absence and the inherently ambiguous nature of the sign, which was established at the beginning of this article. The paradoxical mode of the fictional Coetzee's existence – dead but with us, written into being by Mr Biographer – calls to mind the metanarrative of the author as the originator of the discourse, and the postmodernist response to it:

the author placed under erasure yet never fully obliterated. This presence through absence is telling also for Coetzee's novel, for it is there that the act of bringing to life is actually achieved by means of ironical narrative annihilation of its very protagonist.

The present study of Coetzee's *Summertime* attempted to show narrative dynamics as resulting from the oscillation between fictional and referential readings. Whereas the inclusion of the real-world person or place into a fictional context is not new in the history of literature, it has always implied the existence of a particular contract with the reader, the embodiment of Virginia Woolf's call: "Let it be fiction [...] or let it be fact. The imagination will not serve under two masters simultaneously" (in Cohn 1989: 11). However, the principle of minimal departure such works lived by is no longer binding for anti-mimetic postmodernist authors. Quite to the contrary, their texts gain momentum from the clash between fact and fiction, from imaginative oppositions of propositions to which truth value cannot be easily assigned. Such is the case in *Summertime*. The fictional Coetzee emerges as a conflated character who has to be seen through the prism of double exposure, the sum of two structures of reference – the real author over an image of a character in the presented world – superimposed upon each other. The result is the emergence of a counterfactual persona, a hybrid between two orders, since there is no principle of identity at work that would establish what is and what is not Coetzee.

This counterfactual scheme is textually inscribed into an asymmetrical model of narration. Coetzee is dead, no longer able to respond to personalised stories about him and his life. His fictional character appears as already filtered by interpretative acts of others – histories of those who knew him. These, in turn, become appropriated by the biographer. What is thus incited is a series of perspectives upon perspectives rendered in a typically postmodernist technique of infinite regress. These individualised accounts cannot be conceived of in terms of instabilities or tensions – elements typical to narratives characterised by progression. Instead, by means of transworld migration of the writer into the written, the focus is shifted to the exploitation of the artificiality of the material out of which a character is made.

Works cited

A True and Faithful Account of the Island of Veritas; Together with the Forms of Their Liturgy; and a Full Relation of the Religious Opinions of the Veritasians, as Delivered in Several Sermons Just Published in Veritas. ([1790]). London.

A Voyage to the World in the Centre of the Earth. Giving an account of the manners, customs, laws, government and religion of the inhabitants. Their Persons and Habits described: With several other Particulars. In which is introduced, The History of an Inhabitant of the Air, Written by Himself. With some account of the planetary worlds. (1755). London.

Abrams, M. H. (ed). (1981) *A Glossary of Literary Terms*. Fort Worth, Philadelphia: Harcourt Brace C P.

Agamben, G. (1998) *Homo sacer – sovereign Power and bare life*. Stanford CA: Stanford University Press.

Allen, G. (2000) *Intertextuality*. London: Routledge.

Amanuddin, S. (1989) "Anita Desai's Technique". In R. K. Dhawan (ed.). *The Fiction of Anita Desai*. New Delhi: Bahri Publications.

Andreae, J. V. (1916) *Christianopolis*. Trans. and ed. Felix Held. New York: Oxford University Press.

Archell-Thompson, P. (1997) "Fairytale, Myth and Otherness in Andre Norton's Juvenile Science Fiction". *Foundation* 70 (Summer): 25-31.

Attwell, D. (2008) "Coetzee's Estrangements". *Novel: A Forum on Fiction* 41.2/3.

Auerbach, E. (1968) *Mimesis. Rzeczywistość przedstawiona w literaturze Zachodu*. Trans. Z. Żabicki Z. Warszawa: PIW.

[Bacon, F.]. (1999) *New Atlantis*. In Susan Bruce (ed.). *Three Early Modern Utopias. Thomas More: Utopia / Francis Bacon: New Atlantis / Henry Neville: The Isle of Pines*. Oxford, Oxford UP. 149-186.

Bailey, D. (1999) *American Nightmares: The Haunted House Formula in American Popular Fiction*. Bowling Green: Bowling Green State University Popular Press.

Bainbridge, B. (2003) *Young Adolf*. 1978. London: Abacus.

Bakhtin, M. .M. (2006) *The Dialogic Imagination*. Trans. C. Emerson and M. Holquist. Austin: University of Texas Press.

Bal, M. (2002) *Travelling Concepts in the Humanities. A Rough Guide*. Toronto: University of Toronto Press.

Baldick, C. (2001) *The Concise Oxford Dictionary of Literary Terms*. Oxford: Oxford UP.

Bard, K. A. (ed.). (1999) *Encyclopedia of the archaeology of ancient Egypt*. London: Routledge.

Barnes, J. (1675) *Gerania: A New Discovery of a Little sort of People Anciently Discoursed of, called Pygmies. With a lively Description Of their Stature, Habit, Manners, Buildings, Knowledge, and Government, being very delightful and profitable*. London.

Barrish, Ph. (2001) *American Literary Realism: Critical Theory and Intellectual Prestige, 1880–1995*. Cambridge: Cambridge UP.

Barthes, R. (1974) *S/Z*. Oxford and Malden: Blackwell.

Barthes, R. (1975) "An Introduction to the Structural Analysis of Narrative". *New Literary History* 6.2 (Winter): 237-272.

Barthes, R. (1977) "The Death of the Author". *Image, Music, Text*. London: Fontana Press. 142-148.

Bayley, J. (1987) "The Tall and the True". *TLS* 27 (March): 317-318.

[Berington, S.]. (1737). *The Memoirs of Signor Gaudentio di Lucca. Taken from his Confession and Examination before the Fathers of the Inquisition at Bologna in Italy. Making a Discovery of an Unknown Country in the Midst of the Vast Deserts of Africa, as Ancient, Populous, and Civilized, as the Chinese. With an Account of their Antiquity, Origine, Religion, Customs, Polity, &c. and the Manner how they got first over those vast Deserts. Interspers'd with several most surprizing and Curious Incidents. Copied from the original Manuscript kept in St. Mark's Library at Venice: With Critical Notes of the Learned Signor Rhedi, late Library-Keeper of the said Library. To which is prefix'd, a Letter of the Secretary of the Inquisition, to the same Signor Rhedi, giving an Account of the Manner and Causes of his being Seiz'd. Faithfully translated from the Italian by E. T. Gent*. London.

Bernays, Anne. (1989) *Professor Romeo*. New York: Weidenfeld and Nicholson.

Bianga, M. (1997). "Mit i magia w *Ziemiomorzu* Ursuli K. Le Guin" in: M. Bianga and M. Stawicki. *Mit i Magia. Ursula K. Le Guin*. Gdańsk: Gdański Klub Fantastyki.

Blaim, A. (2013) *Gazing in Useless Wonder. English Utopian Fictions: 1516-1800*. Oxford: Peter Lang.

Blaim, A. and L. Gruszewska. (1994) "Implied Authors, Implied Readers, Implied Texts: A Modest Proposal". In G. Bystydzieńska and L. Kolek (eds.). *Focus on Literature and Culture*. Lublin: Maria Curie-Skłodowska University Press. 145-155.

Brodzka, A. (1964) *Pojęcie realizmu w powieści XIX i XX wieku*. Lódź: Łódzkie Towarzystwo Naukowe.

Brodzka, A. (1967) *O kryteriach realizmu w badaniach literackich*. Warszawa: PIW.

Brooke-Rose, C. (1981) *A Rhetoric of the Unreal: Studies in Narrative Structure Especially of the Fantastic*. Cambridge: Cambridge UP.

Brown, R. (1989) "Little England: On Triviality in the Naive Comic Fictions of H. G. Wells". *Cahiers Victoriens et Edouardiens* 30 (Oct.): 55-66.

Brustein, W. I. (2003) *Roots of Hate: Anti-Semitism in Europe Before the Holocaust*. Cambridge: Cambridge UP.

[Burgh, J.]. (1764) *An Account of the First Settlement, Laws, Form of Government, and Police, of the Cessares, a People of South America: In Nine Letters, from Mr. Vander Neck one of the Senators of that Nation, to his Friend in Holland. With Notes by the Editor*. London.

Byatt, A. S. (1987) *The Game*. 1967. London: Penguin Books.

Byatt, A. S. (2009). *The Children's Book.* London: Chatto & Windus.

Campanella, T. (1981). *The City of the Sun: A Poetical Dialogue [Civitas Solis]*. Trans. and ed. Daniel J. Donno. Berkeley: University of California Press.

Campbell, J. (1968) *The Hero with a Thousand Faces*. Princeton: Princeton UP.

Carpenter, H. (1999) *Inklingowie: C.S. Lewis, J.R.R. Tolkien, Charles Williams i ich przyjaciele*. Trans. Z. A. Królicki. Poznań: Zysk i S-ka.

Carr, M. (1970). "Classic Hero in a New Mythology". *The Horn Book Magazine* October 1970: 508-513.

[Cavendish, M.], Duchess of Newcastle. (1666). *The Description of a New World, Called the Blazing World. Written By the Thrice Noble, Illustrious, and Excellent Princesse, the Duchess of Newcastle*. London.

Chatman, S. (1978) *Story and Discourse: Narrative Structure in Fiction and Film*. Ithaca: Cornell UP.

Coetzee, J. M. (2004) "He and His Man: The 2003 Nobel lecture". *World Literature Today* 78.2.

Coetzee, J. M. (2009) *Summertime. Scenes from Provincial Life*. Harvill Secker.

Cohan, S. (1983) "Figures Beyond the Text: A Theory of Readable Character in the Novel". *NOVEL: A Forum on Fiction* 17.1: 5-27.

Cohn, D. (1989) "Fictional verus Historical Lives: Borderlines and Borderline Cases". *The Journal of Narrative Technique* 19.1.

Collini, S. (2008) Introduction. *Interpretacja i nadinterpretacja*. By U. Eco. Trans. T. Biedroń. Kraków: Wydawnictwo Znak. 5-27.

Colmer, J. (1983) *E. M. Forster: The Personal Voice*. London and Boston: Routledge.

Conrad, J. (1915) "The Partner". In Joseph Conrad *Within the Tides. Tales*. London & Toronto: J. M. Dent & Sons, Paris: J. M. Dent et Fils. The Project Gutenberg eBook (eBook #1053).
http://www.gutenberg.org/files/1053/1053-h/1053-h.htm.

Cowan, M. H. (1968) *Twentieth century interpretations of* The sound and the fury*: a collection of critical essays*. Prentice-Hall: Englewood Cliffs.

Cuddon, J. (1992) *A Dictionary of Literary Terms and Literary Theory*. London: Penguin Books.

Culler, J. (1975) *Structuralist Poetics: Structuralism, Linguistics and the Study of Literature*. London: Routledge.

Dalgarno, E. K. (1975) "The Textual History of Conrad's 'The Partner'". *The Library. The Transactions of the Bibliographical Society* 5-XXX (1): 41-44.

Dannenberg, H.P. (2008) *Coincidence and Counterfactuality. Plotting time and Space in Narrative Fiction*. Lincoln and London: University of Nebraska Press.

Decrees and Orders of the Committee of Safety of Oceana. (1659). London.

DeMott, B. (2007) "How To Write a College Novel". In M. Moseley (ed.). *The Academic Novel. New and Classic Essays*. Chester: Chester Academic Press, 63-75.

Dengel-Janic, E. (2011) *Home Fiction: Narrating Gendered Space in Anita Desai and Shashi Deshpande's Novels*. Wurzburg: Konigshausen & Neumann.

Desai, A. (1978) "Pineapple Cake". In *Games at Twilight*. London: William Heinemann.

Desai, A. (1988) *Baumgartner's Bombay*. London: William Heinemann.

Desai, A. (1999) *Fasting, Feasting*. London: Vintage.

Dobrinsky, J. (1989) *The Artist in Conrad's Fiction: A Psychocritical Study*. Ann Arbor: UMI.

Dobson, J. (1999) *The Raven and The Nightingale*. New York: Doubleday.

Dowden, W. S. (1970) *Joseph Conrad. The Imaged Style*. Nashville: Vanderbilt University Press.

Dunning, S. M. (2000) *The Crisis and the Quest: A Kierkegaardian Reading of Charles Williams*. Carlisle and Waynesboro: Paternoster Press.

Eco, U. (1972) *Pejzaż semiotyczny*. Trans. A.Weinsberg. Warszawa: PIW.

Eco, U. (1996) *Nieobecna struktura*. Trans. A.Weinsberg. P.Bravo: Warszawa: KR.

Eco, U. (2009) "On the ontology of fictional characters: A semiotic approach". *Sign Systems Studies* 37(1/2): 82-98.

Eder, J., F. Jannidis, and R. Schneider. (2010) "Characters in Fictional Worlds. An Introduction". In J. Eder, F. Jannidis, and R. Schneider (eds.). *Characters in Fictional Worlds. Understanding Imaginary Beings in Literature, Film, and Other Media*. Berlin: Walter de Gruyter. 3-64.

Eichenbaum, B. M. (1970) "Jak jest zrobiony 'Płaszcz' Gogola". In M. R. Mayenowa and Z. Saloni (eds.). *Rosyjska szkoła stylistyki*. Warszawa: PIW. 491-513.

Elgin, D. D. (1985) *The Comedy of the Fantastic: Ecological Perspectives on the Fantasy Novel*. Westport, CT: Greenwood Press.

Elliott, A. (2007) *Concepts of the Self*. Cambridge and Malden: Polity.

Encyclopedia of Ancient Egypt. MobileReference. http://books.google.pl. 20.01.2012.

[Evans, A.]. (1719) *The Adventures and Surprizing Deliverances, of James Dubourdieu, and His Wife: Who were taken by Pyrates, and carried to the Uninhabited-Part of the Isle of Paradise, Containing A Description of that Country, its Laws, Religion and Customs: Of Their being at last Releas'd; and how they came to Paris, where they are still living. Also, The Adventures of Alexander Vendchurch, Whose Ship's Crew Rebelled against him, and set him on Shore of an Island in the South-Sea, where he liv'd five Years, five Months, and seven Days; and was at last providentially releas'd by a Jamaica Ship*. London.

Evans, V. (2009) *Leksykon językoznawstwa kognitywnego*. Trans. M. Buchta et al. Kraków: Universitas.

Faulkner, W. (1929) *The Sound and the Fury*. New York: Jonathan Cape & Harrison Smith.

Felenstein, F. (1995) *Anti-Semitic Stereotypes. A Paradigm of Otherness in English Popular Culture, 1660-1830*. Baltimore and London: The Johns Hopkins UP.

Fludernik, M. (2009) *An Introduction to Narratology*. Trans. P. Häusler-Greenfield and M. Fludernik. London and New York: Routledge.

Fokkema, A. (1991) *Postmodern Characters. A Study of Characterisation in British and American Postmodern Fiction*. Amsterdam: Rodopi.

Forster, E. M. (1974) *Aspects of the Novel*. Ed. O. Stallybrass. Penguin: London.

Forster, E. M. (2006) *Howards End*. 1910. London: Penguin Classics.

Frye, N. (1969) "The Mythos of Winter: Irony and Satire". In *Anatomy of Criticism: Four Essays*. New York: Atheneum. 223-239.

Gasparini, Ph. (2008) *Autofiction – Une aventure de langage*. Paris: Le Seul.

Gemmell, D. (1990) *Quest for Lost Heroes*. London: Orbit.

Genette, G. (1997) *Palimpsests: Literature in the Second Degree*. Lincoln: University of Nebraska Press.

George, U. (2008) *William Golding: A Critical Study*. New Delphi: Atlantic.

Gerrig, R. J. (1983) *Experiencing Narrative Worlds: On the Psychological Activities of Reading*. New Haven and London: Westview Press.

Glanvill, J. (1676) "Anti-fanatical Religion, and Free Philosophy. In a Continuation of the New Atlantis". In *Essays On Several Important Subjects in Philosophy and Religion*. London.

Glendinning, V. (1979) "Hitler in England 1912". Review of *Young Adolf* by Beryl Bainbridge. *New York Times*, 11 March. <http://www.nytimes.com/books/98/11/29/specials/bainbridge-adolf.html>

[Godwin, F.]. (1638) *The Man in the Moone; or A Discourse of a Voyage Thither*. By Domingo Gonsales. London.

Golding, W. (1977) "The Scorpion God". In *The Scorpion God. Three Short Novels*. London: Faber and Faber. 9-62.

Goldstein, R. (2000) *Properties of Light*. Boston: Houghton Mifflin.

Goldstein, R. (1993) *Strange Attractors*. New York: Viking Penguin.

Goldstein, R. (1993) *The Mind-Body Problem*. 1983. New York: Penguin Books.

Gopal, N. R. (1995) *A Critical Study of the Novels of Anita Desai*. New Delhi: Atlantic Publishers and Distributors.

[Gott, S.]. (1902). *Nova Solyma. The Ideal City, or Jerusalem Regained. An Anonymous Romance Written in the Time of Charles I. Now First Drawn from Obscurity, and Attributed to the Illustrious John Milton*. Ed. Rev. Walter Begley. 2 vols. London: John Murray.

Greaney, M. (2002) *Conrad, Language, and Narrative*. Cambridge: Cambridge University Press.

Grixti, J. (1989) *Terrors of Uncertainty: The Cultural Contexts of Horror Fiction*. London: Routledge.

Grossberg, L. (1997) *Bringing It All Back Home: Essays on Cultural Studies*. Durham and London: Duke UP.

Gruszewska-Blaim, L. (2012a) "Amerykańska powieść akademicka z duchem kotki w tle". *Acta Humana* 3: 19-36.

Gruszewska-Blaim, L. (2012b) "The Lives of Texts and Academics: With Apologies to M. R. James and James Hynes". In K Pisarska and A. S. Kowalczyk (eds.). *The Lives of Texts: Exploring the Metaphor*. Newcastle upon Tyne: Cambridge Scholars. 7-17.

Gruszewska-Blaim, L. (2014a) "Faculty Gothic in the American College Novel of the 1990s". In A. Kędra-Kardela and A. S. Kowalczyk (eds). *Expanding the Gothic Canon*. Frankfurt am Mein: Peter Lang. 147-172.

Gruszewska-Blaim, L. (2014b) "Exploring / Exploding the Small World: Postmodern Academic Fiction". In D. Fuchs and W. Klepuszewski (eds.). *Academic Fiction Revisited*. Koszalin: Wydawnictwo Politechniki Koszalińskiej. 37-50.

Guerard, A. J. (1958) *Conrad the Novelist*. Cambridge, MA: Harvard UP.

Hadfield, A. M. (1983) *Charles Williams: An Exploration of His Life and Work*. Oxford and New York: Oxford UP.

Hall, S. (1996) "Introduction: Who Needs Identity". In S. Hall and P. du Gay (eds.). *Questions of Cultural Identity*. London and New Delhi: SAGE Publications. 9-17.

Hammond, J. R. (2001) *A Preface to H. G. Wells*. Harlow: Longman.

Hampson, R. (1992) *Jospeh Conrad: Betrayal and Identity*. New York: St. Martin's Press; Basingstoke: Macmillan.

Hardy, S. (1993) "H. G. Wells the Poststructuralist". *The Wellsian* 16:2-23.

Harrington, J. (1656) *The Common-wealth of Oceana*. London.

Harris, W. V. (1979) *British Short Fiction in the Nineteenth Century: A Literary and Bibliographic Guide*. Detroit: Wayne State UP.

Hartley, J. (2003) *A Short History of Cultural Studies*. London: Sage Publications.

Harvey, W. J. (1967) "The Human Context". In Philip Stevick (ed.). *The Theory of the Novel*. New York and London: The Free Press. 231-251.

Hattenhauer, D. (2003) *Shirley Jackson's American Gothic*. New York: State University of New York Press.

Head, D. (1992) *The Modernist Short Story: A Study in Theory and Practice*. Cambridge: Cambridge UP.

Heath-Stubbs, J. (1998) "Charles Williams". In A. T. Tolley (ed.). *The Literary Essays of John Heath-Stubbs*, Manchester: Carcanet Press. 138-164.

Herman, D. (2002) *Story Logic: Problems and Possibilities of Narrative*. Lincoln: University of Nebraska Press.

Herman, D. (2007) "Recontextualizing character: Role-theoretic framework for narrative analysis". *Semiotica* 165: 191-204.

Hewitt, D. (1988) *English Fiction of the Early Modern Period, 1880-1940*. London: Longman.

Higgins, Ch. (2009) "The Princess with Flaming Hair". *The Guardian* (23 May). <http://www.guardian.co.uk/books/2009/may/23/lavinia-ursula-le-guin-review>.

Hochman, B. (1985) *Character in Literature*. London: Cornell University Press.

Hoffman, F.J., and O. W. Vickery (eds.). (1960) *William Faulkner. Three Decades of Criticism*. Ann Arbor: Michigan State UP.

Holmes, F. M. (1997) *The Historical Imagination. Postmodernism and the Treatment of the Past in Contemporary British Fiction*. Victoria: University of Victoria Press.

Howard, T. (1983) *The Novels of Charles Williams*. New York and Oxford: Oxford University Press.

Humphrey, R. R. (1970) „Strumień świadomości – techniki". Trans. S. Amsterdamski. *Pamiętnik Literacki* 4.

Huntington, J. (1979) "The Science Fiction of H. G. Wells". In P. Parrinder (ed.). *Science Fiction: A Critical Guide*. London and New York: Longman. 34-51.

Hutcheon, L. (1988) *A Poetics of Postmodernism: History, Theory, Fiction*. London and New York: Routlege

Hutcheon, L. (2005) *Theory of Adaptation*. New York: Routledge.

Hynes, James. (1997) *Publish and Perish: Three Tales of Tenure and Terror*. New York: Picador USA.

Jackson, S. (2006). *The Haunting of Hill House*. London: Penguin Books. Kindle edition.

Jakobson, R. (1986) "Closing Statement: Linguistics and Poetics". In K. Pomorska (ed.). *Language in Literature*. Cambridge, Mass. and London: Harvard UP. 62-94.

James, E. (2004) "The City Watch". In Andrew Butler (ed.). *Terry Pratchett: Guilty of Literature*. 2nd edition. Baltimore: Old Earth Books.

James, H. (1948) *The Art of Fiction and Other Essays*. Oxford: Oxford University Press.

Jannidis, F. "Character". *The Living Handbook of Narratology*. <http://hup.sub.uni-hamburg.de/lhn/index.php/Character.>

Jędrzejko, P., M. M. Reigelman, and Z. Szatanik (eds.). (2010) *Hearts of Darkness: Melville, Conrad and Narratives of Oppression*. Zabrze: M Studio.

Joseph, M. (2011) "Liminality". In P. Nel and L. Paul (eds.). *Keywords for Children's Literature*. New York: New York UP. 138-140.

Jowitt, C. (2002) "'Books will speak plain'?" In B. Price (ed.). *Francis Bacon's New Atlantis: New Interdisciplinary Essays*. Manchester and New York: Manchester University Press. 129-155.

Jóźwiak, B. (2005) "Strategie narracyjne i wybory językowe we 'Wspólniku' Josepha Conrada". *Con-teksty* 6: 20-31.

Kahane, C. (1985) "The Gothic Mirror". In S. N. Garner, C. Kahane, and M. Springnether (eds.). *The (M)other Tongue: Essays in Feminist Psychoanalytic Interpretation*. Ithaca: Cornell UP. 334-351.

Kasperski, E. (1993) „Sprawa podmiotu. Szkic z antropologii literatury". *Przegląd Humanistyczny* 5.

Kasperski, E. (1998) „Między poetyką i antropologią postaci. Szkic zagadnień". In: E. Kasperski, and B. Pawłowska-Jądrzyk. *Postać literacka. Teoria i historia*. Warszawa: Wydawnictwa Uniwersytetu Warszawskiego.

Kasperski, E. (2006) *Świat człowieczy. Wstęp do antropologii literatury*. Warszawa–Pułtusk: Akademia Humanistyczna im. Aleksandra Gieysztora.

Kędra-Kardela, A. (2010) *Reading as Interpretation: Towards a Narrative Theory of Fictional World Construction*. Lublin: Wydawnictwo UMCS.

Keith, A. M. (2000) *Engendering Rome: Women in Latin Epic*. Cambridge: Cambridge UP.

Killigrew, T. (1720) "A Description of New Athens in Terra Australis incognita. By One who resided many years on the Spot". In *Miscellanea Aurea: or the Golden Medley*. London. 80-118.

King James Bible Online. <http://www.kingjamesbibleonline.org/>.

King, S. (2006) *Danse Macabre*. London: Hodder and Stoughton. Kindle edition.

Knight, G. (1990/2010) *The Magical World of the Inklings: J. R. R. Tolkien, C. S. Lewis, Charles Williams & Owen Barfield*. Cheltenham: Skylight Press.

Kolb, H. H. Jr. (1969) *The Illusion of Life: American Realism as a Literary Form*. Charlottesville: University of Virginia.

Kolek, L. S. (1996) "The Emperor's New Clothes: Or, The Semiotic Pranks in the 'Uniform Scene' in J. Kosinski's 'Cockpit'". In *Approches to Fiction*. Lublin: Wydawnictwo Folium.

Korwin-Piotrowska, D. (2011) *Poetyka: przewodnik po świecie tekstów*. Kraków: Wydawnictwo Uniwersytetu Jagiellońskiego.

Krajka, W. and A. Zgorzelski. (1984) *On the Analysis of the Literary Text*. Trans. A. Blaim. Warszawa: PWN.

Kramer, John E. (2000) *Academe in Mystery and Detective Fiction*, sec. ed. Lanham, Maryland: Scarecrow Press.

Kundu, R. (2008) *Intertext: A Study of The Dialogue Between Texts*. New Delhi: Surup and Sons.

L'Epy, M. H. de. (1689) *A Voyage into Tartary. Containing a Curious Description of that Country, with part of Greece and Turky; the Manners, Opinions, and Religion of the Inhabitants therein; with some other Incidents*. London.

Labuda, A. (1979) „O literackich i nieliterackich obrazach postaci". *Teksty* 4.

Lakoff, G. and M. Johnson. (1999) *Philosophy in the Flesh: The Embodied Mind and Its Challenge to Western Thought*. New York: Basic Books.

Lasdun, J. (2005) "Howard's folly". *The Guardian,* 10 September. http://www.guardian.co.uk/books/2005/sep/10/fiction.zadiesmith

Le Guin, U. (2010) *Lavinia*. London: Phoenix.

[Lee, F]. (1693) *Antiquity Reviv'd or the Government of a Certain island Antiently Called Astreada, In Reference to Religion, Policy, War, and Peace. Some hundreds of Years Before the Coming of Christ.* London.

Leith, S. (2009) "Writing in terms of pleasure". *The Guardian.* April 25. http://www.guardian.co.uk/books/2009/apr/25/as-byatt-interview.

L'Heureux, John. (1999) *Having Everything.* New York: Grove Press.

Lindow, S. J. (2010) "*Lavinia*: A Woman Reinvents Herself in Fact And/Or Fiction". *Journal of the Fantastic in the Arts* 21.2. <http://www.questia.com/>.

Lindsay, B. E. (ed.). (2007) *Great Women Mystery Writers.* Westport: Greenwood Press.

Lodge, D. (1992) *The Art of Fiction.* London: Penguin.

Lodge, D. (2002) *Consciousness and the Novel.* London: Secker and Warburg.

Lootens, T. (2005) "'Whose Hand Was I Holding?': Familial and Sexual Politics in Shirley Jackson's *The Haunting of Hill House*". In B. M. Murphy (ed.). *Shirley Jackson. Essays on the Literary Legacy.* Jefferson, North Carolina and London: McFarland and Company. 150-168.

Lothe, J. (1996) "Conradian Narrative". In J. H. Stape (ed.). *The Cambridge Companion to Joseph Conrad.* Cambridge: Cambridge UP. 160-178.

Łotman, J. (1984) *Struktura tekstu artystycznego*, Warszawa. PIW.

Ludwig, S. (2002) *Pragmatist Realism: The Cognitive Paradigm in American Realist Texts.* Madison: University of Wisconsin Press.

Lukács, G. (1968) *Teoria powieści.* Trans. J. Goślicki. Warszawa: PIW.

[Lupton, T.]. (1580) *Siuqila. Too Good, to be true: Omen. Though so at a vewe, Yet all that I tolde you, Is true, I upholde you: Now cease to aske why For I can not lye. Herein is shewed by waye of Dialogue, the wonderfull maners of the people of Mauqsun, with other talke not frivolous.* London.

Mackail, J. W. (1922) *Virgil and His Meaning to the World of To-Day.* Boston: Marshall Jones Company.

MacKay, L. A. (1963) "Hero and Theme in The Aeneid". *Transactions and Proceedings of the American Philological Association* 94: 157-166.

Margolin, U. (1983) "Characterisation in Narrative: Some Theoretical Prolegomena". *Neophilologus* 67: 1–14.

Margolin, U. (1990a) "Individuals in Narrative Worlds: An Ontological Perspective". *Poetics Today* 11.4. Narratology Revisited II.

Margolin, U. (1990b) "The What, the When, and the How of Being a Character in Literary Narrative". *Style* 24.3. *Academic Search Complete.* <http://web.ebscohost.com/>.

Margolin, U. (1995) "Characters in Literary Narrative: Representation and Signification". *Semiotica* 106: 373–92.

Margolin, U. (2007) "Character". In D. Herman (ed.). *The Cambridge Companion to Narrative*. Cambridge: Cambridge UP. 66-79.

Markiewicz, H. (1984) *Wymiary dzieła literackiego*. Kraków: Wydawnictwo
Literackie.

Markiewicz, H. (1995) *Teorie powieści za granicą, od początków do schyłku XX
wieku*. Warszawa: Państwowe Wydawnictwo Naukowe.

Markiewicz, H. (1996) "Postać literacka". In S. Balbus (ed.). *Wymiary dzieła
literackiego*. Kraków: Universitas. 158-178.

Markiewicz, H. (ed.). (1976) *Problemy teorii literatury* 2. Wrocław: Zakład
Narodowy im. Ossolińskich.

Marovitz, S. E. (2010) "From Desertion Comes Solace – Perhaps: The Stories of
Agatha, Hunilla, Amy Foster and Winnie Verloc". In P. Jędrzejko, et. al.
(eds.). *Hearts of Darkness: Melville, Conrad and Narratives of Oppression*. Zabrze: M Studio.

Mateas, M. and P. Sengers. (1999) *Narrative Intelligence*. http://users.soe.ucsc.
edu/~michaelm/publications/mateas-aaai-symp-ni-1999.pdf.

Matteson, J. T. (2010) "'Unfathomable Cravings' and 'Enchanted Heysts': The
Ironic Rescuer in *Pierre* and *Victory*". In P. Jędrzejko, et. al. (eds.).
Hearts of Darkness: Melville, Conrad and Narratives of Oppression. Za-
brze: M Studio.

Matthaei, L. E. (1917) "The Fates, the Gods, and the Freedom of Man's Will in
the *Aeneid*". *The Classical Quarterly* 11.1: 11-26.

Matthews, J.T. (1982) *The Play of Faulkner's Language*. New York: Ithaca,
Cornell UP Press.

McHale, B. (1994) *Postmodernist Fiction*. 1987. New York and London: Me-
thuen.

McHale, B. (1992) *Constructing postmodernism*. New York: Routledge

McLaren, S. (2004) "A Problem of Morality: Sacramentalism in the Early Novels of Charles Williams". *Renascence* 56.2: 109-127.

Medcalf, S. (1995) "Objections to Charles Williams". In B. Horne (ed.). *Charles
Williams: A Celebration*. Leominster: Gracewing. 206-217.

Meyer Spacks, P. (1979) "Charles Williams: The Fusions of Fiction". In M. R.
Hillegas (ed.). *Shadows of Imagination: The Fantasies of C. S. Lewis, J.
R. R. Tolkien, and Charles Williams*. Carbondale, IL: Southern Illinois
UP. 150-159.

Mieletinski, E. (1981) *Poetyka mitu*. Trans. J. Dancygier. Warszawa: PIW.

Miller, L. (2006) Introduction. In *The Haunting of Hill House*. By Shirley Jackson. London: Penguin Books. Kindle edition.

Miller, T. S. (2010) "Myth-Remaking in the Shadow of Vergil: The Captive(-ated) Voice of *Lavinia*". *Mythlore* 29.1/2: 29-50.

Modrzewski, S. (1992) *Conrad a konwencje. Autorska świadomość systemów a warsztat literacki pisarza*. Gdańsk: Uniwersytet Gdański.

Moorton, R. F. (1989) "The Innocence of Italy in Vergil's *Aeneid*". *The American Journal of Philology* 110.1: 105-130.

Morgan, R. (2010) *The Steel Remains*. New York: Ballantine Books.

Morwood, J. (1997) "Introduction". In *The Aeneid* by Vergil. Trans. John Dryden. Ware: Wordsworth Classics. vii-xvii.

Murphy, B. M. (2005) "Introduction: 'Do You Know Who I Am?' Reconsidering Shirley Jackson". In B. M. Murphy (ed.). *Shirley Jackson. Essays on the Literary Legacy*. Jefferson, North Carolina and London: McFarland and Company. 1-21.

Newfields, T. "Deconstructing Cinderella - Helping students explore their personal myths". <http://jalt.org/pansig/PGL2/HTML/Newfields.htm>.

Newman, J. (2005) "Shirley Jackson and the Reproduction of Mothering: *The Haunting of Hill House*". In B. M. Murphy (ed.). *Shirley Jackson. Essays on the Literary Legacy*. Jefferson, North Carolina and London: McFarland and Company. 169-182.

Nityanandam, I. (2000) *Three Great Indian Women Novelists*. New Delhi: Creative Books.

Norris, C. (2003) "Two Cheers for Cultural Studies: A Philosopher's View". In P. Bowman (ed.). *Interrogating Cultural Studies. Theory, Politics and Practice*. London: Pluto. 76-98.

[Northmore, T.]. (1795) *Memoirs of Planetes, or a Sketch of the Laws and Manners of Makar. By Phileleutherus Devoniensis*. London.

O'Gorman, R. (2009) "Caught in the Liminal: Dorothy Cross's *Udder Series* and Marina Carr's *By the Bog of Cats...*". In I. G. Nordin and E. Holmsten (eds.). *Liminal Borderlands in Irish Literature and Culture*. Bern: Peter Lang. 103-130.

Okopień-Sławińska, A. (1967) „Relacje osobowe w komunikacji literackiej". In *Problemy socjologii literatury*. Wrocław: Zakład Narodowy im. Ossolińskich.

Olszański, T. A. (1996) „Trzy serca i trzy pióra". *Nowa Fantastyka* 2: 66-67.

Oziewicz, M. (2008) *One Earth, One People. The Mythopoeic Fantasy Series of Ursula K. Le Guin, Lloyd Alexander, Madeleine L'Engle and Orson Scot Card*. Jefferson, North Carolina, and London: McFarland and Company.

Pandit, L. (1995) "A Sense of Detail and a Sense of Order: Anita Desai Interviewed by Lalita Pandit". In P. C. Hogan and L. Pandit (eds.). *Literary*

India. Comparative Studies in Aesthetics, Colonialism and Culture. New York: State University of New York Press.

Paris, B. J. (1997) *Imagined Human Beings. A Psychological Approach to Character and Conflict in Literature*. New York: London, 1997.

Parks, J. G. (2005) "Chambers of Yearning: Shirley Jackson's Use of the Gothic". In Bernice M. Murphy (ed.). *Shirley Jackson. Essays on the Literary Legacy*. Jefferson, North Carolina and London: McFarland and Company. 237-250.

Parrinder, P. (1977) *H. G. Wells*. New York: Capricorn.

Peters, B. (ed.). (2002) *AZ Murder Goes...Professional*. New York: Poisoned Pen Press.

Phelan, J. (1989) *Reading People, Reading Plots. Character, Progression, and the Interpretation of Narrative*. Chicago and London: The University of Chicago Press.

[Plattes, G]. (1641) *A Description of the famous Kingdome of Macaria; shewing its excellent Government: Wherein The Inhabitants live in great Prosperity, Health, and Happinesse; the King obeyed, the Nobles honoured; and all good men respected, Vice punished, and Vertue rewarded. An Example to other Nations: In a Dialogue between a Schollar and a Traveller*. London.

Poe, E. A. (1962) *Selected Stories and Poems*. Massachusetts: Airmont Publishing.

Pratchett, T. (1990) *Guards! Guards!* London: Transworld Publishers.

Pratchett, T. (1993) *Men at Arms*. London: Transworld Publishers

Pratchett, T. (1998) *Jingo*. London: Transworld Publishers.

Pratchett, T. (2002) *Night Watch*. London: Transworld Publishers.

Pratchett, T. (2009) *Unseen Academicals*. London: Transworld Publishers.

Pratchett, T. (2011) *Snuff*. London: Transworld Publishers.

Propp, V. (1968) *Morphology of the Folktale*. Texas: University of Texas Press.

Rabinowitz, Peter J. (2011) "'The Impossible Has a Way of Passing Unnoticed': Reading Science in Fiction". *Narrative* 19:(2).

R. H., Esquire. (1660) *New Atlantis. Begun by the Lord Verulam, Viscount St. Albans: and Continued by R.H. Esquire. Wherein is set forth a Platform of Monarchical Government. With A Pleasant intermixture of divers rare Inventions, and wholsom customs, fit to be introduced into all Kingdoms, States, and Common-Wealths*. London.

Redford, R. (2001). "Beryl Bainbridge". *The Observer*. Sunday 11 February. <http://www.guardian.co.uk/books/2001/feb/11/berylbainbridge>

Redpath, P. (1986) *William Golding: a structural reading of his fiction*. London: Vision Press.

Reicher, M. E. (2010) "Ontology of Fictional Characters". In In J. Eder, F. Jannidis, and R. Schneider (eds.). *Revisionen: Characters in Fictional Worlds. Understanding Imaginary Beings in Literature, Film and other Media*. Berlin: Walter de Gruyter. 111-133.

Rembowska-Płuciennik, M. (2012) *Poetyka intersubiektywności: kognitywistyczna teoria narrracji a proza XX wieku*. Toruń: Wydawnictwo Naukowe Uniwersytetu Mikołaja Kopernika.

Richardson, B. (2010) "Transtextual Characters". In J. Eder, F. Jannidis, and R. Schneider (eds.). *Characters in Fictional Worlds. Understanding Imaginary Beings in Literature, Film and other Media*. Berlin: Walter de Gruyter. 527-541.

Rimmon-Kenan, S. (1983/1994) *Narrative Fiction: Contemporary Poetics*. London and New York: Routledge.

Roberts, A. (2009) "*Lavinia* by Ursula K. Le Guin". <http://www.strange horizons.com/reviews/2009/01/lavinia_by_ursu-omments.shtml>.

Rollyson, C. (ed.). (2008) *Critical Survey of Mystery and Detective Fiction*. Pasenda, California: Salem Press.

Rossetti, D. G. (1953) "Sister Helen". In D. S. R. Welland (ed.). *The Pre-Raphaelites in Literature and Art*. London.

Royden, M. (2004) "Adolf Hitler – did he visit Liverpool during 1912-1913?" *Mike Royden Local History Pages* January. <http://www.btinternet.com /~m.royden/mtlhp/local/hitlerinliverpool/hitlerinliverpool.htm>

Rubenstein, R. (2005) "House Mothers and Haunted Daughters: Shirley Jackson and the Female Gothic". In B. M. Murphy (ed.). *Shirley Jackson. Essays on the Literary Legacy*. Jefferson, North Carolina and London: McFarland and Company. 127-149.

Russ, J. (1995) "What Can a Heroine Do? or Why Women Can't Write". In *To Write Like a Woman. Essays in Feminism and Science Fiction*. Bloomington: Indiana University Press.

Rustin, M. and M. Rustin. (2001) *Narratives of Love and Loss. Studies in modern children's fiction*. London and New York: Karnac, 2001.

Scheick, W. J. (1990) *Fictional Structure and Ethics: The Turn of the Century English Novel*. Athens: University of Georgia Press.

Scheick, W. J. (1994) *The Ethos of Romance at the Turn of the Century*. Austin: University of Texas Press.

Schneider, R. (2001)."Toward a Cognitive Theory of Literary Character: The Dynamics of Mental-Model Construction". *Style* 35.4: 607-640.

Scott, J. and J. M. Coetzee. (1997) "Voice and Trajectory: An Interview with J.M. Coetzee". *Salmagundi* 114/155.

Sellar, W. Y. (1965) *The Roman Poets of the Augustan Age: Vergil, Third Edition*. New York: Biblo and Tannen.

Sharma, S. P. (1984) "A Vindication of the Feminine". In R. K. Srivastava (ed.). *Perspectives on Anita Desai*. Ghazibad: Vimal.

Sheehan, B. (2000) *At the Foot of the Story Tree. An Inquiry into the Fiction of Peter Straub*. Burton: Subterranean Press.

Sheppard, Richard. (1990) "From Narragonia to Elysium: Some Preliminary Reflections on the Fictional Image of the Academic". In D. Bevan (ed.). *University Fiction*. Amsterdam: Rodopi. 11-48.

Showalter, E. (2005) *Faculty Towers*. Philadelphia: University of Pennsylvania Press.

Sławiński, J. (1979) „Semantyka wypowiedzi narracyjnej". In *Dzieło-język-tradycja*, Warszawa: PWN.

Smethurst, P. (2000) *The Postmodern Chronotope. Reading Space and Time in Contemporary Fiction*. Amsterdam - Atlanta, GA: Rodopi.

Smith, A. (2009) "Children of the Night: Shirley Jackson's Domestic Female Gothic". In D. Wallace and A. Smith (eds.). *The Female Gothic: New Directions*. Basingstoke: Palgrave Macmillan. 152-165.

Smith, Z. (2005) *On Beauty*. Penguin Books.

[Spence, T.]. (1782) *A Supplement to the History of Robinson Crusoe, Being the History of Crusonia, or Robinson Crusoe's Island, Down to the Present Time. Copied from a letter sent by Mr. Wishit, Captain of the Good-Intent, to an intelligent Friend in England, after being in a Storm in May, 1781 driven out of his course to the Said Island. Published by the said Gentleman, for the agreeable Perusal of Robinson Crusoe's Friends of all Sizes*. Newcastle upon Tyne.

Stanzel, F. (1980) „Typowe formy powieści". Trans. R. Handke. In: R. Handke (ed.). *Teoria form narracyjnych w niemieckim kręgu językowym*. Kraków: Wydawnictwo Literackie.

Stawicki, M. (1997) "Czytelnik w mit wprowadzony". In M. Bianga and M. Stawicki. *Mit i Magia. Ursula K. Le Guin*. Gdańsk: Gdański Klub Fantastyki.

Steiger, E. (1956) *Grundbegriffe der Poetik*. Zurich. Atlantis Verlag.

Stockwell, P. (2002) *Cognitive Poetics: An Introduction*. London: Routledge.

Stout, S. E. (1924) "How Vergil Established for Aeneas a Legal Claim to a Home and a Throne in Italy". *The Classical Journal* 20.3: 152-160.

Straub, P. (1981) *Shadowland*. New York: Berkley Books.

Sturrock, J. (2010/2011) "Artists as Parents in A. S. Byatt's *The Children's Book* and Iris Murdoch's *The Good Apprentice*". *Connotations* 20.1: 108-130.<http://www.connotations.uni-tuebingen.de/sturrock02001.htm>.

Szczepan-Wojnarska, A. M. (2010) "The Tragedy of Trauma". In P. Jędrzejko, et. al. (eds.). *Hearts of Darkness: Melville, Conrad and Narratives of Oppression*. Zabrze: M Studio.

Terentowicz-Fotyga, U. (2013) "The 'Cultural Turn' and the Changing Face of the Humanities in Poland". In J. Fabiszak et al. (eds.). *Crossroads in Literature and Culture, Second Language Learning and Teaching*. Berlin Heidelberg: Springer-Verlag. 519-30.

The Island of Content; or, A New Paradise Discovered. In a Letter from Dr. Merryman of the same Country, to Dr. Dullman of Great Britain. By the Author of the Pleasures of a single Life. (1709) London.

The New Shorter Oxford English Dictionary. (1973) Oxford UP: Oxford. Electronic Publishing: Rotterdam, 1996. Data Version 02.10.96s. CD-ROM.

Trębicki, G. (2005) "The Cultural Syncretism of Andre Norton's *Year of the Unicorn* and Tanith Lee's *Volkhavaar*". In L. Gruszewska-Blaim and A. Blaim (eds.). *Texts of Literature, Texts of Culture*. Lublin: Wydawnictwo UMCS. 111-118.

Trębicki, G. (2007). *Fantasy. Ewolucja gatunku*. Kraków: Universitas.

Trębicki, G. (2009a). "*Fantasy* – ucieczka od cudowności". In T. Ratajczak and B. Trocha (eds.). *Fantastyczność i cudowność. Wokół źródeł fantasy*. Zielona Góra: Wydawnictwo Uniwersytetu Zielonogórskiego. 63-70.

Trębicki, G. (2009b) *The Second Life of Earthsea*. Paper presented at the seminar "Lives of Texts", November 9-10, 2009, Lublin.

Trębicki, G. (2010a) Mythic Scenario: The Motif of Protagonist's Initiation and Maturation in Secondary World Fantasy (to be published).

Trębicki, G. (2010b) Human Identity in The World of "Altered Carbon". In J. J. Copeland (ed.). *The Projected and Prophetic: Humanity in Cyberculture, Cyberspace and Science Fiction*. Oxford: Inter-Disciplinary Press. 119-126.

Trębicki, G. (2011a) "Mythic Elements in Secondary World Fantasy and Exomimetic Literature". In T. Ratajczak and B. Trocha (eds.). *Fantastyczność i cudowność. Mityczne scenariusze: od fikcji do mitu, od mitu do fikcji*. Vol.2. Zielona Góra: Wydawnictwo Uniwersytetu Zielonogórskiego. 63-70.

Trębicki, G. (2011b) *In the Enslavement of the Formula? – A Short Survey of Antagonists in Secondary World Fantasy*. Paper presented at the Conference "Literatura i kultura popularna w kontekście nowych i starych mediów", Wrocław, October 14-15, 2011.

Trocha, B. (2009) *Degradacja mitu w literaturze fantasy*. Zielona Góra: Wydawnictwo Uniwersytetu Zielonogórskiego.

Truffin, Sherry R. (2008) *Schoolhouse Gothic: Haunted Hallways and Predatory Pedagogues in Late Twentieth-Century American Literature and Scholarship.* Newcastle upon Tyne: Cambridge Scholars Publishing.

Turner, V. (1991) *The Ritual Process. Structure and Anti-Structure.* Ithaca: Cornell UP.

Walker, J. M. (1980) "Rites of Passage Today: The Cultural Significance of *A Wizard of Earthsea*". *Mosaic* XIII: 180-191.

Wallace, D. and A. Smith. (2009) "Introduction: Defining the Female Gothic". In D. Wallace and A. Smith (eds.). *The Female Gothic: New Directions.* Basingstoke: Palgrave Macmillan. 1-12.

Van Gennep, A. (1960). *The Rites of Passage.* Chicago: The University of Chicago Press.

Veiras, D. (2006) *The History of the Sevarambians: A Utopian Novel.* Ed. John Christian Laursen and Cyrus Masroori. Albany: State University of New York Press.

Wells, H. G. (1998) *The Complete Short Stories of H. G. Wells.* Ed. J. Hammond. London: Phoenix.

Vergil. (1996) *Aeneid VII-XII.* Ed. D. Williams. Bristol: Bristol Classical Press.

Vergil. (1997) *The Aeneid.* Trans. J. Dryden. Ware: Wordsworth Classics.

Weststeijn, Willem G. (2007) "Towards a Cognitive Theory of Character". *Amsterdam International Electronic Journal for Cultural Narratology (AJCN).* http://cf.hum.uva.nl/narratology/a07_weststeijn.htm; 8.05.2014

White, L. (2005) "Vital Disconnection in *Howards End*". *Twentieth Century Literature* 51.1 : 43-63.

Wignall, B. (1991) "Throwing People to Stories" *Million* 5, September/October. <http://www.co.uk.lspace.org/about-terry/interviews/million.html>.

Wilde, A. (1987) *Horizons of Assent: Modernism, Postmodernism, and the Ironic Imagination.* Philadelphia: University of Pennsylvania Press.

Williams, C. (2003) *Shadows of Ecstasy.* 1933. Vancouver: Regent College Publishing.

Woloch, A. (2004) *The One vs. the Many. Minor Characters and the Space of the Protagonist in the Novel.* New York: Princeton University Press.

Woolf, V. (1996) "Mr. Benett and Mrs. Brown". In M. J. Hoffman and P. D. Murphy (eds.). *Essentials of the Theory of Fiction.* Durham. 23-35.

Woolf, V. (1966) "Mr Bennett and Mrs Brown". In *Collected Essays.* Vol. 1. Ed. L. Woolf. London: Hogarth. 319-337.

Zgorzelski, A. (1984a). "Conradowska nowela grozy". In *O nowelach Conrada. Interpretacje.* Gdańsk: Wydawnictwo Morskie. 50-67.

Zgorzelski, A. (1984b). "On Differentiating Fantastic Fiction: Some Supragenological Distinctions in Literature". *Poetics Today* 5.2. 299-307.

Zgorzelski A. (1996) "Against methodological compromise in literary studies". In L. Kolek (ed.). *Approaches to Fiction*. PASE studies and monographs. Vol.2. Lublin: Wydawnictwo Folium. 231-242.

Zgorzelski, A. (1999) *System i funkcja. Ustalenia metodologiczne i propozycje teoretycznoliterackie*. Gdańsk: Wydawnictwo Gdańskie.

Zgorzelski, A. (2004). *Born of the Fantastic*. Gdańsk: Wydawnictwo Uniwersytetu Gdańskiego.

Żeromski, Stefan. (1949). *Ludzie bezdomni*. Warszawa: Czytelnik.

Index

Contributors

Artur Blaim is Professor of English Literature at the University of Gdańsk. He is president of the Polish Shakespeare Society and Committee member of the Utopian Studies Society – Europe. His major book publications include *Gazing in Useless Wonder. English Utopian Fictions 1516-1800* (2013), *Aesthetic Objects and Blueprints. English Utopias of the Enlightenment* (1997), *The English Robinsonade of the Eighteenth Century* (1990). He co-edited (with Ludmiła Gruszewska-Blaim) volumes: *Texts of Literature, Texts of Culture* (2005), *Structure and Uncertainty* (2008), *Imperfect Worlds and Dystopian Narratives in Contemporary Cinema* (2011), *Spectres of Utopia. Theory, Practice, Conventions* (2012), *Mediated Utopias. From Literature to Film* (2015). He is co-editor of Peter Lang series *Mediated Fictions: Studies in Verbal and Visual Narratives*.

Ludmiła Gruszewska-Blaim is Associate Professor of English and American Literature at the University of Gdańsk. She specializes in narratology, contemporary literature in English, campus fiction, academic mystery novel, and utopian/dystopian cinema. Her publications include monographs on T.S. Eliot's poetry and drama (*Wizje i re-wizje w poezji T.S. Eliota*, [1996]; *T.S. Eliot: "Murder in the Cathedral"* [co-author, 1995]; *Chaos and Cosmos in "The Waste Land" by T.S. Eliot* [1994]) and Jerzy Kosinski's novels (*Gra w SS. Poetyka /nie/powieści Jerzego Kosińskiego* [2005]). She co-edited with Artur Blaim and David Malcolm 7 volumes on literary and film studies. She is co-editor of Peter Lang series *Mediated Fictions: Studies in Verbal and Visual Narratives*.

Kamil Karaś is a doctoral student at the University of Gdańsk working on a dissertation about the fiction of Terry Pratchett. In addition to research on Polish and English fantasy authors, he is particularly interested in angelic fantasy.

Barbara Klonowska is Assistant Professor in the Institute of English at the Catholic University of Lublin. She teaches British literature and culture and has published on contemporary British fiction and film. She is the author of *Contaminations: Magic Realism in Contemporary British Fiction* (2006), and *Longing for Romance. British Historical Romances 1990-2010* (2014). Her academic interests include contemporary literature, magic realism in fiction and film and cinematographic utopias and dystopias.

Marta Komsta is Assistant Professor of English Literature at Maria Curie-Skłodowska University in Lublin. She teaches British literature and has published articles on British contemporary fiction as well as (anti-) utopian narratives. Her main research interests include postmodernist fiction, contemporary Gothic and utopia/dystopia in literature and cinema. She is the author of *Welcome to the Chemical Theatre. The Urban Chronotope in Peter Ackroyd's Fiction* (2015).

Andrzej Sławomir Kowalczyk is Assistant Professor of English Literature at Maria-Curie Skłodowska University in Lublin. He is the author of *The Voice of God, the Voice of Man: Religious Discourse in Late Medieval English Drama* (2007). He also published articles and book chapters on medieval and twentieth-century drama, the supernatural in modern fiction, as well as utopia/dystopia in contemporary literature and film. He is currently working on a book-length cognitive study of Charles Williams's "supernatural thrillers".

Magdalena Kuźniar received Ph.D. at Maria Curie-Skłodowska University in Lublin. Her publications and doctoral dissertation focus on techniques of constructing and construing literary character in A.S. Byatt's fiction.

Halszka Leleń is Assistant Professor at English Department of University of Warmia and Mazury in Olsztyn. Her research interests comprise generic transgression in turn-of-the-century fiction, artistic precepts of the short story, literary use of spatial motifs as well as Polish-English avant-garde. She published book chapters on Thomas Hardy, H. G. Wells, the conventions of fantastic fiction and metaphor. Her book H. G. Wells: *The Literary Traveller in His Short Story Machine* is due to be published in 2015 by Peter Lang.

Żaneta Nalewajk works at the Faculty of Polish Studies at Warsaw University, Poland. She received her Ph.D. in 2008. The main areas of her interest are: history of Polish literature of the 20th and 21st centuries, methodology of comparative and interdisciplinary studies, comparative historical poetics, relations between literature and philosophy or anthropology, and avant-garde literature. She published *Perspectivism's Way. The Issue of Carnality in Prosaic Works of Bruno Schulz and Witold Gombrowicz* (2010). She is the editor-in-chief and co-founder of the quarterly *Tekstualia* as well as a Polish coordinator of the international exchange of literary and scientific translations from Central and Southeastern Europe, and an animator of cultural activities, such as meetings of Polish Writers' Association.

Joanna Pasternak is a doctoral student at the University of Gdańsk working on a dissertation on the fiction of Anita Desai.

Elżbieta Perkowska-Gawlik holds Master's Degrees in Economics and English literature. Currently she is a lecturer in the Institute of English and Ph.D. candidate at Maria Curie-Skłodowska University in Lublin, Poland. She has published articles and book chapters on British and American mystery fiction and utopia/dystopia in new media (in *Crime Scenes: Modern Crime Fiction in an International Context* /2014/, /*Im/perfection Subverted, Reloaded and Networked: Utopian Discourse Across Media* /2015/).

Katarzyna Pisarska is Assistant Professor of English Literature at Maria Curie-Skłodowska University in Lublin, Poland. She is the author of *Mediating the World in the Novels of Iain Banks: The Paradigms of Fiction* (2013) and co-editor of *The Lives of Texts: Exploring the Metaphor* (2012). She has published articles and book chapters on British and American literature and utopian cinema and fiction. Her main research interests include the contemporary Scottish novel, utopian studies and myth in literature and culture.

Patrycja Podgajna received Ph.D. at Maria Curie-Skłodowska University in Lublin. She published book chapters on contemporary literature in English and utopian/dystopian cinema in: *Imperfect Worlds and Dystopian Narratives in Contemporary Cinema* (2011), *Echoes of Utopia. Notions, Rhetoric, Poetics* (2012), /*Im/perfection Subverted, Reloaded* *and Networked: Utopian Discourse Across Media* (2015). Her present research focuses on alternative worlds in film and fiction.

Sławomir Studniarz is Assistant Professor at the University of Warmia and Mazury in Olsztyn. Interested primarily in American literature, he publishes on Edgar Allan Poe's prose and poetry, Peter Straub, Tennessee Williams, Walt Whitman, and Samuel Beckett as well as on ekphrasis in the poetry of Auden, Williams and Ferlinghetti. His major publications include *Tragiczna wizja. Rzecz o nowelistyce Poego* [*The Tragic Vision. A Study of Poe's Short Fiction*] (2008), *Brzmienie i sens w wierszach Edgara Allana Poego* [*Sound and Sense in Poe's Poetry*] (2011) and the most recent *Edgar Allan Poe – artysta i wizjoner* [*Edgar Allan Poe – the artist and the visionary*].

Dominika Szwajewska received Ph.D. at Maria Curie-Sklodowska University in Lublin, Poland. Her academic interests range from fictional multiverses of postmodernist literature to ideologically charged constructs in utopian and dystopian fiction. She has published several articles on the topic, most recently in *Echoes of Utopia. Notions, Rhetoric, Poetics* (2012) and *Academic Fiction Revisited: Selected Essays* (2014).

Urszula Terentowicz-Fotyga is Assistant Professor of English Literature and Culture at Maria Curie-Skłodowska University in Lublin. She is the author of *Dreams, Nightmares and Empty Signifiers: The English Country House in the Contemporary Novel* (2015) and a study of Virginia Woolf's novels (2006). She has book chapters in *Expanding the Gothic Canon: Studies in Literature, Film and New Media* (2014), *Spectres of Utopia* (2012), *Imperfect Worlds and Dystopian Narratives in Contemporary Cinema* (2011), *Voyages Out, Voyages Home* (2010), *Zadie Smith: Critical Essays* (2008), *Structure and Uncertainty* (2008) and *The Athlone Critical Traditions Series: The Reception of British Authors in Europe* (2001).

Karolina Trapp is a tutor and a Ph.D. student at the University of Melbourne, Australia. She publishes on contemporary literature, especially on R.S. Thomas, whose poetry she is exploring in her doctoral dissertation. Her paper "Imagining God: R. S Thomas's 'The Hand'" appeared in *Refashioning Myth* (2011) by Cambridge Scholars Publishing.

Grzegorz Trębicki is Assistant Professor at Jan Kochanowski University, Kielce, Poland. His academic interests include non-mimetic literature (especially secondary world fantasy) as well as theory and genology of literature. He is the author of *Fantasy. Ewolucja gatunku* (1997). His articles and reviews have been published in *The New York Review of Science Fiction*, *Extrapolation*, *Mythlore* and *Science Fiction Studies*. He recently published *Synkretyzm fantasy. Fantasy świata wtórnego: literatura, kultura, mit* [*The Syncretism of Fantasy. Secondary World Fantasy: literature, culture, myth*] (2014) and is currently working on a book-length study: *Worlds So Strange and Diverse: Towards a Genological Taxonomy of Non-mimetic Literature*.

Jadwiga Węgrodzka is Associate Professor in the English Institute at the University of Gdańsk and in Koszalin University of Technology, Poland; she teaches British literature and publishes on medieval and contemporary British literature, fantastic literature, children's literature and fairy story from the eighteenth to the twenty first century. Her publications include *Canon Unbound* (2011; editor), *Patterns of Enchantment: E. Nesbit and the Traditions of Children's Literature* (2007) and *Instructive curiosity: Suspense in C. S. Lewis's Trilogy* (1995).

Andrzej Zgorzelski is *professor emeritus*; he lectured on British literature and literary theory in the English Institute of the University of Gdańsk, where he was the head of Literary Studies Department. He published extensively on fantastic literature, utopia, British fiction and poetry, literary theory and methodology, among others: *Kreacje świata sensów* (1975), *Fantastyka. Utopia. Science fiction* (1980), *O nowelach Conrada* (1984), *Konstrukcja i sens* (1992), *System i funkcja* (1999), *Born of the Fantastic* (2004). He is also the author of a volume of poetry *Doświadczenia* (2006) and a poetic prayer book *Akty niestrzeliste* (2014).

Mediated Fictions

Studies in Verbal and Visual Narratives

Series Editors: Artur Blaim and Ludmiła Gruszewska-Blaim

Vol. 1 Katarzyna Pisarska: Mediating the World in the Novels of Iain Banks. The Paradigms of Fiction. 2013.

Vol. 2 Anna Kędra-Kardela and Andrzej Sławomir Kowalczyk (eds.): Expanding the Gothic Canon. Studies in Literature, Film and New Media. 2014.

Vol. 3 Grzegorz Czemiel: Limits of Orality and Textuality in Ciaran Carson's Poetry. 2014.

Vol. 4 Artur Blaim and Ludmiła Gruszewska-Blaim (eds.): Mediated Utopias: From Literature to Cinema. 2015.

Vol. 5 Justyna Laura Galant: *Painted Devils, Siren Tongues*. The Semiotic Universe of Jacobean Tragedy. 2015.

Vol. 6 Marta Komsta: Welcome to the Chemical Theatre. The Urban Chronotope in Peter Ackroyd's Fiction. 2015.

Vol. 7 Urszula Terentowicz-Fotyga: Dreams, Nightmares and Empty Signifiers. The English Country House in the Contemporary Novel. 2015.

Vol. 8 Barbara Klonowska / Zofia Kolbuszewska / Grzegorz Maziarczyk (eds.): (Im)perfection Subverted, Reloaded and Networked: Utopian Discourse across Media. 2015.

Vol. 9 Jadwiga Węgrodzka (ed.): Characters in Literary Fictions. 2015.

www.peterlang.com